View of Fishbourne looking north from above the creek. The excavation of 1962, over the East Wing, is marked with marginal arrows

Photograph by permission of Dr J. K. St Joseph, Committee for Aerial Photography, Cambridge

Reports of the Research Committee

of the

Society of Antiquaries of London

No. XXVI

Excavations at Fishbourne
1961 – 1969

By

Barry Cunliffe, M.A., Ph.D., F.S.A.

Volume 1 : The Site

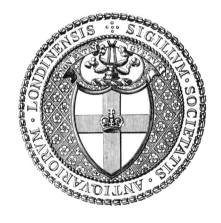

LEEDS

Printed by W. S. Maney and Son Ltd, for

The Society of Antiquaries

Burlington House, London

1971

PRINTED IN GREAT BRITAIN

PREFACE

THE two volumes offered here describe in detail the results of excavations carried out at Fishbourne from 1961 to 1968, with a summary of the 1969 season. The work undertaken in April–May 1969 in the area south of the A27 produced results which came as something of a surprise. Instead of allowing a few loose ends to be tidied up, new and interesting possibilities were suddenly opened up — possibilities which will take several more years to examine satisfactorily. It was decided, however, that rather than hold up the publication of the main site, the new work from 1969 onwards should form the basis of a third report to be published later, thus allowing the first two volumes to appear as scheduled. The division is a happy one: volumes 1 and 2 describe the excavation of the Flavian palace and the earlier features beneath it, while volume 3 will be concerned largely with the environmental setting and will include a discussion of the harbour regions and possibly the large unexplored area east of the palace, which is scheduled for road development in the near future, as well as some consideration of the palace estate.

The division of the first phase of the report into two volumes has been thought advisable because of the bulk of the relevant material requiring publication. The first volume contains a description of the excavated features and their context arranged in chronological order, while the second volume is concerned with a description of the loose finds and scientific appendices. The arrangement should make for easy reference and allow both volumes to be used together, thus overcoming the necessity for the reader to possess an abnormal number of fingers to keep the book open at innumerable places.

ACKNOWLEDGEMENTS

I have often thought the 'acknowledgements' to be the most enjoyable part of many archaeological reports, not the least because they mention people rather than scraps of things: certainly it is the most pleasant section to have to write. At Fishbourne over the last nine years more than a thousand people have laboured, largely as volunteers, on the archaeological and restoration work — sadly, for reasons of economy, only a few can be mentioned by name.

First of all there were the organizers — the Chichester Civic Society's Excavation Committee, under the chairmanship of Miss K. M. E. Murray, who throughout the work have undertaken the full responsibilities of organizing the domestic and financial side of the excavation, after each tiring season responding with willingness and even enthusiasm to requests for yet another major excavation in the following year. Much of the work fell on the shoulders of two people, the secretary, Mr A. H. Collins, and Mrs M. Rule who was instrumental in discovering the site in 1960 and has remained closely associated with all aspects of the work since then.

The increase in the complexity of the excavations ran in parallel with the growth in the number of committees. In 1963 the land containing a large part of the Palace was purchased by Mr I. D. Margary and donated to the Sussex Archaeological Trust, who set up a Fishbourne Management Committee under Mr Margary's chairmanship to direct the policy of reconstruction, leaving the Civic Society to continue to organize the excavations. A little later a Fishbourne Local Committee came into being as an offshoot of the Management Committee to co-ordinate the growing complex of day-to-day matters as the pace of rebuilding and reconstruction intensified. After the opening day, 31 May 1968, the committee structure was reformed, the Fishbourne Executive Committee and the Fishbourne Advisory Committee coming into being, replacing the others. Many of the same people served on all the committees and were therefore responsible for a great deal of the administrative work. There were even times when the present writer felt a little uncertain as to which committee he was actually attending. Nevertheless, the bulk of business transacted in a very short time was enormous.

Perhaps the most difficult task of the Civic Society's Excavation Committee was to raise funds for the excavation which, unlike the building and restoration projects, did not receive large private donations. Over the years, however, a number of trusts, learned societies and other bodies generously contributed to the general fund the sum of £12,140, which covered the entire expenditure not only of the nine seasons' excavation but also the production costs of this two-volume report. It is difficult to see how the work could have been accomplished with greater economy. The bodies to whom our grateful thanks must be recorded are the Society of Antiquaries, the British Academy, the Ministry of Public Building and Works, the Adorian Archaeological and Educational Trust, the Carnegie United Kingdom Trust, the Haverfield Trust, the Marc Fitch Fund, the Pilgrim Trust, the Chichester Corporation and the Sussex Archaeological Society.

From the vast number of people who gave up their summers to work on the excavation, only a few names can be selected. The site supervisors included Miss M. Hall, Miss J. Hatfield (now Mrs B. Morley), Miss C. Picard (now Mrs A. B. Norton), Miss F. Pierce (now Mrs J. P. Wild), Miss J. Wareing (now Mrs P. Webster) and Messrs D. Baker, P. Basset, R. Bradley, G. H. Brown, K. Greene, P. Greene, M. Henig, I. MacLellan, B. M. Morley, A. B. Norton, A. J. Parker, D. Phillipson, J. Saunders, N. Sunter, M. Todd and J. P. Wild. The frequency with which the young ladies married the men shows, perhaps, that the hard work did not entirely overshadow the social life: nor were the marriages solely between the supervisors. Many of the supervisors worked on the site for several years, but none can outshine the Revd. Tony Norton who, from being a first-year undergraduate at Manchester to responsibility for a parish in Bristol, returned for seven years to serve as a much-loved supervisor and Assistant Director. The same meritorious conduct (less the parochial duties) can be recorded of David Baker, whose care with the site photography (often, let it be said, to the frustration of those responsible for cleaning the trenches) can be judged by the quality of the half-tone illustrations in these volumes. The volunteers, too, returned in large numbers year after year, but two especially will be remembered by practically every season of diggers: Philip Burstow, already an old friend, who turned up at the end of the first season to help with the back-filling and hardly missed a week of digging in the following eight years, and William Hogan whose arrival each year from America with a party of carefully picked students was eagerly awaited by us all. I would like to reminisce about many friends made over these years but this is not the place; let us simply record our gratitude to all who were prepared to give up their holidays to work hard and long at Fishbourne for little or no reward save the satisfaction of being a part of the project.

While it is true that the work could not have been completed without the willing labour force engaged in the digging, a considerable staff of workers with other skills was required to deal with the enormous task of cleaning, treatment, recording and illustrating. The organization of the finds on the site was in the hands of my wife; site treatment was undertaken by Mrs Rule and the Institute of Archaeology at London; while the laboratory work following the excavation was, in later years, carried out by Miss J. Draper in the University of Southampton's archaeological laboratories; Mr J. Fisher was responsible for reconstructing the pottery now on show; Professor D. E. Strong co-ordinated the reconstruction of the Corinthian capital at the British Museum's Laboratories and Mr W. Taylor of the Ministry of Public Building and Works undertook to supervise the restoration of the Tuscan column.

The illustrations for these volumes were provided by many willing hands. I would particularly like to remember here Mr Syd Potter, not only for his drawings of the small finds, the painted plaster and some of the polychrome mosaics published below, but for his continued enthusiasm throughout the whole project from the day he helped clear out the site hut at Easter, 1961, until the final touches were added to this report in June 1969. Between these dates he had visited Italy to photograph comparative material, undertaken detailed analyses of the stonework and spent many long hours over the drawing board in order to produce hundreds of fine drawings. He was not alone: Miss E. Amos (now Mrs D. Baker) drew all the marble mouldings together with some of the site drawings and publication drawings of the mosaics — an enormous task, as a glance at the relevant sections will show, and Mr Nigel Sunter undertook to draw the samian pottery as well as producing the fine architectural reconstructions published below. Finally, all the site photographs were taken by Mr David Baker, while the object photography was largely in the hands of Mr David Leigh. In addition to these specialists there were, of course, a host of others who have contributed in one way or another and whose names appear at the heads of their detailed reports published in the second volume. It cannot be particularly easy to possess expert skills in archaeological matters and to be constantly bludgeoned by one's colleagues to produce specialist reports. I would like to thank all those who succumbed to persuasion, not only for their hard work, which speaks for itself, but for their tolerance.

While the bulk of the excavation was carried out on land originally belonging to Mr F. Ledger and later the Sussex Archaeological Trust, many local residents kindly made parts of their gardens available to us in order that details of the south side of the Palace could be traced. Mr and Mrs N. Anderson, Mr and Mrs Blackman, Mrs Blakeney and Commander and Mrs Cundle all generously allowed gaping trenches to be sliced through their attractive and well-kept gardens. Such was their devotion to the project. Commander Cundle even allowed part of his cellar floor to be removed in the same cause. The significance of this work will be apparent in the descriptive text to follow. Further afield, Mrs M. Grey and Mr R. Gribbon at different times volunteered areas of garden at no. 104 Fishbourne Road, where details of a separate building were exposed, and Parkhurst Property Co. Ltd. and Messrs Whitehead and Sons actively encouraged the trial excavation of two fields south of the South Wing of the building. Without the willing help of all the people mentioned here much of value would have been unobtainable.

Although these reports, and therefore the acknowledgements, are concerned largely with the archaeological work something must be said, albeit briefly, of those who contributed to the building and presentation which ran in parallel with the later stages of the excavation. Had it not been for the generosity of Mr I. D. Margary in purchasing the land and financing to a large extent its development, the area would probably by now have become a housing estate. All who enjoy visiting the building as it is now displayed owe an enormous debt of gratitude to him. The Trust's decision to prepare the remains for presentation led to the creation of a small team of professionals, each responsible for a part of the work, but working in close consultation with each other and with Mrs Rule who was present on the site almost daily during the last months. The architects for the cover buildings were Carden, Godfrey and Macfadyen (W. E. Godfrey assisted successively by Sheila Gibson, G. Denniston and A. Berzins) and the builders were H. Horton and Son under the active direction of the late Mr A. Horton. After building had begun the *Sunday Times* came forward with a generous offer to undertake the cost and organization of the Museum interior — an offer gratefully accepted by the Trust. The *Sunday Times* then appointed Mr R. Wade as designer while two of their staff, Miss P. Connor and Mr K. Pearson, acted as the co-ordinators of the team of illustrators and artists responsible for producing details of the display. In addition they gave their advice generously on problems arising in the cover building and the garden. The months of ceaseless and often frantic activity before the site was finally opened provided an invigorating and memorable interlude. A number of specialists were also employed to deal with the problems posed by the conservation of the remains. The Ministry of Public Building and Works provided constant advice and undertook to train Mr Horton's masons who consolidated the exposed Roman foundation while Mr W. Novis of Art Pavements Ltd, personally directed the men working on the conservation of the mosaics.

Finally I would like to mention the help given by my wife at all stages in the work. For eight years (whilst producing two children) she worked full-time on the site organizing the pottery and finds so that by the end of each season everything was clean, marked, recorded and stored, but it was after the dig had ended that her work really began, with the endless tasks of indexing, sorting and analysing necessary to maintain the required progress before the next season began. Throughout this time, particularly towards the end, she translated nearly half a million words of my illegible manuscript into a relatively clean typescript: this in itself was no mean task. Only I can know the full extent and value of her contribution.

A mere handful of names out of the many hundreds are mentioned here. To everyone who took part in the project, whether they are named in these pages or not, my heartfelt appreciation must be recorded.

BARRY CUNLIFFE.

Southampton
June 1969

CONTENTS

PART I
General Background

PART II
The Structures of the First Period, A.D. *43–75*

PART III

The Flavian Palace (Period 2), c. A.D. *75/80–100*

PART IV
The Third Period, c. A.D. *100–280*

PART V

The Destruction of the Building and the Subsequent History of the Site

LIST OF FIGURES IN THE TEXT

ILLUSTRATIONS

LIST OF PLATES

B

BIBLIOGRAPHY

Allen 1944   D. F. Allen, 'The Belgic Dynasties of Britain and their Coins', *Arch.*, 90 (1944), 1–46.

Allen 1961   D. F. Allen, 'The origins of Coinage in Britain: a Reappraisal' in *Problems of the Iron Age in Southern Britain*, ed. Frere (London, 1961), 97–308.

Allen 1962   D. F. Allen, 'Celtic Coins', *Ordnance Survey Map of Southern Britain in the Iron Age* (London, 1962), 19–32.

Benoit 1947   F. Benoit, 'La Maison à double péristyle, le Jardin de Grassi à Aix-en-Provence', *Gallia*, 5 (1947), 98–112.

Biddle 1969   M. Biddle, 'Excavations at Winchester 1967', *Antiq. Journ.*, XLVIII (1968), 250–84.

Blake 1930   M. E. Blake, 'The Pavements of the Roman Buildings of the Republic and Early Empire', *Mem. Am. Ac. Rome*, VIII (1930), 7–160.

Blake 1936   M. E. Blake, 'Roman Mosaics of the second century in Italy', *Mem. Am. Ac. Rome*, XIII (1936), 67–214.

Boëthius 1960   H. Boëthius, *The Golden House of Nero: Some Aspects of Roman Architecture* (Michigan, 1960).

Brion 1960   M. Brion, *Pompeii and Herculaneum* (London, 1960).

Clifford 1961   E. M. Clifford, *Bagendon, a Belgic Oppidum* (Cambridge, 1961).

Colvin 1963   H. M. Colvin, *The History of the King's Works*, II (London, 1963).

Cox 1735   T. Cox, *Magna Britannia* (London, 1735).

Crawford 1931   O. G. S. Crawford, 'The Chiltern Grim's Ditches', *Antiq.*, V (1931), 161 ff.

Cunliffe 1962   B. W. Cunliffe, 'Excavations at Fishbourne, 1961', *Antiq. Journ.*, XLII (1962), 15–23.

Cunliffe 1963   B. W. Cunliffe, 'Excavations at Fishbourne, 1962', *Antiq. Journ.*, XLIII (1963), 1–14.

Cunliffe 1964   B. W. Cunliffe, 'Excavations at Fishbourne, 1963', *Antiq. Journ.*, XLIV (1964), 1–8.

Cunliffe 1965A   B. W. Cunliffe, 'Excavations at Fishbourne, 1964', *Antiq. Journ.*, XLV (1965), 1–11.

Cunliffe 1965B   B. W. Cunliffe, 'Fishbourne, 1961–4', *Antiq.*, XXXIX (1965), 177–83.

Cunliffe 1966A   B. W. Cunliffe, 'Excavations at Fishbourne, 1965', *Antiq. Journ.*, XLVI (1966), 25–38.

Cunliffe 1966B   B. W. Cunliffe, 'The Somerset Levels in the Roman Period' in *Rural Settlement in Roman Britain*, ed. C. Thomas (London, 1966), 68–73.

Cunliffe 1967   B. W. Cunliffe, 'Excavations at Fishbourne, 1966', *Antiq. Journ.*, XLVII (1967), 51–9.

Cunliffe 1968A   B. W. Cunliffe, 'Excavations at Fishbourne, 1967', *Antiq. Journ.*, XLVIII (1968), 32–40.

Cunliffe 1968B   B. W. Cunliffe, ed., *Fifth Report on the Excavations of the Roman fort at Richborough, Kent* (London, 1968).

Cunliffe 1969   B. W. Cunliffe, *Roman Bath* (London, 1969).

Curwen 1954   E. C. Curwen, *The Archaeology of Sussex*, 2nd edn. (London, 1954).

Curwen and Frere 1947   E. C. Curwen and S. S. Frere, 'A Romano-British Occupation site at Portfield Gravel Pit, Chichester', *S.A.C.*, 86 (1947), 137–40.

Dyer 1961   J. Dyer, 'Dray's Ditches, Bedfordshire and Early Iron Age Territorial Boundaries in the Eastern Chilterns', *Antiq. Journ.*, XLI (1961), 32 ff.

Dyer 1963   J. Dyer, 'The Chiltern Grim's Ditch', *Antiq.*, XXXVII (1963), 46 ff.

Dyer and Hales 1961   J. Dyer and A. J. Hales, 'Pitstone Hill — a study in Field Archaeology', *Rec. of Bucks.*, XVII (1961), 49 ff.

Frere 1959   S. S. Frere, 'Excavations at Verulamium, 1958', *Antiq. Journ.*, XXXIX (1959), 1–18.

Frere 1967   S. S. Frere, *Britannia* (London, 1967).

Grenier 1934   A. Grenier, *Manuel d'Archéologie*, VI, pt. 2 (Paris, 1934).

Grimal 1943   P. Grimal, *Les Jardins Romains* (Paris, 1943).

Harden 1937   D. Harden, 'Excavations on Grim's Dyke, North Oxfordshire', *Oxon.*, II (1937), 74 ff.

Hawkes 1940   C. F. C. Hawkes, 'The Excavations at Bury Hill 1939', *P.H.F.C.A.S.*, XIV (1940), 291–337.

Hawkes 1961   C. F. C. Hawkes, 'The Western Third C Culture and the Belgic Dobunni', in E. M. Clifford, *Bagendon, a Belgic Oppidum* (Cambridge, 1961), 43 ff.

Hawkes 1968   C. F. C. Hawkes, 'New Thoughts on the Belgae', *Antiq.*, XLII (1968), 6 ff.

Hawkes and Hull 1947 C. F. C. Hawkes and M. R. Hull, *Camulodunum* (Oxford, 1947).

Hay 1804   A. Hay, *History of Chichester* (Chichester, 1804).

Hodgson 1967   J. M. Hodgson, *Soils of the West Sussex Coastal Plain* (Harpenden, 1967).

Holmes 1961   J. Holmes, 'Excavations at Densworth Farm in 1960', *S.N.Q.*, XV (1961), 242 ff.

Holmes 1968   J. Holmes, 'The Chichester Dykes', *S.A.C.*, CVI (1968), 63–72.

MacDonald 1965   W. L. MacDonald, *The Architecture of the Roman Empire*, I (Yale, 1965).

Mau 1899   A. Mau, *Pompeii, its Life and Art* (London, 1899).

Murray 1956   K. M. E. Murray, 'The Chichester Earthworks', *S.A.C.*, XCIV (1956), 139 ff.

O'Neil 1943   B. H. St J. O'Neil, 'Grim's Bank Padworth, Berkshire', *Antiq.*, XVII (1943), 188 ff.

O'Neil 1944   B. H. St J. O'Neil, 'The Silchester Region in the 5th and 6th Centuries A.D.', *Antiq.*, XVIII (1944), 133 ff.

Painter 1965   K. S. Painter, 'A marble head from Sussex', *Antiq. Journ.*, XLV (1965), 178–82.

Parlasca 1959   K. Parlasca, 'Die römischen Mosaiken im Deutschland', *Römisch-Germanische Forschungen* 23 (Berlin, 1959).

Richardson 1951   K. M. Richardson, 'The excavation of Iron Age Villages on Boscombe Down West', *W.A.M.*, LIV (1951), 123–68.

Richmond 1967   I. A. Richmond, *Hod Hill: Volume Two* (London, 1967).

Richmond and   I. A. Richmond and O. G. S. Crawford, 'The British Section of the Ravenna Cosmo-
   Crawford 1949   graphy', *Arch.*, XCIII (1949), 1–50.

Rolland 1958   H. Rolland. A note on the progress of the excavations at Le Jardin de Grassi in *Gallia*, 16 (1958), 417–19.

'S' 1816   'S' in *Gents. Mag.*, May 1816, part II, 19 ff.

Sabatier 1963   W. Sabatier, *Roman Military Earthworks near Chichester (c. 1798)* (Chichester Papers, 1963).

Sautel 1954   J. Sautel, 'Vaison-la-Romaine', *Gallia*, 12 (1954), 457.

Schönberger 1967   H. Schönberger, 'Das augusteische Römerlager in Rödgen', *Germania*, 45 (1967), 84–95.

Scott 1938   L. Scott, 'The Roman Villa at Angmering', *S.A.C.*, 79 (1938), 3–44.

Scott 1939   L. Scott, 'Angmering Roman Villa', *S.A.C.*, 80 (1939), 89–92.

Smith 1858   H. Smith, 'An account of certain Sepulchral Remains lately Discovered at Densworth in the Parish of Funtington, Sussex', *S.A.C.*, X (1858), 168–80.

Stern 1957   H. Stern, *Recueil Général des Mosaiques de la Gaule*. Tenth supplement to *Gallia*. Vol. I, Province de Belgique: 1, partie ouest.

Stern 1960	H. Stern, *Recueil Général des Mosaiques de la Gaule*. Tenth supplement to *Gallia*. Vol. I, Province de Belgique: 2, partie est.
Stern 1963	H. Stern, *Recueil Général des Mosaiques de la Gaule*. Tenth supplement to *Gallia*. Vol. I, Province de Belgique: 3, partie sud.
Stern 1967	H. Stern, *Recueil Général des Mosaiques de la Gaule*. Tenth supplement to *Gallia*. Vol. II, Lyonnaise.
Thomas 1958	N. Thomas, 'Excavations at Callow Hill, Glympton and Stonesfield, Oxfordshire', *Oxon.*, XXII (1958), 11 ff.
Wheeler 1934	R. E. M. Wheeler, 'London and the Grim's Ditches', *Antiq. Journ.*, XIV (1934), 254 ff.
Wheeler 1954	R. E. M. Wheeler, *The Stanwick Fortifications* (London, 1954).
Wheeler and Richardson 1957	R. E. M. Wheeler and K. M. Richardson, *Hill Forts in Northern France* (London, 1957).
Wheeler and Wheeler 1936	R. E. M. Wheeler and T. V. Wheeler, *Verulamium: a Belgic and two Roman Cities* (London, 1936).
White 1934	G. M. White, 'Prehistoric Remains from Selsey Bill', *Antiq. Journ.*, XIV (1934), 40–52.
Williams-Freeman 1934	J. P. Williams-Freeman, 'The Chichester Entrenchments', *S.A.C.*, LXXV (1934), 65–106.
Wilson 1956	A. E. Wilson, 'The Beginnings of Roman Chichester', *S.A.C.*, XCIV (1956), 100–11.
Winbolt 1932	S. E. Winbolt, 'Roman Villa at Southwick', *S.A.C.*, LXXIII (1932), 13–32.
Winbolt 1935	S. E. Winbolt, 'An Early Iron Age Camp in Piper's Copse, Kirdford', *S.A.C.*, LXXVI (1935), 245–50.

ABBREVIATIONS

Antiq.	*Antiquity.*
Antiq. Journ.	*Antiquaries Journal.*
Arch.	*Archaeologia.*
Arch. Ael.	*Archaeologia Aeliana.*
Arch. Camb.	*Archaeologia Cambrensis.*
Arch. Cant.	*Archaeologia Cantiana.*
Arch. Journ.	*Archaeological Journal.*
B.B.C.S.	*Bulletin of the Board of Celtic Studies.*
B.M.G.	*British Museum Guide to the Antiquities of Roman Britain* (London, 1951).
Bull. Inst. Arch.	*Bulletin of the Institute of Archaeology.*
Cam.	C. F. C. Hawkes and M. R. Hull, *Camulodunum* (London, 1947).
Gents. Mag.	*Gentleman's Magazine.*
J.R.S.	*Journal of Roman Studies.*
J. Sedim. Petrol.	*Journal of Sedimentary Petrology.*
Mem. Am. Ac. Rome	*Memoirs of the American Academy at Rome.*
Norf. Arch.	*Norfolk Archaeology.*
Oxon.	*Oxoniensia.*
P.H.F.C.A.S.	*Proceedings of the Hampshire Field Club and Archaeological Society.*
P.P.S.	*Proceedings of the Prehistoric Society.*
Proc. Camb. Ant.	*Proceedings of the Cambridge Antiquarian Society.*
Proc. Soc. Ant. Lond.	*Proceedings of the Society of the Antiquaries of London.*
Proc. Yorks. Geol. Soc.	*Proceedings of the Yorkshire Geological Society.*
Rec. of Bucks.	*Records of Buckinghamshire.*
R.I.B.	R. G. Collingwood and R. P. Wright, *Roman Inscriptions in Britain*, 1 (Oxford, 1965).
S.A.C.	*Sussex Archaeological Collections.*
S.N.Q.	*Sussex Notes and Queries.*
Surrey A.C.	*Surrey Archaeological Collections.*
T.B.G.A.S.	*Transactions of the Bristol and Gloucestershire Archaeological Society.*
T.L. & M.A.S.	*Transactions of the London and Middlesex Archaeological Society.*
W.A.M.	*Wiltshire Archaeological Magazine.*

SUMMARY

THE site of Fishbourne lies at the head of a tidal inlet about one mile (*c.* 1.4 km.) west of the Roman town of Chichester (*Noviomagus Regnensium*) within the large tract of land defined by the 'Chichester Entrenchments' — a series of defensive earthworks of late pre-Roman Iron Age date.

During the first period of occupation, *c.* A.D. 43–4, the site was developed as a military supply base used in conjunction with the main camp thought to be at Chichester. A likely context for these installations is the campaign fought by the *Legio II Augusta* under Vespasian, which in 43–4 swept across the south-west of Britain. Fishbourne and Chichester were at this time well within the pro-Roman territory ruled by the client king Tiberius Claudius Cogidubnus: as such the area would have been suitable for a rearward supply camp in the initial stages of the advance.

The army soon moved out, but civilian development continued to make use of the old installations — roads were re-metalled, the drainage system improved and several new buildings were put up. To begin with (Period 1 B — late Claudian), timber buildings were erected, one of which was a house of some quality, while another close by may have been a workshop connected with it. Later (Period 1 C — Neronian), the timber structures were replaced by masonry. Two buildings of this period have been recognized. The 'proto-palace', which immediately replaced the timber house, possessed an elaborate bath suite, several ranges of rooms and a peristyle, and was clearly a structure of some standing. The other masonry building, apparently unfinished, lay to the west. In about A.D. 75, when work on the main palace began, the 'proto-palace' was incorporated into the new design.

The main Flavian palace (Period 2) occupied an area exceeding ten acres. It consisted of a formal garden enclosed by four ranges of rooms with a large natural garden to the south extending down to the sea. Of the ranges, the west with its central Audience Chamber was the official and administrative suite, the north comprised private suites arranged around two peristyles, and the south, about which little is known, seems to have been the private residential range facing south across its private garden to the sea. The East Wing was a composite structure containing the Entrance Hall, bath suite, Assembly Hall and private courtyards with rooms attached. Domestic ranges and structures lay to the north and west of the main building. The interior decoration was of a high standard: practically all of the rooms were adorned with mosaics and painted walls. Some were provided with inlaid marble whilst a few were fitted with friezes of moulded stucco. The north garden was laid out with great formality with shrubs and trees, pathways and fountains. The south garden appears to have been far more natural, adorned with pools and streams.

Such elaboration in architecture and design was largely unknown in Britain at the time. It must have been the creation of large numbers of craftsmen imported from the Mediterranean world specifically for the job, and employed by a Romanophile possessing great wealth. Details such as the Audience Chamber, the Hippodromos and the Assembly Hall are best paralleled among the architecture of Domitian's palace on the Palatine.

It is argued that the palace may well have been owned by the local client king Cogidubnus, who by the 70s had probably gained the title *legatus Augusti* implying senatorial rank. It may be that the progression, from timber house to proto-palace to palace, reflected the rise in the king's fortunes.

Towards the end of the first century a slight decline began (Period 3) possibly consequent upon the king's death, but a series of modifications and additions throughout the second and third centuries maintained the old palace on a level in advance of most contemporary country buildings. Two new bath suites were built, one replacing the other, and several new polychrome mosaics were added. Alterations were still under way as late as *c.* 280, when a new hypocaust was being inserted. About 280–90 the occupied part of the building was destroyed by fire. Then followed a period of systematic demolition lasting into the early years of the fourth century.

Later, possibly in the sub-Roman period, a few graves were dug into the ruins. After this the area reverted to farmland, being extensively ploughed in late Saxon to early medieval times. Since the eighteenth century it has served largely as pasture. Archaeological discoveries began to be made in 1805 and have continued sporadically since. In 1960 a trench dug for a water-main sectioned the building, re-focussing attention on the site once more. Large-scale excavation began in 1961.

PART I
General Background

INTRODUCTION

THE HISTORY OF DISCOVERY   (frontispiece, figs. 1 and 2)

ONE mile west of the centre of Chichester is the village of New Fishbourne — a cluster of houses of eighteenth-century and more recent date straddling the main A27 trunk road. To the south, Mill Lane leads down to the once tidal Salt Mill sited on the side of an area of extensive mud-flats lining the upper reaches of Chichester Harbour. North of the main road, modern housing estates are now spreading up to the railway, turning Fishbourne into a suburb of Chichester.

Several finds of Roman material have been made from time to time in the village. The first recorded discovery came in 1805, when, about 20 March, workmen found, '. . . in digging by the road side for the foundation of a house, a tessellated pavement about 13 ft. 6 in. in width. One end runs under a hedge so that the length has not been ascertained. In the middle is a space about two feet in diameter where the workmen found part of the base of a

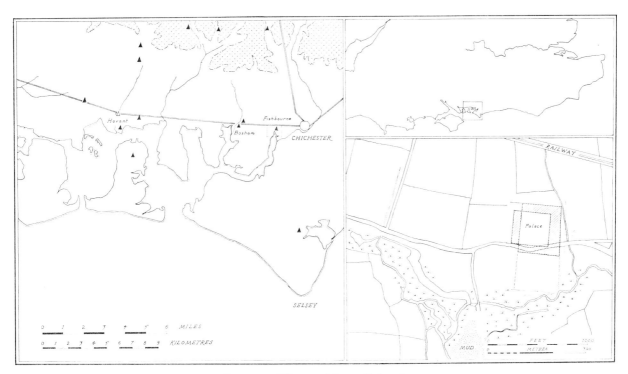

FIG. 1.   The position of the site

column'. (*Gents. Mag.*, 1805, pp. 926–7.) The description goes on to mention that beneath the floor, which was composed of black and white tesserae, a fine spring was discovered. The writer concludes with the advice 'if the discovery were followed up with spirit, some valuable piece of Antiquity might, perhaps, be found'. The precise position of the mosaic is unknown but a year later, on 18 April 1806, the house in question was sold by auction (*Hampshire Telegraph and Sussex Chronicle*, Monday, 7 April 1806). The information given by the notice of sale is, unfortunately, insufficient to enable it to be recognized with certainty today, but it must be one of the houses on the south side of the main road to the east of the Woolpack. Clearly, then, the mosaic referred to belongs to one of the rooms in the South Wing of the palace.

Some years later, reference was made to the remains of a Roman bath and pavement (Smith, 1858, p. 169) without further details being given. Whether these remains were the same as those found in 1805 or a separate later discovery cannot be decided. The recent excavation, however, in the front garden of no. 63 Fishbourne Road discovered part of a bath suite, one room of which had been previously excavated in the nineteenth century. Presumably this was the site of the 1858 find and possibly also of the 1805 mosaic. Later finds of Roman pottery and tiles are recorded on the Ordnance Survey 6 in. maps as coming from the old watercress beds to the south of the village, and from a site over what is now known to be the West Wing of the palace. The information was given to the Ordnance Survey in 1896 by a Chichester resident, Mrs Ayling, but the circumstances and date of the discoveries are unknown.

Seven hundred yards (640 m.) to the east of the site, in the grounds of the old rectory, a quantity of Roman material was found in 1929 by the vicar, Rev. N. Shaw. In a letter to the *Times*, published on 11 February 1929, the material is listed as including samian, dating to the late first century, a mortarium, a quern, a piece of a mosaic and a coin of Domitian. To the south of the road were found waterpipes 3 ft. (0.9 m.) down. Clearly the site is one of considerable potential interest. Unfortunately, when the rectory[1] was demolished in 1964 and a new housing estate erected, permission to watch the excavations could not be obtained. Further work in the area is, however, not impossible.

Returning to the main site, in 1938 two schoolboys, digging in the north end of the garden of no. 80 Fishbourne Road, uncovered part of a black and white mosaic. The find was not published, but local residents still remember the occasion and rumour has it that steps were found at the same time. There can be little doubt that the mosaic lay in one of the rooms of the West Wing of the palace, immediately to the south of the Audience Chamber. The site occupied by the four houses, numbers 74–80, covers the south half of the West Wing. It was in the summer of the same year that Mr F. Ledger, who owned the land until it was purchased by the Sussex Archaeological Trust, laid water pipes to troughs in his fields. Had the pipes been as little as 3 in. (0.076 m.) deeper several of the North Wing mosaics would have been discovered. But there the matter rested.

In 1960, a skin-diver exploring the Mill Pond salvaged a quantity of pottery, which was given to Chichester Museum. The discovery stirred up considerable local interest and when, in April of the same year, a water main was laid through the fields to the north of the

---

[1] There is some confusion between the two rectories: the Old Rectory is in Appledram Lane, the Rectory is in Fishbourne Road, but Roman material is known to have been found on both sites.

village several local residents were present to observe it. The engineer in charge of the project, Mr Burgess, informed by a workman that the machine was digging through a mass of ancient building debris, immediately reported the find to Mrs M. Rule of the Joint Archaeological Committee. A visit to the site showed that the machine had, in fact, sectioned a Roman building of considerable size. Moreover, the pottery rescued from the trench was almost entirely of first-century date.

Informed of the potential significance of the discovery, the Chichester Civic Society approached the owner of the land, Mr F. Ledger, and obtained permission to carry out a limited exploratory excavation at Easter, 1961. The writer was invited to direct the work.[1] As a result of the Easter dig it became apparent that three major periods were represented, a timber building phase of the Claudio-Neronian period, a Vespasianic masonry building and subsequent second-century alterations. The Civic Society, encouraged by these tentative results, obtained permission for an extended summer excavation. But at this stage it became known that the owner was intending to sell the land for building purposes. The summer excavation was therefore planned as a rescue operation with the object of tracing the extent of the building as quickly as possible, and, quite unashamedly, exposing as many of its exotic elements as time allowed in the hope that public opinion would be sufficiently inspired to make further excavation possible. In fact seven mosaics were discovered, the finest, the dolphin pavement, appearing in a narrow trial cutting on the last afternoon. The spectacular nature of the building had thus been demonstrated, and in the following autumn Mr I. D. Margary began negotiations for the purchase of the site, which he was later to present to the Sussex Archaeological Trust.

Whilst negotiations were proceeding, the Civic Society arranged a further season's work in the summer of 1962. With pressure now eased, attention was turned to the large-scale area excavation of the eastern part of the site where previous work had shown there were pre-Flavian timber buildings lying beneath the Flavian masonry structure. The extensive excavation of these established a firmly dated sequence for the site and exposed the plans of superimposed military and civil buildings. By the following summer, with the completion of the purchase, excavations over the North Wing were resumed and part of the newly-discovered West Wing was examined. In 1964 the work continued, making it possible by the end of the season to produce a tolerably complete plan of the site in all it phases. At this stage it seemed as though the work was nearing completion and could be finished in one further season, but towards the end of summer 1965 it became apparent that the central courtyard had originally been laid out as a formal garden, the detailed plan of which was recoverable by archaeological means. It was therefore necessary to organize two further seasons of digging in 1966 and 1967 to complete the examination of this vital area. It was during the 1967 season that the main outlines of the South Wing were discovered. A short session in 1968 completed the outstanding problems on the main site and finally at Easter, 1969 a limited programme of trial trenching was carried out to the south of the building over the upper reaches of the creek.[2]

---

[1] Interim reports have appeared regularly in *Antiq. Journ.* from 1962–8 (Cunliffe, 1962, 1963, 1964, 1965a, 1966, 1967, 1968a, and a summary was published in *Antiq.* (Cunliffe, 1965b)).

[2] The work of Easter, 1969 is only briefly summarized in vols 1 and 2 of this report. At the time of writing (May 1969) further work is being planned.

In 1965, the Sussex Archaeological Trust began to erect a modern cover-building over the entire North Wing of the Roman building. The work was completed in 1966 and in the following year a museum, concourse, and custodian's house were put up. At the end of May 1968 the site was opened to the public.

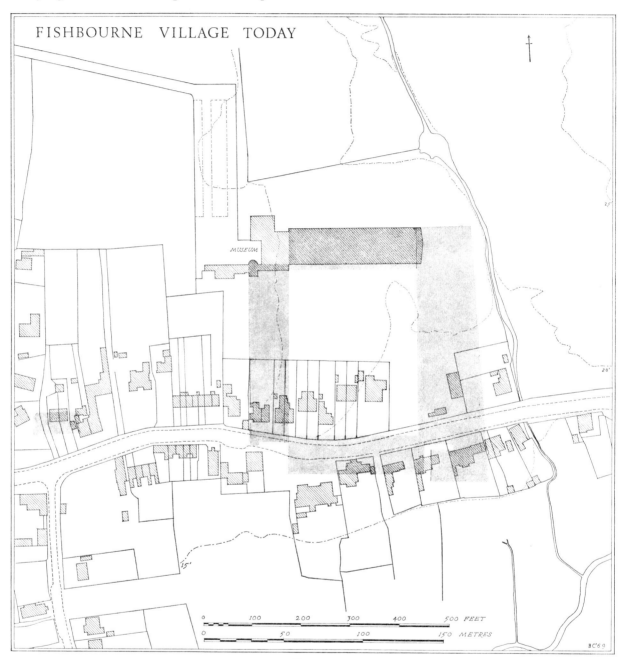

FISHBOURNE VILLAGE TODAY

Fig. 2
(The area of the Second-Period building is stippled)

THE SITE   (fig. 2)

The excavated part of the Fishbourne site covers about 6 acres (24,280 sq. m.): it is but a small sample of a much larger occupied area, the limits of which are not yet precisely known. On the north side of the main site, trial excavation has shown that Roman occupation levels extended for about 350 ft. (107 m.) along the valley; to the north-west, however, soil removal for the access road and car park demonstrated that the area was completely open in the Roman period. Traces of Roman buildings have, however, been found about 350 ft. (107 m.) west of the West Wing, in the garden of no. 104 Fishbourne Road (p. 138 and fig. 41).

To the east, ditches and occupation layers of Roman date turned up in a gas-pipe trench, 600 ft. (183 m.) from the East Wing, whilst remains beneath the rectory, 2,100 ft. (640 m.) away, have already been mentioned. South of the present main road, down to the harbour, Roman material is densely scattered: quantities of pottery were dredged up from the Mill Pond, more turned up when builders dug trial trenches in the field south of the Woolpack and thick occupation layers were sectioned when trenches for gas, water and electricity services were dug along the verges of the Chichester By-pass for a distance of 800 ft. (240 m.) from its junction with Fishbourne Road. Therefore, even excluding the Rectory site, Roman material has been found at Fishbourne over an area of between 35–50 acres.

That excavation has covered perhaps as little as one tenth of the occupied area is an important consideration which must be borne in mind when assessing the significance of the pre-Flavian settlement. In terms of the Flavian building it is less important, for we can be certain of its limits on all but the west side, and while it is fair to assume that unknown domestic buildings lie to the west, the plan of the residential part at least is reasonably complete.

We have been content at this stage to excavate the masonry building and the earlier features lying below it with only the limited trial trenching of the immediate environment. It will be evident from the foregoing paragraphs that much remains to be done, and indeed will be done in future years, but for the present purposes of reporting the first phase of excavation can be regarded as complete. Soon, however, the By-pass will be extended along the eastern limit of the present site: this will demand a considerable preliminary excavation and rescue excavations will also become necessary as the fields to the north and south are developed as housing estates. The next decade should see a renewal of archaeological activity at Fishbourne.

THE PHYSICAL ENVIRONMENT
(Figs. 3 and 4, and pp. 204–5)

The village of Fishbourne lies astride the junction between the Reading Beds clay and the chalk. Although the solid geology is partly obscured by a thin overlay of gravel, the drainage pattern of the area is to some extent influenced by it.[1] This is best shown by the three streams which flow from north to south across the clay band, one close to Salt Mill Lane, one immediately east of the site, and one further east by Appledram Lane. When they reach the

[1] For a useful general survey of the soils of the Chichester region see Hodgson, 1967.

edge of the chalk band they change direction, running at right-angles to their original courses and converging to form the head of Fishbourne Harbour. Between the streams the Reading Beds, here a red and grey mottled sticky clay, are overlain by a superficial deposit of orange gravel which in places has been piped down deeply into it, while the ferruginous salts from the gravel have been partly leached out, discolouring the surrounding clay to a yellowish-brown. A typical soil profile was exposed in the area now occupied by the car park. Here the clay was covered by a layer of gravel varying from 9 to 18 in. (0.2–0.5 m.) in thickness, above which was a layer of green-grey silty soil about 9 in. (0.2 m.) thick, gradually merging with a 12 in. (0.3 m.) thick topsoil. The gravel is part of an extensive Pleistocene deposit which blankets much of this part of the Sussex coastal plain (fig. 4).

Towards the end of the Pleistocene period, when the sea-level was much lower than it is today, the streams running into the sea cut deeply into the underlying clay and chalk, eroding their valleys to the new level. As the sea-level rose again with the onset of Neo-thermal times the lower reaches of these valleys became clogged with silt, whilst further upstream gravel terraces were laid down. Sections across the stream which ran through the Fishbourne site demonstrate this sequence well. Section 1 (fig. 51) across the upper part of the valley shows the original valley profile and the depth of gravel deposited during the aggrad-ing. Section 2 (fig. 51), taken across the eastern creek-end, is more complicated. The original valley-floor of gravel slopes steeply off to the south and on it were deposited several feet of grey silty clay still bearing the impressions of the reeds which were growing whilst the silts were being laid down, presumably under estuarine conditions. This particular section produced an unabraded tranchet axe[1] from the top foot of the silt. At the top the clay merged into a thin, shingly, gravel layer, representing a shore line at c. 10 ft. O.D. (3.05 m.). A few small scraps of briquetage lying on the gravel, and similar to those found in dated sequences elsewhere, allow an Iron Age date to be tentatively suggested. Above this came about 2 ft. (0.61 m.) of redeposited silt streaked and mottled brown to grey, sealed by a gravel lens closely dated to the Roman period by the fact that an early Roman well had been cut from the level of its surface. Finally, the Roman level was sealed by about a foot of grey-brown silt, representing post-Roman flooding. The section therefore demonstrates in a striking manner the way in which the deep late Pleistocene valley was gradually silted to its present state.

From the evidence amassed during the excavations, and from levelling and bore-holes dug since, it is possible to offer a tolerably accurate plan of the local environment of the eastern creek-end at the time of the Roman Conquest (fig. 3). Across the excavated site lay a shallow, gravel-floored valley, through which flowed a rapidly-moving stream. Occasionally, possibly at exceptionally high tide, the valley became flooded, causing lenses of grey silt to be deposited on either side. An identical environment still exists three miles west of Fishbourne at one of the heads of Bosham Creek. The Fishbourne stream flowed south into a wide marshy lagoon, into which another stream issued, coming from the east. It would appear that the joint force of water was sufficient to scour the creek-end, preventing silt from accumulating in the main channels and thus providing a sufficient depth of water to allow ships of normal size to sail close in.

A surface examination of the western creek-end suggests that the drainage pattern here in the Roman period was closely similar to that described for the eastern creek: two streams,

---

[1] This axe, together with another discovery in building work nearby in 1969, will be published in the third volume.

one flowing from the north, the other from the west, converging to form a wide inlet. The creation of a mill pond and later the erection of a pumping station have, however, considerably altered the original lie of the land. Detailed examination of the underlying sediments has not yet been attempted.

It is to some extent possible to clothe the geomorphology of the site with details of the local vegetation. A sample of organic material was taken from the stream bed close to the position of Section 8 (fig. 52). On examination at Kew Gardens it was found to contain well-preserved twigs of hazel, willow, ash and fir, with smaller quantities of oak and blackberry,

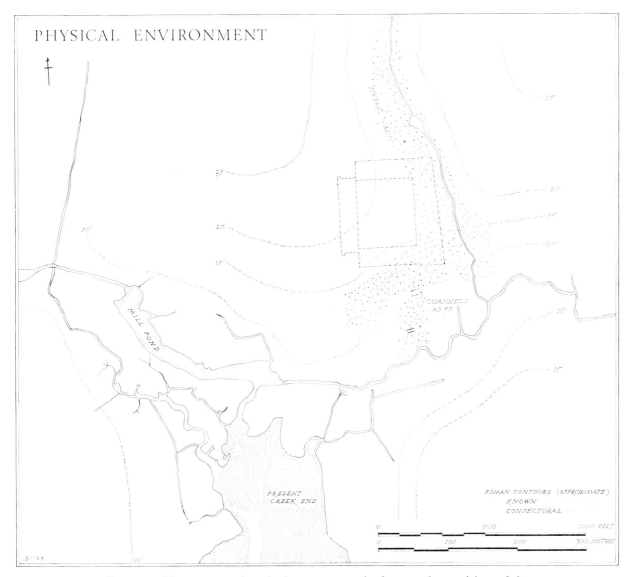

FIG. 3. The present-day drainage system is shown: the position of the palace is indicated by the broken line

C

indicating the type of mixed undergrowth originally growing close to the stream (Vol. II, p. 377). Pollen analysis of soil samples taken from the area to the west of the stream suggests a more open countryside supporting grassland with some patches of bracken, heather and pine. These heathland species are by no means out of place: the slightly elevated patches of gravel between the streams would have provided suitable conditions for growth and indeed bracken and pine still flourish locally in some areas. Further south, towards the creek-ends, marsh-land species would have predominated with phragmites growing on the fringes where brackish water conditions would have prevailed.

This, then, was the scene when the Romans arrived. The site does not appear to have been previously occupied, although a few scraps of Iron Age saucepan pots were found lying about the site, implying sporadic use probably in the first century B.C. (Vol. II, fig. 72 and pp. 158–60). The effects which Roman occupation had on the immediate environment in terms of buildings, roads, etc., are described in detail below; here it is sufficient to examine how this activity affected local conditions. By the end of the first century the stream had been diverted slightly to the east, close to the line which it now follows, and the original valley had been filled with clay and gravel to provide a dry platform for the erection of the Flavian palace. The result of this building activity was to dam up water to the north of the building, but to provide an outlet to the sea by means of the newly-dug drainage ditch. All the time that the ditch was kept clear of sediment the water would continue to flow, but as soon as the ditch was neglected water would tend to pond up to the north of the building. This is precisely what happened in the latter part of the Roman period. Section 3 (fig. 51), taken to the north of the palace, shows how grey-brown mottled silts, layer 3, dating to the third–fourth centuries overlap the make-up layers contemporary with the first-century building. The degree of oxidization which the silt exhibits implies that the area was not permanently waterlogged and, in its later stages, may have been a periodically-flooded meadow. The pond which still exists in the centre of the area is an interesting survival from late Roman times.

The clogging of the stream may have been one factor in the periodic flooding north of the building; another of some importance was a general rise in sea-level in the late Roman and post-Roman period. Evidence for this is provided by Section 2 (fig. 51) which shows clearly that a layer of silt (layer 2) had been deposited above the gravel surface of the early Roman period. Similar evidence was obtained to the south of the South Wing of the palace, where, in Section 4 (fig. 51), silt (layers 3–5) could be shown to overlie the surface of the Flavian terrace which lay between the building and the sea. These layers, and indeed the flats which surround the harbour end, must have been the direct result of the sea-level change. Since the upper limits affected lie at about 13 ft. (3.96 m.) O.D., late or post-Roman high tides must have risen to at least this height. That the top of the silt layer deposited on the north side of the building is at about 17 ft. (5.18 m.) O.D. argues that here the blocking of the outlet stream was the dominant factor, although sea-level rise could easily have contributed. Precise dating for the deposition of the silt layers is impossible, but sufficient evidence is now available from elsewhere in the country to show that flooding was beginning in the late Roman period:[1] the stratigraphy shown in Section 3 (fig. 51) and the associated finds strongly support such a dating. By the eleventh–twelfth century the sea had receded sufficiently to allow the area covered by the palace to be ploughed; indeed traces

[1] For a very brief summary of sea-level change see Cunliffe, 1966b.

of medieval agricultural activity have been found down to the 15 ft. (4.57 m.) O.D. contour. Presumably the land by that time had assumed much of its present form but it was not until the eighteenth century that houses began to spread along the road from the nucleus of the original medieval village to the west.

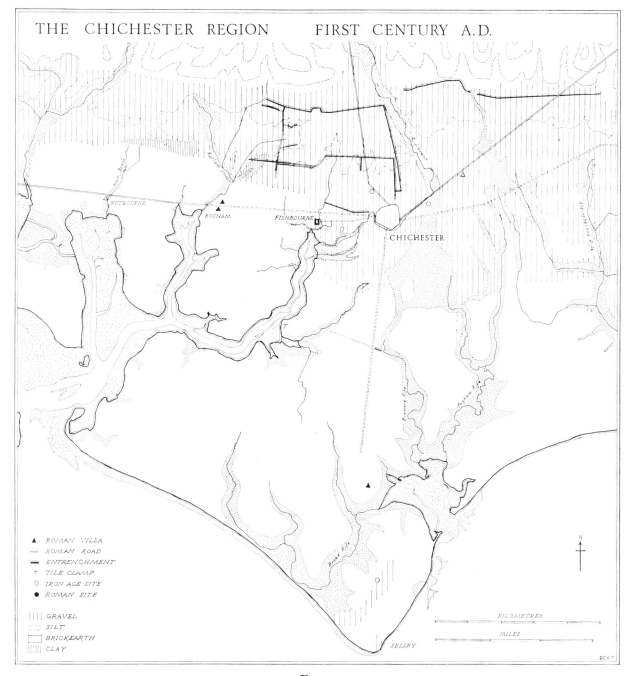

Fig. 4

THE CULTURAL ENVIRONMENT

THE ATREBATES   (fig. 5)

Our knowledge of the early history of the Atrebatic Kingdom is based almost entirely upon the interpretation of coin evidence; as yet archaeology has had little to offer. The flight of Commius from the Romans in Gaul and his arrival in central Southern Britain in about 50 B.C. is marked by the beginning of a coin sequence, inscribed with his name, which closely copy, and presumably supersede, the uninscribed British Q series.[1] If distribution is at all meaningful, the area over which Commius ruled would appear to have stretched from the middle Thames valley south to the Sussex coast. If we assume that the Commius who issued coins was the man who fled from Caesar, the origin of the Atrebatic ruling household can be placed firmly in the middle of the first century B.C.

Tincommius, the son of Commius, succeeded to the throne about 20 B.C., inheriting at first the firm anti-Roman policy of his father. Soon after, about 16 B.C., a complete reversal of policy took place. Old style coins depicting a triple-tailed horse were replaced by new types, evidently the work of a Roman engraver, one of them copying an issue of Augustus minted in 15–12 B.C., and Roman imports began to arrive at Silchester, the northern capital of the tribe. The limited historical evidence available adds support to the idea of a reversal of political views at about this time, for while Horace refers to Caesar's suppliants in Britain, in an ode published in 13 B.C., Dio tells us that fourteen years previously the Britons would not come to terms with Rome. Presumably, then, between these dates at least one British tribe became allied to Rome.

The new pro-Roman policy of Tincommius must have been difficult for the old die-hards of the ruling aristocracy to accept, but the policy persisted, though not without opposition. It seems that at about this time the friendly Dobunni to the north-west became estranged,[2] and finally internal or external pressures became so great that sometime before A.D. 7 Tincommius was forced to flee the country, running, significantly, to the Emperor for support. To reassert the authority of Tincommius would have been unwise. Instead, Augustus allowed him to be succeeded by his brother Eppillus, whom he recognized as *Rex*, a title which appeared on Atrebatic coins from thenceforward. Presumably, by this action, Augustus hoped that the pro-Roman policy would be made more palatable to the tribe, but judging by coin distribution Eppillus soon moved to Kent, ousted, it is suggested, by his brother Verica, whose coins covered much the same areas as did those of Commius.

Verica continued the pro-Roman policies of Tincommius: copying coins of Tiberius, styling himself *Rex* and even displaying his love of things Roman by including a vine-leaf emblem on the reverse side of his coins. But in spite of this blatant propaganda, his military position in the face of Catuvellaunian expansionist policies does not appear to have been strong, and as early as A.D. 25 Epaticcus, a son of Tasciovanus, gained control of the Northern Atrebatic area with its capital at Calleva, leaving Verica with the southern region east of the River Test centred upon the oppidum at Selsey. Continued aggression from the north may well have whittled away Verica's lands still further. In about A.D. 40 the situation worsened when Togodubnus and Caratacus, two active young men, succeeded their father

---

[1] All conveniently summarized in Frere, 1967, ch. 3, and Allen, 1944, 1961 and 1962.
[2] Hawkes in Clifford, 1961.

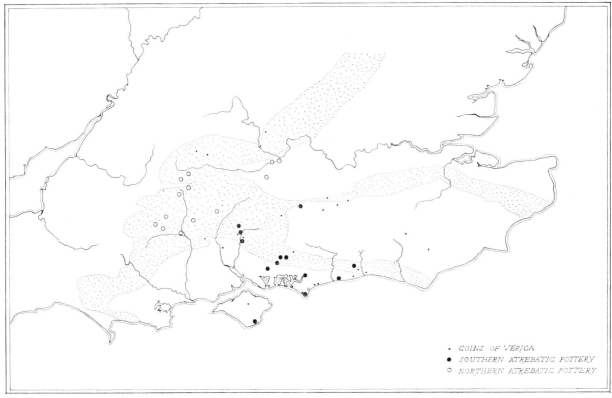

Fig. 5. Distribution of late Atrebatic coins and pottery: the chalk is stippled

Cunobelin as rulers of the Catuvellaunian kingdom. The new impetus given to Catuvellaunian aggression by this event reached crisis point in the south in A.D. 42–3, forcing Verica, who was by now an old man, to flee to Rome to ask the support of the Emperor Claudius.

This much is, in broad outline, the historical framework deducible from numismatic and literary evidence. A closer examination of the archaeological material, however, allows greater geographical accuracy to be obtained and highlights the cultural contrast between the pro- and anti-Roman factions. The late pre-Roman Iron Age pottery of the Atrebatic Kingdom differs significantly from contemporary styles current in surrounding regions. The principal forms include high-shouldered jars with beaded rims, high-shouldered bowls with upright rims, necked jars sometimes with cordons at the junction of neck and shoulder, and shallow dishes often in imitation of Gallo-Belgic imports. The distribution of assemblages containing these types, given in fig. 5, is closely followed by the distribution of coins of the Atrebatic rulers, particularly Commius. A more detailed analysis, however, allows a distinction to be made between a north-west group and a south-east group, the northern area containing elements clearly deriving from a close contact with Catuvellaunian types. Although the evidence is still imprecise, it thus seems possible to distinguish on ceramic grounds alone those areas which came under Catuvellaunian control in the twenty years or so before the invasion. Furthermore, the distribution of coins of Verica closely reflects the area covered by the non-Catuvellaunian pottery, defined here as Southern Atrebatic, adding support to the impression that the pro-Roman Atrebates can be recognized on cultural grounds.

It will be seen from fig. 5 that Atrebatic pottery does not spread east of the River Adur. Instead in East Sussex there is a totally different assemblage currently referred to as 'Southern Third B' which extends from the south coast, across the Weald, and into Kent. Precisely the same distribution pattern is shown by the local 'tin coins', some of which are stratified with the pottery in pits at the Caburn. Clearly, a cultural break occurs in central Sussex, which might represent an eastern limit for the Atrebates. That coins of Tincommius and Verica are rare in the eastern region adds support to this view.

Rather more impressive evidence comes from a consideration of the defended sites. In the area covered by the Southern Atrebatic pottery no site defended or redefended in the period immediately before the Roman Conquest is known. All the excavated forts, St Catherine's Hill, Torberry, Goosehill, Trundle, Highdown and Cissbury, were abandoned long before — surely dramatic evidence for the pro-Roman attitude of the inhabitants of these areas. Immediately outside the Southern Atrebatic area the situation is quite different. In East Sussex, the Caburn was strongly refortified in an up-to-date manner with a wide ditch similar to the anti-Roman defences found in Gaul in Caesar's time. The dating evidence, though slight, suggests a defence against the Claudian army. Several Kentish sites were also put in defensive order at this time. To the west, most of the old hill-forts that have been examined by excavation were brought up to date in the period before A.D. 43. Indeed, Vespasian was forced to destroy twenty of them during his western campaign. The closest that the defended sites are known to come to the kingdom of Verica is the strip of land between the Salisbury Avon and the Test. Here two sites are relevant: Boscombe Down West (Richardson, 1951) and Bury Hill (Hawkes, 1940 b). Both were defended by a double ditch system at the very end of the pre-Roman Iron Age, quite possibly against the threat of Roman attack; nothing comparable has been found east of the Test in the Southern Atrebatic region.

In summary, the archaeological evidence suggests that the kingdom of the Southern Atrebates, at the time of Verica, had been reduced to the region stretching from the Test to the Adur, and from the lower reaches of the Wey to the Channel coast. Apart from the entrenchments around Chichester (see pp. 17–36), the sites were undefended at the time of the Conquest, as would befit a tribe on friendly terms with Rome. They were surrounded on all sides by anti-Roman tribes. To the north and west lay old Atrebatic territories, now ruled by the Catuvellauni, further west were the hostile Durotriges, while to the east flank lived a tribe of unknown name, possibly a branch of the Cantiaci. Several problems remain unanswered. If aggression after the death of Cunobelin was as devastating as we suspect, why were old downland settlements of the Southern Atrebates not refortified against the Catuvellauni? Could it be that attack was so rapid and unexpected that Verica was caught off guard and forced to flee, leaving his lands to the attackers? Or was his flight caused entirely by internal conflicts and in no way connected with outside aggression? These are problems for which we are unable at present to provide satisfactory answers.

TIBERIUS CLAUDIUS COGIDUBNUS

It now seems very likely that the early history of the Fishbourne site is bound up closely with the fortunes of the local client king Tiberius Claudius Cogidubnus, whose capital was at Chichester (*Noviomagus Regnensium*). Cogidubnus is twice referred to in contemporary sources. Tacitus, writing of the early years of the Invasion, says that 'certain states were presented to King Cogidubnus, who maintained his unswerving loyalty right up to our own memory'.[1] The second reference comes from an inscription carved on Purbeck marble, found in Chichester in 1723 (*R.I.B.* 91). It records the erection of a temple to Neptune and Minerva, put up to the honour of the Imperial Household by a guild of craftsmen under the patronage of '*Tiberius Claudius Cogidubnus r(ex), legatus Augusti in Britannia*'. Cogidubnus, then, was a local client king at the time of the invasion, who remained an ally of Rome until at least the Flavian period, some thirty to forty years later. His origins are unknown, but the absence of any coins definitely assignable to him is an indication that he did not rule independently before A.D. 43. It may be that as a young member of the ruling household he kept control of the Atrebatic kingdom between the flight of Verica and the arrival of the Claudian army. A rather more likely possibility is that he had in fact fled the country earlier, perhaps as a child with Tincommius, and was living in exile in Rome while plans for the invasion were being prepared. The arrival of the aged and useless Verica would have provided Claudius with the opportunity of sending the now-Romanized Cogidubnus back to Britain with the invading forces to stabilize the Southern Atrebatic area on the left flank of the advance for sufficient time to allow the military consolidation of the east. If Cogidubnus had been a member of the ruling household, his arrival would have been acceptable to the natives, while his training in Rome would have made him eminently suitable in the eyes of Claudius as an ambassador for Roman culture. That he was both successful as a local leader for a long period, and spent much time in Romanizing his kingdom, are strong indications that these speculations may be close to the truth. Moreover, a manipulation of this kind would have been in keeping with the policies of Claudius. A comparable situation arose in Germany at this time: the Cherusci, having annihilated their nobility by civil war, asked Claudius for a king. Claudius replied by sending the only surviving royal prince, Italicus, a nephew of Arminius, reminding him as he left that he was the first man born at Rome as a citizen to proceed to a foreign throne. There are close similarities between the two events, the main difference being that Italicus eventually failed.

Early in his career as a Claudian supporter Cogidubnus would have been granted Roman citizenship, taking as his praenomen and nomen those of the Emperor, Tiberius Claudius. At what stage he received the much grander title of *legatus Augusti* is far less clear. As an Imperial Legate he would have been eligible to sit in the Roman senate: the upgrading of a client king to so exalted a position was an extremely rare occurrence. There are three possible occasions when he may have gained imperial favour: as a reward for help at the time of the Claudian invasion, for support during the Boudiccan incident, or as a supporter of Vespasian in A.D. 69. If the reward was given by Claudius it would have been in A.D. 48 when, taking advantage of a census, Claudius managed to persuade the senate, not without some difficulty, to elect a number of new members from among the ranks of the Gaulish

---

[1] Tacitus, *Agricola*, 14.

aristocracy. It seems, however, unlikely that Cogidubnus was among them — as a new ally of Rome only recently made a citizen he would surely have been low down on the list of promotions. There were many trusted Gauls with far stronger claims than Cogidubnus. About his part during the Boudiccan rebellion, there is little to say: serious conflict did not spread far south of the Thames and indeed there may have been no opportunity for Cogidubnus to have distinguished himself. Had he done so, it is likely that some reference to it would have been made by the literary sources.

The events following the death of Nero, in 68, provided some chance for loyal support.[1] In Britain the army was clearly divided in its allegiance to the various contenders to the throne, but its support was eventually swung to Vespasian by the efforts of his old legion, the *legio II Augusta*. The attitude of provincial leaders would have been crucial. It is a strong possibility that Cogidubnus led Vespasian's cause. He would have known Vespasian when the *legio II Augusta* passed through his kingdom in the early years of the Conquest, and may well have been a personal friend. Vespasian was generous with the honours which he handed out to his loyal supporters: for example L. Antistius Rusticus, *tribunus laticlavius* of the Second Legion, was given entitlement to a senatorial position as a newly-created legionary legate at this time. Such rapid promotion was unusual. The elevation of Cogidubnus to a similar standing might, in Vespasian's eyes, have been just reward for his active loyalty. Indeed Tacitus might well be referring to this as a specific act of faith when he mentions Cogidubnus' loyalty 'up to our own memory'. The arguments are coherent, if incapable of proof.

Without prejudging the meaning of the archaeological evidence offered below, it is relevant here to draw attention to the development at Fishbourne. The earliest residence on the site was a moderately luxurious masonry building erected about A.D. 60–5 and replaced, in the early Flavian period, by an enormous palatial structure. It is tempting to see the first building as the country house which Cogidubnus used when he was a local king and Roman citizen. In Britain it would have been of exceptional quality, quite suitable for a man of this rank. The palace which superseded it was erected soon after his supposed elevation to the rank of *legatus Augusti*. The new splendours and dignified architecture would have befitted the official residence of a newly-elected senator with a strong desire to surround himself with things Roman. Again, conclusive proof is not available, but the picture offered fits all the known facts and is, at the least, a likely explanation of the evidence.

How long Cogidubnus ruled is unknown, but certainly into the late 70s or 80s of the first century. This would not make him unduly long-lived. On his death his kingdom would have been absorbed into the rest of the province, his heirs, if there were any, passing into obscurity. In 30–40 years of peaceful reign he must have accomplished much in the area over which he ruled. During his lifetime he would have seen a torn native kingdom transformed into a worthy part of the Roman Empire.

THE DEVELOPMENT OF THE CHICHESTER REGION IN THE LATE FIRST CENTURY

The territory of the Southern Atrebates between the Test and Adur consisted of a series of east–west strips of different soils; the clay and sands of the Weald to the north, a fertile

---

[1] I owe this suggestion to Professor Eric Birley.

band of chalk through the centre and a complex of mixed sands, clays and gravels to the south along the coastal fringes. In the Chichester region (fig. 4) the geology was simpler: south of the chalk fringes came a wide band of relatively level gravel, which gave way on the coast to brickearth, a friable clayey silt. The downland strip was the scene of intensive arable farming. A dense scatter of peasant farms, some originating in the early years of the pre-Roman Iron Age, are found in all areas where sufficient field-work has been carried out. Most of them continue in use, little changed, well into the Roman period. The settlement pattern of the gravel and brickearth is not yet well known, although air photographs of the Selsey peninsula indicate the presence of considerable areas of ancient fields. The coastal fringes were also extensively settled by communities who were engaged in the extraction of salt from sea-water. Frequently individual sites can be shown to originate in the middle of the pre-Roman Iron Age and continue in use into the beginning of the Roman period. The basic settlement pattern seems, therefore, to imply the existence of a stable population remaining little changed from the Iron Age well into the Roman occupation. It is extremely unlikely that changing fortunes of the ruling minority had much effect on the everyday life of the bulk of the population; there is certainly no archaeological evidence of upheaval, war or any form of folk-movement in the countryside.

The capital of the Southern Atrebatic rulers and their households is generally thought to lie somewhere in the vicinity of Selsey Bill. Unfortunately coastal erosion has been so rapid in the area that many hundreds of acres of land have been removed by the sea; the pre-Roman capital is likely long since to have vanished, but within the last hundred years erosion has exposed a considerable number of Atrebatic coins together with gold waste, suggestive of a mint.[1] Unfortunately, no excavation has been carried out, nor have structures or occupation layers been adequately recorded and it is now highly improbable that any of the site survives. An occupation site found a mile or so inland in 1931 (White, 1934) produced pottery of the late pre-Roman Iron Age, but it is probably only an outlier of the main occupation area.

Perhaps the most dramatic features of the Chichester region in the first century A.D. were the Chichester entrenchments — about 10 miles (16 km.) of massive earthworks running across the gravel plain to the north of the town. Mr Bradley's survey of the remains is published in detail below (pp. 17–36) and need not be repeated here. Suffice it to say that three phases can be recognized: the first consisted of a defensive line linking the valleys leading to Bosham and Bognor, thus protecting about 60 sq. miles of land (154 sq. km.). The second system reduced the area to about 10 sq. miles (26 sq. km.) around Bosham and Fishbourne harbours, whilst the third strengthened about half the area, omitting the Bosham inlet. Such dating evidence as there is suggests a late pre-Roman Iron Age date. Functionally the entrenchments must be thought of as the defences for the lands and flocks belonging to the Atrebatic capital, that is, they define the territory of the *oppidum*. The fact that defences were considered necessary at all raises interesting problems, particularly as it is now believed that they were not all erected at the same time. It might be thought that they represent successive attempts of the Atrebatic rulers to defend themselves against the rampaging Catuvellauni, but why were the numerous peasant sites left undefended? Could it be that

---

[1] Allen, 1944, 4 and 8; Allen, 1961, 212.

the entrenchments were the work of the Catuvellauni, having captured the area? The fact that the works show successive phases of building would argue against this. A more reasonable explanation is that it was normal practice to define territory of the *oppidum* in this way, the earthworks serving as land divisions and stock enclosures as well as defences. Most of the theoretical difficulties would be overcome if this were the case.

Within the entrenched area there would, no doubt, have been farms and other small settlements besides the main *oppidum*. Sites of this period are known at Portfield (Curwen and Frere, 1947), Densworth (Holmes, 1961) and Whitehouse Farm, and there must be others yet to be discovered. Chichester itself presents a special problem, but at present there is no firm evidence to suggest a pre-Conquest date for its origins. Similarly the excavated part of Fishbourne has produced only a few scraps of 'native' ware — quite insufficient to indicate a pre-Roman settlement.

After A.D. 43 there were changes. At the beginning the army occupied Fishbourne and probably part of the site of Chichester, only to move off a year or two later, as the western campaigns progressed, leaving the area once more to the natives, now under the control of Cogidubnus. There is ample evidence from both Chichester and Fishbourne to show that here civil development was rapid: Fishbourne seems to have developed as a port while Chichester began to flourish as a town named *Noviomagus Regnensium*. Noviomagus (new market) clearly implies that the town superseded an earlier settlement, presumably the oppidum at Selsey. The full name is usually taken to mean 'the new market of the people of the Kingdom' (Richmond and Crawford, 1949, 42), the 'Kingdom' being that ruled over by Cogidubnus and comprising an area much the same as the old kingdom of Verica.

Some difficulties are raised by the statement of Tacitus that 'certain states were given to King Cogidubnus'.[1] Presumably these were not the old Northern Atrebatic regions, for the northern area was reconstituted as the *civitas Atrebatum* with its capital at *Calleva*, whilst the western area was lumped together as the *civitas Belgarum* governed from *Venta*. The states to which Tacitus was referring may well have been the parts of East Sussex and the Weald which we saw earlier were not culturally part of the original Kingdom of Verica. When the administrative boundaries of the new province were worked out it would have been logical to split up these eastern regions, creating the *civitas Cantiacum* in the north and adding the geographically isolated southern areas to the lands of Cogidubnus. The administrative convenience of the move could easily have been presented in political terms as a reward for faithful support.

Cogidubnus was evidently concerned to Romanize his new capital as quickly as possible. Two inscriptions, both carved on Purbeck marble, have been found belonging to this period. The first, the famous Cogidubnus stone, has already been mentioned (p. 13). The second, now lost, was a dedicatory inscription to Nero (*R.I.B.* 92). Both imply a high degree of urban sophistication: they show that within thirty years of the invasion Chichester could boast masonry buildings dedicated to the Imperial household, at least one temple to Roman gods, guilds of craftsmen organized on a thoroughly Roman basis and stone-workers capable of cutting good-quality Roman lettering. Other details of town planning and domestic architecture must await the results of further excavations.

---

[1] Tacitus, *Agricola*, 14.

In the countryside, too, it might be expected to find the effects of the Romanophile Cogidubnus. The Fishbourne palace is a notable example of his influence; the Angmering villa (Scott, 1938) was built at about the same time and there are several architectural details about the plan of the Southwick villa (Winbolt, 1932) which suggest a similar first-century date. The fine marble head of ?Germanicus from Bosham (Painter, 1965) is also indicative of an early structure, perhaps a villa or a shrine, in the neighbourhood. It is therefore reasonable to conclude that during the later part of the first century A.D. the influence of Cogidubnus was making itself felt in the town and countryside of his kingdom. It is against this background of active Romanization that the development of the Fishbourne site should be seen.

A FIELD SURVEY OF THE CHICHESTER ENTRENCHMENTS[1]

By Richard Bradley

INTRODUCTION

The Chichester Entrenchments are a group of fifteen linear earthworks on the gravel plain between the foot of the South Downs and Chichester Harbour. With the exception of two lines, EWA (i) and EWI, they are all within an area to the north and west of Chichester, $2\frac{1}{2}$ miles (4 km.) from north to south and $3\frac{1}{2}$ miles (5.6 km.) from east to west.

Two elements can be distinguished in their layout. The northernmost lines, EWA (i) and (ii), together cut off the entire coastal plain between Bosham and Bognor, including the Selsey peninsula where the dykes are supplemented by EWI. The area enclosed is about 60 square miles. The remaining earthworks form a rough square about the head of Chichester Harbour facing north east and west. In its simplest form this layout includes all the land between the River Lavant and the watercourse discharging into Bosham Harbour, thus taking in the whole Bosham peninsula and apparently enclosing an area of about 10 square miles.

The earthworks are still traceable over woodland and farmland for a total length of $17\frac{1}{4}$ miles (27.5 km.) and where they have not been damaged by agriculture they may survive to a height of up to 10 ft. (3 m.). The average width of the ditch is 20 ft. (6 m.) and that of the rampart is between 20 ft. (6 m.) and 30 ft. (9 m.). The dykes are almost exclusively on gravel, and, if we take this average cross section we may estimate the total volume moved in their construction as approximately 237,500 cubic yards. Its mass may be estimated as 340,000 tons. If we make allowance for the necessary vertical and horizontal movement of the excavated material, the labour demanded to construct the whole system would be roughly equivalent to 1,500,000 man hours or the labour of 410 men working a 10-hour day every day for a year.[2]

Though certain of the dykes are first referred to in the thirteenth century (Holmes, 1968), they first attracted academic notice early in the eighteenth century, and Cox (1735) describes several earthworks then surviving to the north of Chichester. The first survey was carried

---

[1] The writer has dealt separately with his differences of opinion with Mr Holmes who has suggested that the Entrenchments were all medieval deer leaps (*S.A.C.*, 107, 137–40).

[2] The calculation is based upon the method employed by Holden, 1967, p. 116, and incorporates data from the Overton Down experiment (Jewell, 1960).

out by William Sabatier in 1797 who set down his conclusions and a map of the Entrenchments in a useful manuscript paper published only recently (Sabatier, 1963). We have less
lucid accounts of the earthworks from three Sussex antiquarians writing in the nineteenth
century, Hay (1804), 'S' (1816), and Smith (1858). Finally we have a full survey of the
Entrenchments published by Williams-Freeman in 1934. His conclusions have since been
summarized by Curwen (1954) and Winbolt (1935), both of whom had suggestions as to
their date.

Several doubtful earthworks within their area have been marked by different editions of
the Ordnance Survey and these were included in a map of the Entrenchments published by
Miss K. M. E. Murray, F.S.A., in a report on a section cut through EWA (ii) in 1955 (Murray, 1956). One further section only recently published was cut through EWA (i) in 1965,
by J. R. Holmes, F.S.A. (Holmes, 1968).

A variety of suggestions have been put forward as to the date of these earthworks.
Attractive analogies can be drawn with the dykes about the late Iron Age oppida of
Bagendon, Calleva, Verulamium, and Camulodunum (Curwen, 1954; Frere, 1967). The
strongly rectilinear layout of the Entrenchments led at one time to the view that they were
all of a Roman military origin (Sabatier, 1963), a huge square 'camp', defences for
Chichester or even a model for Hadrian's Wall, while further suggestions have been made of
a sub-Roman date. It is possible to argue that their relationship to Stane Street to the east
and to the track from Chichester to the downland ridgeway to the west is reminiscent of
Grim's Bank to the north of Silchester (O'Neil, 1943 and 1944). Alternatively they are
claimed as the beach head of Aella's invasion of Sussex in A.D. 471 or as territorial boundaries
similar to the Froxfield Entrenchments, 15 miles (25 km.) to the north-west. A context in the
seventh-century conflict between Wessex and the South Saxons also has its advocates.
Finally it has been suggested in a recent paper that the earthworks are all of a medieval
origin and were constructed as deer fences, several of them to enclose the Forest of Chichester
in the thirteenth century (Holmes, 1968).

In view of so much speculation it was decided to re-examine the Entrenchments as part
of the Fishbourne project. It soon became apparent that no existing survey was entirely
adequate and accordingly a full field survey was carried out by the present writer in 1966
and 1967. With the exception of one small area, where the landowner was unwilling to
co-operate, the complete line of every earthwork was re-examined on the ground. Finally
EWA (i) was examined by excavation.

The writer wishes to thank all the landowners for permission to carry out this survey.
Thanks are also due to Professor C. F. C. Hawkes for an extended discussion of his work on
the Colchester Dykes in advance of publication, and for many valuable suggestions. I am
particularly grateful to the Goodwood Estate Company for permission to excavate on the
line of EWA (i).

The earthworks will be referred to throughout by the numbering given them by Williams-
Freeman and followed by all subsequent writers. Where necessary this system has been
expanded to include new lines. It should be noted in particular that the two lengths of
earthwork usually considered together as EWA will now be treated separately as EWA (i)
and (ii). EWD will be similarly divided. The earthworks of this group will therefore be
referred to as follows:

East–West   A   (i)   Boxgrove (926085) to E. Lavant (866086).

                             (ii)   Mid Lavant (859082) to W. Stoke (824084).

                 B   Summersdale (863066) to Sennicotts (842067).

                 C   W. of Chichester Walls (853050) to Fishbourne (843053).

                 D   (i)   Northlands (838064) to Ashling (818066).

                             (ii)   Northlands (838064) parallel to and to the south of EWD (i).

                 E   N. of Oakwood Park (832070).

                 F   N. of Densworth House (832075).

                 G   S. of Lie Wood (825081).

                 H   Bishop Otter College (863057).

                 I   Kipson Bank (858009) to ?Manhood End (843013).

North–South   1   ?Bishop Otter College (864057) to Mid Lavant (859082).

                 2   ?NE of Chichester walls (862052) to Summersdale (863066).

                 3   E. Broyle Copse (852065).

                 4   Sennicotts (842067) to Northlands (838064).

                 5   W. Stoke (830082) to Clay Lane (826062).

As well as the earlier accounts set out above, all relevant estate and tithe maps were consulted and in addition a full examination was made of air photographs of the area. The 1934 survey made little detailed use of early maps and took no account of the evidence of aerial photography. Sabatier's valuable account of the earthworks was at that time unknown.

The interpretation of the earthworks given in this paper relies strongly upon a reconsideration of details of their layout. However, since Williams-Freeman's first aim was to give a full account of the line of each earthwork, it will only be necessary here to supplement or modify the views expressed in his admirably lucid report. Where no comment is offered his views are accepted in their entirety.

These modifications being complete, the junctions of the lines will be treated separately on pp. 27 f., possible entrances on pp. 28 f., and a revision of the accepted view of the relevant surface geology will be offered on pp. 29 f.

THE LINES OF THE ENTRENCHMENTS RECONSIDERED

(Fig. 6)

EWA (i)

(92180846). The line is traceable to within 340 yards (310 m.) of the edge of a steep north–south valley. Beyond this point all trace of the earthwork has been removed by ploughing which has also removed part of a large complex of undated lynchets spreading into the same area.

(91220844). Between this point and (89390838) the line of the earthwork was used as the south boundary of Halnaker Park. It has been much damaged and the unusual width of the ditch in places suggests recutting. The line seems also to have been used as an early road and appears on certain estate maps as 'Pippe' or 'Peepe Street' (? pippel street (O.E.) = pebbled road).

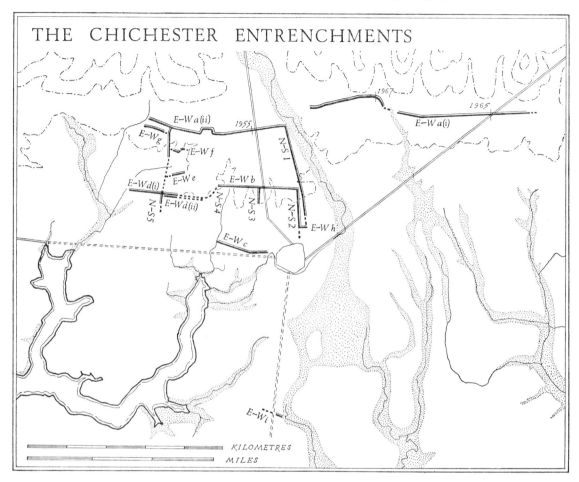

THE CHICHESTER ENTRENCHMENTS

Fig. 6

(89600839).   At this point all trace of the line is lost in pasture over a distance of 135 yards (123 m.), but despite the deceptively rounded end to the earthwork to the west the line is shown as continuous at this point on a survey of the Goodwood Estate of 1791. The present estate wall is in any case sinking into the filling of the vanished ditch.

(89300838).   The line is similarly lost in the cutting for the cross-roads at Waterbeach. However, the impression given by certain maps that a branch ran off from this line in a north-westerly direction is misleading and results from confusion of the main earthwork with a modern boundary bank. This is emphasized by a slight but original change of alignment in the dyke at this point.

(89000845).   Though Williams-Freeman states that the line at this point was destroyed entirely in the laying out of Goodwood Park, Sabatier shows the earthwork as continuous for a further 300 yards (274 m.). Its line can still in fact be traced as far as the Goldings (88780845) as a broad belt of gravel in land now under the plough.

(88700847).   The line is lost in the Goldings but since this point has recently been shown to have been on the line of a major watercourse, it is suggested the line was not continuous.

(88570848). The line is again lost between the western limit of the Goldings and the Cottage (88450860) where Williams-Freeman was able to locate the earthwork running approximately NNW. The hedge lines marked at this point in Yeakel and Gardner's 1791 survey suggest the change of alignment occurred about 200 yards (183 m.) west of the former point.

(88200889). The short break to the east of the Chichester road was not an original feature and was caused by chalk digging. The line was apparently continuous at this point in 1791.

(87200875). Though Williams-Freeman was vague on this point, the earthwork is in fact traceable through the whole of Valdoe Coppice as far as Lavant Lodge (87100870).

(87100870). The line seems to have run under the Lodge and though Williams-Freeman suggests that its line immediately to the west was destroyed in 1779 it does in part survive in the hedgerow to the south of the lane to East Lavant.

(86540858). This line seems to have ended against a slight north–south valley branching off the main valley of the River Lavant. Air photographs suggest no further extensions.

This line runs for a total length of 3¾ miles (6 km.). As far west as the Goldings it runs across open country at an even height of 150 ft. (44 m.) and it is probably this factor which determined the straightness of its line. To the west of the break at the Goldings it meets more uneven ground and its abandonment of straight lengths is perhaps the result of again following the natural contours. Its line may also be explained by the surface geology of the area. Except for one quite short length, it lies entirely upon gravel and closely follows the edge of the Downland chalk. Thus it appears to be laid out deliberately to enclose the largest possible area of the gravel plain to the south. This observation also applies to the next line to be considered.

It may be possible to identify the junctions between the work of three, possibly four, distinct gangs in the section between East Lavant and the Goldings.

EWA (ii)

(85960818). The eastern limit of this line is not, as most writers have suggested, at the northern end of NS1 but a few yards to the east at the edge of the Lavant valley. This modification is supported by Sabatier's account.

(84060800). At this point the earthwork leaves its alignment and forms three sides of a rough trapezium to the north. The lie of the land suggests the existence of a spring in the north-east corner of this 'salient'. There is no trace of a south side to this feature, nor of any occupation site in the area.

(83180810). At this point Williams-Freeman lost the line of the earthwork. To explain this apparent gap he suggested it had followed the line of the original West Stoke parish boundary, and formed a second 'salient' or 'bastion', this time, curiously, deviating from the main alignment to the south. However, the line is in fact faintly traceable at this point and the earthwork is plainly marked as continuous on a map of 1791. Further, of the three sides postulated for this 'bastion' only the west side (NS5) is a linear earthwork at all. The east side is merely a wide and overgrown hedgerow and the south side is a modern lynchet.

(84300836). The end of this line is just below the crest of a north–south valley in Lie Wood. Suggestions of further extensions to the west in the early accounts receive no support in the field or from an early map of the wood.

Like EWA (i) this line runs at a roughly even height between two north–south valleys and just below the exposure of the chalk. Except for the 'salient' to be discussed on pp. 33 f., this earthwork runs in four straight alignments of uneven lengths.

It is suggested that the two lines, though certainly never joined as some writers have suggested, do form part of the same system. The factors determining their layout are the same and their lines lack the inflexibility of those of the other dykes. Again, at several points on the line of EWA (i) unusual numbers of flints were noted on the remains of the rampart. The uniformity of their sizes suggested strongly that they had been deliberately selected. In the field this feature was only noted again in the 'salient' on EWA (ii). Miss Murray observed a similar phenomenon in her section through the latter line at West Lavant and suggested that such flints had been collected to 'cobble' the rampart; she found no trace of internal timbering. Two fortuitous sections cut by farm tracks through EWA (i), (91990845 and 89200840), are support for the view that the rampart was of ordinary dump construction probably over a low core used as a marking out bank.

EWG

This line was discovered and fully traced by Williams-Freeman. It runs from the valley in Lie Wood at which the last line ended eastwards as far as NS5.

EWF

(83080754). The line is traceable to the west to within 70 yards (64 m.) of NS5; beyond this point it has been destroyed by gravel digging. It is very probable that the two lines joined, though this is no longer provable.

(83380765). To the east it seems to end at the edge of a small valley but a further slight depression on the line of the ditch close to its bottom may indicate a further extension.

The earthwork runs on three distinct alignments, two of them roughly parallel and the third joining them at an angle of about 120°. The reason for this is obscure. The change in line may have been to avoid some former obstacle or it may have been to enclose an occupation site to its south which produced a surface sherd of the first century A.D. (Smith, 1858; Holmes, 1961). On the other hand, it is quite as likely that this site could owe its position to the shelter offered by this curious arrangement and so be secondary to the earthwork.

A third possibility is that this is all that remains of a second 'salient' similar to that on EWA (ii). This cannot be proved.

EWB

(86250665). All ambiguity among the early accounts as to the eastern limit of this line is now removed by the publication of Sabatier's map which shows that the line begins at the northern limit of NS2 and does not branch off NS1.

(84250665). At this point the line is lost. Hay's account suggests that it continued to join NS5 at a point west of Densworth House, 1580 yards (1444 m.) to the north–west (829074). This is probably because he favoured the view that the Entrenchments were of a rectangular 'Roman' layout and already knew of a (recent) earthwork running west from this point. 'S', perhaps from reading Hay, describes the line as turning south to Fishbourne Harbour at a non-existent Densworth Common, but here we should adopt Williams-Freeman's suggestion that this is an error for Saltbox Common, where it ends today. In any case Densworth is not north of Fishbourne. In preference to these two accounts we should accept the earlier evidence of Sabatier and of the Goodwood Estate survey that the line ended at this point. Smith in 1858 puts the same view.

Though it might be suggested the eastern end is dictated by a marshy valley to its north-east, the western limit can only be explained by reference to other earthworks in the area. Discussion of this line will therefore be postponed to p. 26.

EWE

(83360700). The line is first traceable as a vague fold in scrub running between two gravel pits. To the west it crosses a corner of Oakwood Park as a marked terrace. It is again cut away by a disused gravel pit but reappears to its west as a steep scarp in undergrowth a little north of the Park boundary.

(83000692). Beyond this point its line is doubtful and cannot be traced for dense undergrowth.

The east end of this line was discovered by Sabatier. Otherwise except for a short length noted but mapped incorrectly by Williams-Freeman this is a new line. The east end is probably original, and it is suggested it was designed merely to cut off the Oakwood Plateau from the valley below. The line runs a little below the crest of the ridge, and would in this case have joined NS5 at a point where the latter is no longer traceable.

EWD (i) and (ii)

(Most of this line could not be examined on the ground.)

EWD (i)

(82800646). Probably because of recent damage there is now some doubt whether the line was continuous between its western end at (81880657) and this point. However, Sabatier tells us: 'It runs [east] uninterruptedly forming a boundary line between two estates for about 1000 yards', that is to say as far as (82800646), thus resolving the problem entirely.

EWD (i) and (ii)

(82650646). At this point an air photograph has revealed the junction between this line and NS5. This is to be discussed on pp. 31 f. It shows that immediately to the east of the latter line the main earthwork is supplemented by a second line of defence to the south EWD (ii). The main line at this point is also visible as a continuous crop mark and therefore the suggestion that this was an entrance of Roman tutulus type is not well founded. In any case an entrance of this form would be defended on the outside and not the inside.

(82800646). The line east from the latter point to (83740639) was again the boundary of two estates. Though the earthworks do not survive it is suggested that the course of EWD (i) is represented by a hedgerow running east from a point a little beyond its present eastern end (83000643) and by a change of alignment in the Fishbourne parish boundary (83930628). The course of EWD (i) is possibly represented by a crop mark at (83800635). If that is the case it turned from its original straight line towards the north at this point.

In the enforced absence of fieldwork this account gives more breaks in the line than are probably justified. The line seems to run east from a stream discharging at Bosham, and it may be assumed on a geological basis that the area beyond it to the west was heavily wooded. Its eastern limit is best seen in relation to other dykes and so discussion of it will be postponed to p. 26.

EWH

This line was described by Sabatier and included in his map of the Entrenchments. Otherwise it was almost completely unknown. It appears that it ran between NS2 and the probable southern limit of NS1. It faced north and if his map is correct its site is probably covered now by Bishop Otter College (863057). If its relationship to the two north–south lines has been suggested correctly, it now explains a difficult passage in Hay's description of the system: 'The outer line [NS1] strikes out or separates

D

from the inner line [NS2] at the Watery Line.' The Watery Line, which Williams-Freeman failed to locate, was a spring north of the city walls. Sabatier defines its position in relation to this line when he says: 'Troops might have been furnished with water from a very fine spring . . . exactly at the spot where the little connecting line [EWH] terminates to the west.'

This line will be further discussed on pp. 31 f.

EWC

This line has at times been taken as the agger of a Roman road. This view is no longer acceptable since Williams-Freeman was able to show that the line did not end, as was once thought, at Chichester Westgate and that it was bounded to its north by a ditch.

(856050). A resistivity survey carried out in playing fields to the west of Chichester Walls suggested that the line did not continue as far as the city and therefore cannot, as Hay implied, have been set out from 'the north-west corner of the city wall'. It is suggested that its line is better explained in relation to the original course of the River Lavant which formed a wide bend to the west of the city as recently as the seventeenth century.

(84400527). At this point the damaged line of the earthwork was reused as the Fishbourne parish boundary. A false impression of its date is given by a low bank added to the crest of the rampart. This is either a boundary bank or upcast from a drainage ditch to the north.

(84810507). The rectangular mound described by Williams-Freeman as projecting from the line to the south was destroyed by building before the survey began. The Fishbourne tithe map shows it as being surrounded by a ditch at least to the south and east. It was probably a medieval moated home-stead with the characteristic internal platform.

(83900557). The disturbance south of Clay Lane at this point which Williams-Freeman claimed as an extension to the line is best explained as the result of clay digging.

This is clearly the line that Hay wrote of as: 'The Roman Bank (a bank and ditch so called in the meadows a little NW. of Mr Newman's Nursery) . . . which terminates at the north-west corner of the city wall.' 'Mr Newman's Nursery' which Williams-Freeman failed to locate lay a little south of the line at (85120493).

The eastern end of the line was, it is suggested, at the River Lavant. Its western limit was probably at a water course discharging into Fishbourne Harbour to the south. In that case the dyke was surely intended to cover the head of the harbour.

EWI

Curwen (1954) has brought forward convincing documentary evidence for a dyke of some date crossing the Selsey peninsula. The line he suggests from this evidence is unsatisfactory both in the field and for a defensive purpose.

(85760090 to 85580098). It is tentatively suggested that a truer line is represented by a short length of rampart with a linear pond to its north at Kipson Bank. Further ponds and a parish boundary occur exactly on this line which if continuous would cross the Selsey peninsula at its narrowest point. Unfortunately, the junction with the Roman Road south from Chichester does not survive and so we have no indication of its date.

NS1

(85930818). This line was butted on to EWA (ii) with the junction 25 yards west of its eastern limit. It is therefore misleading to think of the line as turning at this point. See further, p. 27.

(86450600). The true end of this line is in some doubt. No trace of it has ever been found further to the south and early maps of the area suggest no further extensions. Sabatier's map shows the line as ending at this point, and the other early accounts are divided between that of Hay, quoted above, who says that the earthwork branched off NS2 by means of EWH, and 'S' who claims the line started at Chichester Eastgate. Since Sabatier speaks of EWH as a 'connecting work', it is evident that he accepted Hay's view. 'S's' account throughout is consistent only in error. At all events, if EWH were not joining the end of this line to the other north–south dyke, it would be hard to see any reason for its existence. If it were only intended to cut off the space between two continuous lines it would be placed at the junction of NS2 and EWB.

The significance of this arrangement will be discussed further on pp. 31 f.

NS2

(86250665). This line is clearly marked in the Goodwood Estate survey of 1791. Its site has now been taken by a line of claypits and not as Williams-Freeman suggested by the lane to their west.

(86180586). The line is again traceable through the grounds of the Police Training School on exactly the same alignment.

(86170570). Sabatier's account suggests no further extensions to the south but Hay traces its line to 'the north-east corner of the city walls opposite the Mount in the Friary'. This is a reference to the damaged motte in Priory Park. There are, however, two angles in the wall here that could be taken as the north-east corner of the city defences. The line wrongly adopted by Williams-Freeman was aligned exactly on the more easterly of these (86330522) and he claimed to have found traces of the line at this point. Nothing appears today and it may well be that he was mistaken. The correct line is aligned equally exactly on the other point (86260523) and since Hay speaks of no change of alignment this course is to be preferred.

No trace of the line has been found further to the south but no excavation has been recorded in the city on quite this line. If it did run on to the south to meet the River Lavant it would have met the city wall to the south in between two curiously close bends in its line. It could thus have provided the otherwise missing north–south axis of the city's defences and have cut off a wide bend of the river to the east. However, this is to imply a possible date for the line for which no evidence has been presented. Further discussion will therefore be postponed to pp. 31 f.

NS3

(85270624). The only problem concerning this line is its southern limit. No trace of any extension beyond this point can be found in the field or from documentary sources. Sabatier marked its end as within 15 yards (14 m.) of its present limit. On the other hand it might have been aligned upon the change of course in EWC further to the south at (85080500). If it were intended to join this line we must regard it as incomplete. On the other hand it is only one of a number of short lines projecting from the main dykes on the inside — EWF is another example — and it is perhaps better to treat these together and to look for some common explanation for them all. This will be attempted on p. 33.

The earthwork as a whole is almost certainly unfinished even over the length now visible. In East Broyle Copse (852065) the ditch consists only of a number of irregular pits. Farther to the south the line of the ditch has unfortunately been obliterated. For discussion of the significance of this see p. 34.

NS4

(83990658). The slight earthwork recorded by Williams-Freeman to the east of Salthill Road was sectioned by cable trench at this point. This showed that the ditch was cut through an eighteenth-century brick kiln and thus of no archaeological significance.

(83700544).   A further mains trench at this point running across the entire area from east to west showed that the only earthwork on Williams-Freeman's line was a slight ditch containing a modern brick low in its filling. No other features appeared.

(83570503) to (83530473).   The entire 'earthwork' along this line represents the remains of a line of claypits of no great antiquity.

These observations raise the question of whether there was ever any relevant earthwork on this line. Our sole authority apart from Williams-Freeman is 'S', who says of EWB: 'Forming an acute angle on Densworth Common it proceeds south to the head of Fishbourne Harbour.' The reference to Densworth Common has already been discussed on pp. 22 f., above. 'Acute angle' is a term he uses again elsewhere with a bold disregard for its meaning. If we consider the line as a whole he could have made the same errors as Williams-Freeman.

However, this leaves us with the line of the Fishbourne parish boundary to explain. This runs north from the head of the harbour to the apparent western end of EWB on two straight alignments, the change of line coinciding with the suggested course of EWD. If its complete line can no longer be said to represent an earthwork might it not equally plausibly follow the line of a trackway north from the harbour? This is beyond proof.

Apart from 'S's' account, the sole explicit evidence for an earthwork on any part of this line is the crop mark mentioned in the discussion of EWD (ii) on p. 23, above. If, as this implied, that line turned to the north at this point, then it would be reasonable to envisage a connection between this and the end of EWB. Both run straight across open country at an even height of 100 ft. (30 m.) and a line on this course linking the two dykes would continue to follow the contours. It is perhaps significant that both Sabatier and Smith regarded EWD as belonging to the same line as EWB.

Though it is suggested that EWB, this line and EWD formed one continuous earthwork, it is best on the present evidence to retain Williams-Freeman's numbering for the three separate sections.

NS5

(82980816).   Hay wrote of this line: '[It] turns southwards and [running] to the west of Densworth House . . . [it] passes through lands belonging to Mr Blagden of Chichester [and] goes through part of Clay Lane Common.' Williams-Freeman was unable to locate Mr Blagden's lands and substituted Saltbox Common to the west of the apparent limit of EWB for Clay Lane Common. In fact a map of 1842 shows that the lands in question were the area now comprising Oakwood Park. The road to the south of the park is still called Clay Lane so the other reference need give us no difficulty.

Between the two points given above, the line is apparently visible as a crop mark crossing the line of EWD and making a very slight change of alignment at that point.

There is no evidence of the line to the north between here and the point west of Densworth House to which Williams-Freeman was able to trace it (82920738). To the south too we must rely on Hay's description. Though he went on to suggest that the line turned eastwards to join EWC this was evidently a guess based again on the theory that he was dealing with a rectangular Roman 'camp'.

We do have one further clue. This dyke is apparently one referred to in a document of 1225, as running north from Fishbourne 'through Bichebrook to the Winchester highway' (Holmes 1968). For reasons already given, it is unlikely that any earthwork ran north from the harbour, but we should remember that the Roman palace is strictly speaking at New Fishbourne and that Old Fishbourne lies further to the west and closer to the known line of NS5. Bichebrook and the 'Winchester Highway' cannot be identified. Even so its limit remains in doubt.

SPURIOUS ENTRENCHMENTS

These are earthworks sometimes included among the Entrenchments which must now be considered to be of a recent origin.

(i) (89100820) to (88120817). This line is that of a late eighteenth-century ha-ha forming a boundary of Goodwood Park.

(ii) (87640886) to (87270827). This is merely a parish boundary bank which has been butted on to the earlier line of EWA (i).

(iii) (87470849) to (87690818). This line is that of a wide shallow gully. It is clear that it is secondary to the boundary bank described above.

(iv) (85160804) to (85210789). The causeway at this point represents the remains of the original drive of West Lavant House, so placed to avoid a toll-gate on the Mid Lavant–Chichester road.

(v) (85110635) to (85240616). We should accept Williams-Freeman's view that the 'ditch' at this point is the 'holloway' left by the original Chichester–West Stoke road.

(vi) (83200810) to (83000703). This line was seen by Williams-Freeman as the east side of a second 'salient'. For this see pp. 21 f. To the south the line is continued after a break of 400 yards (366 m.) as a terraced farm track with a modern boundary bank to its west and 400 yards (366 m.) further south again as a lynchet of recent formation. The whole line is therefore to be regarded as suspect.

(vii) (83200793) to (82950799). The south side of this hypothetical 'salient' has been treated on pp. 21 f.

(viii) (82920736) to (82530737). This line appears for most of its course as a sharp high bank, with a ditch to its south just short of its western limit. Its profile is therefore suggestive of a recent boundary earthwork. Against this it must be admitted that it does start from an apparent bend in the line of NS5. On the other hand, unlike all the accepted east–west lines, it faces south rather than north.

(ix) Curwen's EWI. See p. 24.

THE JUNCTIONS OF THE LINES

In this section it is intended to present the direct evidence upon which the suggested sequence of construction on pp. 30 f., is based.

EWA (ii) and:

(i) NS1 (85930817). The junction survives intact though the ditch of NS1 is missing and its rampart is damaged. The rampart of the east–west line seems to have been cut away by the ditch of NS1 which was thus linked with the other ditch. Faint traces of EWA (ii) exist for 25 yards (23 m.) to the east of this junction.

(ii) NS5 (82970814). No junction survives. It is possible that the north–south line ended some yards short of the other line. All that can be said is that the ditch of NS5 did not cut the east–west rampart as in the case above.

EWG and:

NS5 (82970798). For the entire field west of this junction EWG is now missing. However, exactly on its line there is a low mound of the rampart of NS5. It may then be assumed that the ditches of the two lines met and that the east–west rampart was carried across and butted on to the rampart of the other line.

EWF and:

NS5 (82930753).   No trace survives of this (hypothetical) junction.

EWE and:

NS5 (828069).   No trace survives of these lines at this (again hypothetical) junction.

EWB and:

(i)   NS2 (86250665).   Though this junction is now built over it is possible on the evidence of the 1791 Goodwood Estate Survey that the two lines did not quite meet. See further, p. 29.

(ii)   NS3 (85280663).   Little of this junction survives because the east–west line is breached at this point by a track of unknown date which has now removed any trace of a north–south ditch. On this see p. 29.
All that can now be said is that the rampart of NS3 rides up over the tail of the east–west rampart.

(iii)   NS4 (840067).   Though no trace survives at this point it is suggested the line would have made a simple angle.

EWD (i) and (ii):

(i)   NS4 (839064).   This angle too is missing. Here it is suggested that EWD (ii) ended and EWD (i) made a simple angle.

(ii)   NS5 (82660646).   This crucial junction is entirely invisible on the ground, and so we must rely on the evidence of an air photograph. From this it appears that the north–south line cuts the east–west line. EWD (ii) begins a short distance to the east of the junction.

EWH and:

(i)   NS1 (86480575).   This junction does not survive.

(ii)   NS2 (86220576).   This junction does not survive.

POSSIBLE ENTRANCES

This section is concerned with all those interruptions in the lines that could be claimed as part of the original layout.

EWA (i):

(91550843).   Probably caused by modern gravel digging.

(91230842).   The junction of this line and Roman Stane Street. Excavation at this point in 1965 was insufficient to determine their relationship. *Contra* see Holmes, 1968, and for critical comments on that paper as a whole see *S.A.C.*, 107, 137–40.

(89320838).   The present gap is the result of a road junction. Whether the line was originally continuous is not known.

(887084).   Probably original. See pp. 33 f.

(88230893).   The line is badly disturbed but may possibly have been crossed by a causeway at this point.

(87640888).   Badly disturbed. The line is cut by a medieval or later 'ride' and a parish boundary bank is butted on to the rampart (ii on p. 27). This corresponds with a change of line in the earthwork. Though the question must remain open it is probably an original feature.

(86890868).   Probably an original feature. The entire layout between (87050867) and (8670861) should represent an entrance.

EWA (ii):

(85520816).   Probably the crossing point of the Roman Chichester–Silchester road. No evidence on their relationship is yet available.[1]

(85150807).   The result of levelling to improve the view from West Lavant House.

(83830810).   A narrow terrace or causeway but bounded by a recent parish boundary bank. Probably an original feature.

EWB:

(86250665).   The gap between this line and NS2 marked in the Goodwood Estate survey may be original, but this cannot be proved.

(85700674) and (84560677).   In both cases the line is absent today but was marked as continuous in the Goodwood Estate survey. Both points are the junctions of lines with streams and on this point it is possible the map was inaccurate. The picture is further confused by gravel digging. The question must be left open.

(85100664).   The gap had been caused by gravel digging by the time of Sabatier's survey.

(84000679).   As mentioned above the angle between this line and NS4 does not survive. However, Sabatier wrote of the apparent end of EWB: 'At this spot there is every appearance as if a highway had gone through the work.' There may therefore have been an entrance in the angle between the two lines.[2]

(85280663).   The gap in the angle between this line and NS3 already referred to on p. 28 may be an original feature. This is uncertain because of recent gravel digging.

EWF:

(83200756).   A narrow break in the line. Heavily overgrown but could be original.

NS1:

(86280676).   A gap is marked at about this point in the Goodwood Estate survey corresponding to the gap between EWB and NS2. This is now built over and so its origin too is in doubt.

NS5:

(82980816).   The origin of this break in the line is entirely uncertain.

THE GEOLOGY REVISED

No account of the Entrenchments has given much attention to the surface geology of the area over which they are found. Since this is relatively uniform this has been entirely

---

[1] It will be noted that this line for the Roman road is at variance with that proposed by Margary (1953). This course is supported by both field and documentary evidence.

[2] It should be noted that Sabatier thought the gap was caused by a Roman road which he locates on his map to the south west running on a line towards Bosham. There is now no supporting evidence.

excusable. On the other hand the pattern of rivers to which the earthworks are to be related is of basic importance. It is here that a major change in the long-accepted picture is required.

Every account of the Entrenchments has recognized to some extent the importance of the River Lavant. It has been accepted that with only minor variations its present course is original. The recent publication of a new summary of the surface geology of West Sussex shows this assumption to have been mistaken (Hodgson, 1967). It appears instead that the original line of the river was southwards from Chichester bisecting the Selsey peninsula and meeting the English Channel to the east of Selsey Bill.

The date at which its course was changed may be inferred with some confidence. Its long-accepted line departs from the original flood plain where it meets the early Roman Stane Street and runs alongside the road until it reaches the Roman town. Here it skirts the defences to the south. The new channel probably joined an existing stream discharging into Chichester Harbour close to the present city wall. It is more than likely that it was to provide a source of water for the developing town that the river was first canalized. A date in the first century A.D. seems the most likely.

Because of this, the area which we may see the Entrenchments as having enclosed changes radically according to the date proposed. In the final section therefore, the two questions must be regarded as intimately connected.

DISCUSSION

These modifications to previously published plans of the Entrenchments have the effect of making some of the discussion of their purpose in earlier accounts irrelevant. If we may return briefly to two of the main suggestions summarized in the first section, this point can be simply illustrated.

With the suggested modifications to the lines of NS1 and 2 and EWC, it is hard to see the lines as being related to the city of Chichester. This view demands that both these north–south lines be set out further to the east and does nothing to explain the concentration of east–west dykes north-west of Fishbourne. This being so, we may also dismiss Williams-Freeman's suggestion that the dykes defended Chichester and Fishbourne together as one unit.

In the same way it is now quite clear that the exactly rectangular layout spoken of by most of the accounts from Cox onwards, was an illusion and that each of the lines was in fact closely related to the pattern of rivers and to surface geology. This releases us from the need to think of all the Entrenchments as being necessarily contemporary and as belonging to one layout.

It is at this point that we may refer back to the evidence presented on pp. 27 f. Here we have set out a complex set of chronological relationships between certain of the individual lines. It must now be asked whether these reflect merely the sequence of construction of one overall layout or the junctions of elements of several separate systems.

The best starting point for this discussion is EWA (i). With the modifications set out above this is the only line of the Entrenchments to the east of the River Lavant. It can be distinguished from all the other lines but EWA (ii) by being basically a 'contour dyke' and by running on straight alignments only where to do this is to follow the lie of the land. EWA (ii) is of very much the same type and it has been argued above (pp. 21 f.), both from their relationship to the edge of the chalk and from details of their construction, that they can be treated together. This view was also taken by Williams-Freeman and Sabatier.

If this basic argument can be accepted we should again consider the purpose of these two lines. As has been said they linked the watercourses discharging at Bognor and at Bosham and cut off the coastal plain to the south including the Selsey peninsula. Here at least the course of the Lavant need give us no difficulty. No other lines relate to so extensive an area.

We may now turn to the remaining dykes which are all to the west of the Lavant. It can, it is suggested, be shown that NS1 is later than both EWA (ii) and NS2, and that NS2 is itself later than both the lines just discussed. Similarly each of the north–south lines but NS2 depends on the prior existence of the east–west lines, with the exception only of NS4 which is really part of such a line and of NS5 which has been seen to cut and thus to post-date EWD (i). In the same way EWE, F and G were apparently butted on to NS5 after the latter's construction.

Since it seems that the other, more rectilinear, lines within this area are related to EWA (ii) alone we must remember that taken in isolation it links only the Bosham watercourse and the River Lavant. Of the two remaining east–west lines only that consisting of EWB, NS4 and EWD together shares this same general basis. It is therefore reasonable to adopt the hypothesis that this line was intended to supplement EWA (ii). On the other hand its eastern limit was not in fact the Lavant itself but the northern limit of NS2 which cut off a wide bend in the river to its east. Since neither dyke can be explained without the other, perhaps we should take NS2 and EWD as contemporary, and yet there is some difficulty in assuming that this layout was of the same date as EWA (i) and (ii), for in a sense it is screening the area of Chichester and Bosham Harbours from other lands enclosed by the latter line. The fact that this was thought necessary implies a change of design: the nucleus of the Entrenchments surely shifts to the area centred upon Fishbourne and Bosham, and Selsey is only included at all if the system pre-dates the canalization of the Lavant.

The overall sequence becomes much clearer when we consider NS1. It is evident that this line was butted on to NS2 by means of EWH and joined to EWA (ii) by cutting through part of its rampart. It is therefore later in date than either line. If we take it in conjunction with NS2 we see that earthworks now cover the whole line of the Lavant southward to Chichester and leave the area enclosed by EWA (i) outside the new system.

If we turn now to the western length of EWA (ii) we find a closely similar earthwork running south and supplementing the streams at the west of the enclosed area. Unfortunately the junction of this line with EWA (ii) does not survive but it has been shown by air photography that it cuts the second east–west line, at this point EWD (i). The effect of this line, NS5, which runs up to a mile inside these streams, is to exclude Bosham Harbour from the new system.

It is probably this that explains the construction of EWG which has been shown to post-date the new line. This line supplements the final length of EWA (ii) and thus covers the excluded area from the north. The other two shorter lines, EWE and F, can only be explained by the prior existence of NS5 and so we can fairly assume that they were butted on to it even though their junctions do not survive. EWD (ii) which starts immediately inside the new line should also belong to this phase and so might the unfinished NS3 which was butted on to EWB and clearly post-dates it. The date of EWC is not certain but the fact that it covered only Fishbourne Harbour may indicate that it formed part of this final system. The date of EWI cannot be determined.

To summarize: the first layout consisted of EWA (i) and (ii) and cut off the sixty square miles of coastal plain between Bosham and Bognor.

The second layout consisted of EWA (ii), EWB together with EWD (i) and NS4, and NS2. This cut off the 10 square miles between the Lavant and the Bosham watercourse. If the system pre-dates the first century A.D., the western half of the Selsey peninsula may be added, thus increasing the total area to 25 square miles.

The third and final layout consisted of the following dykes in addition to those just set out: NS1 and 5, EWE, F and G, EWD (ii), NS3 and EWC. If the system pre-dates the first century A.D. it enclosed the 20 square miles between NS1 and 5 and the land to the south between Chichester Harbour and the original course of the Lavant. If later, the system was confined to the land between Fishbourne and the two north–south dykes and enclosed only five square miles. The system at first excluded Bosham Harbour though some attempt was later made to provide it with cover from the north.

Fortunately there is now some evidence for the date of this activity. Miss Murray's section through EWA (ii) produced two sherds datable to the mid first century B.C., one in the primary filling of the ditch and the other sealed below the rampart (Murray, 1956). These of course, provide only a *terminus post quem* for this line and could in isolation be cited in support of any of the theories summarized in the introduction to this paper.

However, in August 1967 it was possible to examine the tail of the rampart of EWA (i) in Goodwood Park (88270892). At this point where the line turns through an angle of roughly 100 degrees, a Roman building was found by the writer at a point approximately 90 yards (82 m.) inside the earthwork (88230885). The distribution of surface sherds after ploughing suggested that the Entrenchment had been used as the boundary of the occupied area.

Here again the material of the rampart sealed two sherds of the later pre-Roman Iron Age. A shallow scoop was also found at the back of the rampart containing within its filling a sherd of the first-century A.D. Iron Age. This feature was surely intended to provide material for the heightening of the rampart but whether it was contemporary with the initial construction of the dyke is uncertain. The line of the rampart had, as anticipated, been re-used as the boundary of the Roman building compound. Two parallel ditches were found following the line of the dyke, one cutting away the tail of the rampart and the other cutting through the main body of the earthwork. Neither contained pottery later in date than the early second century A.D. For a full account of this excavation see the appendix (pp. 34 f.).

Secondly it does seem from the distribution of surface 'pot boilers' that first- and second-century A.D. occupation in the area to the south of EWF was delimited by the line of the rampart. This may, more doubtfully, suggest a *terminus ante quem* in the second century A.D. for our final phase. This general dating of each phase can be carried further by comparison with other linear earthworks of a similar period.

The new survey fully justifies earlier comparisons with the Colchester dykes (Hawkes and Hull, 1947, 8–16). Since 1934 it has been shown that here, as at Chichester, the earliest earthworks were of contour type but that they gave place to strikingly rectilinear dykes. On both sites the earlier systems were closely based upon the pattern of rivers but in the later phases it became necessary to reinforce many of these natural obstacles as well. A common ancestry in certain continental promontory forts is not unlikely (for example, see Wheeler and Richardson, 1957, 130).

Within these and similar systems certain details call for comment. At Camulodunum as at Chichester, a number of the entrances are of a distinctive type, being placed inside sharp or right-angled bends in the earthworks. An example at Chichester is the entrance to the 'salient' on EWA (ii) and this layout is again represented at Verulamium, examples being the two entrances to Enclosure A at Prae Wood (Wheeler and Wheeler, 1936, pl. XVI). As set out in Section E there are five further cases where we may suspect this to have occurred at Chichester. Another distinctive entrance type among the Entrenchments occurs close to the western end of EWA (i) and might be called an 'out-turned entrance'. This closely resembles the entrance near to the south-west corner of the Prae Wood system. Thirdly, the possible entrance in Valdoe Coppice is of much the same type as those at Oram's Arbour at Winchester (Biddle, 1969) and possibly Dover Castle (Hawkes, 1968, 10, and Colvin, 1963, fig. 53). Reference has been made to the 'salient' on EWA (ii). Though it is generally thought to be unique, a larger but otherwise precisely similar arrangement exists on the South Oxfordshire Grims Ditch (Crawford, 1931). I have argued elsewhere[1] that this earthwork may be dated to the first century B.C. but it must be added that in part that argument rests upon my view of the Chichester system. Both examples may have covered the junction of two trackways but a primary function as cattle compounds is hard to resist. Again the siting of some of the lines at Chichester a little short of the crest of a slope is a feature that the Entrenchments share with apparently similar earthworks in Middlesex (Wheeler, 1934), in particular the Pinner Ditch which unpublished excavation has suggested to be of Iron Age date.

The wide spacing of EWD (i) and (ii) is reminiscent of the layout at Colchester about the Trinovantian site at Gosbeck's Farm and on the Chiltern Grim's Ditch on Pitstone Hill in Buckinghamshire (Dyer and Hales, 1961, and Dyer, 1963). The type is probably to be related to that of the earlier Iron Age Drays Ditches near Luton, where the intervening space contained a layout of upright posts (Dyer, 1961).

Similarly, the curious way in which EWH and NS1 cover part of the length of NS2 rather resembles the relationship of Gryme's Dyke at Colchester to the earlier Chestnut Farm Dykes though here the sequence of earthworks was not the same. One final feature of the Entrenchments which demands some comment are the three short earthworks projecting from the main lines on the inside, EWE, EWF and NS3. Though tactical explanations within a context of chariot warfare are easy to come by, a more satisfactory primary purpose might be in protecting and delimiting grazing areas. Such an arrangement is essentially similar to the overall layout at Prae Wood.

Even from this it is clear that we may include the Entrenchments among a growing number of linear dyke systems of later Iron Age date. In particular the layout of the last two phases is so similar to the later systems at Colchester, both in overall plan and in certain details, that we might suspect a broadly similar date. The latter systems are associated with the occupation of the Sheepen peninsula from about A.D. 10 onwards.

[1] *Oxoniensia*, 33 (1968), 1–13 (published 1970).

This leaves one question unanswered. Even if we associate the first phase at Chichester with the Selsey oppidum, what is the purpose of the later layouts in which the nucleus partially shifts? Surely the answer has been given us by Professor Frere when he invites us to consider the linear dykes of this period not simply as the outer defences of oppida but also as the limits of large tracts of settled land (Frere, 1967, 46). There is no reason why such an area should not offer refuge to inhabitants and livestock in the same way as earlier hillforts. This being so we need not envisage the gradual eclipse of Selsey or a projected oppidum near Fishbourne. A system of comparable dykes without an oppidum occurs for instance in North Oxfordshire (Harden, 1937, Thomas, 1958, and Hawkes, 1961). This principle is one which again finds expression in a Brigantian context at Stanwick (Wheeler, 1954).

EWA (ii) has been claimed as the work of the Atrebates shortly after their arrival in southern Britain, but this view was based upon two sherds which could only provide a *terminus post quem* (Murray, 1956). With this was coupled the suggestion that the parallel east–west dykes might represent progressive clearances of the hinterland. As has been seen, this sequence can no longer stand. In any case though a connection between that dyke and the Selsey oppidum is almost certain the latter itself is not securely dated, since the evidence is largely that of coins washed up on the present foreshore. Allen has suggested that some of this material may be derived from a single hoard (Allen, 1961, 289–90), and in principle this could apply to any selection of coins from this limited area. We still need in any case to offer some explanation of the later reductions in the enclosed area and the protection given above all to the harbours.

Here it may be well to recall that Allen's work on coin distribution (Allen, 1944) has also indicated that this area of the West Sussex coastal plain represented the final nucleus of Atrebatic power at a time of intense Catuvellaunian pressure and latterly expansion from the north. Surely the best context that can be suggested for at least the second and the possibly unfinished third phase of the Entrenchments is Verica's reaction to this southward pressure which was to culminate in his flight from Sussex to Rome.

APPENDIX

A SECTION THROUGH THE DEVIL'S DITCH IN GOODWOOD PARK (Fig. 7)

Fieldwork in March 1967, on the line of the Devil's Ditch, EWA (i), in Goodwood Park, showed that there had been a small Roman building at a point 90 yards (82 m.) inside a bend in the earthwork at (88230885). From surface sherds of second- and third-century A.D. pottery brought to light by ploughing it seemed that associated occupation had been confined to the area partially enclosed by the earthwork and had been absent from the land outside its ditch.

In August 1967, one section, 20 ft. by 6 ft. (6.1 m. × 1.8 m.) was cut through the tail of the rampart to relate it stratigraphically to any levels associated with the Roman occupation of the site. One small extension, 5 ft. by 4 ft. (1.5 × 1.2 m.) was added 8 ft. 8 in. (2.6 m.) to the north to locate the inner lip of the ditch.

The rampart, though much disturbed by tree roots, was clearly entirely of dump construction over a low core of humus which had been deposited directly on the natural ground surface after the removal of the turf. The main core of the rampart at this point was of tips of chalk rubble. The earthwork had been badly denuded and survived to a height of only 3 ft. (1 m.). The distance between the tail of the rampart and the inner lip of the ditch was 21 ft. (6.4 m.) but there was evidence to suggest a berm of unknown width.

One sherd of first-century B.C. date was found securely stratified on the original surface below the rampart. A second, rather later, Iron Age sherd was found in a similar position below the tail of the rampart but the stratification of this second sherd was less satisfactory because it may have owed its position to root disturbances at this point.

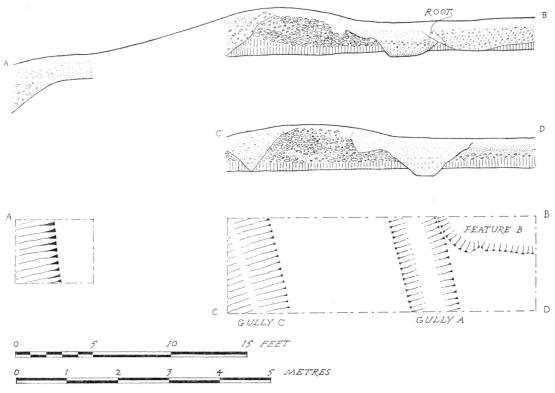

FIG. 7.   Section through the Devil's Ditch in Goodwood Park

To the back of the rampart part of a shallow scoop cut up to 6 in. (0.15 m.) into the natural clay was cleared. This contained one body sherd of the first-century A.D. Iron Age and appears to represent quarrying to heighten the rampart either on its original construction or somewhat later. A similar phenomenon was found at Densworth (Holmes, 1961).

This feature was entirely sealed by a barren layer which was in its turn overlain by a level containing pottery of the second century A.D. This latter layer could be associated with a flat-bottomed gully up to 4 ft. (1.2 m.) wide and 1 ft. 8 in. (0.52 m.) deep, which followed the line of the earthwork and cut away the very tail of the rampart. This is best seen as a boundary earthwork associated with the Roman building to the south.

Running parallel to this gully and 6 ft. 6 in. (1.9 m.) to its north, was a V-profile ditch, 5 ft. (1.5 m.) wide, and cut through the rampart and the underlying clay to the chalk marl to a depth of 2 ft. 8 in. (0.81 m.). This contained pottery of a similar date in its secondary filling. The disturbed surface over the rampart contained a scatter of further Roman sherds but no Roman material was found in the material of the earthwork itself. In the same way Roman pottery was only present in the uppermost filling of the ditch.

This limited excavation has thus established that EWA (ii) was constructed at some time between the first century B.C. and the first century A.D.

PART II

The Structures of the First Period, A.D. 43–75

INTRODUCTION

PERIOD 1 covers all features and structures erected during the time between the Roman invasion of A.D. 43 and the erection of the large palatial building, described here as Period 2, sometime about A.D. 75–80. It therefore spans more than 30 years of formative development and it is only to be expected that considerable change is the hallmark of the period. The size of the excavated area and the processes of levelling carried out in preparation for the Second Period palace sometimes create difficulties of correlation between one part of the site and another but, apart from the relative lack of dating evidence for the features in areas 6 and 7, the main sequence can be offered with assurance.

It is abundantly clear that modification and rebuilding were carried out almost continuously throughout the period. A close consideration of the sequence in areas 2 and 3 shows that at least three separate phases of change were here represented. These have been called Periods 1 A, 1 B and 1 C, and the chronological framework thus provided is used as a basis for the description of the entire excavated site. There are obvious dangers inherent in using subdivisions of this kind rigidly for a large area; these have been seen and avoided as far as possible but even so it is important to state at the outset the meaning and significance of each subdivision. Period 1 A is used to refer to the first group of Roman structures to be erected on the site, which, it will be suggested, date to the very beginning of the Roman occupation and are of military character. Period 1 B marks the first series of alterations carried out sometime before A.D. 50, when the settlement takes on a civilian aspect, whilst Period 1 C represents the final stage of development reached before most of the known buildings were demolished in preparation for the erection of the palace. The periods are therefore better regarded as *stages* in the development of the settlement and it would be quite incorrect to think of them as anything more.

For ease of description the excavated area has been divided into seven areas, nos. 1–5 covering the eastern part of the site with 6 and 7 covering the western. Between the two is an unnumbered strip from which all trace of Period 1 levels has been removed by the large-scale levelling of the land prior to the building of the palace. Composite detailed plans of each area are offered (figs. 8–10, 12–15, 17–19) with the exception of area 2 where the complications of superimposed buildings demand three separate plans. The features of each stage are summarized on three period plans (figs. 11, 16, 20). For purposes of description the individual structures and their relationships are considered under period headings, the dating evidence for each being summarized. Where constructional material is relevant to the understanding of a building, supporting data is published separately as appendices. All small objects and pottery are described in the second volume. To end the section on Period 1 certain observations of a more general character are offered under the heading of historical summary.

THE SITE

The geomorphological development of the area has already been described (pp. 5–9). At the time of the invasion the most obvious attraction of the area would have been the lagoon-shaped harbour at the north-eastern extremity of the Fishbourne inlet, kept free from silt by the constant scouring of the two streams which flowed into it. The surrounding land was tolerably well-drained and even the edges of the streams and inlet were floored with a hard gravelly clay. There can be little doubt that it was the potentially valuable harbour that attracted the first Roman settlers: its significance would have overcome any minor disadvantages caused by the relatively high water-table.

Prior to the Roman period there is little trace of settled occupation on that part of the site which has been excavated. A Mesolithic axe was found deep in the silted channel below the harbour (p. 6) and several struck blades of flint hint at the early use of the area by man. Evidence is a little more plentiful for the pre-Roman Iron Age. Fragments of briquet-age have been found on the contemporary beach and several sherds of pottery dating to the first century B.C. have turned up on the original ground-surface below the main site, but they are so few in number that they clearly do not represent a settlement unless one lies beyond the limits of the present excavation. Several sherds of a later type currently classified as South Eastern Third B were also recovered (Vol. II, p. 160), but since the type was in use at the time of the Roman Conquest there is no need to regard them as indicative of a pre-Roman settlement.

FEATURES OF PERIOD 1 A

ROADS AND PATHS (figs. 8–11)

Two major roads run partly across the site in an east–west direction; they are parallel and lie 110 ft. (33.53 m.) apart. Both were constructed of local gravel laid on an un-prepared surface to a thickness of 12 in. (0.30 m.) in the centre, cambering to a few inches at the edges. The widths of the roads vary. The northern road is 18 ft. (5.49 m.) wide to the east of the stream, but widens to a maximum of 33 ft. (10.05 m.) as soon as the stream is crossed. This peculiarity can, however, be explained in terms of the store-building which lies immediately to the north, which would have demanded a gravelled apron in front to allow vehicles to back up and turn for unloading. The southern road also widens to the west of the stream from 33 ft. to 46 ft. (10.0–14.0 m.) though why this should happen is by no means clear.

Both roads crossed the stream by means of fords. The northern crossing, the repaved version of which survived beside a new bridge in Period 1 B, proved to consist of occasional sandstone and limestone blocks packed around with small flints and gravel. The southern ford had been completely destroyed at the beginning of Period 1 B, when the stream bed was regraded (p. 46).

On the eastern edge of the site traces of a linking north–south road survive, metalled with similar gravel to the two major roads but of thickness not exceeding 3 in. (0.076 m.). At their known western extremities the two east–west roads and some of the underlying natural clay and gravel had been shaved away by the levelling for the Period 2 palace, but

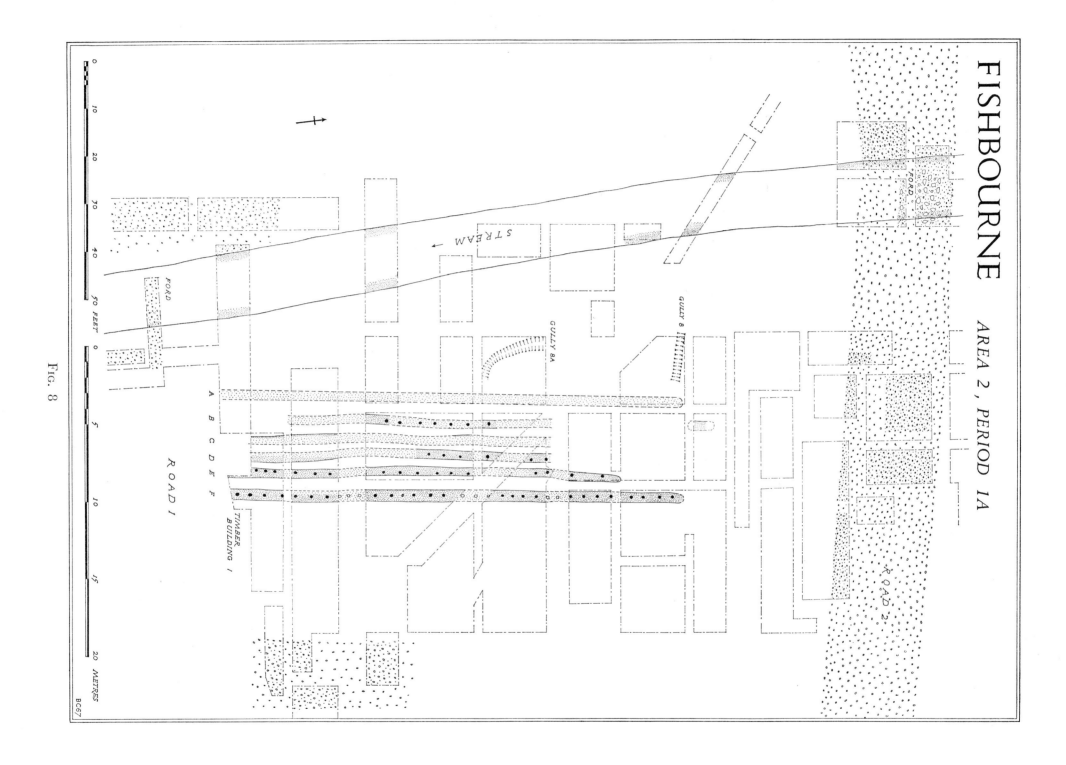

FISHBOURNE

AREA 2, PERIOD 1A

FIG. 8

beyond the negative terrace to the west, where the original surface still remains, no trace of the metalling survives. Clearly, then, the roads ended somewhere in the levelled area, either simply stopping or, more likely, joining a now destroyed north–south road. Several features of the later development of the site suggest that this presumed north–south road remained an important axis for some time.

North of the northern road, flanking the north side of Building 2, lay a pathway 15 ft. (4.57 m.) wide, defined by two gullies. Metalling was sparse but at the low-lying end, close to the stream, tips of sandstone blocks and gravel had been spread to consolidate the surface. The western half of the path lay across a natural soil consisting of green-grey silty soil into which had been trodden many fragments of broken roof-tiles. It is difficult to see why tile should have been laid deliberately as metalling; a more reasonable explanation is that they represent fragments which, throughout a period of time, weathered off the tile roof of the adjacent timber building and were trampled into the soil by constant use of the path. It is significant that the tile fragments were not found beyond the western limit of the building.

The dating of the roads depends largely upon their stratigraphical position. Both lie on the original ground-surface with no trace of occupation levels below. The north road, however, runs across an early gully (gully 14, area 4), the deliberate filling of which contained a single fragment of an amphora. This is the only feature to pre-date the first phase of the roads, and presumably was connected in some way with the earliest building activity. Its vertical sides and deliberate clay filling show that it was short-lived. The roads can, however, be shown to be early by virtue of the facts that they were both overlaid by subsequent remetallings and that they clearly relate to timber buildings which are themselves the earliest structures on the site. Since no datable artifacts were found in the metalling or beneath it, no direct dating evidence can be offered, but as the subsequent additions are late Claudian (p. 46) the first metallings of the roads must date to the beginning of the Roman occupation.

TIMBER BUILDING 1   (fig. 8, p. 206 and pl. 1a)

Building 1 lies between the two roads to the east of the stream on a subsoil of grey gravelly clay. Since, in later periods, drainage gullies and masonry walls were aligned on the same axis, there has been much destruction of the ground-plan of the original building and, as the plan will show (fig. 8), even reconstruction is difficult. However, certain facts are clear. The building consisted of probably six roughly parallel rows of foundation trenches about 2 ft. (0.61 m.) wide and dug to a depth of 2–2½ ft. (c. 0.69 m.) below the surface of the natural gravel: of these, four (rows B, D, E and F) were traced wholly or partly by excavation and the edge of another (row C) was seen in two places where its course diverged from that of a later wall-footing. Only row A is wholly conjectural having, it is suggested, been obliterated by the digging of a Period 1 B gully, gully 10; it is likely to have existed on the grounds of plan alone. The trenches served to support rows of vertical timbers held in position by the spoil from the original trenches, which was packed back around them. It is often extremely difficult to distinguish between the gravel *in situ* and the same material which had been dug out and replaced almost immediately. The distinction depended largely upon differences of texture, which were apparent particularly when the disturbed gravel

E

was seen against the rather more silty top of the undisturbed natural soil (pl. 1a). Sections cut across the foundation trenches at intervals showed no trace of a buried sill-beam and it must therefore be supposed that none existed. The most likely arrangement of the floor would have been for the vertical timbers to have supported a framework of joists some 2–3 ft. (0.6–0.9 m.) above ground, upon which the raised floor and the superstructure of the building would have been based. Such an arrangement is identical to that suggested for the buildings found at Richborough in an early military context, where the structures seem to have been granaries, the raised floors keeping the corn away from the damp ground and allowing the air to circulate freely beneath. A similar, though larger, structure was found at Rödgen, near Bad Nauheim, in a supply base of Augustan date (Schönberger, 1967).

The post-holes for the timbers in rows B, C and E were, on average, 4–6 in. (0.10–0.15 m.) in diameter and were spaced at intervals of about 3 ft. (0.91 m.). The posts in row A (and presumably the destroyed row F) were larger, measuring about 9 in. (0.23 m.) across, implying that greater strength was needed along the sides to support the weight of the walls and roof. The slighter piles, taking the floor, were nevertheless closely spaced presumably in order to bear the load of the stores kept within. The nature of the superstructure must remain unknown, but the quantity of roof tiles lying around and incorporated in Period 1 B walls suggests that the roof had been tiled in order to cut down the risk of fire. Rainwater running off the roof must have collected in ground-level gutters lying along the sides of the building, but in both places later features have destroyed all evidence except at the north-west corner where a short length of gully (gully 8) was found, leading away towards the stream.

In plan the building is elongated, measuring 22 ft. (6.71 m.) by about 100 ft. (30.5 m.), proportions closely comparable to the Richborough examples, but in detail the structures from the two sites differ. At Fishbourne the northern end of the building does not appear to have been floored at a raised level, or if it was the floor was not supported by the close-spaced piles which lay beneath the other part of the building. The implication may be that heavy goods were not placed in this area. It is possible that a loading-bay of complex type lay at this end, the foundation trench projecting from the north end being part of the support for a loading-platform. If so, it could mean that the front part of the building was kept clear of stores to facilitate loading and unloading, in which case elaborate sub-floor structures would not have been required.

That the building was one of the first to be constructed on the site is shown clearly by the fact that the foundation trench fillings were devoid of artifacts and occupation material, implying that they had been dug and refilled before settlement rubbish began to accumulate. It can also be demonstrated stratigraphically that the timbers had either rotted at ground-level or had been sawn off at this point, leaving the stumps in position, before floors of the Period 1 B building were laid, for the stumps had eventually rotted causing the later floor to slump into the voids. Stratigraphically, then, Building 1 was the earliest to be erected in area 2. As might be expected, no occupation rubbish found its way below the building and much of the debris which accumulated outside was contaminated by similar rubbish deposited in Period 1 B, which became mixed with the earlier material by the constant passage of vehicles and people. In one area, however, to the north-east of the building a thin occupation layer was found sealed beneath a Period 1 B floor. It contained fragments of Claudian girth and butt beakers and a few fragments of samian of the same date. Analysis of the general Period 1 A and 1 B occupation material shows that, of the samian pottery recovered, a considerable amount dates from pre- and early Claudian times (Vol. II, pp. 260 ff.) pointing to a date in or soon after A.D. 43 for the initial occupation.

TIMBER BUILDING 2   (fig. 9, p. 206, appendix 2, and pls. 1b, IIa)

Immediately to the north of the northern road, on the west side of the stream, lay a timber building measuring 97 ft. by 52 ft. (29.56 × 15.85 m.). Although it was buried beneath the North Wing of the Second-Period palace it has been possible to examine a substantial part of it, because the late floors in this area had fortunately been largely destroyed in antiquity, thus offering no ethical hindrance to excavation beneath. In those rooms in which the floors are still preserved (rooms N 20 and N 21) the subsidence of their make-up into the post-holes of the early building allows the plan of the obscured structure to be reconstructed in some detail.

In its original form the building consisted of six east–west rows, each consisting of thirteen posts, placed at a distance of 8 ft. (2.44 m.) from each other. Since the rows are also 8 ft. (2.44 m.) apart, the resulting plan is of a grid of 78 equally-spaced timbers. Along the south side, fronting the road, was another row of posts placed in rectangular post-pits, but not aligned with the main north–south rows. These may represent the supports for a veranda or loading platform. Typically, each post was a squared timber about 12 in. (0.30 m.) across, set upright in an individual post-pit 3–4 ft. (0.9–1.2 m.) in diameter and about 4 ft. (1.2 m.) deep. Around each vertical the spoil from the pit had been packed back and rammed hard. In two places, shown on fig. 9 in rows B and F the impressions of horizontal sill-beams placed on the ground-surface could be traced. In spite of a careful search no other beam impressions were found, presumably because of the disturbance of the original ground-surface in the subsequent Period 1 B. It now seems probable that the beams belonged to the earliest phase of the building and that they performed the important function of binding the vertical timbers rigidly together at ground-level. The extent of this ground-beam framework cannot unfortunately be traced.

Consideration of the superstructure of the building poses serious problems. The size of the vertical timbers strongly suggests that they were more than just piles to support the substructure of the floor — a timber 12 in. (0.3 m.) across is more likely to have stood to roof height, and moreover the regular spacing of the verticals (which contrasts with the somewhat haphazard spacing of the piles below the floor of Timber Building 1) implies that a uniform module was required for the internal divisions of the building. That the floor was raised above ground, presumably on joists attached to the sides of the verticals, is strongly suggested by the total absence of floor-levels on the original ground-surface and also by the fact that the dampness of the ground would have called for a raised and ventilated floor. Whether it was based on the ground-beam framework or on separate joists several feet above cannot now be decided.

To judge by the quantity of roof-tile fragments found around the building, particularly trampled into the path to the north, the roof would have been tiled. Rainwater was collected on the north side in a ground-level gutter (gully 3), but no similar provision seems to have been made on the south. Here, instead, two pairs of posts have been found, parallel to the main building but not aligned with the main north–south rows of timbers. The simplest explanation is that they formed part of the support for a veranda opening on to the road. This also raises the problem of whether or not the northernmost row of posts (row A) also supported a veranda. As the plan will show, they are slightly irregularly spaced in relation to rows B–F and could in theory be interpreted in this way but the matter is beyond proof.

The function of the building is debatable, but two possibilities present themselves: either it was a store-building with a loading-bay on the south side, the vertical timbers providing a framework between which temporary partitions could be inserted, or it was a pair of barrack buildings placed back to back, each with a flanking veranda, the verticals taking permanent partitions dividing one *contubernium* from another. Both suggestions offer a possible explanation of the known facts and both types of building would be acceptable in a military context. Similar buildings, thought to be barracks, are known from the early military supply-base of Rödgen (Schönberger, 1967) where the spacing of the verticals is 3 metres. On the other hand, the closest parallel to the Fishbourne structure comes from the Claudian fort at Hod Hill (Richmond, 1967) where a building, clearly the granary of the fort, was constructed on a grid of timbers 5 ft. apart. On balance a store building is the more likely explanation.

Stratigraphically the building was the earliest to be erected in area 4. Its post-pits were dug at a time before occupation material had accumulated on the ground-surface, and their refilling was accordingly clean, with the exception of one pit (no. D 3) low down in the filling of which a thin lens of black occupation material was found, containing a few un-datable sherds of early Roman coarse ware and part of a jar in the native Southern Third B tradition (Vol. II, fig. 72, no. 9). The packing of the pits taking the veranda posts on the south side of the building was overlapped by the metalling of the earliest version of the northern road. The building can be shown to have been destroyed in the Neronian period. Some of the posts (summarized in Appendix 2) had either rotted at ground-level or had been sawn off, leaving the stumps in position to rot slowly, allowing the overlying soil to slump into the void, thus taking up the shape of the original post. The nature of the subsidence beneath the later mosaic floor in room N 21 suggests that here, too, the stumps had not been removed (pl. xxv*b*). Other post-holes show clear evidence of the posts having been dug out (summarized in Appendix 2). In nearly every case the sides of the original post-pit had been destroyed by the demolition pit, which was usually larger. In these cases, of course, all trace of the position of the original post had usually been removed, but in pit D 3 the timber had become so embedded in the soft natural clay at the bottom of its pit that the impression made by its squared base survived destruction. The demolition pits were refilled with the material dug out interspersed with lenses of occupation material which were parti-cularly thick in the tops of the pits. The pottery recovered from these layers is all Claudian-Neronian, and leaves little doubt that the building was destroyed during Period 1 B. In summary, the dating evidence implies that the building was erected in the Claudian period and that it functioned for relatively few years before being demolished. It may have been used in Period 1 B, but if so this could only have been for a short time. The small rectangular pit, 3 ft. 3 in. (0.99 m.) deep, cut into B 3 was filled with mortary clay. It post-dated the demolition of the building and was filled rapidly before the occupation material of Period 1 B began to accumulate.

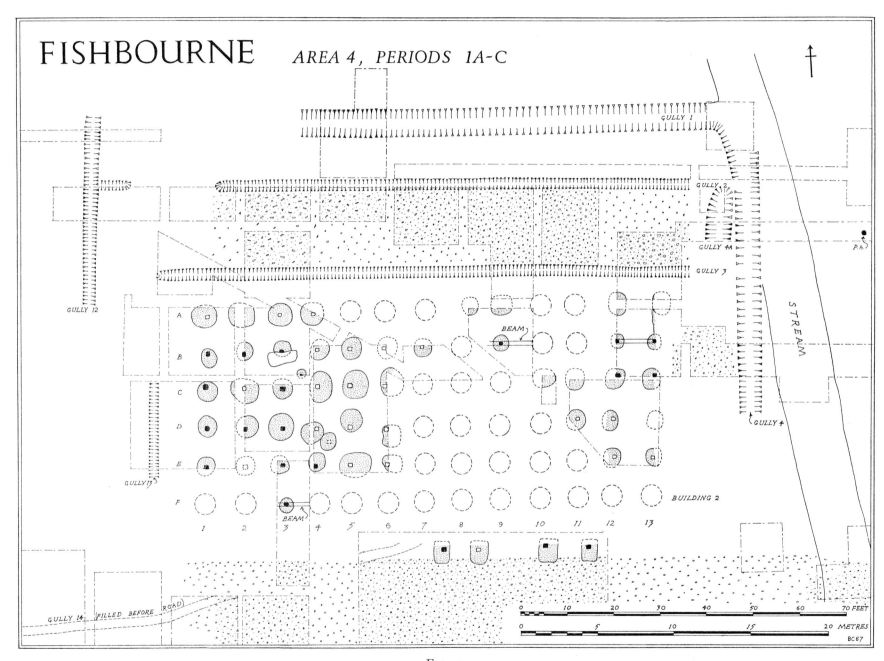

FISHBOURNE

AREA 4, PERIODS 1A-C

GULLY 1

GULLY 12

GULLY 2

GULLY 4A

P.h

GULLY 3

STREAM

A

BEAM

B

C

GULLY 4

D

E

GULLY 13

F

BEAM

BUILDING 2

1 2 3 4 5 6 7 8 9 10 11 12 13

GULLY 14 FILLED BEFORE ROAD

0 10 20 30 40 50 60 70 FEET

0 5 10 15 20 METRES

BC 67

FIG. 9

OTHER FEATURES

BUILDING 3

To the south of the southern road on the east side of the stream (area 3), limited excavation brought to light two bedding trenches sealed beneath Period 1 B floors. The nature and extent of the building to which they belong is completely unknown.

DRAINAGE GULLIES   (figs. 8–10, p. 206, and pls. 11b, va)

Several drainage gullies, probably originating in Period 1 A, have been discovered. They are characteristically 2–2½ ft. (c. 0.7 m.) wide, of U-shaped profile, and are usually not more than 2 ft. (0.61 m.) deep. The nature of their filling and subsequent history differs.

Gullies 2 and 3: area 4 (fig. 9, p. 206). These gullies run parallel to each other, 16 ft. (4.88 m.) apart, to the north of Timber Building 2, delineating a lightly metalled pathway. Gully 3 presumably served as a drain for rainwater accumulating from the roof of the building. Gully 2 continued to the west to meet gully 12, with which it is contemporary. A gap of 18 ft. (5.49 m.) appeared in its line opposite the end of the building, no doubt to allow easy access to the north. Gully 3 ended a little beyond the western limit of the building. Both gullies were on average 2 ft. (0.63 m.) deep. The primary silting, derived from the eroded sides, was barren except for fragments of roof-tile and occasional sherds of pottery. Above this lay a thick mass of occupation rubbish continuous in places with the layer which spread across the pathway and over the post pits of the demolished timber building. The pottery ranged in date from Claudian to early Flavian and represents a rubbish deposit which accumulated during Periods 1 B and 1 C, after the abandonment of the earlier features. No attempt was made to keep the gullies clear of rubbish after the building had been demolished.

Gully 5: area 1 (fig. 13) consists of two lengths of shallow gullies joining at right-angles and filled during the same period with grey gravelly silt and some occupation material. No closely datable finds were recovered but the gully was cut by gully 6 which contained Neronian pottery. It will be seen from the general plan (fig. 11) that the east–west length lines up with gully 2, with which it is thought to be largely contemporary.

Gully 8: area 2 (fig. 8).   A short length of an early gully 2 ft. (0.6 m.) wide and 15 in. (0.4 m.) deep was found close to the north-west corner of Timber Building 1. It may well have served to carry off excess rainwater from the side gutters to the stream. The filling was of grey gravelly silt and it had been cut through by gully 10 in Period 1 B.

Gully 8 A: area 2.   A short curving gully 15 in. (0.4 m.) deep was found near the centre of the west side of the building. It was without finds and could possibly be of pre-Roman date.

Gully 12: area 4 (fig. 9, p. 206) runs in a north–south direction across the end of the northern path; its limits have not been traced. Originally it was 3 ft. (0.9 m.) wide and 2½ ft. (0.8 m.) deep with a flat bottom. The ditch had been allowed to silt up with material washed from its sides, but apart from fragments of roofing tile no artifacts were found in the primary levels. In Period 1 B a thick layer of occupation material had been allowed to

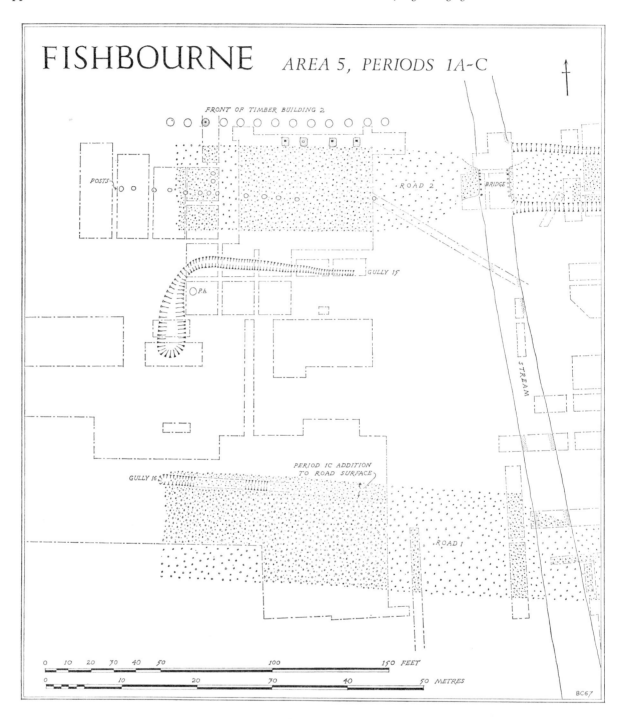

FISHBOURNE *AREA 5, PERIODS 1A-C*

FRONT OF TIMBER BUILDING 2

POSTS

ROAD 2

BRIDGE

P.h.

GULLY 15

STREAM

GULLY 16

PERIOD 1C ADDITION
TO ROAD SURFACE

ROAD 1

0 10 20 30 40 50 100 150 FEET
0 10 20 30 40 50 METRES

BC67

Fig. 10

accumulate over the area, sealing the ditch and containing pottery dating from Claudian to early Flavian times. The north end of the gully had been cut by the Period 1 C gully 1.

Gully 13: area 4 (fig. 9, p. 206) lies parallel to the western limit of Timber Building 2; it was U-shaped, 1½ ft. (0.46 m.) deep and was filled deliberately with redeposited natural clay and silt. Although no dating evidence was recovered, and all sealing Period 1 B layers had been removed by later levelling, it seems probable that the gully was laid out to drain the area close to the side of the timber building during its original occupation.

Gully 14: area 4 (fig. 9, p. 206) was straight-sided, 2 ft. (0.6 m.) wide and 2 ft. (0.6 m.) deep. It had been deliberately filled with clay very soon after it had been dug and before erosion of its sides could occur; the metalling of the northern road sealed it. The only artifact from its filling was a large sherd of a pre-Flavian amphora. It must be supposed that the gully served some temporary drainage purpose while the building was being erected and that it was abandoned and sealed on the completion of the work.

Gully 15: area 5 (fig. 10, p. 206, pl. 11b) lies to the south of the northern road. It varies in size from 4 ft. (1.2 m.) wide at the west end to 2 ft. (0.6 m.) at the east; at the western limit of the east–west arm it turns to the south, but the section beyond the corner has been recut at a later date (see p. 58), destroying most of the original feature. The filling of the original section is of green-grey silty clay washed from the natural subsoil; in the silt were found a large number of fragments of roof tile closely similar to those found further to the north in association with Timber Building 2. In the western part of the ditch the silt had been sealed with redeposited natural clay. No dating evidence was recovered, but the later recutting of the north–south section in Periods 1 B or 1 C suggests an early date, which is supported by the discovery of the Period 1 A roof tiles in the lower silting. A further relevant factor is that the ditch turns south opposite the west end of the building, on which line gully 16 also ends. It seems probable therefore that a north–south axis of some significance existed here to which the Period 1 A features were aligned. Just inside the north-west angle formed by the ditch was a single large post-hole 3 ft. (1 m.) in diameter and 4 ft. (1.2 m.) deep; the post had been dug out and the hole refilled immediately.

Gully 16: area 5 (fig. 10, p. 207) is a road-ditch flanking the north side of the earliest southern road. It has not been fully traced, but at the points excavated it can be shown to have been 5 ft. (1.5 m.) wide and 2 ft. 6 in. (0.76 m.) deep. It had been allowed to silt up while the road was in use, and when an angle of rest had been reached a turf-line 2 in. (0.05 m.) thick had accumulated. Later, in Period 1 C (see p. 55), the road had been widened and the ditch sealed beneath the new layer of metalling. Although no direct dating evidence was obtained, the sequence of silting and the relationship of the road to the early settlement suggest that the ditch, and the road to which it belongs, should be assigned to Period 1 A.

The only remaining feature which might be of Period 1 A date is what appears to be a foundation trench running in an east–west direction across the western part of the site, and aligned with the southern side of Timber Building 2. It consists of a V-shaped trench 3 ft. (0.9 m.) wide and 3 ft. (0.9 m.) deep, filled with redeposited natural gravel (p. 207).

Although a careful search was made, no post-holes could be located within the filling; it must, however, be admitted that if fence-posts had existed and had been uprooted it would have been possible for the holes to have become filled with the surrounding packing in such a way that little trace survived. No positive dating evidence exists to show to which Period 1 phase the feature belongs. Its alignment with the timber building, and the fact that it is slightly askew to the adjacent Period 1 B ditch, hint at a Period 1 A date but of this there is no proof.

FEATURES OF PERIOD 1 B

THE ROADS, THE BRIDGE AND THE STREAM   (fig. 12, p. 207, and pl. III)

Period 1 B is marked by a series of changes, of which the reorganization of the road system is one of the more important. The northernmost road continued in use and throughout the period remained an important thoroughfare. To the east of the stream a new layer of gravel metalling, up to 9 in. (0.3 m.) thick in the centre, was laid and similar, though less continuous, resurfacing occurred to the west.

At the stream a new form of crossing was devised which combined both a bridge and a ford (fig. 12), thus allowing a pedestrian to cross in comfort while carts could splash through the shallow water. The main lateral elements of the new bridge consisted of a row of seven timbers flanking each of the stream banks. Six of the timbers on the western bank were examined by excavation (pl. III*b*) and were found to consist of circular oak piles, 8 in. (0.2 m.) in diameter, rammed into the stream-bed in a row 1–1½ ft. (0.3–0.45 m.) apart. All that now remained were the stumps still preserved below the water-table, but originally they would have projected at least 2 ft. (0.6 m.) from the stream-bed. The eastern row of posts were largely obscured by part of a Period 3 bath building (which could not be removed) but a limited trial trench located one of the timbers preserved in position below water. Behind the timber revetments rough blocks of a glauconitic sandstone were piled up, and behind these a causeway of flints, gravel and sandstone lumps was constructed, leading to dry land on either side. The causeway was surfaced with a layer of gravel metalling which merged in with the road-surfaces of either end.

The nature of the superstructure of the bridge itself must remain conjectural, but it seems reasonable to suppose that the two rows of lateral timbers each supported a horizontal beam at a level a little below the top of the causeway, and that these in turn took the planking which spanned the stream. It is unlikely that central supports were required, for the total span was only 11 ft. (3.4 m.). Immediately to the north of the bridge was a ford about 12 ft. (3.7 m.) wide floored with a layer of gravel and sandstone difficult to distinguish from the earlier surface. On the banks the metalling sloped gently up, beside the causeway of the bridge, to merge with the adjacent road surfaces.

Dating depends partly on sequence and partly on associated finds. The remetalling of the roads and the rubble of the causeway sealed the Period 1 A road surface, and was in turn buried beneath the construction levels of the Period 2 palace. In the stream-bed, however, below the make-up was a thick deposit of grey silty clay mixed with occupation

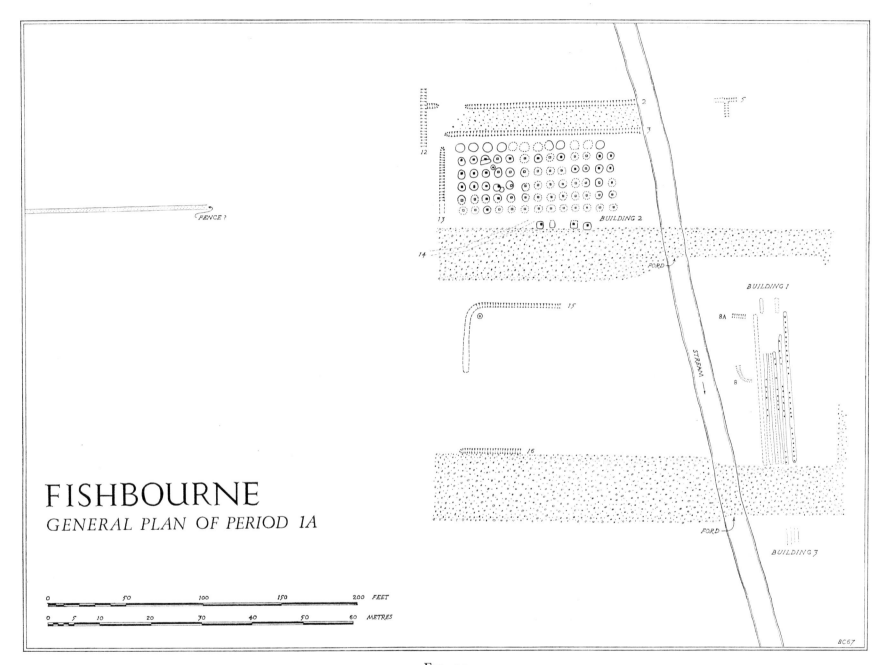

FISHBOURNE

GENERAL PLAN OF PERIOD 1A

FIG. 11

material sealing the old ford and containing pottery dating to Neronian-early Flavian times. This layer, it will be argued below (p. 55), accumulated in Period 1 C when the stream was blocked to the south. Thus the bridge and ford functioned after the first road had been laid, and before the stream was filled in — a period which can be dated broadly to the reign of Nero.

The southern road seems to have been temporarily abandoned in Period 1 B. Indeed, at the point at which it originally forded the stream the stream-bed had been regraded by the cutting of a deeper channel, thus removing the old ford (fig. 52). Moreover, immediately to the east of the stream, gully 10 had been cut across the road and next to this the end of Timber Building 5 had been allowed to encroach. The evidence, therefore, clearly points to the fact that the road was no longer in use during Period 1 B. It will, however, be demonstrated below that it was brought back into use for a short time in Period 1 C, before the palace was constructed.

Of the other early roads there is little to be said. The linking road which had earlier joined the two major roads remained in use, though it was not remetalled, and the timber building, described below, appears to have fronted on to it. The pathway on the north side of Timber Building 2 was abandoned soon after the building had been demolished and an occupation layer of the Neronian-early Flavian period was allowed to accumulate over it.

THE TIMBER BUILDINGS IN AREA 2 (fig. 12, p. 207, and pls. v, vi)

The Period 1 A Timber Building 1 was soon demolished and two new buildings of timber were erected in its place. Both were constructed on a system of horizontal sill beams laid on the ground and both shared a common frontage, but in plan and function they differed.

Timber Building 4 (p. 207 and pls. vb, via). The northern building of the pair consisted of a single range of five rooms 9 ft. (2.7 m.) wide, with two additional rooms, one longer, attached to the north end. The entire ground-frame was constructed of sill beams between 9 and 12 in. (0.2–0.3 m.) wide, into which would have been slotted the vertical timbers of the superstructure. The beams have rotted, but the different materials used for flooring the rooms on either side define clearly the original positions of the timbers. At one point on the north wall, where the ground was very wet, actual traces of much-rotted timber were preserved *in situ*, but survival of this kind was unusual. The main eastern wall of the building was laid, for part of its length, along the line of the post forming the eastern limit of the earlier building. It should not, however, be supposed that the old timbers formed an integral part of the new structure, for as we have seen they are unlikely to have been more than piles. It is more reasonable to suggest that the old posts were sawn off at ground-level and the new beam laid along their length. That no attempt had been made to remove the stumps before the new building was erected, can be shown by the way in which make-up layers post-dating the 1 B buildings had slumped into the beam-slots and into the voids of the posts beneath them indiscriminately.

Each room was floored, three with a layer of Reading Beds clay 3 in. (0.076 m.) thick, one with a fine yellow silty clay of similar thickness, two with white chalky mortar barely 1 in. (0.025 m.) thick, and one with trampled earth. Some of the floors, particularly those of mortar, showed evidence of considerable wear, but in no case was a room ever refloored.

Outside the eastern wall of the main range lies what appears to be a working area, 14 ft. (4.25 m.) wide, delineated by a row of posts each approximately 9 in. (0.23 m.) in diameter, set in post-pits 18 in. (0.46 m.) across. The stratigraphy on either side of the line of posts differs in such a way as to suggest the presence of a wall or at least a fence of timber dividing the working yard from the outside world. The nature of the superstructure of this area is problematical, but one possible explanation is that it could have been roofed with a lean-to springing from the main range and supported around its edges by the posts. In the south-east corner of the area were the battered remains of a simple oven, and close to it a pit 2½ ft. (0.76 m.) across and 2 ft. (0.6 m.) deep, which may have been used to store fuel. The oven was so completely destroyed that its form cannot be ascertained, but it may well be that it was used for bronze-smelting, for the surrounding area was heavily besprinkled with droppings from bronze-working, and from close to the pit a large fragment of copper-slag was recovered (Vol. II, p. 371).

About 15 ft. (4.57 m.) north of the southernmost wall of the building lay an entrance, represented now by an area of paving consisting of broken tiles and slabs of stone. In line with the entrance, on the west side of the building range, two beam slots were found running towards the edge of gully 10 and surrounded by a layer of compact angular gravel. The junction between this feature and the gully had been largely destroyed by the trench dug for a modern water-main and further evidence is not available, but one possible explanation is that the timbers spanned the gully to form a bridge, thus creating a passage right through the building to the entrance. Further support for this view comes from a consideration of the floor of the main range which, at this point, had been worn away, suggesting the through passage of traffic.

Timber Building 5 (p. 207).   The southern building was constructed on the same principle, with sill beams forming the ground-frame of the structure. The floors were of Reading Beds clay, yellow clay and mortar — all carefully laid of even thickness, showing no signs of patching or relaying. In plan the building consisted of a single range of rooms 18 ft. (5.51 m.) wide and more than 55 ft. (16.71 m.) long, the southern limit having not quite been reached. Three rooms ran the full width of the range, the remaining four were of approximately half the width. There is little that can be said of the superstructure, but one feature of considerable interest is that the walls of rooms 3 and 4 were plastered with a white chalky mortar and painted red and white. Only a few fragments of plaster were recovered, but they are sufficient to indicate a building of some significance, for wall-painting at this early date is rare in Britain.

Attached to the east side of the building, at the north end, was a veranda 7 ft. (2.1 m.) wide and 18½ ft. (5.64 m.) long with its roof supported on a series of timber uprights 9 in. (0.23 m.) in diameter. The entire east side of the building and veranda was curbed with blocks of stone set in gravel (pl. va). The stone varied, but the most common type was a glauconitic sandstone, which could have been quarried in the Weald or on the Isle of Wight. Also present were waterworn boulders of Mixon Reef limestone, collected from the shore at Selsey, and less frequently erratic boulders of igneous rocks (see Vol. II, p. 2).

A drystone footing of similar materials was laid parallel to both Buildings 4 and 5 (pl. va) with a short length returning at an acute angle along the north side of Building 4

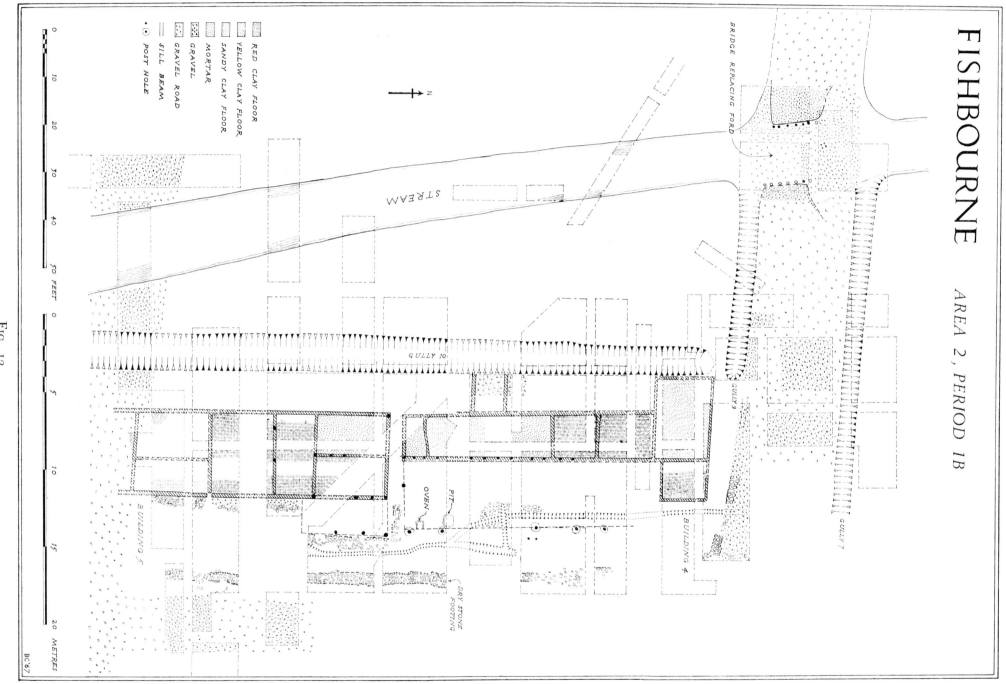

FISHBOURNE

AREA 2, PERIOD 1B

FIG. 12

BC '67

(pl. iv*a*). Beyond the footing, to the north and east, lay the gravel surfaces of the northern road and the side road. Thus the footing divided the area occupied by the buildings from the roads. In detail it measured some 2½ ft. (0.76 m.) across and was constructed of two lines of roughly-faced stone blocks laid on the surface of natural gravel and infilled with smaller stones; no mortar had been used. The footing may have been laid simply as a curb to the road, but it is not impossible that it was intended to support a façade common to both buildings. A large number of semi-circular and quarter-circle tiles and blocks of stone, 14 in. (0.35 m.) in diameter, have been found in Period 1 B levels in the vicinity (Vol. ii, p. 44) which were, in all probability, used as the basis for stuccoed columns. It may be that the columns stood on the footing. Such an arrangement would have posed certain problems of roofing, but these would not have been insuperable. Functionally and aesthetically a colonnaded façade would have been attractive, providing a dry walk along the front of both buildings and linking them visually at the same time. The nature of the evidence does not allow us to be dogmatic on the point, but some such explanation may well be near the truth.

Between the façade and the buildings several lengths of shallow gullies were found (fig. 12), serving perhaps to remove any surface water. They were clearly not all dug at the same time, but their detailed sequence and relationship to the building is beyond demonstration. All that can be said is that they would appear to respect the walls of the Period 1 B buildings but could possibly belong to the Period 1 C arrangement.

There is a considerable body of evidence available for the dating of the Period 1 B features described above. The clay floors of some of the rooms can be shown to overlie the post-holes of the Period 1 A building. Indeed, in several cases the floor has later slumped into the void formed after the stump of the early post had rotted. The buildings are therefore later than the demolition of the Period 1 A structure. At the end of the Period 1 B occupation the floors, demolished walls and associated features were covered by builders' debris which, it is suggested below, belongs to the construction of the Period 1 C building. The same construction debris seals a thick occupation layer which accumulated principally to the west of the timber buildings, and which is continuous with the lower filling of gully 10. The dating evidence from the material in this layer is given in detail below (Appendix 3): in summary it may be said that both pottery and coins range from late Claudian to late Neronian times.

TIMBER BUILDING 6: AREA 3 (fig. 16, p. 207)

Limited trial trenching in the garden at the back of no. 56 Fishbourne Road enabled the First Period levels to be examined in the area to the south of the southern road, east of the stream. The excavation was on a very small scale, but sufficient survived to show that a timber building, similar in structure to Buildings 4 and 5, existed here replacing an earlier Period 1 A structure (p. 43). The western wall of the building was supported on a drystone footing 15 in. (0.38 m.) wide, while the rest of the walls were based on ground-level sill beams. Two floors extended into the excavated area, one of Reading Beds clay and the other of gravel. A little to the south a further trial trench sectioned another clay floor which may have belonged to another room of the same building. Stratigraphically the building is of the same period as those immediately to the north, and may indeed be part of them.

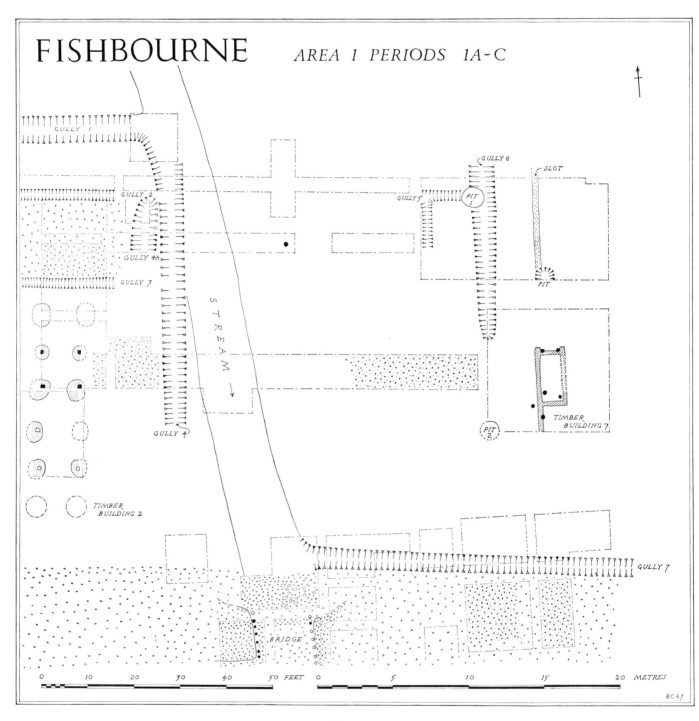

FIG. 13

TIMBER BUILDING 7: AREA 1 (fig. 13, p. 207)

The area lying north of the northern road and east of the stream (area 1) has not been extensively excavated, but limited work has demonstrated the existence of a timber structure based on sill beams 9 in. (0.23 m.) wide, slotted into a shallow trench cut 3–4 in. (c. 0.1 m.) deep into the natural gravel. The beams define a single rectangular unit 4 ft. 6 in. by 9 ft. 6 in. (1.37 × 2.90 m.), projecting to the east of a longer beam. No floor-levels survived. In and around the structure six post-holes, each supporting timbers 8–9 in. (c. 0.2 m.) in diameter, were found apparently broadly contemporary with the beams; their function is problematical, as indeed is that of the entire structure.

To the north, and on the line of the main north–south beam, a linear trench 1½ ft. (0.46 m.) wide and 15 in. (0.38 m.) deep was found cut into the natural and filled with redeposited clayey gravel. Although no post-holes could be traced, it is not impossible that the trench had been dug to bed fence-posts, since removed. The trench had been cut by a shallow gravel-filled pit, unfortunately containing no datable objects. Some dating evidence, in the form of pottery recovered from associated occupation levels, shows that the features were in use in the Neronian period.

THE SITE OF TIMBER BUILDING 2: AREA 4 (fig. 9, p. 207)

The demolition of Timber Building 2 has been described in a previous section and it is clear from the occupation material contained within the demolition pits that destruction took place some time towards the beginning of the Neronian period. After this the entire area, including the early gullies and the pathway, was used as a tip for rubbish, which sometimes attained a thickness of 12 in. (0.30 m.). The pottery recovered from this deposit dates from late Claudian to early Flavian times.

DRAINAGE GULLIES IN AREAS 1–5 (figs. 12–16, p. 208)

The continued use of the low-lying area on the banks of the stream throughout the Neronian period necessitated a considerable modification to the earlier system of drainage gullies. The narrow 2 ft. wide (0.6 m.) gullies of Period 1 A soon became silted up under the particularly wet local conditions; thus when the new gullies were designed they were usually dug at a standard width of 4–5 ft. (1.22–1.37 m.) with a shallow U-shaped profile scarcely more than 2 ft. (0.6 m.) deep.

Gully 6 (fig. 13) continues the line of gully 10 to the north of the northern road. It appears to cut through the earlier gully 5 and is in turn sealed by a layer of sandstone blocks and gravel, which is further cut by a large pit. Thus the gully was dug after Period 1 A and before the deposition of metalling assigned below to Period 1 C. Its filling of grey silty clay contained little dating evidence, but the pottery recovered is consistent with a Neronian date.

Gullies 7 and 9 (fig. 12) were dug along the edges of the eastern part of the northern road in order to carry off surface-water to the stream. Gully 9 begins opposite the end of gully 10 but the limit of gully 7 has not been traced. The profiles of both suggest that they had been cleared out at regular intervals and may even have continued to drain the road during Period 1 C, for very little rubbish and silt had been allowed to accumulate before the Period 2 make-up was laid across them.

Gully 10 (fig. 17) was the principal north–south drain running across areas 2 and 3 along the east side of the row of timber buildings. It began close to the termination of gully 9 and has been traced for 175 ft. (53.3 m.). Its southern end is not known but in all probability it emptied into the lower reaches of the stream. Its filling is characteristically grey silty gravel mixed with large quantities of occupation debris derived from the adjacent houses. Datable material occurs in quantity and is described in Appendix 3. Here it is sufficient to say that it dates largely to the Neronian period, but a quantity of Claudian samian and coins suggests a beginning in late Claudian times.

THE DITCHED ENCLOSURE: AREA 6 (fig. 14, p. 208, and pl. 11*b*)

In the north-west corner of the excavated area a substantial east–west ditch (ditch 21) was discovered and sectioned on several occasions (Sections 27, 29). Typically the ditch measures 17 ft. (5.18 m.) across and $5\frac{1}{2}$–6 ft. (*c.* 1.75 m.) deep. Its shallow U-shaped profile seems to be a reaction on the part of those who dug it to the local clay bedrock, for had the sides been more vertical, serious slumping would have taken place. On the north side of the ditch a shallow bank of gravel and clay had been built, 12 ft. (3.66 m.) wide and surviving now to a maximum height of 2 ft. (0.3 m.). Its southern face, actually on the lip of the ditch, has been revetted with a pile of turfs.

The filling of the ditch varied from section to section, but usually consisted of a thin layer of occupation rubbish lying on the bottom, sealed by primary silting derived from the weathering of the ditch sides. Above this, tips of gravel, clay and rubble had been thrown in to level up the ground in preparation for the erection of the Period 2 palace. A few scraps of pottery recovered from the lowest level of the ditch show that silting began sometime in the late Neronian period (Appendix 3). Therefore, although certain features, particularly the turf-revetted bank, might be thought to hint at early military construction, the dating evidence suggests a Period 1 B or even Period 1 C date. It could, of course, be argued that the ditch was early and had been recut, but in the absence of confirmatory evidence this is special pleading.

The eastern end of the ditch runs below the west end of the North Wing of the later palace, the floors of which are 4 ft. (1.2 m.) below the level of the natural surface at this point. The upper part of the ditch, beneath the building, has therefore been cut away but its course can be traced across rooms N 3 and N 4 by noting the subsidence of the mosaic floor over the soft ditch-fill. On this evidence the ditch would appear to turn to the north to join up with a length of ditch (gully 18), the truncated remains of which were examined below the floor of room N 2. The section at this point showed the filling to consist of a deliberate deposit of clay and sandy gravel 20 in. (0.5 m.) thick, upon which lay a thin lens of occupation rubbish containing a sherd of Claudio-Neronian samian. Although this filling is not typical of the main east–west ditch, it is likely that both form part of the same system. The northern limit of the gully has not been defined.

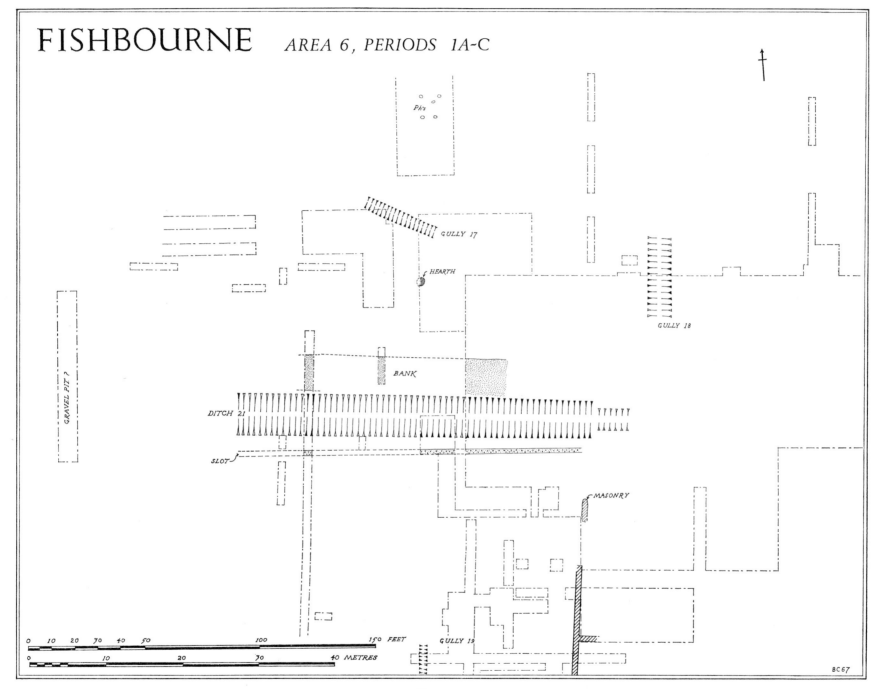

FISHBOURNE *AREA 6, PERIODS 1A-C*

Ph's

GULLY 17

HEARTH

GULLY 18

GRAVEL PIT ?

BANK

DITCH 21

SLOT

MASONRY

GULLY 19

0 10 20 30 40 50   100   150 FEET

0   10   20   30   40 METRES

BC 67

FIG. 14

Within the angle defined by the two lengths of ditch a considerable area has been excavated both archaeologically and by building contractors working under archaeological supervision. Most of the area, however, was barren with the exception of a length of gully (gully 17), and a hearth (fig. 14).

Gully 17 was partly excavated, its limits remaining undefined. In section it was 2 ft. (0.3 m.) deep and 5 ft. (1.5 m.) wide. It had been cut into the natural green-grey silty clay and filled with a 9-in. (0.33-m.) thick layer of dark occupation rubbish containing a quantity of pottery and oyster shells. Above this the ditch and the surrounding area had been sealed by clay make-up dating to Period 2. The pottery from the filling dated consistently to the Claudio-Neronian period.

To the south of gully 17 a thin and discontinuous occupation layer spread out over the surface of the natural clay, disappearing before the bank was reached. No structures could be identified, with the exception of a hearth which consisted of a 3-in. (0.08-m.) thick layer of baked clay, 3 ft. (0.9 m.) in diameter. Over part of the area to the north-east of the gully was a layer of gravel metalling, the extent and precise date of which are undefined.

AREA 7 (fig. 19)

Area 7 seems to have been largely open in Period 1 B since the surface of natural is totally devoid of occupation material. Only one ditch can tentatively be assigned to the period.

Ditch 22 runs in an east–west direction across the southern part of the area, terminating at the east. It was 4 ft. (1.2 m.) wide and was cut with almost vertical sides to a depth of 1 ft. 6 in. (0.46 m.) below the top of natural soil. In the bottom was a 2-in. (0.05-m.) thick layer of dark-grey gritty silt followed by 8 in. (0.20 m.) of brown silty clay, upon the top of which lay a lens of crushed chalk 1 in. (0.025 m.) thick. Above this the gully had been filled with yellow clay make-up related to the Period 1 C building activity. The most remarkable feature about the gully is that no artifact was found anywhere in its filling, nor was there any trace of occupation material nearby. The reason for assigning it to Period 1 B rests entirely upon the fact that stratigraphically it pre-dated the Period 1 C building, while the nature of the silting below the make-up shows that the ditch could not have been open for long.

THE AREA TO THE SOUTH OF THE MODERN MAIN ROAD (figs. 3, 39, p. 208)

South of the A27 the Roman ground-surface sloped down towards the sea. Very little large-scale excavation has been possible in the area, largely because of the proximity of modern buildings and their gardens, but in April 1969 a series of rapid trial excavations were carried out prior to and in connection with housing development on the land south of the 'Woolpack' and the two houses next to it, numbers 67 and 69 Fishbourne Road. Since the work is still in progress, a detailed report on the area is not yet possible; suffice it to say that the original ground-surface of shingly water-washed gravel overlaid by a thick peaty turf-line was traced over much of the area. It had been crossed by several channels (fig. 3), one of which was provided with a revetted side rather like a small quay-side,

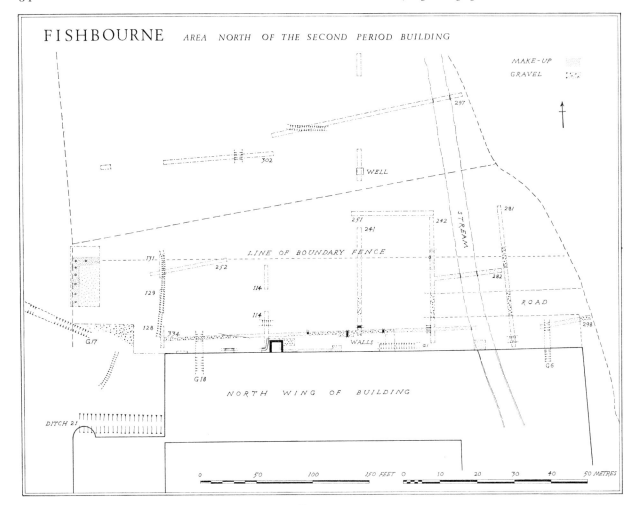

FIG. 15
(Trench numbers are indicated)

made of tips of large greensand and limestone blocks. No trace of timber revetting was seen but this does not prove its absence. Much more work is needed before the significance of these discoveries can be fully assessed.

Further to the north, in the excavations carried out in the garden of no. 65 Fishbourne Road, below the floor of room 11 of the later masonry building, two rows of stake-holes on average 2 in. (0.05 m.) in diameter were found, joining at approximately a right-angle. Space did not permit a fuller examination of the feature, but it seems possible that the stakes might form part of a fenced enclosure pre-dating the Period 1 C masonry building. No datable artifacts were recovered.

THE AREA NORTH OF THE MAIN SITE   (fig. 15, p. 208)

The area which lies to the north of the Second Period palace has been examined only by widely-spaced trial trenches dug by a mechanical excavator both for archaeological and

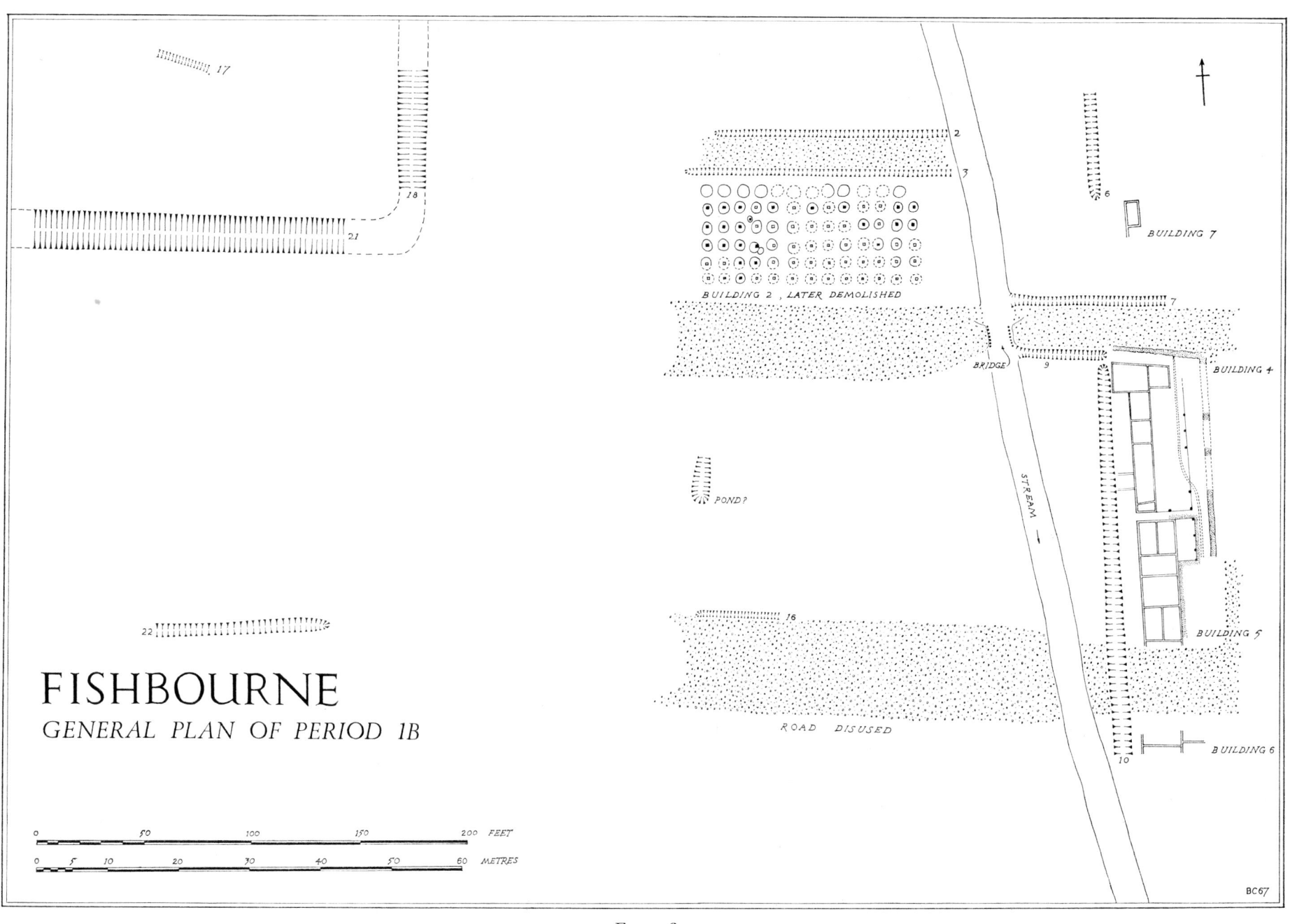

FISHBOURNE
GENERAL PLAN OF PERIOD IB

BUILDING 2 , LATER DEMOLISHED

BUILDING 7

BUILDING 4

BUILDING 5

BUILDING 6

POND?

STREAM

BRIDGE

ROAD DISUSED

| 0 | 50 | 100 | 150 | 200 FEET |
| 0 | 5 10 | 20 | 30 | 40 | 50 | 60 METRES |

BC67

Fig. 16

constructional purposes. The principal early features are summarized on the plan (fig. 15) and also on section 3. Features of post-A.D. 75 date are described separately below (p. 135).

Generally it may be said that the whole of the western part of the area, west of trench 241, was without trace of intensive occupation. The eastern area, however, particularly towards the centre of trench 297, yielded a considerable amount of occupation material and traces of first-century timber buildings. It is these regions which must eventually be totally excavated. Until this is done a brief summary of the principal features will suffice.

In the central section of trench 241 a timber-framed well was discovered, constructed in a pit 6 ft. (1.83 m.) square dug to a depth of 5 ft. (1.53 m.) below the contemporary ground-surface. The framework, of roughly adzed stakes *c.* 4–6 in. (0.1–0.15 m.) across, was laid horizontally, each pair of timbers overlapping the ends of the pair beneath. The filling of the well consisted of layers of clay and gravel together with blocks of greensand mixed with occupation material containing sherds of first-century A.D. pottery. In trench 297 a complex of occupation levels, together with an east–west gully 12 in. (0.3 m.) deep, were discovered. The assessment and description of this area must await more extensive excavation. To the west, in trench 302, occupation levels had ceased except for a single gully 15 in. (0.38 m.) deep and 6 ft. (1.83 m.) wide, which contained a barren, brown, stony silt. The line of trench 241 was continued north to the railway in a series of short discontinuous stretches, showing that occupation levels continued for about 200 ft. (61 m.) north of the well.

FEATURES OF PERIOD 1 C

THE ROADS AND THE STREAM (figs. 17 and 20, p. 208, and pl. VIb)

The principal alteration to be made to the drainage pattern of the site in Period 1 C was the abandonment of the old course of the stream and the digging of a new channel some way to the east. The sequence can be seen most clearly at the point where the southern road originally crossed the stream in Period 1 A, and where in the following period a new channel was cut through the old ford (p. 47, and fig. 52). After a foot or so of silt had been allowed to collect, a new road-surface of rammed gravel and sandstone blocks was laid across the old course, completely damming it (pl. VIb). The effects of this can be seen upstream, where a little to the north of the road a thick black peat had accumulated on the stream-bed in the now stagnant water. The abandonment of one course meant that another channel had to be dug. It seems that this was done to the east of the known buildings, almost along the line followed by the stream today, where a single trench sectioned a wide ditch, 2 ft. 4 in. (0.7 m.) deep, which was later recut during Period 2. The exact course of the diversion beyond this point is unknown, but it must have joined the original channel well upstream somewhere outside the limit of excavation. The abandoned length of old stream-bed, running north from the crossing to at least 40 ft. (12 m.) north of the bridge, was now filled in with tips of yellow clay and, less frequently, grey gravelly clay, so thoroughly that apart from occasional subsidences the original course would have been impossible to see.

The re-making of the southern road across the old stream has just been mentioned. Elsewhere along its line, particularly to the west, there is further trace of remetalling. Here the

F

old line was widened by the addition of a 10-ft. (3-m.) wide strip along the north edge of the original road, covering the now-silted side ditch and bringing the new width of the road at this point to about 45 ft. (13.7 m.). There is no comparable evidence for the remetalling of the northern road, but as stated above it seems probable that the side ditches were kept free from silt, suggesting continued use. The side-road leading between the two east–west roads, however, underwent modification (fig. 17). The section beside the new stream shows some remetalling with cobbles and gravel, and further to the north a new path 6 ft. (1.83 m.) wide of tightly-rammed gravel was laid diagonally to join the northern road, destroying the supposed Period 1 B colonnade and sealing its footing.

AREAS 1 AND 4 (figs. 9 and 13, p. 209, and pl. IV*a*)

With the blocking of the stream, it seems that some provision had to be made to drain the area to the north of the northern road. This was done by digging two gullies, nos. 1 and 4, at right-angles to each other in such a way that surface-water was drained towards their junction at the north-east corner and thence into the old stream-bed to the north. That gully 4 post-dates the abandonment of the stream is clearly shown by Section 6 (fig. 52) in which it will be seen that the gully was dug after clay had been packed into the stream. The bottom of the gully at this point was some 3 in. (0.076 m.) above the old stream-bed, whereas a little to the north (Section 5) the gully-base was several inches below. Consideration of the O.D. heights show that water could have flowed northwards. Similarly, the grading of gully 1 was such that the lowest point was to the east.

The gullies ranged in width from $4\frac{1}{2}$ to $5\frac{1}{2}$ ft. (1.4–1.7 m.) and in depth from $2–2\frac{1}{2}$ ft. (0.6–0.8 m.). The filling varied considerably, but in general very little silting had accumulated before deliberate packing with clay, gravel and rubble took place in preparation for the erection of the palace. Sufficient pottery has been recovered to show that gully 1 was open at the very beginning of the Flavian period (Appendix 3), and although little has been recovered from gully 4, a coin of Nero was found in the primary silt, close to Section 5. From stratigraphical evidence, then, it is possible to show that the gullies post-dated the functioning of the earlier stream and that they were open for only a short time before the Second Period palace was built. The dating evidence supports this view and suggests a late Neronian or early Flavian date for their construction.

Close to the west side of gully 4, a short length of a gully of similar proportions, gully 4a, was discovered. After a thin primary silt of 1–2 in. (0.05 m.) had been allowed to accumulate, the gully was filled with thick clay make-up dating to the beginning of Period 2. It is therefore likely to be of Period 1 C date, but its function is uncertain.

To the east of gully 4, little seems to have happened in Period 1 C. The earlier gully 6 had by this time silted up and a layer of gravel incorporating blocks of sandstone 9 in. thick had been laid over the entire area, presumably to counteract the problems of flooding. Even so, a sterile layer of grey silt up to 3 in. (0.076 m.) thick had accumulated on the gravel as the result of one or more inundations (Section 32, fig. 56).

The latest pre-Period 2 features in the area are two circular pits approximately 3 ft. (0.9 m.) in diameter (fig. 13, pits 1 and 2). Both were cut through all early levels and well into natural, to a depth exceeding 3 ft. (0.9 m.). They were filled with tips of occupation

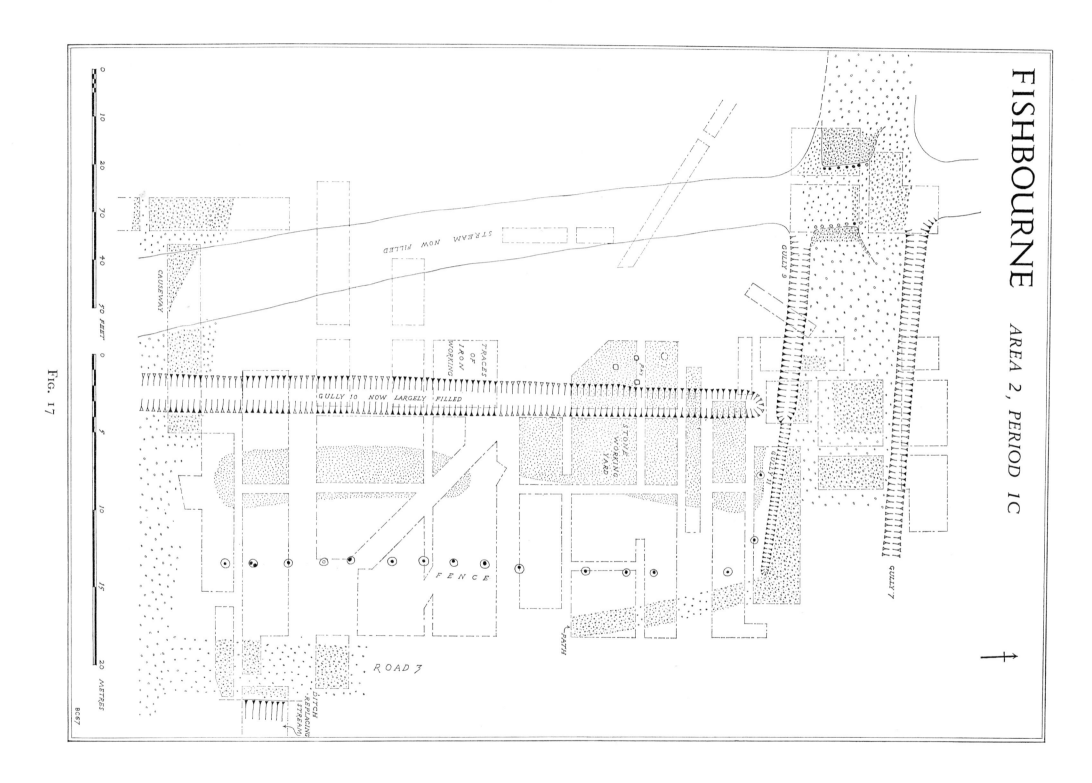

FISHBOURNE AREA 2, PERIOD 1C

Fig. 17

rubbish, gravel and clay and were sealed by the make-up layers from the floors of the palace. While it is possible that they were simply rubbish pits, the possibility remains that they may once have supported posts, later dug out. Several blocks of the red siltstone brought in for use in the proto-palace at the beginning of Period 1 C were found in the upper filling of pit 1.

THE FENCE AND GULLIES IN AREAS 2 AND 5   (fig. 17, p. 209, and pl. va)

The demolition of Timber Buildings 4, 5 and 6 will be considered in detail below — here it is sufficient to say that at the beginning of Period 1 C the entire site was cleared, all vestiges of structure being swept away. An area was then fenced off in preparation for the initiation of a new building programme.

The eastern arm of the fence has been excavated almost in its entirety. It consisted of a series of posts approximately 9 in. (0.23 m.) in diameter set in individual post-pits 2 ft. (0.6 m.) across and about 2 ft. (0.6 m.) deep. They were aligned roughly north–south and were spaced somewhat irregularly at intervals of between 6 and 9 ft. (1.8–2.7 m.). A distinctive characteristic was that the posts had been wedged in position, using large blocks of waste stone such as Purbeck marble and a pink siltstone brought in for the stone-masons who were about to begin construction work on the first masonry building. Although direct stratigraphical evidence was not always available, the new posts could generally be shown to be associated with the layer of builders' debris which sealed the destroyed Period 1 B buildings. At its northern limit the fence turned westwards to take up an east–west alignment along the south side of the northern road. Fortunately the two easternmost posts were found to be cut through the sill beams and floor of the Period 1 B building, again demonstrating the relative sequence of construction in the area. Immediately to the north of these posts, alongside the road, a new length of drainage gully had been dug (gully 11), 2 ft. (0.6 m.) wide and 12–15 in. (0.3–0.4 m.) deep, linking with the end of gully 9 and destroying part of the Period 1 B kerb (pl. iva).

The east–west fence continued in a straight line beyond the west bank of the old stream (fig. 20). The posts in this sector had been dug into the earlier road-surface, cutting off a strip 15 ft. (4.57 m.) wide on the south side and reducing the northern part of the road to a width approximating to that on the east side of the stream. Although only part of the line has been examined by excavation, the posts and their pits are of similar size to those of the north–south fence, the only difference being that they were packed with blocks of sandstone rather than with marble or siltstone. Their assignment to Period 1 C is not proven, but since the holes were dug through the Period 1 B road-surface and sealed by the clay make-up for the garden of the Period 2 palace, and were closely similar in construction to the Period 1 C post-holes of the north–south fence, it is not unreasonable to assume the two lines to be of the same date.

The limits of the fence are not known. To the west the post-holes have been destroyed by later levelling, while to the south excavation has not been possible, but it will be seen from the plan (fig. 20) that the north–south fence aligns exactly with the north-east corner of the first masonry building, with which it is known to be contemporary. It seems likely therefore that the fence delimits an area of land belonging to the building.

Apart from the builders' working yard, to be described below, the only feature within the fenced area known to belong to Period 1 C is the southern part of gully 15, which seems to have been re-excavated and considerably widened at this time. It may be quite fortuitous that the Period 1 C feature coincided with the end of the earlier gully, which we have seen is likely to have originated in Period 1 A. The late recutting created a hollow 4 ft. (1.2 m.) deep and 13 ft. (3.9 m.) wide, the function of which is not immediately apparent, but the most reasonable explanation is that the feature served as a pond. The water-table is so high that today, even in the middle of summer, 3 ft. (0.9 m.) of water soon accumulates. Further-more the nature of the silting strongly suggests that the hollow had been waterlogged in the Roman period. A pond would have been a valuable asset if cattle had been kept within the fenced enclosure. Dating depends on the discovery, in the primary silt, of two diamond-shaped *opus sectile* elements which did not appear on the site until Period 1 C. The few scraps of pottery recovered from the filling again suggest a late Neronian–early Flavian date. The upper levels of the hollow had been deliberately filled with clay and rubble before the period when the palace garden had been laid out. The lower part of the garden topsoil still seals the top of the hollow.

THE BUILDERS' WORKING YARD: AREA 2 (fig. 17, p. 209, and pl. viia)

The timber buildings of Period 1 B were demolished in preparation for the erection of the first masonry building, sometime towards the end of the Neronian period. A detailed consideration of the processes of demolition is not, unfortunately, possible on the available evidence but certain general points can be made. The relative lack of demolition debris over the floors and the presence of large quantities of even-textured yellow clay thrown into the old stream-bed and spread around elsewhere, suggest that the superstructure may have been of wattle and daub. If so, when the buildings were pulled down, loads of daub were probably carted away to level up adjacent areas — the useful timbers being stockpiled for later re-employment. It is difficult to see whether or not the sill beam had also been salvaged. One of them at least, the one along the north side of Timber Building 4, was left in position, no doubt because of its rotten state; the fate of the others is uncertain.

It was at this stage that the fence described above was erected; then followed the develop-ment of a stone-masons' yard in which the decorative stonework and marble-work to be used in the masonry building was prepared. Archaeologically the phase is represented by a layer of sand varying between 1 and 14 in. (0.025–0.35 m.) in thickness and interspersed with thin lenses of occupation rubbish. Scattered densely throughout lay large quantities of waste material, principally rough blocks, off-cuts and broken objects together with a number of ironstone rubbers used to smooth the stone. The working area lies along the western side of the fence between the two roads and extends westwards to gully 10, which by this time was largely silted up. It is divisible into two separate floors, one lying to the south of the other. The southern floor, measuring some 50 ft. by 10 ft. (15 × 3 m.), is marked by a layer of dirty white sand seldom exceeding 2 in. (0.05 m.) in thickness. The fragments of waste material were largely restricted to blocks of red siltstone and Purbeck marble, and also flakes of the same stones created by the hammer-dressing of rough lumps into square-sided blocks. In the same area a rather rarer stone, a breccia from the Côte d'Or, was worked through all stages to create highly-polished slabs.

The northern floor was evidently the main working area. Here the various stones were sawn and smoothed into finished objects and veneers. The commonest types of rock employed were red siltstone, a hard white chalk, a grey shaley siltstone from the Weald and blue Purbeck marble; white Carrara marble was found, though in much smaller quantities. On the northern fringes of the area the yellow and purple lamina from the red siltstone were more commonly worked, together with slabs of Kimmeridge shale (Vol. II, pp. 24 ff.). The waste material represented all stages in the production processes from the roughly-dressed block to the finished object. First the block was cut into sheets, between $\frac{1}{2}$ and 1 in. (0.015–0.025 m.) thick, by means of a multiple-bladed saw; the faces of the sheets were then smoothed and polished, using rubbers of ironstone, until a satisfactory finish was obtained. Next, the required shape was scored on the surface and the line pecked with a chisel to create a key for the sawing process which followed. When the saw had cut almost through the slab, the edges were snapped off and any burr remaining was removed with a hammer (Vol. II, pls. VIII, IX).

The finished objects varied in type (Vol. II, pls. VII-X). The commonest were strips of Purbeck marble for use in wall and floor decoration, and geometric shapes such as squares, triangles, kite-shapes and diamonds in blue, white, yellow, grey and red, which would have formed the elements of *opus sectile* floors (Vol. II, pl. VII). Carrara marble was used exclusively for veneers and mouldings, the small quantity of waste material recovered no doubt reflecting the value placed on even small scraps. Other mouldings were made of Purbeck marble, which was also used to make mortars and pestles (Vol. II, p. 40 and fig. 23). Quantities of much finer inlay, $\frac{1}{4}$ in. (c. 0.6 cm.) thick, principally of red, white and grey stone and, occasionally, a blue-green slate, were recovered in various stages of completion. A selection of the more common shapes is shown (Vol. II, fig. 19); they include peltas, skittle-shapes, hollow-sided triangles and bucrania, too fine for floor or wall inlay but quite possibly intended for use as veneering for table-tops.

The recovery of so large a quantity of waste material has thrown a great deal of light on the tools employed by the masons. Evidently three types of saw were in use: the multiple-bladed saw for cutting blocks into sheets, a single blade for slicing the sheets into strips, and a type approximating to a modern hacksaw for cutting out the small shapes for furniture inlay. The actual process involved is vividly described by Pliny:[1] the saw blades, probably untoothed metal strips, were swung backwards and forwards, rubbing wet sand against the surface of the stone in such a way as to wear a groove deeper and deeper into the block, the blade providing the energy, the sand the abrasive power. The method requires, in addition to the saw, a plentiful supply of sand and water. The masons at Fishbourne were provided with both; indeed, in the area where the offcuts suggested that a maximum amount of sawing had taken place, the accumulation of the used sand had reached a depth of 14 in. (0.35 m.). The position of the water-supply is a little more problematical, but it may well be that water was piped to the area by means of a wooden water-pipe bedded in the north–south gully a little to the east of the working floor. Admittedly no trace of a pipe or of iron joints was recovered, but had they existed they would surely have been removed when the preparation had finished.

[1] Pliny, *Nat. Hist.*, XXXVI, 51 ff.

It is not known whether the saws were held and motivated by two men, or whether they were suspended from a framework and swung. Probably both techniques were used, for the multiple-bladed saw would have been too heavy to man-handle. At any event, some kind of trestle or framework is demanded. The only possible trace of one came from the centre of the sawing area, where three post-holes were found in a triangular setting, between $5\frac{1}{2}$ and 6 ft. (c. 1.7 m.) apart. Each hole was found to be carefully lined and floored with stones to take a square post 9 in. (0.23 m.) across, but the nature of the superstructure is beyond recovery. A fourth post a little to the north may also have belonged to the feature.

Other types of tools used by the masons would have included hammers, chisels, scribers and rubbers, but of these there is little to be said. The working on certain of the blocks implies the existence of at least two widths of chisel-blade, a narrower type for pecking the line in preparation for sawing and a wider blade $\frac{3}{8}$ in. (c. 1 cm.) across for carving mouldings and other three-dimensional objects. Smoothing was carried out with pieces of ironstone of a size suitable to be held easily in the hand. Several of these were found discarded in the masons' area.

The working floor can be shown to overlie the destroyed remains of the Period 1 B timber buildings and in turn to be sealed by the layers of clay and gravel used to make up the ground-level for the floors of the Period 2 palace. The few datable sherds of pottery associated with it support a late Neronian–early Flavian date, but are not closely datable. Previously the floor was assigned to the masons preparing stone for the Period 2 palace, but such an interpretation no longer seems possible and it must now be suggested that the stonework was for use in the first masonry building which lies immediately to the south. The reason for this change of view can be summarized as follows: the yard was concerned largely with the production of elements of *opus sectile* floors but no *opus sectile* work has been found *in situ* in the Period 2 palace or in subsequent rubbish deposits. On the other hand, several decorative elements with pink mortar adhering to them have been found in make-up layers below Period 2 floors. The implication must therefore be that they were used in a floor pre-dating the Period 2 palace and this is most likely to have been in the Period 1 C masonry building. A further factor is the type of marble used. Two foreign marbles occur in the working area, the breccia from the Côte d'Or and Carrara marble. Neither are known among the mass of inlay recovered from the Second-Period palace, where the two commonest imported stones are a white Turkish marble and a green-veined marble from the Pyrenees — types which are not found in the working area. There is therefore little in common between the marbles and veneers found in the working yard and those known to have been used in the later palace. The evidence now strongly suggests that the stone worked in the masons' yard was not used in the Period 2 palace, and that in all probability it ornamented the first masonry building of Period 1 C.

While the experienced marble-workers were engaged to the west of the fence, ordinary masons responsible for the main structure of the building were stockpiling and facing blocks of upper greensand. Their debris, a heavily trampled layer of greensand chippings and dust, 2–3 in. (0.05–0.076 m.) thick, covered much of the area east of the fence and spread for some distance along the southern road — the route along which the worked stone would have been taken to the building site. The layer occupies the same stratigraphical position as does that belonging to the marble-workers.

To the west of the now largely filled gully 10 a quantity of iron slag was recovered (fig. 17) mixed with charcoal to form a discontinuous layer up to 6 in. (0.15 m.) thick in places. It may well represent waste from iron smelting nearby, but no traces of furnaces of any kind have come to light (Vol. II, p. 372).

THE FIRST MASONRY BUILDING: AREA 3   (fig. 18, p. 209, and pls. VIIb, VIII)

Area 3, which lies to the south of the southern road, is now encumbered by a number of recent buildings, making excavation extremely difficult. Through the centre of the site runs the modern Folkestone to Honiton trunk road (the A27), in the vicinity of which digging is totally impossible. To the north is a group of farm buildings belonging to the Sussex Archaeological Trust and an eighteenth-century house and garden, whilst to the south lie two more houses of eighteenth- and early nineteenth-century date, both with moderately large gardens. Fortunately the owners of all three houses have taken a very active interest in the archaeological work and have made substantial areas of their gardens and their cellars available for excavation. Thus, over a period of seven winters, it has been possible to examine, piece by piece, the entire garden areas, leaving the lawns and concrete drives untouched. Although small-scale excavation of this kind leaves much to be desired, a great deal of information has been accumulated and the general form of the building is now known. All this is due to the enlightened forbearance of the local residents, who each year have looked on not only tolerantly but with interest whilst their flower-beds have been ravaged.

In so far as excavation to natural gravel has been possible, there appears to have been no extensive Period 1 A or 1 B occupation, with the exception of the small fenced enclosure previously described (p. 54). This implies that no major demolition had to be undertaken before building work could proceed. Indeed there seems to have been little preparation of the site except perhaps for the consolidation of the ground over the line of the old stream and Period 1 B gully — details of which are not available.

In plan, the building can be divided into four parts: to the north is a courtyard surrounded by verandas, to the south a bath suite and, along the east side of both, a range of rooms flanked by corridors. Traces of a south-western range have also come to light but much more work remains to be done here. The basic structure of all four units was the same: first a foundation trench was dug into the natural clayey gravel and in it a footing of stone blocks, usually ironstone and greensand but occasionally of igneous erratics, was laid without mortar. (pl. VIIIb). The facing stones of the footing were regularly laid in courses, the infill between them being of smaller blocks placed at random. Footings were of two widths: 2 ft. (0.6 m.) wide for the walls of the verandas and the range of rooms, and 3 ft. (0.9 m.) wide for the rooms of the bath suite, the greater width being necessary here because the walls would probably have been built in masonry to roof-level and may even have supported stone vaulting. Very little of the structure survived above the footings, and indeed in many areas even the footings themselves had been removed, but the 'buttress' on the north wall of room 11 (pl. VIIIa), the inner (i.e. east) wall of corridor 2, and a small piece of structure in the south end of corridor 7, stood above footing-level, showing the superstructure to have been built of neatly-squared blocks of upper greensand set in a white chalky mortar, lenses of which had been slopped on the surrounding ground-surface at the time of construction. No trace of external plastering survived.

The courtyard and surrounding verandas

Although the general plan of the courtyard is known, later alterations, extensive robbing and the lowering of the ground in the nineteenth century have combined to remove most of the evidence which would have given some idea of the architecture of this part of the building. Several general points, however, are clear. The courtyard, measuring 58 ft. (17.7 m.) across, was bordered on the east side by a 10-ft. (3.0 m.) wide corridor (corridor 5) which linked the three elements of the building together. It may reasonably be supposed that in relation to the courtyard, the corridor was treated as a veranda opening inwards towards the enclosed area, perhaps through a colonnade. Similar verandas bordered the north and east sides of the court, but since they were essentially decorative rather than functional passages they were laid out at a narrower width, of 7 ft. (2.1 m.).

The northern part of the courtyard was made up with a layer of clayey gravel 8–9 in. (c. 0.2 m.) thick, but similar metalling does not appear to have been laid uniformly over the area, for at the southernmost point examined no make-up at all was found. Gravel and clay make-up was also deposited within the verandas but in no case did a contemporary floor-surface survive.

On the extreme eastern side of the building there appears to have been another 7 ft. wide (2.1 m.) passageway (corridor 1), possibly a west-facing veranda, represented now only by a robber trench; its northern termination is conjectural owing to the presence of a large recent cess-pit. A similar veranda also ran along part of the north wall, but its full extent has not been traced. The function of corridor 1 may have been to link the SW range to the rest of the building.

The major problem still remaining is the nature of the south side of the courtyard. The presence of a mortar-floored room on the south side of the modern road implies that the courtyard terminated somewhere towards the centre of the road, but how the limit was effected, whether by a veranda or a simple cross-wall remains unknown.

The eastern range. The range of rooms forming the eastern element of the building is known only in bare outline. All that can safely be said is that it consisted of a strip of rooms 19 ft. (5.8 m.) wide and at least 170 ft. (52 m.) long, flanked on the east by a 14 ft. wide (4.3 m.) corridor (corridor 7) of greater length than the range of rooms. There is no evidence yet of cross-walls dividing the range into individual rooms, nor does any trace of a contemporary floor survive in the limited area it has been possible to examine. In the corridor, however, yellow clay make-up 12 in. thick (0.3 m.) had been laid between the walls. The southern limit of the range has not been excavated, but limited trial trenching has demonstrated complications of an unexpected form. The eastern corridor can be shown to carry on beyond the southern limit of the bath unit, and within it lies a free-standing masonry structure built of walls 18 in. (0.46 m.) thick, abutting a stone block 3 ft. (0.9 m.) in length and 1 ft. (0.3 m.) thick. Without further excavation, interpretation is impossible.

The bath suite. The original bath suite, and the subsequent alterations made to it, have suffered seriously from the activities of stone-robbers at various periods. Very little remains of the original floors and even less of the walls. If complete assessment of function is not possible, at least some attempt can be made to describe the individual rooms.

Room 8 now lies almost entirely beneath the modern main road and its sidewalks. Much of the remaining part has been ruined by eighteenth- and nineteenth-century excavations, but sufficient survives to show that its southern and eastern walls were lined with pink mortar and that similar material, resting on a make-up of greensand blocks, floored a strip 18 in. to 2 ft. (0.46–0.6 m.) wide at the base of the walls (pl. viib). Beyond this the floor make-up was replaced by a rubble-filled hollow. From the corner of the room and across the corridor ran a drain, floored with tiles, now largely destroyed. The use of pink mortar and the provision of a drain strongly suggests that the room was an integral part of the bathing facilities. One explanation is that it served as a cold plunge bath, the pink mortar feature representing a bench around the walls. A closely similar structure was found in the contemporary bath building at Angmering (Scott, 1939), with which the Fishbourne example has many features in common.

Room 9, lying immediately to the south, was excavated and totally wrecked sometime in the nineteenth century, its filling consisting now of redeposited Roman building rubbish mixed with recent slate and wine-bottle fragments. It may be that this is the room referred to in the article published in 1858 (Smith, 1858). Since everything has been destroyed to a depth of 20 in. (0.5 m.) below the surviving surface of the adjacent corridor floor, it is difficult to assess the function of the room but the depth of excavation alone might suggest that it originally contained a hypocaust. In the north-west corner a small piece of pink mortar survived at the depth suitable for a hypocaust basement floor.

Rooms 10–12 are a range of three adjacent units of approximately equal size, each measuring 19 ft. by 15 ft. (5.8 × 4.8 m.). *Room 10* was only partly examined, most of it lying now beneath a garage and a concrete drive-way. Its floor is now missing, but the floor make-up of large loose-packed greensand blocks up to 10 in. (0.25 m.) long was still in position, lying on natural gravel. From the rubble above was recovered a quantity of small pieces of wall-plaster painted in green and white, and a number of white tesserae. *Room 11* was completely sectioned, but here again the floor had been destroyed, only the make-up of large sandstone blocks surfaced with greensand chippings surviving. The rubble filling the room contained large quantities of building rubble, including small sections from a black and white mosaic floor, much broken box-tile, two pieces of Purbeck marble inlay and pink wall-plaster, some pieces painted red and white, others green of various shades on a white background. Pink mortar and box-tiles are strongly suggestive of a hypocaust fitting. There is little to be said of *Room 12*, which now lies wholly beneath no. 63 Fishbourne Road. Trial trenches beneath the cellar floors of the house located the east and west walls but, with the exception of the lowest few inches, even the greensand floor make-up had been removed by the cellar floor.

Room 13 is best regarded as a passage or an ante-room leading from the heated rooms 10 and 16 to room 14, thought to be a cold room. Again the floor was missing, but the make-up was sectioned showing it to consist of large rough blocks of greensand placed on a layer of flint nodules which had been rammed into the underlying natural gravel. The rubble filling the room contained little of interest, except for a few small fragments of wall plaster painted red.

Room 14 lay immediately to the south: it was largely unexamined. Two small trenches have, however, overlapped its eastern wall. The southern trench sectioned only floor make-up of greensand set in clay, whilst the northern trench discovered a well-laid floor of tiles bedded in a stiff orange clay. In the north-east corner of the room several tiles had been mortared on to the floor with a hard white gritty mortar. The function of such a feature is obscure, but some kind of bench may have been intended. Since a hypocaust was absent, and the room was therefore unheated, it may have served either as a *frigidarium* or an *apodyterium*. The latter is unlikely on the grounds that the room is rather inconveniently placed with regard to the rest of the suite; furthermore its tiled floor would have better served a cold room.

Room 15 served as a corridor along the south side of the building. It was floored with a red mortar 2 in. (0.05 m.) thick laid on a make-up varying between flint cobbles and greensand chippings. At a later stage, in Period 2, its northern wall had been demolished and a new floor laid joining the corridor with the room to the north (see below p. 119).

Room 16 lay in the centre of the bath suite. It measured 20 ft. (6 m.) from north to south, but its length is unknown, indeed it is possible that a cross-partition occurred somewhere east of the limit of the present excavation. The sub-floor stratigraphy was a little more complex than that found elsewhere in the building, for along the southern wall a trench 4 ft. (1.2 m.) wide had been dug and then filled with sandstone blocks, similar to those used in the wall footings, presumably to act as a soakaway for surface-water. Over this had been laid a 9 in. thick (0.23 m.) make-up of greensand blocks mixed with chalk, which was in turn sealed with a spread of rough white chalky mortar between 3 and 6 in. (1.07 m.) thick containing small chips of greensand. This mortar spill served as a floor upon which a hypocaust had been built. Subsequent alterations had removed most of it, but against the northern walls the bases of *pilae* and a continuous bench-like projection along the wall survived together with a wall of tiles laid out on the arc of a circle. The 'bench' and *pilae* clearly supported a raised floor, but the function of the semi-circular feature is less certain, unless it framed a small sunken plunge-bath. Unfortunately, the proximity of the modern house prevented a more extensive investigation. The rubble filling the room contained quantities of black and white *tesserae*, a few pieces of wall plaster painted red and white, and much broken flue-tile.

Although our knowledge of the bath suite is still far from complete the general concept behind the arrangement of the rooms can be assessed in broad terms. Rooms 10 to 12 probably formed the main dry *caldaria* and *tepidaria*. These were linked through a warmed ante-room (no. 9) to a cold plunge-bath beyond (no. 8). To the south lay a further set of rooms of which one, no. 16, was provided with hot damp heat, while close by lay a *frigidarium* (no. 14) where a bather might have been able to douche himself in cold water. Thus it seems that two types of bathing were catered for, one akin to the Swedish sauna bath, which provides an intensely dry hot atmosphere, followed by a plunge in cold water, and the other, of Turkish bath type in which hot steamy rooms are created, often containing subsidiary hot baths, for use in conjunction with tepid and cold rooms through which the body would be allowed gradually to acclimatize to normal temperatures again. If this interpretation is correct in general terms, it will be seen that the first masonry building was provided with a luxurious suite paralleled in its elaboration only by the contemporary baths at Angmering.

So limited an excavation could not hope to discover all the details of the plan, such as positions of drains and flues. One drain, however, has already been mentioned, leading from the supposed plunge bath in room 8. The others are completely unknown. Similarly, there is no good evidence for the siting of the flues, but these must have stood somewhere along the north or east walls of the bath suite in order to serve the rooms in which hypocausts have been found. A 'buttress' of masonry projecting from the north wall of room 11 may well be a cheek-wall for a flue — unfortunately further investigation here is impossible. The adjacent area had been metalled with a spread of gravel 12 in. (0.3 m.) thick indicating, perhaps, the presence of a stoking yard.

Beyond the north-west corner of room 10 a single excavation trench sectioned a pit cut to a depth of 2 ft. 3 in. (0.69 m.) below the level of the adjacent natural gravel and filled with rubble, including many tile and greensand fragments and charcoal. It is possible that the pit once contained the flue by means of which room 10 was heated. If so, it had been totally robbed at some subsequent period.

Trial trenching to the south, west and north of the baths has produced details of the environment. The southernmost trench in the garden of no. 65 Fishbourne Road located the contemporary shore-line, defined here by a clean loose shingle, at a depth of 5 ft. 5 in. (1.66 m.). Thirty feet (9.1 m.) to the north, close to the south side of the building, the ground-surface was 20 in. (0.5 m.) higher. Immediately above the sloping ground lay a wedge of grey silt, containing fragments of Roman building material. At the southern limit of the excavation the layer reached a thickness of 34 in. (0.87 m.) but gradually thinned out towards the building as the land rose. Since the nature of the silt shows it to have been deposited below water — a fact supported by the rolled nature of the rubble fragments found within it — the inescapable conclusion must be that water at one time reached the southern limit of the building. It is possible that a pond was sited here in the Second Period (p. 132). That the silt had accumulated largely before the final destruction of the building, is shown by the section immediately to the south of the south wall where a thick layer of building collapse lay over the silt.

The area west of the bath block

A series of trial trenches in the west end of the front garden of no. 65 Fishbourne Road demonstrated the existence of further Period 1 C walls in the area (see fig. 18), defining two small rooms nos. 17 and 18. It is possible that these are the eastern extremity of an otherwise undefined West Wing. Until further excavation can be carried out to the west, its extent and form must remain unknown.

Constructional details

The building materials commonly incorporated in the Period 1 C masonry building have been mentioned in the descriptive text above. In summary, they consist of a miscellany of stone types, including Wealden sandstone, upper greensand and igneous rocks for the wall footings, squared upper greensand blocks for the superstructure of the walls, and tiles for the roofs. Whether or not the heated rooms of the bath suite were vaulted, and if so with what, are problems which cannot easily be solved. The thickness of the walls is certainly indicative of a heavy superstructure, but no certain traces of fallen vault were found although the broken box-tiles from within some of the rooms may well be from such a structure.

It is not proposed to discuss here details of the types of tiles found in association with the building. A consideration of the major elements will be found below (Vol. II, pp. 43 ff.).

The existence of verandas presupposes columns but only one fragment has been found in direct association with the building, lying in a Period 2 make-up layer in the centre of corridor 2. It is a length of drum $3\frac{1}{2}$ ft. (1.07 m.) long and 14 in. (0.35 m.) in diameter, roughly chiselled from a block of glauconitic sandstone of Wealden origin (Vol. II, p. 15). It shows no trace of having been turned on a wheel, indeed its roughly chiselled surface might suggest that it had been prepared ready for wheel-finishing but never actually turned. It is, however, important to remember that sandstone of this kind would not stand up well to weathering and the possibility remains that the roughly-finished drum was, in fact, a core which may have once been stuccoed. Other, smaller, fragments of similar, apparently unfinished, drums were found in post-holes below the North Wing of the Period 2 palace (Vol. II, p. 15). It may be argued that all were roughouts intended for the later palace, but rejected because of breakage during manufacture. The stratigraphy would allow such a suggestion, but when it is remembered that all the finished column fragments belonging to the second period were of limestone, the argument in favour of the glauconitic sandstone columns belonging to Period 1 C becomes much stronger.

A further point for consideration is the order to which the columns belonged. There is no direct evidence but if the drums were stuccoed it may hint that they were also fluted. Fluted pilasters were certainly employed in internal decoration, as we will see later. Moreover, in some of the post-holes belonging to the Period 2 garden, many fragments of elaborate Corinthian capitals were found, used as packing around the posts (Vol. II, pp. 11–12). Clearly they must have come from some earlier structure, since on stylistic grounds alone they would have been out of place in the Flavian palace. Their most likely place of origin is the first masonry building here under discussion.

These fragments of evidence may be weak individually, but together they point to an early masonry building adorned with elaborate and unusual Corinthian columns composed of oolitic limestone capitals on fluted, stuccoed shafts.

Interior decoration

The magnificence of the exterior was matched by the formal quality of the internal decoration, hardly apparent from the summary of miserable remnants described in the general text above. The building had been so raked and ravaged since its abandonment that little of its former grandeur could be deduced from the odd tesserae and painted plaster fragments that now survive. Two sources of evidence, however, throw some light on its original state, first, the half-finished marble elements from the builders' working yard (above, p. 59), and second, a large amount of painted plaster from walls demolished prior to the construction of the Period 2 palace.

One of the principal products from the masons' yard was geometric elements for *opus sectile* floors. Since a detailed analysis of the individual examples is offered below (Vol. II, pp. 33 ff.), it is sufficient here merely to summarize the main types in production. Triangles were the commonest form, being made in red, grey, blue and white. Several variants of shape and size were manufactured — in white stone, for example, nine different forms were noted, usually measuring between 10.5 and 11.5 cm. across the base and of similar height, though more flattened examples were not uncommon. Squares were made in all four types of stone in three basic sizes: 10.5 cm., 12 cm. and 16 cm. Far less common were the kite-shaped elements known only in red, yellow and blue. Diamonds were made in red and white, and hexagonal slabs only in white and blue. In addition to the geometric shapes, simple strips and bars for outlining the main design were frequently produced, principally in grey and blue. From so great a variety of elements many permutations of design are possible — as will be seen from the illustration (Vol. II, pl. VII) which is based on patterns commonly occurring in Italy. It gives some idea of the range of variants open to the designers using the basic shapes available at Fishbourne. Although *opus sectile* work was relatively widespread in Italy in the first century A.D., it is rare in Britain: the only site where it is known to have been used extensively is Angmering, 16 miles away. Other British sites have produced only occasional fragments. Where exactly the sectile floors were originally laid at Fishbourne cannot now be discovered but most likely they were in the rooms of the eastern range. It may be that in the original building all of the fine rooms were floored with *opus sectile* and that the mosaics, represented by loose tesserae, were added later in the Second Period. The problem is not one which can now be solved. The large number of used elements found in the rubble deposits dating to the construction period of the palace, however, strongly suggests that some, if not all, of the sectile floors were ripped up in the period of rebuilding, which was soon to follow.

The masons' yard also produced mouldings, usually in Purbeck marble, for use as cornices above doors and windows, but at this stage no other type of marble wall-inlay seems to have been made, wall surface decoration being confined to painting.

When, some years later, the early building was incorporated in the palace, a new floor-level, 3 ft. (0.9 m.) above the original floors, was created. This necessitated the deposition of layers of make-up, both within and without the old building, particularly on the north and west sides where new ranges of rooms were abutted. For make-up the builders used, among other things, building rubble obtained from the demolition of parts of the old building which were now defunct. To the north and west excavation revealed thick layers of fine, even-textured yellow clay mixed up with large quantities of painted wall-plaster. The plaster was sometimes as much as 3 in. (0.076 m.) thick, the backs of some pieces showing the marks made by laying the plaster against a roughly-keyed clay wall. The layer, therefore, probably represents the demolished remains of timber-framed daub walls which had been heavily-plastered and painted. A comparison between figs. 18 and 34 will show that several of the Period 1 C corridors were torn down in Period 2; others may well have been rebuilt from foundation level in masonry. At any event, it is likely to be from the northern part of the building that the wall plaster was derived.

The painting and finish of the plaster was of exceptional quality. The plaster surface had been prepared from a coarse white lime mortar, containing crushed crystals of calcite, applied in layers to the daub wall. When the final layer had dried, the whole face had been rubbed down to a smooth, almost polished surface, before the paint was applied. Most of the fragments recovered from the make-up layer had been broken into fairly small pieces, but a sufficient quantity was recovered to enable the general design to be reconstructed. A detailed analysis is given below (Vol. II, pp. 52–6); here it is sufficient to consider the broad outlines of the scheme.

The walls were divided into panels, each painted blue-black, yellow or red in bold clear colours outlined with a white frame $\frac{3}{8}$ in. (1.0 cm.) wide. The red panels were ornamented with a white or cream line $\frac{3}{16}$ in. (0.5 cm.) thick, forming an inner frame 2 in. (5.0 cm.) from the outer border. The other coloured panels were treated in the same way, the blue-black areas lined with yellow, the yellow areas with brown. The background against which the panels were set was of an even green colour, usually over-painted with elaborate floral designs in white, and occasionally other colours. The surviving designs are fragmentary. Often they represented flowering plants drawn with simple foliage and stems in white lines, the flowering heads being frequently painted in red and white with carefully shaded orange fruit attached. So far as it is possible to tell, the flowers lay in the wide green borders adjacent to yellow panels. The green borders between the black and red panels were restricted to unadorned strips 2 in. (5.0 cm.) wide. In addition to flowers, green areas were also painted with fish and mammals — one fragment bears a representation of a goldfish, an even smaller piece shows the dorsal fin of what is probably a dolphin.

The top of the area of green background was finished with a painted moulding, a few sections of which were found. The moulding is an accomplished piece of painting, using white and various shades of pink to depict a cornice in such a way that it appears to be viewed in a warm evening light. Above the cornice was a plain white frieze.

Blue-black was also used as a background colour and many fragments were found over-painted with floral designs depicting green and yellow fronds sprouting from the ground, with white blobs at their tips representing flowers. The painting was carried out with bold brush-strokes, usually 2 cm. wide, in strong contrast to the delicate floral paintings on the green borders. Painting of this kind would have been suitable for a dado below general eye-level, running along the bottom of the wall, with the main coloured panels and green surround above. While there can be little doubt that blue-black was generally used for the dado, in one case the colour appeared next to a red panel, showing that here at least it had been used as an over-all background colour above dado-level.

By far the largest percentage of the surviving painting falls into the categories just described. There are, however, other colours and relationships which cannot be directly related to the main design. White was relatively common, the fragments recovered being quite frequently ornamented with inscribed circles 3 in. (8.0 cm.) in diameter, painted internally with simple petals in red or green. It is possible that plaster treated in this way came from ceilings. Other colours include orange, purply-brown and purple splashed with red and white to simulate marble.

The general picture to emerge from a consideration of the wall-plaster is of rooms or corridors with blue-black foliage-decorated dados surmounted by large panels of red, yellow and black set against a green background delicately painted with flowers and sprigs of leaves, which grow between and around the panels. The design is capped with a cornice,

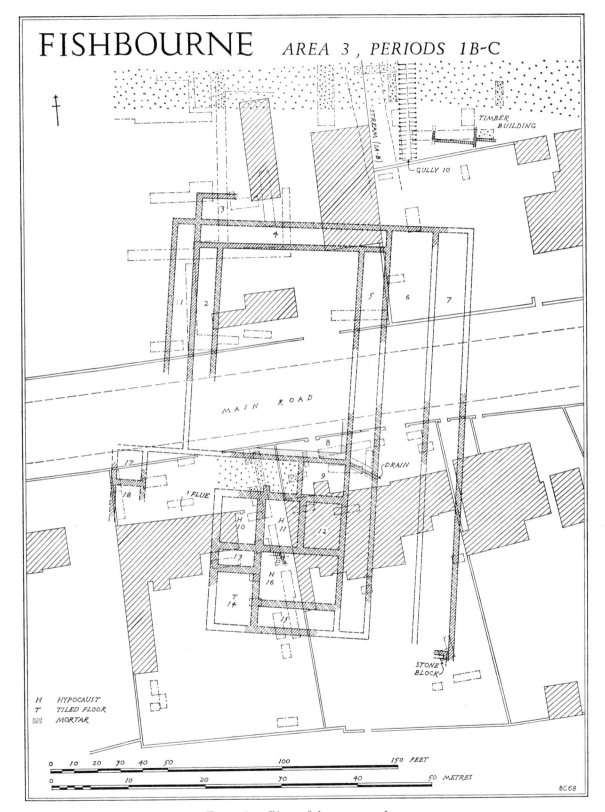

FISHBOURNE AREA 3, PERIODS 1B-C

TIMBER BUILDING

STREAM (1A-B)

GULLY 10

3

4

1 2 5 6 7

MAIN ROAD

8

DRAIN

17

9

18 FLUE

H 10 H 11 12

13

H 16

T 14

STONE BLOCK

H HYPOCAUST
T TILED FLOOR
MORTAR

0 10 20 30 40 50 100 150 FEET

0 10 20 30 40 50 METRES

BC 68

FIG. 18. Plan of the proto-palace

above which is a white frieze and ceiling. The arrangement is one of considerable elegance which, combined with the high quality of the painting, would not have been out of place anywhere in the metropolitan area. Style and execution are so refined that one must suppose a group of continental painters to have been present at Fishbourne, along with the other specialists required by the building programme.

Amid the large quantities of painted plaster recovered from the make-up layers were found a number of fragments of stucco-work belonging to fluted pilasters (Vol. II, fig. 26). The fragments were too small to provide a complete section through a pilaster but the size of the fluting alone indicates a width in excess of 2 ft. (0.6 m.). Three small fragments of stucco ornamented with curvilinear motifs were also found; they are too small to identify with certainty but they may have come from ornamented capitals. It is impossible to say, from the available evidence, where in the original building the pilasters might have stood, except that they are more likely to have ornamented the rooms of the east range than corridors.

The date of the building

Direct dating evidence is not plentiful, but the stratigraphical position of the building can be used with some precision to give dates to the period during which it was occupied. It has been shown above (pp. 58–9) that masons' working debris lay above the destroyed remains of timber buildings dating to the Claudio-Neronian period, and that the debris was in turn sealed by make-up belonging to the erection of the Period 2 palace which, it will be shown, began to be built sometime about A.D. 75. It will also be shown below that the early form of the building was modified and, in parts, substantially altered at the time when the palace was put up. The original building must therefore pre-date A.D. 75, and from the dating and coin evidence sealed beneath the working yard it must post-date much of the Neronian period. A construction date sometime between A.D. 65 and 70 would therefore seem most likely. The relatively few sherds directly associated with the construction phase of the building offer a no more precise agreement.

THE SECOND MASONRY BUILDING: AREA 7 (figs. 19–20, pp. 209–10, and pls. IXb–XI)

Beneath the West Wing of the Period 2 palace the corner of a substantial masonry building was discovered. Its foundations, laid in foundation trenches 2 ft. 6 in. (0.76 m.) wide and dug to a depth exceeding 3 ft. (0.9 m.), were of small flint nodules set in a cream-coloured concrete. The plan is incompletely known, partly because mosaic floors of the later palace prevent excavation down to the earlier surface, and partly because the building extends beyond the south and west limits of the available site. The surviving fragment is therefore the north-west corner of the structure.

The building comprises two ranges of rooms at right-angles with a group of smaller rooms set at the junction. The North Wing is represented by two parallel walls 20 ft. (6.1 m.) apart, between which presumably lay a series of cross-walls defining individual rooms. Most of the cross-walls have not been traced; the room sizes are therefore generally undefined but the easternmost room is known to be 14 ft. (9.27 m.) across. The spacing of the other known wall would allow the range to be composed of units of approximately equivalent size. Too little of the east range lies within the excavated area for individual room divisions to occur;

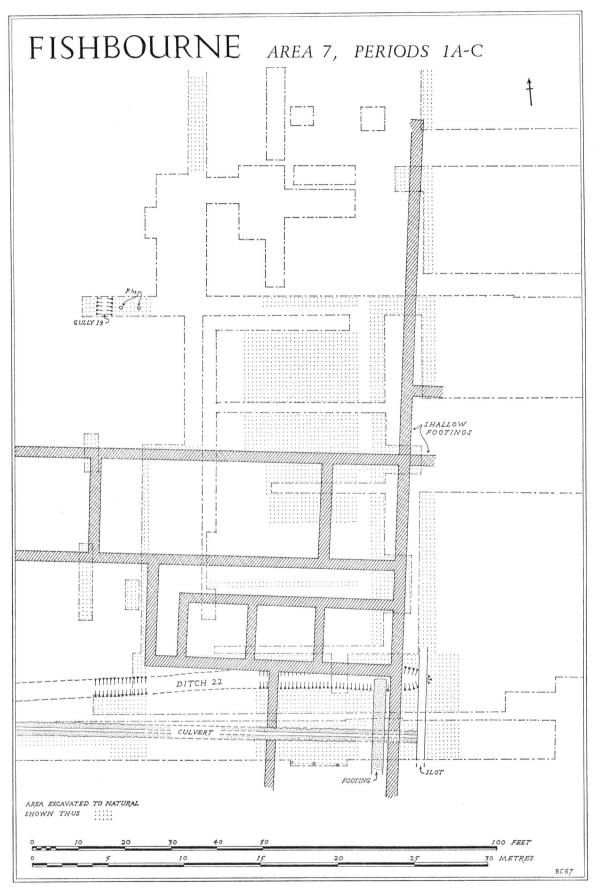

FISHBOURNE AREA 7, PERIODS 1A-C

P.hs.

GULLY 19

SHALLOW FOOTINGS

DITCH 22

CULVERT

FOOTING

SLOT

AREA EXCAVATED TO NATURAL
SHOWN THUS

| 0 | 10 | 20 | 30 | 40 | 50 | | 100 FEET |

| 0 | 5 | 10 | 15 | 20 | 25 | 30 METRES |

BC67

Fig. 19. The second masonry building

the rooms were, however, 24 ft. (7.3 m.) wide. In the angle between the two wings lay a strip of three smaller rooms linked by an L-shaped corridor.

To the north-east corner were attached a series of minor walls running north and east, and differing from the walls of the main building in that their foundations were only 12 in. (0.3 m.) deep. They could not have supported much weight and may have functioned only as boundary walls. The exact plan will never be recoverable, since immediately to the east, the levelling for the garden of the palace has removed the subsoil to a depth of 5 ft. (1.5 m.).

Several other features are associated indirectly with the building. The most impressive of these is a culvert (pl. IXb) running across the southern part of the site, constructed of two walls of sandstone blocks set, unmortared, on the ground-surface with capstones placed across the 9 in. (0.23 m.) space between them. The blocks were largely of Wealden sandstone and, from the traces of white mortar adhering to them, had evidently been re-used from an earlier building. The culvert was traced for more than 100 ft. (30 m.) running from beyond the western limit of the site to the edge of the scarp formed by Period 2 levelling. Its relationship to the walls of the building is at one junction confused by extensive robbing, but at the other it can be shown to pass through a ragged gap cut through the footing, and thus is structurally later.

Two unexplained features lie at the south-east corner: one is a length of footing parallel to, and inside the east wall of the east range, and the other is a slot or trench 20 in. (0.5 m.) wide and 5 in. (0.13 m.) deep lying 4 ft. (1.2 m.) to the east of the wall. In so far as evidence is available, they would appear to be broadly contemporary with the building. The function of the wall is difficult to explain, but the slot may well have once held a timber-lined drain. The fact that the culvert ends in line with it is purely fortuitous, for the destruction in the area was such that the culvert could once have continued beyond the slot and have been later removed.

Within the eastern range a line of five stake-holes were found measuring 5 in. (0.13 m.) across and 12 in. (0.3 m.) deep. They were aligned with the main building-axis and were sealed by a layer of yellow clay make-up.

The foundations of the masonry building were sealed directly beneath the floors of the palace, and between the palace period floor make-up and the natural subsoil lay a 9-in. (0.23-m.) thick layer of yellow clay with a discontinuous lens of chalk within it. The clay layer was deposited after the wall footings had been constructed and at several points overlapped the top of the footing. At the place where the culvert had cut through the western foundation, clay continuous with the main layer had been used to make up the ragged gap between the footing and the side of the culvert. Elsewhere the clay could be shown to postdate the construction and the culvert, and to fill and seal the slot beyond the east wall of the building. The sequence is therefore clear: first the footings were constructed, together with the 'slot', then the culvert was laid through gaps cut in the footings, and finally clay was laid over the whole area, sealing the culvert and making up the ground-level to the top of the footings, sometimes sealing the footings partially or completely. It is a remarkable fact that, in spite of extensive excavation to the natural subsoil, not a single sherd of pottery was recovered from the layers below the Period 2 make-up, so that all can be said is that the pre-palace features are earlier than c. A.D. 75, the date at about which the construction of the palace began.

G

To summarize: all the evidence points to the masonry building being unfinished. Its footings were completed to a few inches above ground-level, but before the superstructure could be erected plans changed and instead a culvert was laid, cutting through the foundations at two points. The ground-level was then raised by between 9 in. and 12 in. (0.23–0.3 m.), burying the culvert and in some places covering the tops of the footings. A further relevant factor is that in several places the footings had been carefully finished with a smooth layer of mortar, apparently in preparation for the superstructure, but no evidence was observed to indicate that walling had ever been erected nor was any building rubble found to suggest destroyed superstructure.

The area lying north of the north range and west of the shallow wall-footing was entirely open and devoid of occupation, with the exception of a gully and two stake-holes. The gully (gully 19) was 2 ft. 6 in. (0.76 m.) wide and 9 in. (0.23 m.) deep, and contained a few fragments of pre-Flavian pottery. The post-holes were 7 in. (0.18 m.) in diameter and on average 12 in. (0.3 m.) deep. The clay layer referred to above sealed the post-holes but was cut by the gully, showing that while the posts were contemporary with, or earlier than, the early building, the gully was of the same relative date as the culvert.

SUMMARY AND SYNTHESIS OF THE FIRST PERIOD

The main facts concerning the features and buildings of the First Period have now been given, and it remains to consider them in their local and national context. But before this is done, it must be stressed that the excavations have examined only a small part of a very much larger site, for evidence of early occupation is known to stretch over a considerable area in all directions from the main excavation. The sample which has been examined is, in all probability, large enough to represent fairly the general sequence of development but the fact remains that it may be atypical. This should constantly be borne in mind.

The nature of the late pre-Roman Iron Age occupation is still uncertain. Scraps of pottery dating from about the first century B.C. onwards have been found, but only in small quantities. This does not, of course, mean that the Fishbourne harbour was little used before the invasion; quite the reverse seems to be implied by the history of the Chichester entrenchments as elucidated by the new survey carried out by Mr Bradley for this report. We can only suppose that occupation sites remain to be discovered.

With the onset of Roman occupation we are on surer ground. The structures belonging to the initial settlement include two timber buildings of military type, of which one (Timber Building 1) is represented at the military supply-base at Richborough, where at least twelve examples are known (Cunliffe, 1968b, fig. 27), similar in both size and structure to the Fishbourne building. At Richborough they have long been identified as granaries, on the grounds that their plan implies a raised timber floor suitable for keeping stored grain away from damp and rodents. Much larger versions of the same type were found in the forward supply-base at Rödgen near Bad Nauheim, east of the Rhine (Schönberger, 1967). The second timber building at Fishbourne poses certain difficult problems of interpretation which have been set out in some detail above (p. 41). Two explanations present themselves: either it was a store-building or, less likely, a pair of barracks. While it is difficult on internal

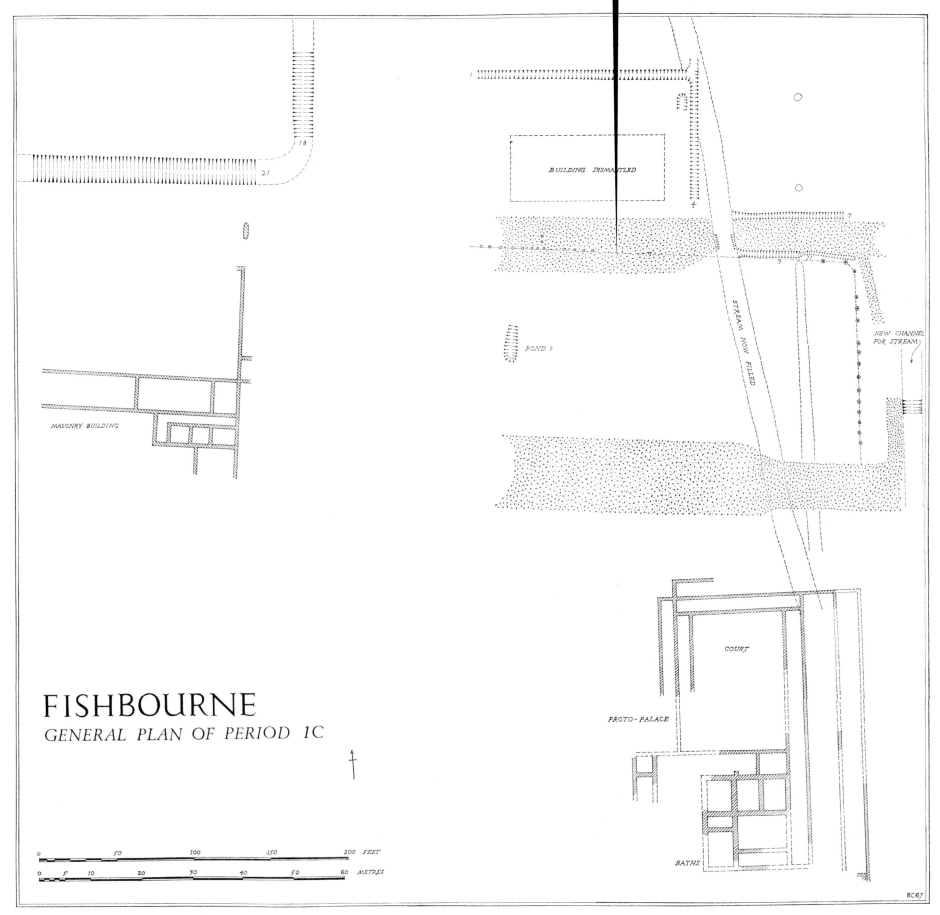

18

21

BUILDING DISMANTLED

4

7

5

STREAM NOW FILLED

NEW CHANNEL FOR STREAM

POND ?

MASONRY BUILDING

COURT

PROTO-PALACE

BATHS

FISHBOURNE

GENERAL PLAN OF PERIOD 1C

0		50		100		150		200 FEET

0	5	10	20	30	40	50	60 METRES

BC67

FIG. 20

evidence to decide which explanation is the more likely, the close similarity of the building to the granary of the Claudian fort at Hod Hill suggests a storage function. The only other major features of the early settlement are the roads which serve as a link between the buildings.

The earliest settlement, then, contains structural elements found elsewhere only on military sites. This fact, combined with their early Claudian date and the presence of a few articles of military equipment, is strong evidence in favour of the site having been used, initially, as a military supply-base.

Historically, two possible contexts exist for the creation of such a base. Either it was used early in A.D. 43 as one of the invasion beach-heads, or, a little later in the year, as a spring-board for the western advance under Vespasian. Since no archaeological dating evidence is ever likely to provide us with so precise a distinction, we must rely on a consideration of the contemporary political and military scene. At the moment of invasion Aulus Plautius, we are told, divided his force into three so that a unified landing should not be opposed.[1] The statement implies that three separate landings were made, probably in the region of Richborough, but since it is highly unlikely that a competent general would have allowed his force to be split for long, it is generally supposed that the separate units rapidly converged on one spot for the main offensive along the north Kentish coast. Several commentators, however, have followed Hübner's lead in suggesting that one at least of the forces sailed west to land somewhere on the west Sussex coastal plain.[2] This, they argue, is a fair interpretation of Dio's description of how the ships were guided west by a comet. The argument is itself weak, but a very good case can be made out for a landing in this area in terms of the probable political situation. The Southern Atrebatic area, centred on Chichester, was potentially friendly to Rome, though the flight of Verica implies that dissident elements were at work. It was vital to the success of the early advance for this region to remain at least neutral, to serve as a temporary buffer against the hostile tribes of the west. It would have been logical, and indeed prudent, for Plautius to have despatched a small landing force to the kingdom simply to ensure that the politics remained pro-Roman, either by giving support to Cogidubnus if he was already there or, more likely, by bringing him in with them from the continent. If a landing of this kind had taken place, it would not have been necessary to supply a particularly large force — merely a sufficient body to create a feeling of military presence. Where such a contingent would have been based is completely uncertain: Fishbourne is one possibility but so is the site of Chichester itself, where several indications of military remains have recently come to light.

A second possible context for military occupation is provided by the campaign fought by the *Legio II Augusta* under Vespasian. It is known that the Isle of Wight was taken, followed by the destruction of two powerful tribes in the south-west. Since the campaign, which was largely in the form of a landward thrust, would have relied upon amphibious support, a supply-base on a good harbour in friendly territory would have been essential. Fishbourne harbour was one of the best in the area and it is surely to this phase that the main use of the military buildings belongs. Admittedly, two buildings do not make a supply-base but it

[1] Cass. Dio, *History of the Romans*, book LX, pp. 19–23.

[2] E. Hubner, *Römische Herrschaft in West Europa* (1890), 16 ff.; B. H. St J. O'Neil, *Arch. Journ.*, CIX (1952), 23–38.

should be remembered that the area of higher and drier land immediately to the east of the buildings is totally unexplored, in fact only the fringes of the military settlement may have been excavated. Furthermore, the traces of military occupation found beneath Chichester could belong to the main base, the Fishbourne buildings being only the harbour warehouses. Much more excavation will be needed both at Fishbourne and Chichester before answers to these questions can be provided.

Vespasian's onslaught seems to have been rapid and successful. By A.D. 44 or 45 bases such as Fishbourne, now far in the rear of the advance, would have become obsolete and new supply centres like those at Hamworthy and Topsham would have taken over. At Fishbourne there must have been substantial harbour-works which, together with the road grid, would have made the site immediately attractive to merchants and small traders alike. With the site at Chichester developing rapidly as a provincial Roman town under the patronage of Cogidubnus, the commercial significance of the harbour is obvious. Unfortunately, practically nothing is known of the harbour area, but the presence of water-worn boulders of igneous rocks from Cornwall, the Channel Islands and Armorica, brought in quite possibly as ballast in merchant ships, is sufficient to point to the direction of the overseas trading contacts (Vol. II, p. 12). Where exactly the nucleus of the harbour settlement lay is not yet clear, but it could equally well have been at either of the two creek-ends.

On the excavated site there is clear evidence of demolition and re-building at about this time, resulting in the abandonment of the military buildings and the erection of a series of new timber structures. That one of them, Timber Building 4, was evidently a workshop with an oven, fuel-pit and traces of bronze working, led originally to the tentative conclusion that the buildings of this period were connected in some way with commercial development. This view must now be re-examined. Knowledge of Timber Buildings 6 and 7 is at present too fragmentary to be relevant to the argument, but the plan of Timber Building 5 is now sufficiently well-known to show that it was unusually elaborate for its extremely early date, with at least six rooms, painted walls, a veranda and possibly even a colonnade of brick and stucco. Assessment of its function and status is impossible with so little comparative material available from the rest of the country, but compared with the pre-Boudiccan shops at Verulamium (Frere, 1959, fig. 2) (similar in many ways to Timber Building 4) it was positively luxurious, and must surely have been a house of some importance. If a domestic function is now proposed, the nature of Timber Building 4 must be considered, for the two were evidently laid out as part of the same concept. There can be no doubt that it served as a workshop, but it need not have functioned commercially, instead it could easily have been a combination of workshop, store and servants' quarters belonging to the house. Thus we are left with two likely interpretations: either Buildings 4 and 5 formed a single unit belonging to a wealthy owner or one was a house, the other a workshop, neither connected with each other but both fronting on to a common arcade. On balance and in view of the later development of the area, the former explanation is preferred.

This does not mean that there were no commercial buildings at all. Extensive traces of timber structures were found well to the north of the main excavation, and to the east, close to the upper reaches of the eastern creek, thick occupation layers came to light during road-works. In both areas pre-Flavian and Flavian pottery was abundant. Nor should we forget the large group of pottery recovered by a skin-diver from the bottom of the Mill Pond. This, too, was largely pre-Flavian to Flavian, and since it lay some considerable distance from the main excavation, it can hardly be rubbish survival from the known settlement area. It is far more likely to have come from buildings yet undiscovered. In summary, it may be said that by the end of the Neronian period the occupied area measured at least 2,500 ft. (760 m.) from east to west by 1,000 ft. (300 m.) from north to south. The development of the settlement was probably largely dependent upon the growing prosperity of Chichester.

Towards the end of the Neronian period a major rebuilding programme was initiated, involving the demolition of two of the old timber buildings and the erection of an elaborate masonry house on an open site to the south. Demolition and building must have been linked, for although the new building did not physically replace the earlier structures, its masons' working-yard spread across the old site, implying that the entire tract of land belonged to one owner. If, as suggested above, Timber Building 4 was a house belonging to a man of wealth or importance, the simplest explanation of the new building is that he, or his heirs, decided to rebuild their 20-year-old house in stone on a much grander scale. The hypothesis is attractive and would fit the facts, but is totally beyond proof.

The new house, more than 25,000 sq. ft. (2,300 sq. m.) in area, was substantially larger than the timber buildings, but in terms of living-space for the owner's family and servants there was little difference. Where it exceeded the size of the previous house was in the addition of spacious luxuries such as a colonnaded courtyard and a bath suite. Enough has been said of the building in the descriptive text above to emphasize that its quality was exceptional. Its very existence implies the presence of such specialists as architects, masons, sculptors, marble-workers, mosaicists, stucco-workers and painters, all of whom practised skills largely unknown in the province at this early date.

Although this masonry building and its decorative features were enormously sophisticated, and indeed unique, in comparison with the contemporary architectural scene, individually many features of the work can be paralleled elsewhere. Sixteen miles to the east, at Angmering, lay another bath house of comparable size with black and white mosaics and *opus sectile* floors, which, though not precisely dated, is broadly contemporary with the Fishbourne building. It is evident that precisely the same sources, both of stone for sectile pavements and tiles for the fittings of the bath suite, were being used by the builders on both sites. So striking are the similarities that one must assume a very close connection — even perhaps that the same team of specialists was employed. Clearly there was more than one person among the first-generation Regnenses able to afford Roman luxuries. Other decorative details belonging to the building are more difficult to parallel. The wall-painting is similar in style and execution to that found in a late first-century town house at Leaholm Gardens, Cirencester, in 1962,[1] but no other examples are known, and the fluted pilasters of stucco and the Corinthian capitals are quite unique.

The driving force behind the construction must have been someone with a strong desire for things Roman, supported by considerable wealth. Here we must anticipate the next section of the report, by saying that within a short time the masonry building or, better, 'proto-palace' was vastly expanded to create a palace of unsurpassed magnificence which, it will be argued, may well have belonged to the local client king, Cogidubnus. Could it not

[1] Reconstructed and displayed in the Corinium Museum, Cirencester.

be that the progression from timber house to proto-palace, over the period *c.* 45 to *c.* 75, represented the gradual increase in wealth and status enjoyed by the king? An explanation in these terms would make good sense of both the observed sequence and what little written evidence there is, but it could never be proven.

The period following the construction of the proto-palace was one of rapid change. To the west a new building on a monumental scale was begun, but never finished. The small fragment of surviving plan does not readily suggest a function, but it may be that the new building was intended to replace the proto-palace on an even grander scale. Another possibility, not without its attraction, is that it was to be an administrative or official structure of some kind. Without more evidence further speculation is worthless.

By the mid 70s a totally new concept was emerging which was to transform the site beyond all recognition, engulfing the existing proto-palace and unifying the environment in one enormous scheme.

PART III

The Flavian Palace (Period 2) *c.* A.D. 75/80–100

INTRODUCTION

ABOUT A.D. 75 a massive programme of rebuilding was initiated, resulting in the erection of a huge palace covering an area of at least 10 acres including the gardens. The basic arrangement of the building was simple but effective: it was composed of four wings placed around a central garden, 250 ft. (76 m.) across, with a second large garden of comparable size to the south. The wing closing the west side was built on the original ground-surface (covering the unfinished masonry building) but in front of it up to 5 ft. (1.52 m.) of natural subsoil was removed and thrown over the low-lying eastern area to form an almost level platform at a lower level, upon which the garden and the other three wings were laid out. The east front of the wing had therefore to be retained by a 5-ft. (1.52-m.) high revetting wall which also acted as a base for a continuous colonnade. Similar colonnades, at the level of the lower terrace, enclosed the remaining sides of the garden; behind them lay the North, East and South Wings.

It will be seen from fig. 21 that the East Wing is of a somewhat irregular nature. This is because it was built so as to incorporate most of the proto-palace at its southern end. Its detailed construction sequence will be considered fully below, but here it may be said that there is reason to believe that the Aisled Hall at its north end was built early on. If this were so, the centre section of the wing would have been forced to fit between two existing structures and to marry them together. In the centre of the wing lay the main Entrance Hall served, it seems, by a road leading direct from Chichester. On reaching the building, the main road joined a minor service road which ran the full length of the wing, and met, at its northern end, with an east–west service road leading perhaps to the kitchen area somewhere to the west.

The North Wing fitted neatly between the corner of the West Wing and the Aisled Hall. Structurally it is best considered to be a self-contained unit built around two small courtyards and thus turned in upon itself, but linked both physically and visually to the rest of the building by means of its fronting colonnaded walk.

The South Wing occupies a similar position, lying regularly between the West and East Wings, but its conception is different, for although it too is made an integral part of the main building by a north-facing colonnaded veranda, its principal aspect is to the south, facing across a sloping terrace to the sea beyond.

In general terms, then, it may be said that the palace consisted of three self-contained ranges: the North, East and South Wings each with their own courtyards or terraces, together with the West Wing which clearly formed a functional and visual continuation of the great central garden.

While the known elements of the palace can all be explained in terms of residential or official functions, it is true to say that little evidence of either servants' quarters or out-buildings has come to light. Accommodation of this kind would have been essential for the efficient functioning of so large a building, and clearly it must exist. The most likely site lies 300 ft. (91 m.) to the west of the West Wing, where traces of masonry were seen (p. 138), but the area is now heavily built up and further exploration is, for the present, impossible.

Much is known of the main palace, of its plan, superstructure, decoration and garden. In the following sections each of the structural elements will be described in turn, followed by a consideration of the dating evidence; finally, some comments will be offered on the significance and function of the building.

STRUCTURAL DETAILS

THE PREPARATION OF THE SITE   (fig. 21, p. 210)

Before building work on the palace could proceed far, it was necessary for the construction teams to undertake a scheme of massive land-levelling in order to create approximately level terraces for the building to stand on. Although the natural slope of the land was not particularly great, the floor area of the building was such that the amount of soil which had to be moved to level the site was enormous. Since the western limit lay at *c.* 25 ft. (7.6 m.) O.D. and the lowest eastern parts were, before levelling, about 15 ft. (4.6 m.) O.D., the builders decided to create a lower terrace at *c.* 20 ft. (6.1 m.) O.D. by removing subsoil from the western part of the site and dumping it over the low-lying eastern area: in all more than 36,000 cu. yds. (27,600 cu. m.) of clay and gravel would have had to be moved. The result was the creation of two platforms, the lower 20 ft. (6.1 m.) terrace upon which the garden and the north, east and south wings were built, and a higher terrace of untouched ground at the west end for the West Wing.

The actual process of levelling was more complicated. First, it seems that the top-soil was removed from the western half of the lower terrace and stock-piled so that when the levelling was complete it could be replaced on the newly-levelled surface to form the soil of the garden. Gradually the underlying gravel and clay was carted to the eastern area, but whilst this process was going on the walls of the East Wing were being erected, for the archaeological sections show clearly that the trench-built foundations of the range were generally dug from close to the pre-levelling ground-surface and that on them, free-standing walls of ashlar masonry were erected. Only after they had reached a height exceeding 4 ft. (1.2 m.) had the thick layers of clay and gravel make-up been spread between them. The economy of this method is evident, for had the ground been levelled first and the wall foundations laid later, the foundation trenches would have needed to be excessively deep to reach load-bearing gravel through the overlying made-earth. Further efficiencies were involved in that spoil from the foundation trenches could be heaped up in the centres of the rooms, thus reducing the quantity of make-up required. Similarly, chippings created by squaring off the ashlar blocks for the walls were simply allowed to accumulate in piles, only to be buried by tips of clay brought in from outside.

The levelling of the eastern area posed certain problems in relation to the already existing proto-palace, the floor levels of which were close to the original ground-surface. When work began on the new palace some of the wattle and daub walls of the existing buildings were demolished and the plaster and clay of which they were made was spread out between and around the upstanding walls to raise the floors to the new level, but, even so, additional clay and gravel had to be brought in to increase the level sufficiently to match that of the newly-constructed East Wing.

Although little is known of the South Wing, it is evident that the ground sloped naturally south to the shore of the inlet. Here, too, a considerable thickness of make-up was needed, not only for beneath the building itself but also for the terraced area to the south of the wing, between it and the sea. Much of the clay and rubble used came from the destroyed walls of the proto-palace. The area occupied by the main central garden and the North Wing required relatively little making-up, with the exception of the eastern edge of both where clay and gravel were tipped.

The drainage problems raised by so much disturbance of the clayey ill-drained sub-soil were considerable. Already, in Period 1 C, a major improvement had been made by diverting the stream to the eastern boundary of the site. This system continued in use in Period 2 and the minor irritations posed by surface-water accumulation were easily overcome by raising the ground-level. The result, however, was that water tended to pond up in the old valley to the north of the building and throughout the useful life of the building the area must have remained boggy, in wet seasons turning into a lake. The pond, which still survives here, is a shrunken remnant of its Roman predecessor.

Beyond the West Wing, the ground continued to rise slightly in such a way that surface-water would have drained down towards the building. To prevent the foundations from becoming waterlogged a drainage ditch had been dug parallel to the west wall a few feet away, serving not only to collect surface-water but also to remove the eaves-drips from the building. The ditch sloped south towards the sea. It is clear, therefore, that the builders went to considerable pains to prepare a site that was both level and reasonably well drained. Details of the internal drainage required by the building itself will be described below.

THE BUILDING SEQUENCE

A building of such enormous size could not have been constructed quickly, and indeed a close examination of the surviving structure shows that several well-defined stages are apparent. The proto-palace was already in existence and the way in which the walls of the later East Wing join it shows beyond doubt that the basic structure of the early building was incorporated totally into the new palace. How far west, into what was to become the South Wing, the rooms of the proto-palace extended is unknown, but the general siting of the wing must have been largely dependent upon the position of the earlier building.

The Aisled Hall, which lies in the junction of the East and North Wings, is placed askew to the end of the North Wing in a way which might suggest that it was already in existence, but there is no positive evidence for this and indeed the nature of its structure and foundations and their relation to the newly-created ground-level shows conclusively that the Hall was part of the main phase of building and not an earlier free-standing structure, as was the proto-palace. It might, however, have been built at an initial stage and served as a point from which the North and the East Wings were laid out.

A striking example of the way in which the Period 1 C features influenced the plan of the palace is shown by the alignment of the Entrance Hall, which was built exactly over the line of the early road. Although it may be true to explain this as a nostalgic desire on the part of the builders to monumentalize an early thoroughfare, a more practical explanation is that the early road, which was probably linked direct to Chichester, was utilized as the main approach road to the palace. It would therefore have been convenient to site the Entrance Hall astride it. In this way an east–west axis was created which determined the plan not only of the West Wing but also of the garden.

The ground plan itself and the considerations outlined above imply a predetermined conception, but within the scheme it is clear that the West Wing was built first, for not only is it of a different construction from the rest of the building, but at its north-east corner the North Wing can be shown to abut its earlier masonry. It is hardly surprising that the West Wing was built first: its terrace needed no preparation and the building could be put up immediately, whilst the levelling of the rest of the site was in progress. When the lower terrace had been created all that was required was the addition of the revetting wall to retain the West Wing platform. But as we have seen (above, p. 78), the foundations of the East Wing were begun before the mass of the clay make-up was deposited; thus the most likely sequence of work is: (*a*) West Wing foundations and superstructure built first, (*b*) East Wing and possibly much of the North and South Wing foundations laid at the same time, (*c*) removal of clay from the west and its deposition around the foundations of the eastern part of the building, (*d*) the construction of the West Wing revetting wall, and (*e*) the erection of the superstructure of the North, East and South Wings. Within this broad programme there were several sub-phases. In both the North and the East Wings, for example, the major structural walls were built first and the partition walls added later, and in the area of the proto-palace deposition of clay make-up could have occurred at any time within the sequence. Apart from the decorative finishes, the last of the structural work to be carried out was evidently the laying of the shallow foundations for the stylobate supporting the colonnades, since in all cases the foundations could be shown to have been dug through the highest layer of floor make-up. In the final stage the stock-pile of topsoil was spread out over the area which was to be laid out and planted as the formal garden, while the gravelling of the road must have taken place at about the same time.

BUILDING MATERIALS AND TECHNIQUES (pl. XII, p. 210)

A considerable uniformity in constructional detail exists between the wings of the palace which were built on the lower terrace, but the style of the West Wing on the higher terrace differs in several significant points from the others and is best described first. The range was constructed on trench-built foundations of concrete $2\frac{1}{2}$–3 ft. (0.75–0.9 m.) wide, composed of fist-sized nodules of flint set in a white pebbly mortar. Most of the superstructure, and indeed in some places the footings themselves, had been later destroyed but at several points the lowest course of ashlar masonry survived. The stone chosen for the free-standing structure was a fossiliferous limestone from the Mixon reef which now lies off the shore at Bracklesham Bay, some seven miles south-east of Fishbourne (pl. XXXIII). A closer examination of the facing stone shows that all were water-worn slabs, collected presumably from below high-tide

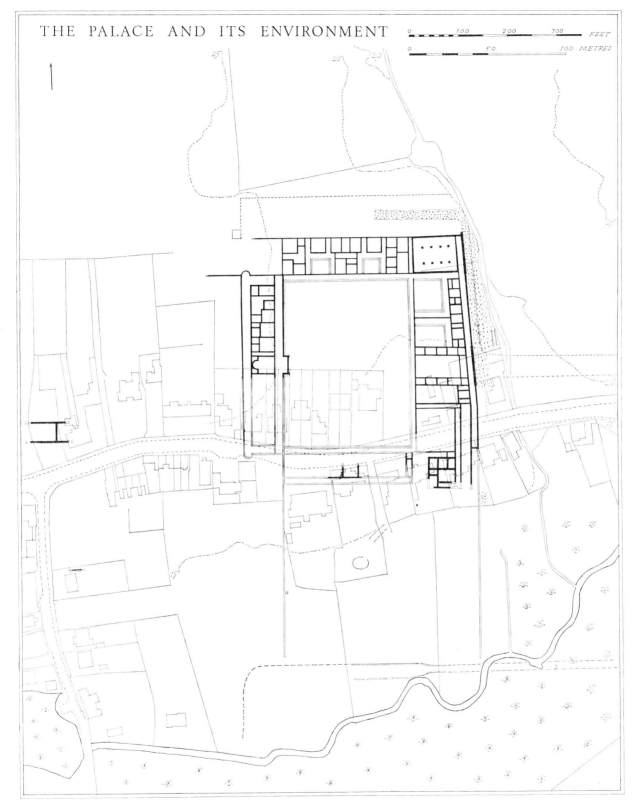

THE PALACE AND ITS ENVIRONMENT

FIG. 21. (Modern boundaries and features are shown in outline)

level. In preparing them for the building the masons had merely struck off one edge to give a fresh vertical face, and then squared up the sides.

The revetting wall in front of the wing was built in a different way, in two separate sections, the junction coming at about 70 ft. (21 m.) from the north-east corner. South of this point the wall had been built free-standing with its inner (i.e. western) face constructed indiscriminately of flint and limestone, while the outer face was built of regular courses of limestone blocks. The core work between was largely of coursed flint set in a copious matrix of white pebbly mortar. North of the junction, the inner face was built of coursed limestone blocks in the same manner as the outer while the core was almost entirely of limestone slabs. There is no great significance in the difference between the two styles: they are best regarded as the work of two different gangs of builders using different stock-piles of material.

The East, North and South Wings were built of different materials and in a slightly different manner. To begin with, a foundation trench 2½–3 ft. (0.76–0.9 m.) wide was dug into the natural clay or gravel to a depth of about 3 ft. (0.9 m.) and into the bottom were driven pointed piles of oak 6–9 in. (0.15–0.23 m.) across and 2 ft. (0.6 m.) long. From what little evidence survives, the piles would seem to have been placed in pairs, the centre of each post being 1½ ft. (0.46 m.) from the next. The foundation trench was then filled with a footing of flint cobbles laid in a yellow gritty mortar (pl. xiia). The superstructure was of carefully-coursed blocks of Upper Greensand set in the same yellow mortar, with the core infilled with greensand chippings and occasional flints (pls. xiia and c). The number of fragments of brick found in the destruction rubble suggest that bonding courses may have been employed and indeed a row of tiles was found close to the base of the south wall of room N 16, but this may have been merely levelling for a door-sill. The wall between rooms N 3 and N 4, which stands to a height of 2½ ft. (0.76 m.) has no tile course. The footings were sufficiently substantial to support a masonry superstructure to roof-height. There is no evidence whatsoever of timber framing to the upper part of the walls.

The stylobates (pls. xxx, xxxiii) in all parts of the building were laid on a relatively unsubstantial foundation made by digging a trench 2–3 ft. (0.6–0.9 m.) wide and 2 ft. (0.6 m.) deep and filling it with rubble of various kinds, including greensand, chalk and flint loosely bound together with mortar. It had not been considered necessary to take the footings down to load-bearing sub-soil. The stylobate blocks themselves varied in size, averaging from 2–4 ft. (0.6–1.2 m.) long by 2 ft. (0.6 m.) wide by 15 in. (0.4 m.) thick. They were invariably of Bembridge limestone obtained from quarries at the eastern end of the Isle of Wight. The gutter blocks, of similar dimensions, were laid without foundation. Two types of stone were employed: Bembridge limestone was used along the north and east colonnades of the garden, and a glauconitic sandstone from the Lower Greensand beds was used along the west side of the garden and in courtyard 4 in the East Wing. The precise origin of the greensand cannot be discovered, but similar stone outcrops in the Weald near Pulborough and on the Isle of Wight. In view of the enormous weight of the quantities required, the Isle of Wight is the more likely origin since sea transport would have been easier.

The columns themselves were made of various stones which cannot be exactly identified (Vol. ii, p. 1) but all appear to be of limestone, some originating in Jurassic outcrops of the West Country, some imported from Caen.

The logistics of the building work cannot be discussed fully here, but a few figures are informative: about 2 miles (3 km.) of wall were built, 1,600 ft. (490 m.) of stylobate blocks were required with an equivalent length of gutter blocks, and about 165 columns, each weighing 4 tons, were erected.

Very little is known of the roof structure in detail but all roofs, with the possible exception of those in the bath block, were of a timber framework covered by tiles. Furthermore, the ground-plan makes the general arrangement of the roof lines tolerably certain, but details of this kind will be considered in the description of each wing, given below.

Finally, something must be said of the general construction of the floors, all of which were laid in much the same way. First a layer of greensand blocks, usually pitched on end, was placed over the clay and gravel make-up; this was sealed by a bed of mortar 4 in. (10 cm.) thick, containing chippings of greensand. When the mortar had dried a screed of fine pink mortar, $1\frac{1}{2}$–2 in. (4–5 cm.) thick, was laid. If a mosaic was to be constructed, a very thin slurry of white cement was washed over the semi-dry pink mortar and into this the tesserae were pushed, the pink mortar still being sufficiently plastic to allow the tesserae to be levelled up while the white cement acted as an adhesive. Since most of the floors of the palace were mosaic-covered, the description is generally applicable but where a pink mortar finish was required, the mortar was usually laid 2–3 in. (5–7.5 cm.) thick. The veranda floor was not elaborately prepared and mostly had to make do with a 2–3 in. (5–7.5 cm.) thick surfacing of white mortar laid immediately on the clay make-up.

DESCRIPTION OF THE BUILDING

THE WEST WING
(Figs. 22–25, p. 210)

The West Wing consists of a single range of rooms, 48 ft. (14.6 m.) wide and approximately 316 ft. (96.3 m.) long, of which a little more than half lies within the area available for excavation, the remainder being below the houses and gardens of nos. 76 to 80 Fishbourne Road. The plan of the known half and the general arrangement of the other wings suggest a certain degree of regularity in the planning, which might imply that the wing was symmetrical about its central axis. However, with a total absence of evidence concerning the plan of the southern half of the wing, the matter is best left open until further excavation is possible.

In the centre of the wing stood a large square room with an apsidal recess at one end serving, it will be suggested below, as an Audience Chamber. The room was isolated from the adjacent suites by side corridors beyond which, on the north side at least, lay a block of twelve rooms. Before considering the architectural and functional implications of the plan it is necessary to describe the surviving features of each room individually.

DESCRIPTION OF THE EXCAVATED FEATURES

Room W 1. The floor had been almost totally destroyed, with the exception of one or two rows of white tesserae surviving in short lengths against the walls. No evidence of doors was recovered, but a way through into room W 3 is likely.

Fragments of painted wall plaster included areas of mock marbling in pink and purple splashed with white and black (Vol. II, p. 81).

Room W 2. The original mosaic floor survives in a few patches along the edges of the room, but never more than five rows of plain white tesserae were left in position. Although the foundations do not remain high enough to show traces of door-sills, it is reasonable to suppose that at least one door opened on to the eastern veranda.

The room appears to have been decorated with a dado of pink splashed with deep purple and black to simulate marble. Above this were areas of dark red. Complex patterns incorporating bright blue were also represented in small fragments (Vol. II, p. 81).

Room W 3. The room was irregularly shaped, occupying a position between rooms W 1, W 2, W 4, W 5 and W 6. The possibility remains that it had originally been divided by wooden partitions, or screens, into smaller units but since much of the floor had been destroyed the problem must remain open. A substantial piece of the original mosaic survives in the southern part of the room (pls. XIIIa, LXXV). The design was composed of square panels linked by, and alternating with, areas of Greek key pattern. The known panels all differ: two are infilled with Greek key patterns drawn in thinner lines than those of the main linking design, another contains squares placed corner to corner around a quadruple arrow motif, whilst the others, too destroyed to be decipherable, appear to depict complex box motifs. The entire decorated area was enclosed within concentric wide black bands. The survival of so much of the floor is due largely to the fact that in a later period a wall, which had been built across the room, was laid directly on the top of the mosaic. When, still later, the tesserae had been removed for use elsewhere the strip below the wall was left untouched, together with a small area in the south-west corner of the room.

One doorway survives in the south-west corner. It was 6 ft. (1.83 m.) wide and the surviving remains of the charred door-sill showed its step to have been 1 ft. 9 in. (0.53 m.) wide. Constant use had worn a small hole in the mosaic, which had subsequently been neatly patched with large tesserae of red brick. The positions of the other doors are unknown, but it seems likely that the northern part of the room served as a corridor linking east and west verandas, and therefore would have required doors in the positions suggested on the reconstruction plan.

The painted wall decoration incorporated adjacent areas of mock marbling, one of a blue-grey smeared with wide brush-strokes, another of purple splashed red and white, divided from each other by a simply-painted moulding. Areas of plain colour were also represented (Vol. II, p. 80).

Room W 4. No trace of flooring survives nor are the positions of doorways known. It would seem likely that the room opened on to the eastern veranda.

Room W 5 (pls. XIIIb, LXXIV). In the north-west corner of the room, a small area of mosaic pavement survived, depicting the end of a running scroll which would have formed a panel 2 ft. (0.61 m.) wide running the length of the room — a similar arrangement to that found in room W 8 (pl. XIV). The individual tendrils are shown growing out of nodes outlined in black and infilled with coloured tesserae, the one surviving in this case being yellow. Presumably here, as in room W 12, the nodes were alternatively red and yellow. The main panel of the mosaic had been totally destroyed. Together with the tendril panel it was enclosed within a wide black band.

No doorways have been found, nor can their positions be suggested with certainty, but in all probability the room opened on to the eastern veranda.

Room W 6 (pls. xvi*b*, lxxiv). A substantial part of the mosaic floor survived in the south-west part of the room. The design was composed of two panels, one serving as a 'mat' along the western wall, the other as the main 'carpet' filling the rest of the room: each was considered as a separate entity. The 'mat' consisted of a complex chequer pattern of white squares on black and black on white. It had been laid out with its two short sides converging slightly on each other to give an impression of perspective. Little survived of the main 'carpet' but one corner showed a band of triangles arranged base-to-apex, set within an outer border of double wide black bands. Both mat and carpet were laid against a plain background of white tesserae set diagonally to the walls and the main design.

At some date, possibly well after the original construction, a quarter-round moulding of pink mortar had been laid at the junction between the floor and the wall. The room was served by only one door, opening from its north-west corner into room W 3.

Very little painted plaster was recovered, but some fragments depicted areas of pink over-painted with bold purple designs, while others were in plain red, pale blue and purple (Vol. ii, p. 80).

Room W 7. The position and size of the room suggest that it was of some importance and is likely to have been floored with a fine mosaic; unfortunately nothing now remains except for a few patches of pink floor matrix along the edge of the western wall. The whole of the eastern part of the room had been severely mutilated by the action of ploughing in medieval and later times. The main door, 13 ft. (3.96 m.) wide, lay in the centre of the east side and opened on to the eastern veranda. The sill, presumably of timber, has long since disappeared, but its foundation of loosely-packed stone blocks survived to show its original position. It may be that, like the other door-sills in the wing, it had been destroyed by fire but no certain sign of this was seen. A second, smaller, door opened from the north-west corner of the room into a corridor, room W 9. Its charred sill, 5 ft. (1.5 m.) long, still remained in position.

Room W 8. Substantial areas of the mosaic which originally covered the room still survive along the south and west walls. The central area was covered with a highly repetitive pattern based on the box-within-box theme. Indeed, the design is so repetitive that a diagrammatic reconstruction of the entire floor is possible, even though only a relatively small percentage of the total area survives (pls. xiv, lxxvi). On two sides the geometric area was lined with narrow elongated panels containing running tendrils drawn in black with the nodes infilled alternatively with red and yellow. Although the central area of the panels does not survive, it is certain from the arrangement of the tendrils that they were shown sprouting from a vase placed in the middle of the panel.

The walls of the room have been so robbed that no trace of doorways could be expected to survive. Even so, the plan implies the existence of a major door placed centrally within the eastern wall, giving access to the eastern veranda.

Room W 9.   Room W 9 is likely to have served as a corridor leading between room W 7 and the western veranda, in effect giving access through the wing from east to west. The door in its east end has already been mentioned; a similar door probably existed at the west end but no trace was seen. The room was floored with a coarse-grained pink mortar, 1½ in. (4 cm.) thick, laid on a white pebbly concrete continuous with the wall footings. A door in the south-east corner, 5 ft. (1.5 m.) wide, led into room W 10.

Room W 10.   The room was entered from room W 9 by the door just mentioned and was presumably linked to room W 11 by a door in the south wall, of which all trace has now disappeared. It was floored in a similar way to room W 9 with a 1½-in. (4-cm.) thick spread of pink mortar laid on a screed of concrete.

Room W 11 (pl. xv).   This room is the only example in the entire Flavian palace of under-floor heating used in domestic rooms, as opposed to the baths. The basement floor of the hypocaust lay at a depth of 2 ft. (0.6 m.) below the level of the adjacent floors. It was surfaced with a thin layer of pink mortar continuous with the pink mortar rendering of the walls. The suspended floor, also of pink mortar, of which fragments were found lying in the rubble filling the room, had originally been supported on regularly-spaced pilae built of hollow box-tiles, filled with clay, and placed on a single horizontal brick mortared to the floor. Since the walls did not survive to a height above the level of the suspended floor, it is not possible to say how the necessary jacket of flue tiles was set into the super-structure. Heat was supplied by means of a flue opening through the south wall, from room W 12.

The upper wall surfaces were rendered with pink mortar and painted in areas of plain white and plain red. At the junction of the two colours a thin black line was painted. The red probably formed the dado with the white serving as the main wall colour. There is some evidence of an elaborately painted cornice shown above the white areas. Smaller quantities of blue-green also occur, but how they fitted with the main design is uncertain (Vol. ii, p. 81).

Room W 12 (pl. xvia) served as a stoking chamber for the hypocaust in room W 11. It was floored on the same level as the adjacent hypocaust basement with pink mortar, with which the walls were also plastered. The flue opened through the centre of the north wall. It was 15 in. (0.38 m.) wide, splaying out to the south, and was floored with tiles continuous with an apron of tiles which projected from its southern opening into the room. The chamber was entered from corridor W 13 through a doorway 6½ ft. (1.98 m.) wide in the south wall. The charred timber still remaining in the sill socket would have incorporated at least one step down from the higher level of the corridor.

Corridor W 13 (pls. xviia, lxxiv).   Corridor W 13, 5 ft. 6 in. (1.68 m.) wide, ran the full width of the wing, allowing access between the east veranda and the west, and at the same time isolating the Audience Chamber from the adjacent rooms. At both its east and west ends there would have been doorways, but while impressions of the western door-sill survive, all trace of the east end had been removed by later ploughing. The corridor was floored with black and white mosaic of simple form consisting of two concentric black bands enclosing an area of plain white tesserae set diagonally to the edges. The floor had been subjected to considerable use, for it had worn out in places and been patched on at least two separate occasions with areas of pink mortar.

Room W 14 (fig. 22, pl. XIX) — the Audience Chamber — measures 31 ft. by 35 ft. (9.4 × 10.7 m.) with an apsidal recess 20 ft. (6.1 m.) in diameter opening out of its west wall. Originally the room was floored with a mosaic pavement of exceptionally fine character, but almost the entire floor has been destroyed by medieval and later ploughing, with the exception of small areas of white border which lie close to the west wall. In the north-east corner of the apse, however, the extreme corner of a black-on-white design survives, depicting the tip of a stylized leaf or shoot. Further towards the centre, another small fragment 6 in. by 8 in. (15 × 20 cm.) remained *in situ*, this time showing part of a twisted or braided guilloche in black, yellow and red. A similar fragment survived close by. From the ploughsoil which had accumulated in front of the West Wing opposite the room were recovered quantities of tesserae, sometimes in small slabs still mortared together, derived ultimately from the Audience Chamber floor. The highest percentage were white, but black, yellow and red

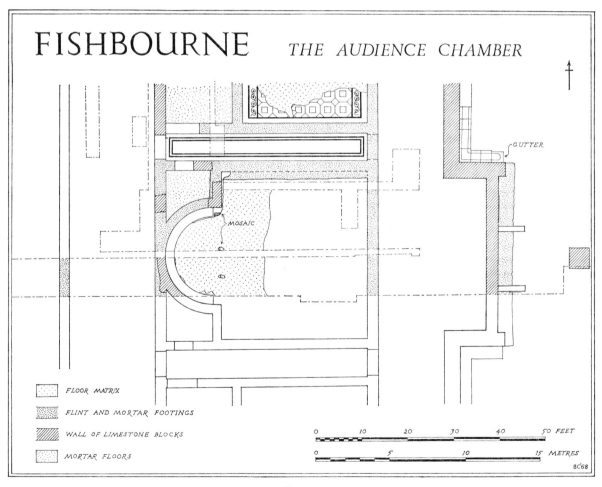

FIG. 22

H

occurred frequently. All were small, seldom more than $\frac{3}{16}$ in. (0.5 cm.) across, and the quality of the workmanship was excellent. There can be little doubt that the floor would once have been the finest in the palace.

The tesserae marking the edge of the floor in the apse stop 2 ft. (0.6 m.) away from the wall in a manner suggesting the one-time presence of a bench lining the apse. The material of which such a structure would have been built is unknown, but most likely it was of timber. In the angle between the edge of the bench and the corner of the apse wall, part of a column-drum was found standing on the floor. The absence of a prepared foundation and the fact that it obscured part of the mosaic design argues strongly that it was not intended to stand here as part of the original architectural concept; at what period it was added remains unknown.

The Audience Chamber would, no doubt, have been entered through a large opening placed centrally in the east wall. Unfortunately extensive robbing and the destruction wrought by the plough have removed all trace of the original entrance.

In the discussion to follow below (p. 91) it will be suggested that the entire room was roofed with a barrel-vault. One of the principal structural arguments for this is that the north wall footing (and presumably also the south) was exceptionally massive, measuring 4 ft. (1.2 m.) wide by at least 5 ft. (1.5 m.) deep. Such strength would have been necessary only if it had been the intention to support a substantial weight, such as that exerted by a masonry vault. This does not imply that the walls retained a thickness of 4 ft. (1.2 m.) to their full height, indeed the edge of the mosaic floor in the north-west corner of the room shows that at this point the wall was only the standard 2 ft. (0.6 m.) thick. More likely the extra width foundation was to spread the load and possibly to take supporting internal pilasters. These problems are, however, discussed below.

Within the apse a small quantity of decorative plaster survived, much of which must have come from the stucco surface of the vault, for it was ribbed, and although the pieces were small a slight curvature was discernible. It might be thought that the stucco was more likely to have derived from the semi-dome of the apse, but its finish was too rough to allow close scrutiny; it would, however, have looked perfectly satisfactory high up in a vaulted roof where the effect of the white ribs against a background of bright blue, purple and red would have appeared, to say the least, dramatic.

Rooms W 15 and W 16. Within the space formed between the junction of the apse and the west wall of the range were two small rooms floored with a plain white mortar and entered by means of doors leading from the flanking passages. Only the northern room has been excavated.

Room W 17 or W 18. In 1938 two boys, digging at the end of the garden of no. 78 Fishbourne Road, uncovered what is said to have been an area of black and white mosaic. The exact find-spot is not known, but the floor must either have belonged to a corridor flanking the south side of the Audience Chamber or to the room immediately to the south. No further information is available, nor is anything known of the rooms further south in the wing.

The east veranda (pls. XVII*b*, XXXIV). It has already been stated that the West Wing was built on the original ground-surface while the ground to the east was terraced to a maximum depth of 5 ft. (1.5 m.). This necessitated the construction of a retaining wall 3 ft. (0.9 m.) thick, which thus formed the eastern front of the West Wing. The wall must originally have supported a colonnade based on a stylobate level with the West Wing floors, but extensive ploughing has removed not only the top courses of the wall but also all trace of the floors immediately adjacent to it. A few fragments of the columns belonging to the colonnade have been recovered from rubble layers in front of the retaining wall (Vol. II, p. 81). They are clearly similar in size and style to those found elsewhere in the building, the only exception being that their abaci were usually horizontally ribbed.

In front of the Audience Chamber the revetting wall was brought forward to form a wide platform, 24 ft. (7.3 m.) wide by 33 ft. (10 m.) long. Here again all floor-levels have been removed by ploughing and much of the masonry has been robbed in late Roman or medieval times, but sufficient survived to indicate the presence of a flight of timber steps leading up from the garden to the platform level. All trace of timber had, of course, disappeared but the two supporting cheek-walls, built of greensand blocks, remained in position, projecting 6 ft. (1.8 m.) into the garden, a sufficient distance to allow four 18 in. (0.46 m.) wide steps each rising 12 in. (0.3 m.). As the reconstruction plan will show, the steps would have exactly occupied the space between the two centre columns of the main front. The cheek-walls and the adjacent faces of the revetting wall were rendered in a waterproof pink mortar painted in a blue ground, upon which are depicted architectural paintings in various shades of brown. Very little is still in position, but quantities of broken fragments lie around (Vol. II, p. 81).

The north and west verandas. The western side of the range is flanked by a continuous corridor, 17 ft. (5.2 m.) wide, running the full length of the known part of the building and terminating at its northern end in an apsidal recess (pl. XVIIIa). It is likely that the southern end possessed a similar feature, but the crucial area is now below the pavement in front of the village post office, and cannot be excavated. The northern recess is lined with an 18-in. (0.46-cm.) wide bench built of stone and rubble and faced with a coating of pink mortar painted red. Only the bottom few inches of the foundations survive, but enough to have protected the adjacent floor-surfaces from ploughing. It is therefore surprising that no made surface remains anywhere in the corridor, but the explanation here, as in the North and East Wings, may be that the corridors were floored only with a thin layer of mortar which subsequent use and erosion have caused to disintegrate completely. From the relatively large quantity of painted plaster recovered from the corridor it is possible to say that it was decorated in much the same style throughout. The lower part of the walls was painted with a a pink dado splashed with white, black and ochre to simultate a grained marble, at the base of which was a narrow deep red skirting. Above the dado the walls were painted with white panels bordered by deep red bands and framed internally with thin black frame lines. Within the apse were panels of yellow framed with thin brown lines. Other colours were only rarely used (Vol. II, p. 79).

THE SUPERSTRUCTURE   (figs. 23–5)

Although the walls nowhere survive to above two courses in height, and in most places are completely destroyed to their footings, the relative simplicity of the plan enables much

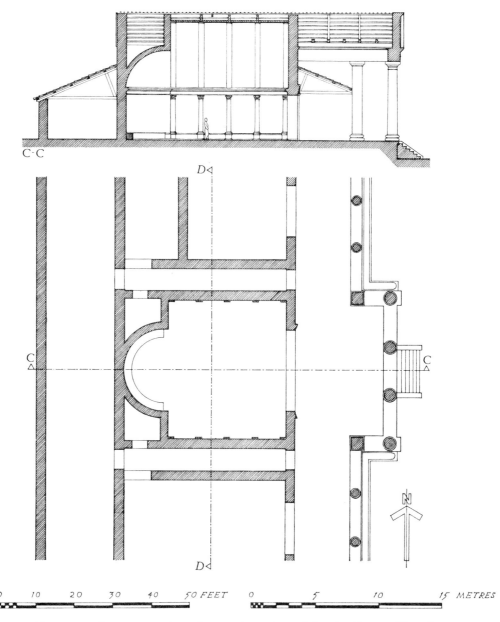

Fig. 23. Reconstruction plan and section of the Audience Chamber
(by N. J. Sunter)

to be said of the superstructure of the wing. The rooms are so arranged that they may be thought of as a single range some 50 ft. (15.2 m.) wide and 354 ft. (107.9 m.) long enclosed beneath a simple single-ridge roof, broken in the centre only where the Audience Chamber demands a special treatment. The colonnade, which flanked the east side, gives a tolerably accurate indication of general roof-height, for from our knowledge of the column diameter and spacing (p. 121) it follows that the height of the veranda architrave would have been about 12 ft. (3.66 m.) and therefore, if we allow a sloping veranda roof and provision for clear-story lights into the rooms behind, the eaves would have stood at about 25 ft. (7.62 m.) above floor-level.

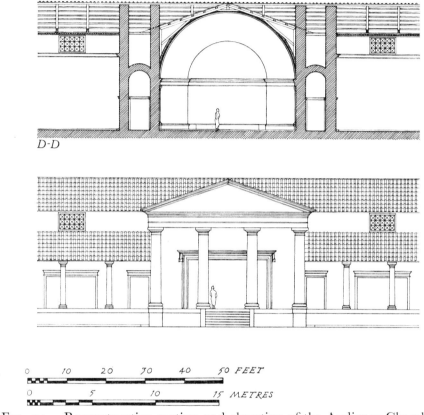

FIG. 24.   Reconstruction section and elevation of the Audience Chamber
(by N. J. Sunter)

The roofing of the Audience Chamber poses a number of problems. Of primary importance is the question of whether the main chamber was roofed with a plain ceiling or with a vault. On balance a vault would seem to be more likely when it is remembered that the north wall footing (and presumably also the south) were considerably wider and more massive than any other in the building, presumably because of the weight and thrust which a heavy vaulted roof would exert upon them. The recovery of fragments of ribbed stucco from within the room is also suggestive of vaulting but the possibility that they came from the semi-dome covering the apse cannot, however, be completely ruled out (see above, p. 88). A good example of a contemporary ribbed vault of stucco occurs in the Women's Thermae at Herculaneum (see Brion, 1960, pl. 39, for a clear illustration). It is no surprise that structural fragments of vaulting have not been found: late Roman robbing and subsequent ploughing have so completely destroyed the room that even the floor make-up has been removed over much of the area.

If the possibility of a vaulted roof is accepted, it remains to consider its form. The simplest, and most acceptable, arrangement would have been a simple barrel-vault sprung from the north and south walls. Its east–west alignment would thus have enhanced the main axis around which the entire palace was planned. Moreover, if the corridors to the north and south were roofed with tunnel-vaults, as seems likely, they would fall neatly into position as the essential buttressing masses necessary in such an arrangement (fig. 24). The materials and the structure of the vault must remain unknown, but we should remember as one possibility the method described by Vitruvius for suspending light stuccoed false vaults from a hidden timber ceiling.[1] The span across the Audience Chamber, 35 ft. (10.66 m.), would not be too great for such a construction but the massive footings of the lateral walls imply a more solid treatment in masonry.

The height of the vault poses more difficult problems. However, the nature of the revetting wall and its colonnade in front of the room implies a tetrastyle pedimented front which, adopting the proportions applicable elsewhere, strongly suggests that the cornice-level approximated to the level of the adjacent roof. Thus the crest of the pediment would be equal in height to the ridge of the main roof, which could therefore pass unbroken across the Audience Chamber. An elevation based on these principles (fig. 24), though modest in appearance, is visually highly acceptable. But the implications which this reconstruction carries for the proportions of the Audience Chamber are less happy. As the reconstruction shows, the enclosed volume is rather too low in proportion for its width. The matter is not one of great importance and it may well be that the feeling of boundless space, both vertically and laterally, thus created was thought desirable in the context of an Audience Chamber. These matters will be returned to in more detail below (p. 151).

The precise function of the rest of the rooms in the northern half of the wing is unknown, but their position alone implies use as state apartments. The ground-plan suggests a division into two units: rooms W 1–W 6 constituting one, arranged around a communal hall (room W 3), and rooms W 7 to W 12 forming the other, consisting of two large east-facing rooms, one of which leads to a heated suite beyond. No special roofing details seem to be required and all are therefore likely to have been of similar pattern with timber ceiling and provision for clear-story light either from the east or west, depending on their position within the wing.

The western corridor, which runs the full length of the wing and terminates at its north (and probably south) ends in an apse, raises a series of extremely interesting questions. Functionally, a service passage in this position would not have been necessary, and even if it were a width of 17 ft. (5.2 m.) would have been regarded as unduly wasteful. Its position, plan and proportions cannot fail to call to mind the *hippodromos* of Domitian's palace in Rome[2] and the similar structure which Pliny describes adorning his villa.[3] Insufficient survives of the west wall at Fishbourne to show whether it supported a colonnade or balustrade overlooking a further garden or open area to the west, but some form of lighting from this direction would have been essential, making the 'corridor' a warm sunny place in which it would have been pleasant to stroll or take exercise in the late evening.

---

[1] Vitruvius, *de Architectura*, Book VII, iii, 1 ff.   [3] Pliny, *Letters*, Book II, letter 17.
[2] For a useful plan and discussion see MacDonald, 1965.

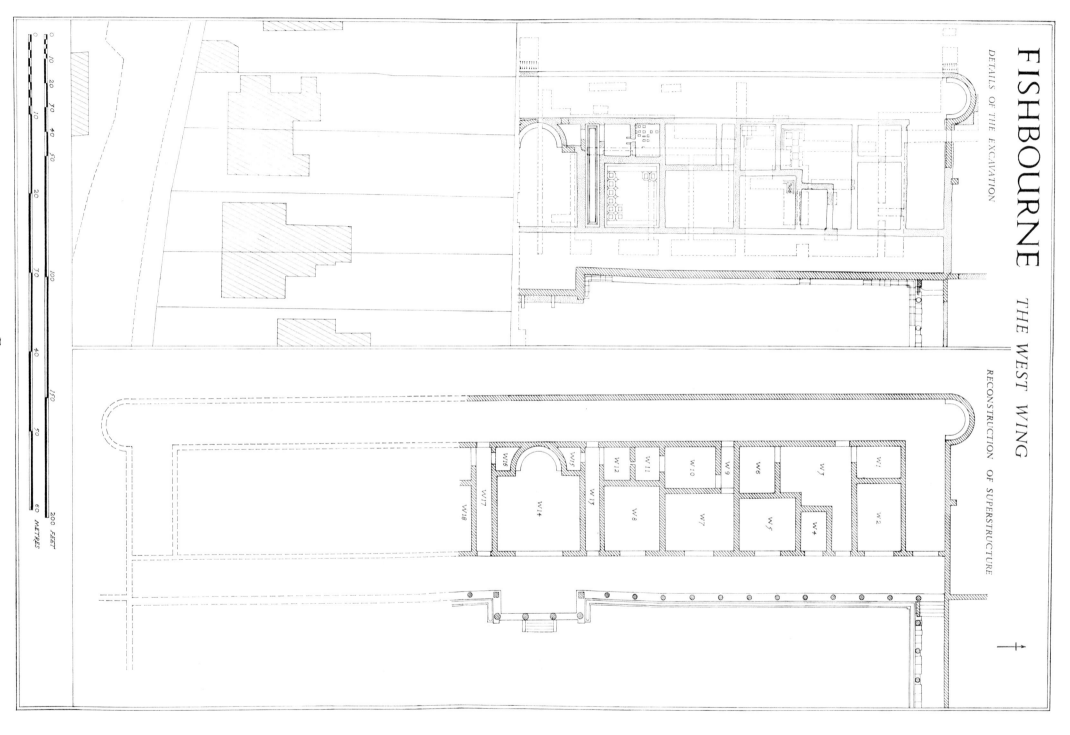

FISHBOURNE

THE WEST WING

DETAILS OF THE EXCAVATION

RECONSTRUCTION OF SUPERSTRUCTURE

W1 W2 W4 W5 W6 W7 W8 W9 W10 W11 W12 W13 W14 W15 W16 W17 W18

FIG. 25

THE NORTH WING

The plan of the North Wing is simple and effective, the overriding desire of the architect being to create private enclosed spaces around which blocks of rooms were arranged. The resulting plan is like a letter E, the spaces between the short arms representing the open courtyards. Although the wing is linked visually and physically to the garden and the adjacent wings by means of a colonnaded walk flanking the south side, it must be thought of as an isolated unit functionally detached from the rest of the palace.

DESCRIPTION OF THE EXCAVATED FEATURES   (fig. 26, p. 211)

Room N 1.   Part of the original floor is still in position in the eastern part of the room, between the channels of the later hypocaust. The fragment is small but the design is sufficiently repetitive to suggest that the area was divided into nine squares, each of which probably contained complex square-within-square motifs drawn largely in black on white, but with the use of red and blue as infilling in some at least of the squares. The panel was enclosed within a triple border to black bands (pls. xxa, LXXIX). None of the surviving painted plaster is of Palace-period date (Vol. II, pp. 58 ff.).

The room was entered by means of a door in the south wall leading into the hall (room N 5). It is possible that another door led into room N 2 but the wall in this area has been so extensively robbed that no evidence is available.

Room N 2.   There is practically nothing to be said of this room in its original state. A few rows of white tesserae survive in the south-west corner beneath the later floor make-up, but the rest of the design has been destroyed. Similarly, the walls are so robbed that the positions of the doorways must remain unknown, but the plan would suggest at least one door in the south wall leading to the hall. No original painted wall plaster survived.

Room N 3 (pls. xxb–xxI).   Rooms N 3 and N 4 are both tolerably well preserved in their original state, largely because in the later periods they were converted to store-rooms or workshops and were not therefore refloored as were the rooms which continued to be used for living elsewhere in the wing. The original mosaic floor is two-thirds complete (pl. LXXVIIa). It is basically white with a design of evenly-spaced boxes linked by a simple square and diamond pattern. The boxes contain one of three standard designs based on squares: a simple black square, a white square within a larger black one, or a multiple motif composed of five squares. A quarter-round moulding of pink mortar survives in most places at the junction of the wall and floor, but it may well be a later addition.

Part of the floor has subsided noticeably over the soft filling of an early ditch which crossed this part of the site (p. 52). The waterlogged nature of the ditch filling must have caused a large damp patch to form in the room even during the early years of the building's life, and it may have been this that decided the later occupants to abandon the room for living purposes and use it as a store.

The positions of three doors are known: one opened through the north wall into the western part of the hall; the others lead through the east wall, which still survives to a height of five courses, one into room N 4, the other into the southern part of the hall. Two doorways into the hall are excessive, but most likely the northern door, which is represented now only by a masonry sill rendered with pink mortar, was cut through the wall at a later date when several major modifications were being made to the building (see p. 161). In support of this view it may be said that a mortar-rendered sill is not found elsewhere in doorways which can be assigned to the original palace; normally a timber sill was employed set in a slot, the bottom of which was several inches below the adjacent floor-levels. The other door into the hall is of this type and the relationship of its sill-recess to the adjacent upstanding masonry leaves little doubt that it was original. The third door, leading to room N 4, was also original but at a later period it had been blocked with ashlar masonry. No original painted wall plaster survived.

Room N 4 (pl. XXI)   A considerable area of the original mosaic floor remains in position, but the construction of a later oven and continuous wear, which necessitated extensive patching with pink mortar, have removed about two-thirds of it. The design, however, is simple and repetitive (pl. LXXVII*b*) consisting of a regular chequer-board of black squares of two different sizes on a white ground. The whole is contained within a triple black border. In addition to the door already mentioned which led into room N 3, the room was served by another door in the north wall which gave access from the hall. The north wall had been dismantled during the Third Period, when the room was enlarged, but even so the position of the original door-sill can still be traced.

The painted plaster recovered from the room is probably of Third-Period date and is described below.

Room N 5.   Room N 5, by nature of its irregular shape and the relationship of the adjacent rooms to it, seems to have served as a hall or concourse for the westernmost block of rooms. In character and function it is not unlike room W 3 in the West Wing. Originally it was floored with a mosaic pavement, but there has been so much re-use and reflooring that only a very small fragment, showing a black band on a white ground, exists, bordering the extreme western end of the room (pl. LXXX*b*).

The main door opened into the hall through the centre of its eastern wall, opposite the veranda which enclosed the western courtyard. Through this door everyone wishing to use the rooms in the western block would have had to pass. The room was so extensively re-modelled in the Third Period that it is unlikely that any of the original painted plaster survived.

Room N 6.   Room N 6 is one of a group of four rooms or corridors of elongated form which flank the two large central rooms in each half of the wing. Later modifications were so extensive that no indication of original flooring survives, nor is it possible to say whether the south side of the room was closed by a timber partition.

From the rubble filling the room was recovered a small quantity of wall plaster painted over a pink undercoat, with over-painted flowers in brown and green and areas of bright blue. This treatment is identical to the Flavian plaster dumped outside the North Wing and must therefore represent the original decoration.

Room N 7.   The room, like room N 16, occupies an important position overlooking one of the enclosed courtyards. In the later period it was to be fitted out with one of the finest floors in the building, emphasizing its importance, and we must suppose that it was similarly treated in its original state, but no details of its primary floor are available. It may be that substantial parts of it survive below the later dolphin mosaic, but if so they must remain sealed until the upper floor is lifted. That the room did in fact possess an early mosaic was shown when the fillings of the robber trenches around the floor were removed, and it became possible to examine in section the layers below the dolphin mosaic. The matrix of the original floor could be clearly traced and in some places a row of white tesserae remained, but the impression gained was that the original floor had been thoroughly robbed before the new floor was laid.

The door positions cannot be located with certainty, but in all probability the main door lay in the south wall overlooking the courtyard. In the later period the original opening was probably remodelled on a grander scale (see p. 163).

A mass of painted wall plaster was found within the room and in the robber trenches for the surrounding walls, but it seems more reasonable to assign it to the Third Period when it is known that the room was completely redesigned.

Room N 8. Room N 8 occupies a position similar to room N 6, but here again extensive Third-Period alterations have combined to destroy all evidence of the original flooring, layout and function. None of the painted wall plaster is likely to be original.

Room N 9 (pl. XXIIIa). Although the room was completely refloored at a later period, a small part of the original mosaic survived in the south-east corner and at various points around the perimeter rows of white tesserae could be seen projecting into the sections left after the fillings of the robber trenches had been removed, but in no case did more than three rows survive. The fragment of design in the south-east corner shows a black chequer pattern on a white background, enclosed by a thin black line. The decorated panel began only 7 in. (0.17 m.) out from the wall, which is unusual considering that a white surround 18–24 in. (0.46–0.6 m.) wide was normally employed. The most likely explanation is that the surviving piece was the corner of a 'mat', like that found in room W 6 in the West Wing; indeed the two designs are very similar. This arrangement raises certain problems concerning the positions of the doors, for although a reasonable plan would be to provide one opening from the south side, on analogy with room W 6 it might be that the room was in fact entered through a door at the south end of the east wall, from room N 10. If this were so a visitor would walk through on to the 'mat' and be able to stand clear to view the main panel of the floor, which would be laid out on his right. No further evidence relevant to the door positions is available.

Quantities of painted wall plaster show that the room had been provided with a mock marble dado, about 3 ft. (1 m.) high, painted in tones of red surmounted by a cornice moulding of toned green-brown between tighter framing mouldings of black and white. Above this the wall had been divided into a series of panels which were either plain, of red, orange, or blue splashed with green, or were more complicated, simulating inlaid marble. Sufficient remains of one of the latter to show that it was composed of a 'slab' of blue-grey veined marble set within a complex frame of strips of brown and green textured 'marble' and plain red 'stone', all divided by simple white-black-white 'mouldings'. The panels were in turn surmounted by a simple frieze in black and white. Other, more fragmentary, painting is summarized below (Vol. II, pp. 63 ff.). Dating is difficult but the elaboration of the composition, choice of colours and general quality of the work would indicate a Flavian rather than a later date.

Room N 10 lies centrally in the middle block of rooms within the wing. No trace of the original mosaic floor survives below the later tessellated floor, with the exception of the matrix in which the mosaic had once been set, and the occasional rows of white tesserae which remain in position along the extreme edges of the floor where they were visible in the sides of the robber trenches. Entry was most likely gained from the hall to the south by means of a central door, but no positive evidence of this survives the extreme robbing of the masonry footings. As we have seen above, it is not impossible that access was also provided to room N 9. If so, room N 10 might be thought of as an inner entrance hall serving the two flanking rooms, but of this there is no certainty.

At the time of its destruction the northern part of the room was decorated with an area of inlaid marble, described below (pp. 144–5, and Vol. II, p. 26), which may well date back to its original phase of decoration. A quantity of painted wall plaster was also recovered (Vol. II, p. 66), but it is impossible to say whether or not it belonged to the early period.

Room N 11 is of similar size to room N 9 and balances it across the central north-south axis through the building. Here again most of the original mosaic had been destroyed before the later tessellated floor was laid, but a small patch in the north-east quarter of the room escaped destruction. Insufficient remains to give a clear idea of the design except to show that it was of a white geometric pattern on a black background — the reverse of the normal style. Nothing is known for certain of the position of the doorways, but their arrangement is likely to be close to that of room N 9.

Although it is difficult to be certain, the style of the painted wall plaster found within the room suggests that it may have retained its Flavian decor throughout. The room was provided with a dado of contrasting mock marble panels, one painted in streaks of blue and green, another with grey splashed with flecks of dark grey and white. Above, the wall surface seems to have been painted with plain panels of deep red, orange-red and deep blue. The colour range is very close to the painting in the pre-Flavian proto-palace (Vol. II, p. 66).

Room N 12. This room contains the best preserved of the early mosaics in the entire palace (pls. XXIV, LXXVIII). The main panel is decorated with a series of cross motifs infilled either with solid bands of black or with triangles arranged base to apex. Between the crosses are square boxes ornamented in a variety of ways: some, the most common, contain the square-diagonally-within-square pattern, others are filled with stylized rosettes or more complex fleur-de-lis arrangements. The crosses and boxes are linked with a square-and-diamond background cleverly designed to give the impression of incomplete perspective. The result is kaleidoscopic. The main panel is enclosed by two wide black bands arranged concentrically, beyond which on both the north and south sides are further elongated panels infilled with simple repetitive arrangements of oblongs within squares drawn in a thin black line on a white ground. Apart from a later wall which divides the room into unequal halves and areas of disturbance in the north half, the floor is remarkably well-preserved considering that it was only 18 in. (0.46 m.) below the surface when found. The floor had evidently been damaged during the Roman period in several small areas, particularly in the north and south panels, but the holes had been carefully, if not always accurately, patched. Coarser patching with red tesserae, close to the main door-sill and on either side of the door which opened through the partition wall, belongs to a later period.

The only known door lay in the centre of the north wall, giving access from room N 14. Its timber sill, burnt by the late third-century fire, is still preserved in position.

Although the room was eventually divided into two by a timber partition, the same style of painted wall plaster was recovered from both halves, suggesting that the room had not been redecorated after division. Moreover the style was close to that of the pre-Flavian painting of the proto-palace. The room was provided with a dado of pink splashed with deep red to simulate marble, areas of which still survive in position to a maximum height of 1 ft. 10 in. (0.56 m.). Several other areas of different types of marbling occur, including deep red with splashes of black and white, streaky pink, splashed purple, yellow with red veins, speckled deep blue and green and white with red veins. These more exotic veined and textured types were edged with bands of plain colour and occasionally strips of mock marble or painted mouldings, and must represent the decoration of the upper part of the walls above the plainer dado. Visual relief was provided by intervening areas of plain red and deep blue. The overall effect must have been opulent in the extreme and would have contrasted well with the plain black and white of the floor (Vol. II, p. 67).

Room N 13 (pls. xxiii*b*, lxxx*c*). Originally the room contained a black and white geometric floor, but much of it was destroyed before a new mosaic was laid in the early second century. Fortunately a fairly large sample remained undisturbed in the centre of the room at just the point where later ploughing had eventually destroyed the upper floor. The surviving fragment shows that the design was composed of large squares infilled with black rectangles and squares, alternating with areas of Greek key pattern. Much the same arrangement occurred in the West Wing, in room W 3. Some parts of the floor showed signs of discoloration caused by fire. This can have nothing to do with the burning of the building in the late third century, for at this time the later mosaic, or at least its matrix, would have protected the underlying fragment. It is far more likely that the marks were caused by a brazier being placed too close to the surface during the first phase of the building's life.

The only door to be identified lay in the centre of the north wall, opening on to room N 14. The door-sill has long since been ploughed away but the underlying ashlar masonry still survives unrobbed.

Fragments of very finely painted plaster have been recovered from the rubble filling the room, the quality and style of which suggest a Flavian date. It would appear that the room was provided with a mock marble dado of orange-red splashed with green, above which were areas of plain colours, particularly red, and also perhaps of more finely painted marbles, surrounded by painted fillets and mouldings of marble (Vol. II, p. 68).

Room N 14 (pl. lvi*b*) is an L-shaped room lying between rooms N 9–11 and 12 and 13. It seems to have served both as a passageway allowing access between the two courtyards and as a concourse out of which opened all the surrounding rooms. In the first stage it was mosaic-floored, but all that is known to have survived the later extensive refloorings was a small area of white tesserae laid against the north wall of room N 13 and a somewhat larger patch laid in diagonal rows, close to the north-east corner of room N 12. Elsewhere later floors have sealed any other fragments which might still remain *in situ*. It may be significant to mention here the floor which now occupies the southern part of the room (p. 166). It is so similar in design to the mosaic in room N 12 that originally it was thought to belong to the early palace, but later work showed that it had been laid 4 in. (0.1 m.) above the earlier floor-surface and that in one place the tesserae of the original floor ran beneath it. Furthermore the quality of the workmanship, when studied in detail, can be shown to be inferior to that of the early group of floors. It therefore appears that the surviving floor is either a relaid version of the original or a later, and more elaborate, imitation of the floor in room N 12 constructed out of re-used materials. At any event, it is interesting that the later owners should have wanted a design so out of fashion.

The doors leading from the adjacent rooms have already been mentioned. One other is known for certain at the west end, where the charred door-sill is still in position; another is likely in the corresponding position in the east wall but here extensive robbing has destroyed the entire wall down to the level of the footings.

One length of painted wall plaster still survives in position, on the north face of the north wall of room N 12. It is likely to be of early date because it begins at the lower floor-level, the later tessellated corridor floor obscuring the lower 3 in. (0.076 m.). Admittedly it could be argued that in the late period the process of redecorating the walls precedes the laying of the new floors, but on balance an earlier date seems more likely. The surviving piece, some 9 in. (0.22 m.) high, is painted in pink splashed with blue and red to simulate a marble-inlaid dado with the joins between one sheet and the next painted as a black line.

Other types of marbling include pinkish-red over-painted with streaks of darker red, deep pink splashed finely with red, deep red splashed with pink and red-brown. All seem to have served as dado decoration. Above were a series of panels painted in plain rich colours including green, yellow, orange-red, red, deep blue and white. Each of the panels was decorated with thin internal frame lines of various contrasting colours. The style and colour range is closely similar to that of the Neronian proto-palace (Vol. II, p. 68).

Room N 15.   There is little to be said of the form or decoration of the room. All trace of the surface-rendering has long since disappeared and even the top of the floor make-up has been so disturbed as to remove any evidence of door-sills or timber partitions.

Room N 16.   Room N 16 corresponds in size and position to room N 7, in the western half of the wing. In such a position, overlooking the courtyard, it must once have served an important function and would have been elaborately ornamented. Unfortunately ploughing has removed all evidence of the floor and its matrix down to the greensand blocks which form its make-up, and all that survives are large numbers of black and white tesserae scattered in the ploughsoil. The positions of the doorways are unknown, but the principal entrance would almost certainly have been placed centrally in the south wall where a levelling course of tiles was found.

Room N 17.   Like room N 15, nothing survives to give an indication of its original function or decoration. Medieval and later ploughing have destroyed everything.

Room N 18. Here again ploughing has destroyed the original floor surface, but the large numbers of loose black and white tesserae in the overlying ploughsoil strongly suggest that the room was once floored with a mosaic. Door positions are unknown, but a door leading to room N 19 would seem to be essential.

Room N 19 (pl. xxv*a*). The water-main trench of 1960 cut diagonally through the room, destroying part of its mosaic floor, but even before this ploughing, possibly preceded by a period of destruction or wear, combined to remove much of the original surface. Nevertheless sufficient survives to show that the room was originally floored with a simple geometric mosaic composed of overlapping rectangles drawn in thin black lines on a white background (pl. LXXX*d*).

The walls have been destroyed to such an extent that all trace of the original doors has vanished, but the position of room N 19 is similar to that of rooms N 14 and N 5, suggesting that it may have served as a hall giving access to the neighbouring rooms in the way suggested on the reconstruction plan. Further than this it is impossible to go.

Room N 20 (pls. xxvi, xxvii, Lxxxi, xci). Room N 20 contains the most striking and unusual of the first-century mosaics to be found in the palace. It consisted of a central circular panel, now completely destroyed, surrounded by a circular band depicting rosettes alternating with leaves. Both were drawn in red, yellow and white outlined in black, and were set on a white background. Beyond lay another circular band of comparable width bearing a multicoloured twisted guilloche on a black background. The outer border of the circle almost touched at four points the square framework of black bands which enclosed the decorated panel, thus defining four corner spandrels each of which was ornamented in a different fashion. The north-west corner contained two dolphins facing a central vase, out of the base of which sprang simple tendrils. The arrangement in the south-east corner was similar, except that the dolphins were here replaced by fish. The remaining two corners contained central vases with high square-topped handles with large exuberant tendrils growing from their bases. The relative freedom of the design and the lavish use of not only bright simple colour but also subtle tones, serves to distinguish this pavement from the more restrained monochrome floors which adorned the rest of the palace at this period. Its significance will be further examined below.

The floor suffered a certain amount of damage early during its life, partly because some sections subsided over the fillings of earlier post-holes beneath, and partly because of continuous wear unchecked by repair. Eventually some attempt at patching was made, first with tile and later with clay, but by then much of the centre had been destroyed. Medieval ploughing caused a little more damage, particularly of the south and west edges, but fortunately much of the floor escaped destruction until finally in 1960 the water-main cut across the north-east corner, removing a small area from the border and spandrel.

The positions of the doorways are unknown. The simplest possibility is that the room was entered from the veranda through its west wall, but such an arrangement is unknown elsewhere in the wing. Another possibility, shown on the reconstruction plan, is that the room was linked to those adjacent to it by means of doors in both the north and south walls. The problem must, however, remain open.

Room N 21 (pls. xxv*b*, LXXXII). Room N 21 is the smallest of the North Wing rooms and may have functioned only as an ante-room to room N 20. Its mosaic floor was very well preserved. Like the fragment still surviving in room N 11, it is in reverse (i.e. white on black instead of black on white). The design is simple, consisting of alternate squares of plain red or blue enclosed in a framework of interlocking white lines. Close to the wall in the south-east corner a simple diamond, outlined in white tesserae, has been set into the black border. Clearly it is not part of the design but may well be the signature of the mosaicist. Subsidence has occurred in two places, both corresponding with the positions of posts belonging to the Period 1 timber building. Presumably the stumps were still in position when the floors were laid and only later did they rot, creating a void into which the floor sank.

The east wall of the room incorporates, at floor-level, a layer of broken roofing tile which in all probability represents the seating or a levelling-up course for a timber door-sill. A door in this position strengthens the impression that the room served as an ante-room to room N 20, which would therefore have been entered through a door at the western end of their dividing wall. The striking contrast between the restrained colour of the mosaic in room N 21 and the bright floral arrangement in room N 20 must have been deliberately contrived to surprise and impress.

Room N 22 (pl. XXIII*c*). The mosaic floor in room N 22 had been largely destroyed either deliberately in the Roman period or, more likely, by subsequent ploughing. The surviving patches, however, make it clear that a decorated panel existed in the form of a simple black design on a white ground, not dissimilar to the floor in room N 19. An unusually wide white border occurred along the northern side, hinting at the possibility that the panel was square and had thus to be set unevenly within the rectangular room (pl. LXXX*a*).

The positions of the doors are unknown, but on functional grounds alone there is a strong likelihood that access was provided to room N 19. Another door may have opened into room N 23, but the possibility is beyond proof.

Room N 23. The nature of the floor of room N 23 is uncertain. A strong foundation had been prepared as in the rooms which were to contain mosaics, but no trace of floor-surfacing survived nor were there many tesserae in the overlying ploughsoil. It was clear, however, that in the later period the general area of the room had been used as a yard, over which a considerable mass of occupation debris had been allowed to accumulate. It remains a strong possibility that before this was allowed to happen any mosaic would have been ripped up and the materials perhaps used elsewhere.

Only one door is known for certainty — the door which led into room N 21. Another probably opened from room N 19, but of this there is no trace.

Very little of the original painted plaster remains, but several fragments show that the walls were painted with elaborate mock marble panels, of which traces of two survive, one painted in pale green with the texture and grain picked out in tones of green and white overlaid by fine red veins, the other in purple, flecked with ochre and white (Vol. II, p. 69).

The eastern corridor (N 24). Immediately to the east of the North Wing and between it and the Aisled Hall described below (p. 106) lay a corridor or alleyway 67 ft. (20.3 m.) long and varying from 8 ft. 6 in. (2.6 m.) wide at the north end to 10 ft. (3.0 m.) wide at the south end. Only the southern third had escaped the extensive modification made necessary when a later bath building was inserted, but all indications are that the floor make-up of clay and greensand was left unsurfaced. This fact, together with the structural considerations outlined below (p. 106 ff.), imply that the corridor was unroofed and may have been merely a space between the two different structural units. It may have provided access between the main colonnade surrounding the garden and the area north of the North Wing.

The western courtyard (Courtyard 1) (pl. xxiia). The rooms at the western end of the building are arranged around three sides of the courtyard, the fourth being enclosed by a blank wall. Originally the courtyard was bounded on the west, north and east sides by a stylobate of large Bembridge limestone blocks, but only the western row now survives, the rest having been removed during the period of late Roman robbing. Sometime in the second century the colonnade, standing on the stylobate, was pulled down and replaced by walls. For this reason no fragments of the original colonnade survived in position, nor were many found in adjacent rubble deposits. In front of the stylobate there would originally have been a gutter, but all that now remained were a few fragments of flanges knocked off and discarded as useless, presumably at the time when the blocks were removed for re-use. The rain-water accumulating in the gutter was directed by means of a carefully arranged gradient, to the south-east corner of the courtyard, whence it passed through a tile-built drain below the floor of the veranda flanking the southern side of the wing, and was emptied into the gutter surrounding the garden.

The colonnade fronted a veranda 8½–9 ft. (c. 2.6 m.) wide. Only along the western side, where later reflooring was absent, did evidence of the original floor survive in the form of a 3-in. (0.076-m.) thick layer of cream mortar spread directly on the underlying clay make-up. Since corridor and veranda floors elsewhere in the palace were treated in this way we can only suppose that in general no more durable or more decorative form of surfacing was employed.

The walls facing in towards the courtyard were all plastered and painted with elaborate designs in bright colours. The west wall and parts of the north wall were painted with pink and purple backgrounds over-painted with bold foliage in blue and green. Areas of white and red were also included but how they were arranged is unknown. There is no certainty that this design belonged to the original Flavian scheme and it may be thought that since it differed considerably from the Flavian painting known elsewhere in the building that the painting is of a later origin. The problem must be left open. The north-west corner did, however, produce painting identical in style and colour range to the Neronian and Flavian work found elsewhere. It depicted a dado composed of two adjacent slabs of mock marbling, one purple splashed with red the other of mottled green painted over red. Above was a simply-painted moulding surmounted by a band of red dividing the dado from two upper panels, one of plain deep blue, the other of green. The painting on the east wall, of which much more survives, is in a similar style. The dado is composed of four differently painted marbles: purple with red splashes, blotchy red, green mottled with blue, and yellow-brown overpainted mottled red. The panels were framed with simple mouldings. Along the top ran a band of red toning into yellow representing a cornice, above which were bands of deep blue, bright green and red. The red may, in fact, be the beginning of an upper panel but insufficient survives to be sure (Vol. II, p. 70).

The eastern courtyard (Courtyard 2).   The eastern colonnade was closely similar in size and arrangement to the courtyard just described. It had, however, suffered considerably both from robbing and from subsidence into the soft fillings of earlier underlying features, and all that now survives are the footings for the stylobate and the robber trench which marks the position of the ground-level gutter. Rainwater had been removed from the courtyard by a tile drain identical to that which served the western courtyard.

The only architectural fragment to be recovered was part of a column drum, which lay in the rubble filling the north-east corner of the gutter robber trench. Since it is clear that the eastern part of the wing had been demolished during the second century before any rebuilding took place, it is probable that the fragment belonged to one of the columns of the original courtyard. In size and form it is identical to the columns which surrounded the garden (p. 121). Only one fragment of painted plaster, depicting a skilfully painted garden scene, survives to give some idea of the quality of the early decoration (Vol. II, p. 72, and pl. XIIIc).

Masonry structure north of room N 11 (pl. xxiib).   A masonry projection of uncertain function was discovered to the north of room N 11, butted on to the north wall of the palace. It consisted of an area of tiles supporting two parallel walls 15 in. (0.38 m.) apart, one projecting for a distance of 3 ft. (0.9 m.) and ending neatly with tile-built corners, the other projecting at least 18 in. (0.46 m.) further but with its northern continuation destroyed by the water-main trench. Structurally the masonry is identical to that of the palace and quite unlike the later Third-Period masonry; for this reason alone it is best to consider it as a first-century feature.

One possible explanation is that the structure was part of a small latrine serving the North Wing and reached through a door at the north end of room N 15. Unfortunately, the water-main trench has destroyed much of the surrounding stratigraphy.

THE SUPERSTRUCTURE   (fig. 26)

The ground-plan alone of the North Wing leaves little doubt that the roofed area was E-shaped, arranged around two open courtyards, each of which was enclosed on three sides by a colonnaded veranda, the fourth being a blank wall continuous across the south side of the wing. The general rules governing the proportions of the colonnades will be discussed in detail below; here it is sufficient to state that the columns were placed at 12 ft. (3.66 m.) centres and that the height from base to cap was in the order of 12 ft. (3.66 m.). The height is important, for if we allow a sloping roof over the veranda, it implies that the clear-story lights, with which it was necessary to provide the adjacent rooms, could not have begun much below 16–17 ft. (*c.* 5 m.); gable height would therefore have been at about 20 ft. (6.1 m.). The standard spacing of the columns recorded along the north colonnade of the great garden fits well the proportions of the courtyards, as the reconstruction plan will show, allowing a column at each of the northern corners with two others along each of the three sides. The southernmost columns might be thought to be too close to the wall, but the arrangement commonly recurs in Pompeian peristyles of this kind and is not altogether unattractive. Although no positive evidence survives, it seems likely that the south ends of the verandas would have been provided with doorways leading into the garden, thus giving the residents

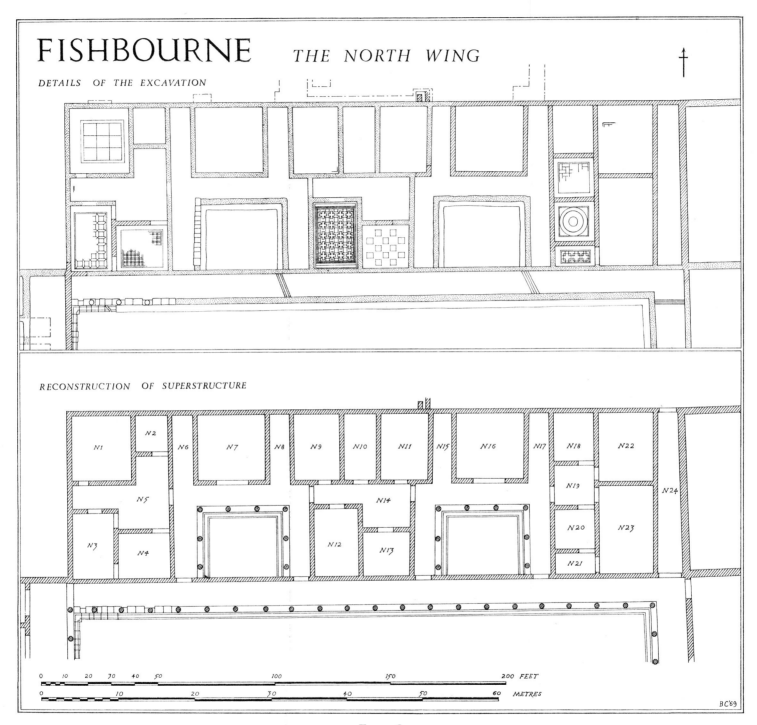

FISHBOURNE *THE NORTH WING*

DETAILS OF THE EXCAVATION

RECONSTRUCTION OF SUPERSTRUCTURE

Fɪɢ. 26

of the North Wing access to the rest of the palace. The function of the courtyards would therefore have been to provide a recreational area, to allow light into adjacent rooms and to give access between one part of the building and another. The courtyards themselves would probably have been laid out with flowers and shrubs, but in spite of a careful search no trace of bedding-trenches or root-holes survived.

The roof-lines above the rooms could have been arranged in a variety of ways, but without knowledge of the pitch and substructure of the individual sections it is impossible to offer a reconstruction with any degree of assurance. The happiest arrangement from a visual point of view would have been to roof the three blocks, rooms N 1–5, N 9–14 and N 18–23, as separate units with north–south ridges, thus providing three imposing gable ends overlooking the garden. The intervening rooms, nos. N 6–8 and N 15–17, could then have been provided with an east–west ridged roof abutting the main roofs. If this arrangement were adopted, the east–west ridge would have necessarily been lower than the north–south ridges unless its roof was of a much steeper pitch, which seems unlikely. Other arrangements are equally possible on structural grounds, but from a visual standpoint they would have been monotonous in comparison.

There is little more to be said of the superstructure of the individual rooms. The descriptions given above show that all were elaborately decorated, but no room seems to have been singled out for special treatment nor is there any evidence of vaulted ceilings. The impression given is of an evenness in character and function.

THE SOUTH WING

The South Wing now lies largely beneath the main road (A27) and the houses and gardens which line its southern side. Some hint of this was given by the discovery, in 1805, of a black and white mosaic pavement, 13½ ft. (4.1 m.) wide, while building work was being undertaken in the village close to the road. Although it is now impossible to locate the spot closely, the strong possibility exists that the floor belonged to the eastern half of the South Wing. It was not until the summer of 1968, several years after excavation had begun, that traces of the wing were discovered, giving for the first time a firm idea of its plan and extent.

The only extensive excavations so far possible have been restricted to the garden of no. 69 Fishbourne Road, with more limited work in the front garden of no. 65. Sufficient has been done to show that the original floor-levels have been totally destroyed, for in the front gardens of both houses clay and gravel floor make-up exists only 6–9 in. (c. 0.2 m.) below the present topsoil. The implication is that beneath the main road and the car-park in front of the 'Woolpack', both of which are almost a foot lower than the adjacent gardens, even the floor make-up will have been largely removed. Trenches dug by G.P.O. and Gas Board workmen in front of no. 69 confirm this view. Nevertheless the Roman wall footings were constructed in trenches dug to a depth of more than 3 ft. (1 m.) below the contemporary ground-surface and even the deepest recorded levelling will not have destroyed them.

DESCRIPTION OF THE EXCAVATED FEATURES (fig. 27, p. 211)

At three points in the front garden of no. 69 Fishbourne Road the foundations of Roman walls were found, built of courses of flint set in a yellow gritty mortar. The two north-south

I

walls were preserved to approximately the height of the original natural surface (pl. xviii*a*) but the east–west wall had been completely robbed. This was fortunate, for the robber trench contained a quantity of rubble including a few black and white tesserae and fragments of red and white-painted plaster. The three walls defined three rooms, one measuring 26 ft. (7.9 m.) across, the others of unknown size. The floor-surfaces and the upper levels of the floor make-up had been totally destroyed but some mortary rubble, churned up by recent gardening activities, still survived in the western room. The black and white tesserae and small fragments of painted wall plaster found here give some idea of the former decoration.

A single trial trench, immediately to the south of the modern house, sectioned what is evidently the rubble foundation for a stylobate, in front of which lay a shallow robber trench of exactly the correct proportions to take a masonry gutter. As if further proof were required, a small fragment of the flange of a greensand gutter-block was actually found in the rubble filling the robber trench. There can be little doubt, therefore, that the features discovered here represent a south-facing colonnade identical to those surrounding the main palace garden.

Very limited trial trenching in the front garden of no. 65 Fishbourne Road produced trace of the eastern end of the wing. The limiting north–south wall and the walls of the two adjacent small rooms were in fact of Period 1 construction and have been described above (p. 65). At the time when the palace was built it is clear that much of the Period 1 structure was incorporated into the South Wing of the new building and that layers of clay and soil make-up were deposited to raise the ground-surface to the level adopted elsewhere in the palace. The extent of the Period 1 building westwards and the degree to which it influenced the plan of the South Wing are problems that cannot be examined without further excavation, which at present is not possible.

Extensive, if intermittent, trial trenching south from the colonnade was possible in the flower beds on either side of the lawn of no. 69, in the garden of the 'Woolpack' and across the large area of land to the south. The results of this work showed conclusively that the South Wing of the palace was provided with a vast terraced area, probably a garden, stretching for a distance of 350 ft. (106 m.) south from the building to the sea. Brief details of the area will be given below, pp. 132 ff.

RECONSTRUCTION OF THE PLAN AND THE SUPERSTRUCTURE (fig. 27)

At first sight it might be thought impossible to say much about the plan and super-structure of the South Wing, but in fact a remarkable amount can be deduced from the few surviving fragments. In the first place, if it is assumed that the Audience Chamber lay in the exact area of the West Wing and that the West Wing was symmetrical about its centre point, the position of the north wall of the South Wing can be plotted. That this supposed position aligns exactly with a known wall in the East Wing (figs. 27, 34), to which on structural grounds it would have been convenient for it to join, is strong supporting evidence that the wall actually existed where it is thought to have been. Assuming this and knowing the position of the south wall found by excavation, the width of the Wing can be given as 51 ft. 6 in. (15.7 m.) — a measurement closely similar to the width of the West Wing. Furthermore, since the western limit of the wing should align with the east front of the West Wing, and

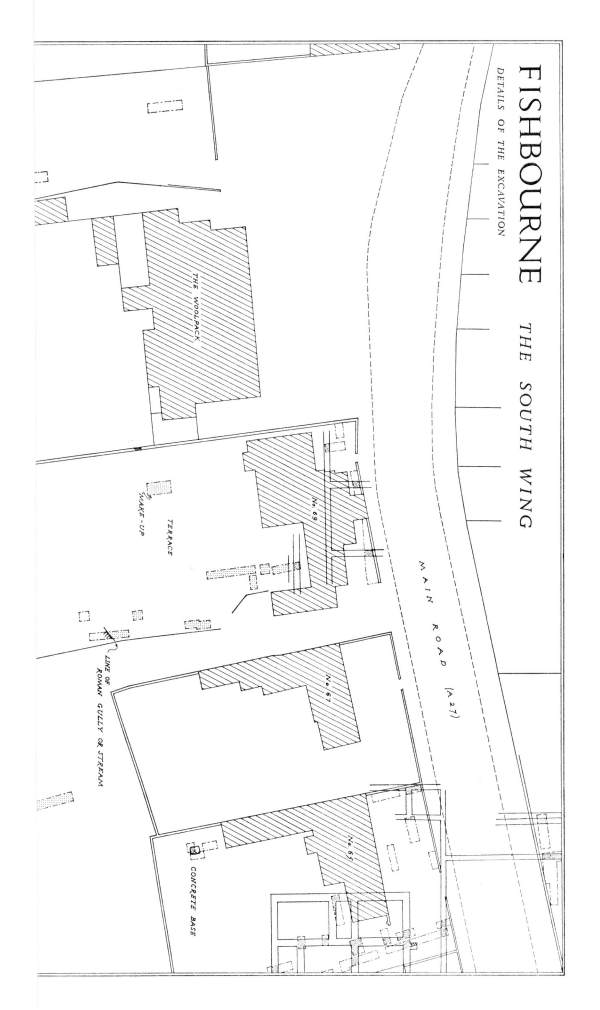

FISHBOURNE THE SOUTH WING

DETAILS OF THE EXCAVATION

THE WOOLPACK

SHAKE-UP

TERRACE

No. 69

No. 67

No. 65

MAIN ROAD (A 27)

LINE OF ROMAN GULLY OR STREAM

CONCRETE BASE

the eastern limit has been found in its expected position by excavation, the length of the range can be estimated as 262 ft. (79.9 m.).

The general proportions of the range suggest that it was roofed beneath a single ridge in much the same way as the West Wing and that, unlike the North Wing, there were no internal courtyards. Of the arrangement of the rooms, there is little to say. The three rooms partly examined in the centre of the wing were all comparable in size to those found elsewhere in the palace, but they are unlikely to have stretched the full width of the building. It is far more reasonable to suppose that the arrangement approximated to that in the West Wing, where smaller rooms lay behind a range of large front rooms. Nothing more can be said at present, but eventually it may become possible to excavate in the garden of no. 67 Fishbourne Road, where some of the outstanding problems will no doubt be answered. Digging for service pipes and cables beneath the main road will also provide useful details of the general plan, if an adequate watch can be kept over the next few decades.

The general symmetry of the palace garden implies the existence of a north-facing colonnade along the north side of the wing, continuous with the eastern colonnade and abutting, at a lower level, the colonnade in front of the West Wing. No opportunity has arisen to trace it by means of excavation, for it lies beneath the main road, its northern side-walk and the front garden hedges of the houses on the north side of the road. Even so, one can hardly doubt its existence. What was more surprising was the discovery of a south-facing colonnade flanking the south side of the wing. Although only a very small section of it has been examined by excavation, it is identical to those found elsewhere in the building and may imply that the entire south side was provided with a colonnaded walk overlooking the terrace which led down to the sea.

The further implications are attractive, for just as the North Wing rooms were arranged around their own private courtyards and were, strictly, isolated from the main garden, so too was the South Wing provided with a private garden, needing no connection with the main building and garden to the north. For this reason we may suppose that all the major rooms faced south towards the sea, the north colonnade being nothing more than a visual and semi-functional way of completing the square of the main garden.

THE EAST WING

The East Wing consists of an amalgam of several separate architectural units placed side by side and linked only by means of the verandas flanking the east and west sides. The central feature, both physically and visually, was the huge Entrance Hall which would have dominated the wing however it was approached. South of it lay a short range of rooms serving as a link between the Hall and the earlier proto-palace which, in a modified form, served as an integral part of the later palace. On the north side of the Entrance Hall were two peristyles backing on to a continuous range of eleven rooms. Beyond, at the extreme northern end stood a large Aisled Hall. As the plan (fig. 34) will show, most of the area north of the Entrance Hall is open land belonging to the Sussex Archaeological Trust, where large-scale excavations could be carried out. The Hall itself and the northern part of the proto-palace were more difficult to excavate partly because of the destruction caused by the recent farm buildings, and partly because the eastern part of the site lies below a private house and its garden, to which only limited access was possible. The remainder of the proto-palace was even more difficult to examine, for not only were three recent houses standing above it, but the modern A27 passed through the centre.

Unlike the other three wings, the East Wing is best described in sections dealing individually with the constituent architectural units.

THE AISLED HALL (figs. 28–30, p. 211, and pl. xxviii*b*)

Description of the remains

The Aisled Hall is a single unit, measuring internally 88 ft. by 66 ft. (26.7 × 20 m.) with its roof supported on four pairs of piers. The footings of its walls, which would have taken some of the thrust from the roof as well as the compression load of the walls themselves, were rather more massive than those found elsewhere in the palace, measuring 3–3½ ft. (about 1 m.) wide instead of the usual 2–2½ ft. (*c.* 0.7 m.) but they were constructed in the normal manner of flints set in yellow mortar with a superstructure of greensand-block masonry. In 1969 a sewer trench was cut through both the north and the south walls of the Hall, exposing the massive timber piles beneath the concrete footings. The piles, each a complete trunk 12–14 in. (0.3–0.35 m.) in diameter, were arranged in pairs with centres at intervals of about 1 ft. 9 in. (0.53 m.). The pier bases were also extremely solidly constructed (pl. xxviii*b*). First, a roughly-square pit measuring 6 ft. (2 m.) across had been dug to a depth exceeding 3 ft. (1 m.) which was then filled with a foundation of flints laid in courses in a matrix of yellow mortar. On this a square foundation of greensand masonry was built, free-standing, to a height of 12 in. (0.3 m.) (two courses). Above the masonry came a triple course of tiles. The entire foundation was then buried to the level of the top of the tiles by a mass of clay and gravel make-up deposited in the Hall to bring its floor-level up to the desired height. The make-up would also have imparted a certain rigidity to the footings. On the tile course, capping each foundation, a single block of masonry had been placed. The two that survive are 14 in. (0.35 m.) thick and measure 3 ft. square (0.9 m.). These would have formed the bases for the piers.

The original floor-surface within the Hall has been much mutilated by later alterations and re-use, but it survives in patches as a 3–4 in. (*c.* 0.1 m.) layer of cream mortar laid directly on top of the clay and gravel make-up. No attempt had been made to construct a more substantial foundation of the kind found below the mosaic floors of the rooms elsewhere in the building.

Excavations through the floor make-up close to the westernmost pier base of the northern row produced evidence of a surface of pink mortar, ½ in. (1.3 cm.) thick, set haphazardly with isolated black and white tesserae, which lay within the layers of make-up. It had clearly been deposited here before the foundation pit for the pier base had been dug, and looked superficially like a floor-surface of an earlier phase. Since further excavation failed to trace the layer, or an equivalent surface, for more than about 8 ft. (2.4 m.) and brought to light no further indication of early features, and since the layer was thinly spread without substantial make-up, it is more reasonably explained as a builders' spread in which loose tesserae had accidentally been mixed.

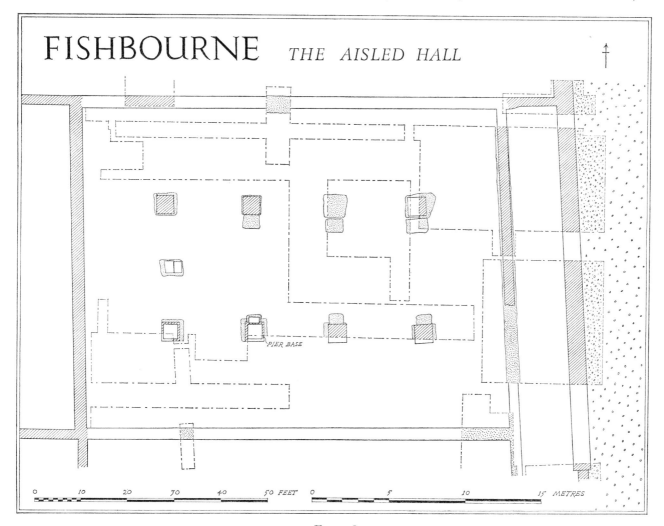

FIG. 28

Sometime after the construction of the Hall had been completed, but before the Third Period remodelling began, a minor phase of alteration occurred during which additional concrete bases were constructed in front of the first three pairs of piers from the east end. These new bases consisted of a foundation of flints in yellow mortar laid in a pit, usually about 2 ft. (0.6 m.) deep, cut through the floor of the Hall. One stone base, a block of Bembridge limestone 15 in. (0.4 m.) thick, survived in position in the south row. The westernmost pair of piers were not treated in this way, but instead an isolated foundation of similar construction was placed between them, upon which stood two adjacent stone blocks.

There is no evidence to show what the new bases supported. They do not seem to have been substantial enough to have supported additional piers, nor is there any reason to suppose that supports were needed. The focal position of the axial base, on the other hand, suggests that they may have taken ornamental features, possibly statuary. A group standing at the

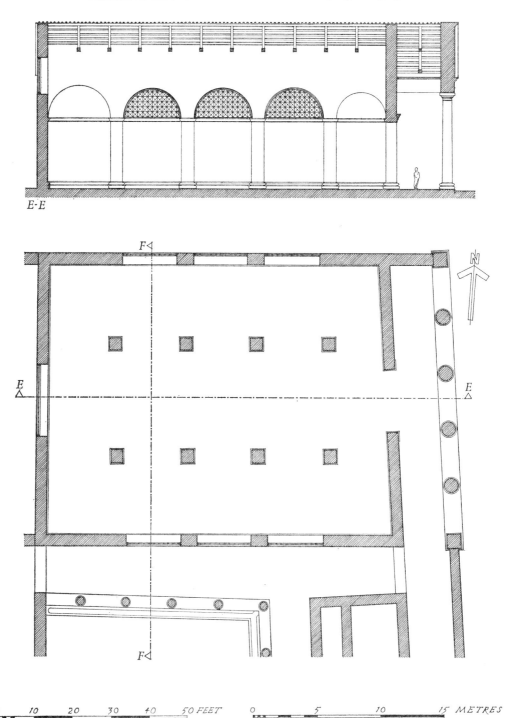

E-E

F◁

E △   △ E

F◁

0   10   20   30   40   50 FEET   0   5   10   15 METRES

FIG. 29.   Reconstruction plan and section of the Aisled Hall
(by N. J. Sunter)

end of the Hall and others standing against the piers would have been visually both acceptable and dramatic, but of their positive existence there is absolutely no proof — the matter
must be left open.

Quantities of painted wall plaster were recovered from the southern part of the Hall,
showing that areas of plain red and white predominated but grey-black, yellow, streaky
green and pink also occurred. Marbling based on white and pink occurred sparingly. The
detailed relationships of the colours are discussed below (Vol. II, pp. 74 ff.).

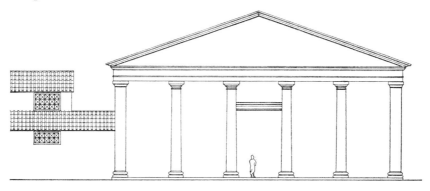

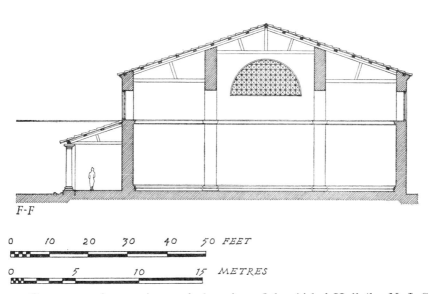

FIG. 30.   Reconstruction section and elevation of the Aisled Hall (by N. J. Sunter)

Reconstruction of the superstructure (figs. 29–30)

A hall of this kind could have been roofed in one of two ways: either the entire floor area
was spanned by a single pitch, the piers providing internal support for the rafters, or the
'nave' was roofed at a higher level than the 'aisles' so that clear-story light could be provided

through lunettes above the piers. Both styles would have been visually acceptable and both are structurally possible on the evidence of the ground plan alone. The hall, however, is fronted on the east by a wide and substantially built footing which implies the existence of a monumental facade similar to that which fronts the Entrance Hall (p. 111). In such a position the most satisfactory arrangement would have been a hexastyle front supporting a pediment above, identical in fact with that with which, it is argued, the Entrance Hall was provided. In this case the column centres would have to be about 13 ft. 6 in. (4.11 m.) apart. If we adopt the proportions used elsewhere within the Palace the entablature would come at about 26 ft. (7.9 m.) with the pediment rising to about 42 ft. (12.8 m.). The end columns are shown on the reconstruction as square in section. There can, of course, be no certainty about this, but columns of this type would have facilitated the abutment of the adjacent walls and colonnades. If one accepts the single pedimented front of monumental proportions it is difficult to see how the body of the hall could have been roofed at two heights: it is far simpler to suppose that the entire area was spanned in one, in which case the height of the eaves, approximately equivalent to that of the entablature at about 26 ft. (7.9 m.), would have allowed ample height for lunettes in the side walls to provide light, obviating the need for clear-stories above the piers. The function of the piers would therefore have been simply to act as supports for the rafters.

Several internal treatments are possible but the most acceptable would have been for the piers to support an entablature serving as a frame for two side arcades springing between the piers in a manner similar to the treatment of the Great Bath at Bath (Cunliffe, 1969, fig. 40). This would have allowed the nave to be provided with a ceiling at a greater height than the two side aisles had such an arrangement been considered visually desirable. Lighting would have offered no problem since the structural isolation of the hall allowed windows to be set in the north, west and south walls. A large lunette in the west end-wall would have had the additional advantage of providing a focus of interest in an otherwise gaunt but impressive shell.

The function of the Hall poses even more problems. It has been suggested that it served a storage purpose, being close to the service road and internally of apparently unprepossessing decoration, but now that the plan of the palace is better known it seems unlikely that a store-building would be placed in such isolation and so far from the servants' quarters and kitchen areas. Furthermore, the sheer magnitude of the structure makes it more suited to higher things. The roughness of the pier bases need no longer worry us for, as we have seen, they are likely to have been incorporated in arcading which would have been plastered and elaborately painted. The quality of the building, then, is determined by the magnitude of its architecture not by its internal decoration. Two possible uses suggest themselves, either for public assembly or for worship. Without more evidence it is impossible to go further.

THE ENTRANCE HALL   (figs. 31–33, p. 211, and pl. XXIX)

The Entrance Hall lies in the centre of the East Wing. Its function was simply to provide access from the outside world to the garden, from where all other parts of the palace could be reached. Structurally it can be divided into three elements: the Hall itself, the rows of chambers flanking its north and south sides, and the colonnades across the east and west approaches.

Description of the remains

The main Hall measures 44 ft. (13.4 m.) across by nearly 100 ft. (30 m.) long and is divided into two entrance bays and a central area, 44 ft. by 65 ft. (13.4 × 19.8 m.), by two north–south walls. Of these the western wall is sufficiently well preserved to show that originally it served as a sleeper foundation supporting the bases of two piers. Although all trace of the superstructure has long since disappeared, there can be little doubt that the piers supported a triple-arched opening consisting of a wide central arch and narrower, and therefore correspondingly lower, side arches. The function of the feature was thus to provide a perforated screen wall to divide the main Hall from the western entrance bay (pl. xxix*a*). A similar foundation, which crossed the eastern side of the Hall, was no doubt originally treated in the same fashion but extensive robbing has removed all trace of superstructure to well below floor-level.

The western entrance bay opened through the main west wall of the building on to the flanking colonnade. The nature of the opening is difficult to reconstruct, but the absence of pier bases corresponding to those on the eastern foundation, and the existence of a short length of standing masonry in the south-west corner (pl. xxix*c*), strongly suggest that the opening was trabeated. This would imply a lintel 30 ft. (9.1 m.) long, but with suitable structural relieving arches above there would have been no inherent difficulty in constructing such an arrangement. The unusually wide opening was necessitated by the construction of a rectangular pool in the entrance bay, overlapping the western foundation. It was so placed as to force the pedestrian, coming from the Hall and wishing to pass through to the garden, to deviate either to the north or south.

The pool was constructed on a foundation of pitched rubble laid at the same time as the surrounding floor make-up (pl. xxix*b*). Internally it measured 8 ft. 6 in. by 11 ft. (2.6 × 3.6 m.) and was surrounded by a 3-ft. (0.9-m.) wide ledge of pink mortar raised 9 in. (0.23 m.) from the base of the pool, and lined inside and out with a coating of a similar pink mortar. The exposed vertical surfaces were neatly finished and painted red, but the horizontal surfaces both of the ledge and the floor of the pool were rough, suggesting that the lining, perhaps of marble, had at some stage been removed. It may be that the slabs of re-used marble found in the Third-Period cold plunge bath in the East Wing had come from the pool (p. 177). They would have fitted well and pink mortar from an earlier structure still adhered to them, but there can be no proof of their original position. Even in its mutilated state it was still possible to trace the positions of the inlet and outfall leading to and from the pool (fig. 31). The trench for the inlet was only 5–6 in. (*c*. 0.15 m.) across, implying that a lead pipe had been used. Although its exact line could not be fully traced, it seems that the pipe passed through the concrete footing of the stylobate and in all probability joined with the inner ceramic ring-main which served the fountains in the northern half of the garden. The trench for the outfall pipe was large enough to take a ceramic pipe. From its direction it would appear to have emptied into the main gutter of the garden.

Of the eastern entrance bay little is known, but in broad terms the architecture is likely to have been closely similar to that of the western bay. Excavation was not possible in the central area and it cannot therefore be said whether a pool occurred here, but in all probability the bay would have been left unencumbered. For the Entrance Hall to function

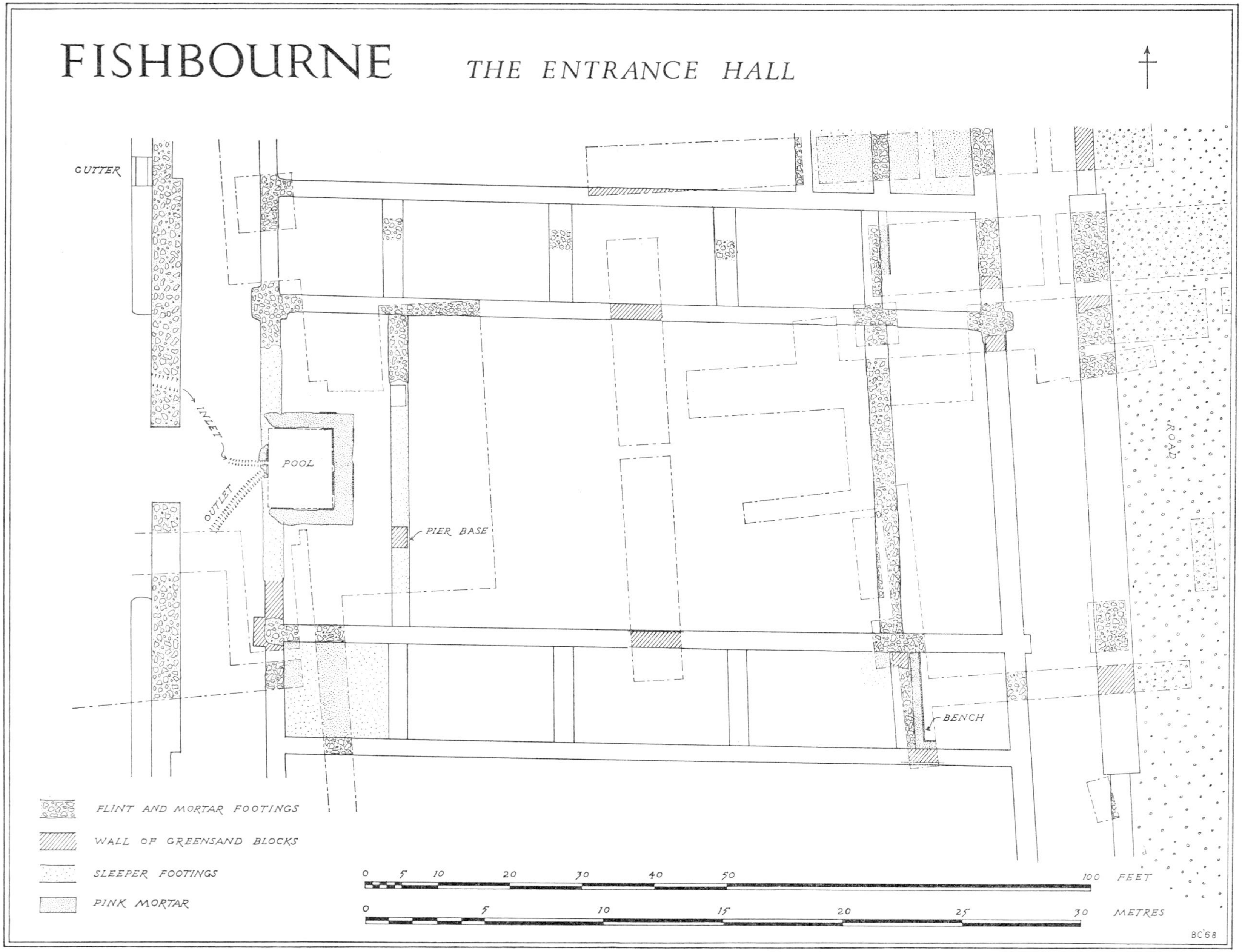

FISHBOURNE   THE ENTRANCE HALL

ROAD

BENCH

PIER BASE

POOL

INLET

OUTLET

GUTTER

FLINT AND MORTAR FOOTINGS

WALL OF GREENSAND BLOCKS

SLEEPER FOOTINGS

PINK MORTAR

BC68

FEET
METRES

0   5   10   20   30   40   50   100
0   5   10   15   20   25   30

FIG. 31

efficiently visitors would have needed to be ushered quickly into the main Hall: any large ornamental feature in the eastern bay would only have impeded their progress.

The Hall was flanked along the north and south sides by long narrow units once thought to be corridors, but now known to have been divided, each into five rooms, three opening off the central Hall and one off each of the entrance bays. Very little has been left of the superstructure and even where ashlar masonry has escaped robbing it nowhere survives high enough to give an indication of the architectural treatment above floor-level. Nevertheless, as we will see below, certain possible reconstructions emerge when the Hall is considered as a structural unit (p. 115). The two small rooms flanking the eastern bay were both provided with a narrow masonry bench attached to the walls and rendered in pink mortar. It is tempting to think of them as rooms for porters or guards; their position would suit them admirably for such a function and the palace must have been provided with accommodation of this kind. Of the other rooms, two on the south side had floors of pink mortar and it may well be that the others were originally floored in this way. Unfortunately late Roman and more recent disturbance has removed all evidence.

Along the west front of the main structure of the Hall was a colonnade, represented now by a footing of flint rubble which once supported a stylobate fronted by a trench for a gutter. The colonnade was continuous along the full length of the East Wing, but at the point opposite the Entrance Hall the footing, here of flints set in yellowish mortar, widened out to a width of 4 ft. (1.2 m.); in the middle was a gap 11 ft. (3.35 m.) wide on the centre axis opposite the pool. The trench for the gutter could be traced, but it terminated well clear of the central line giving unimpeded access from the Hall to the garden. The structural significance of this plan will be considered below (p. 115).

The eastern side of the wing was treated in a similar fashion. Here the foundation widened out to a width of 4 ft. (1.2 m.) opposite the Hall, but the central point could not be examined by excavation and extensive robbing has removed all but a few patches of ashlar masonry to well below the contemporary floor-levels.

Although considerable later wear has destroyed large areas of the original floor-surface, patches of cream mortar 2–4 in. (c. 0.1 m.) thick survive in both verandas showing that the floors were probably unadorned. While it remains a possibility that the mortar served as the bedding for marble, flags or tiles, the areas examined show none of the impressions which would be expected if slabs had been inset. Indeed in some places the surface of the mortar had been carefully smoothed to provide an even, sealed surface.

Reconstruction of the superstructure (figs. 32–3)

Any discussion of superstructure must begin with a consideration of the western façade erected on the 4 ft. (1.2 m.) wide masonry foundation which divides the Hall from the garden. Since the foundation is physically and visually continuous with the colonnade surrounding the garden, it is reasonable to assume that this central element also incorporated columns, for any other treatment would have appeared incongruous. Similarly, it may be argued that a position of such importance would have been treated more grandly than the flanking colonnades, with larger columns and presumably a pedimented front. The arrangement of the foundation and of the structure of the Hall behind leaves little doubt that the

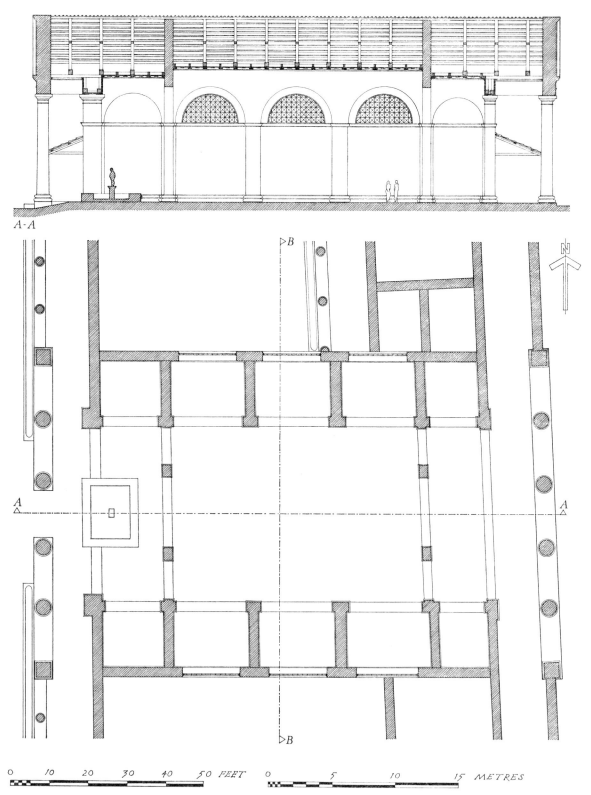

A-A

B

A   A

B

0   10   20   30   40   50 FEET   0   5   10   15 METRES

Fig. 32.   Reconstruction plan and section of the Entrance Hall (by N. J. Sunter)

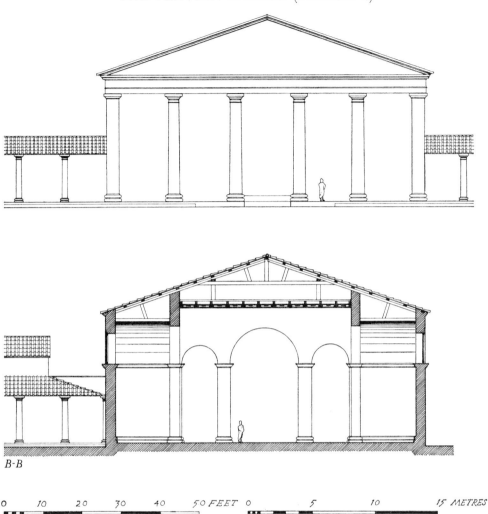

FIG. 33.   Reconstruction section and elevation of the Entrance Hall (by N. J. Sunter)

façade was hexastyle with columns based at approximately 15 ft. (4.6 m.) centres. The recon-struction plan shows how well such a system fits the known ground-plan. If we adopt the proportions evident elsewhere in the palace, the height of the entablature in such a case would be at approximately 26 ft. (7.9 m.) above which the only acceptable treatment would be a pedimented front rising to an apex at about 47 ft. (14.3 m.).

The implication which follows is that the mass of the Hall must have been incorporated behind the front. The most satisfactory way of doing this would have been to enclose both the Hall and its flanking ranges of rooms beneath a single roof in the manner shown in fig. 33. Such an arrangement creates problems of lighting, for in so large a unit side lighting would have been essential in addition to the light which could have penetrated the east and west openings. The problem is neatly overcome by assuming that the side rooms were open to the Hall and that their external walls were perforated by large lunettes (fig. 32). Thus from within the Hall the visual impression gained would have been of a rectangular unit, enclosed by regular side arcades with the ends partially screened by walls broken by large central openings flanked with smaller side arches, tending to emphasize the main east–west axis. Beyond the arcades on all sides would have been brightly lit areas inviting visitors to explore the incomplete and enticing views which the architect had constructed.

Roofing the Hall offers few problems. It is most unlikely that the central area was vaulted, since to cover the span a vaulted ceiling would have been too high to fit behind the façade. Moreover the foundations of the side walls are of the normal width and depth, far too insubstantial to take the weight and thrust of a vault, however lightly built. We can therefore confidently suggest that the Hall was roofed with a timber ceiling which may have been coffered to break the monotony of so large an area. The treatment of the side rooms is less certain: vaulting or coffering would have been equally acceptable and there is no evidence to suggest which was employed. If vaulted, each would have had a north–south vault supported on the side walls to allow space for sufficiently large lunettes in the external walls. It may be that their side walls were also perforated with arched openings allowing east–west circulation, but the point is beyond proof.

The treatment of the eastern façade was probably identical to the western. The known foundations would have allowed this and the need for an imposing entrance viewed from the outside world, would have demanded it. Since no structural problems arise we may safely assume a bilateral symmetry about a north–south axis, as well as the east–west axis.

While it is possible to say much about the superstructure of the Hall, the quality of its internal decoration must remain largely unknown. A few fragments of evidence, however, survive. A small quantity of marble inlay was found in rubble deposits in front of the western colonnade, but this may have been dumped here at any time during the late Roman period, as could the marble cornice moulding found in the Hall (Vol. II, fig. 8, no. 9).

Painted wall plaster was rare, except in the eastern room of the north side of the Hall where a large fallen slab was found. It depicted a panel of magenta-red ornamented with an internal frame line, next to a wide yellow band streaked with green, beyond which was an area of greyish-white. The piece presumably comes from the panelling of the wall above a dado, unless it is supposed that the greyish-white represented the dado (Vol. II, p. 76).

The reason for the survival of so little decorative material is no doubt that the Hall remained in use throughout the period of occupation, and even after its tiled roof had fallen, traffic continued to pass, grinding the tiles smooth. So much activity with so little concern for the structure would have allowed widespread dilapidation, during which marble surfaces may have been removed while the painted plaster peeled off and was trampled underfoot. The problems of later re-use are considered in detail below (pp. 182–3).

THE PERISTYLES   (fig. 34, p. 211, and pls. XXX–XXXI)

Between the Aisled Hall and the Entrance Hall are two colonnaded courtyards backed by a range of eleven rooms along their eastern side.

The northern courtyard consisted originally of a stylobate, supporting a colonnade, enclosing three sides of a large courtyard (pl. XXX) the fourth side of which was closed by a blank wall. The stylobate, constructed of large Bembridge limestone blocks, is fairly complete along its southern side and many of the individual blocks of the eastern side are still in position, preserved largely by the later re-use of the area (pp. 172 ff.). The corner block in the south-east corner still bears the mark of a cross and a T-shape carved on the upper surface as guide-marks for the builders who were erecting the columns. Fortunately, several fragments of capitals were found in rubble layers, showing that the size of the columns, and therefore presumably their spacing, was identical with those of the colonnade surrounding the main garden. As the reconstruction plan will show, the standard spacing fits the courtyard satisfactorily. On the garden side of the stylobate it was possible to trace the trench in which the gutter had been laid (pl. xxx). Two gutter blocks survived in position in the south-east corner, but since both had lost their inner flanges it is not impossible that they had been relaid in this position sometime during the period when the courtyard and its colonnades were turned into a bath suite. In the north-east corner, however, the original corner gutter block survived, cut with a channel leading from its corner to the mouth of a drain which lay below the corner stylobate block (pl. xxxic). Elsewhere along the north side of the courtyard, the gutter robber trench was packed with broken fragments of gutter blocks which remained after the complete stones had been removed for re-use elsewhere.

The slope of the gutter was such that rain-water collecting in it ran to the north-east corner and was emptied into a tile-built drain 1 ft. (0.3 m.) wide and about 2 ft. (0.6 m.) deep, constructed beneath the veranda floor. The drain passed through the eastern wall of the building and would then have run beneath the road, emptying into the ditch beyond, but all trace of it in this area has been removed by robbing (pl. xxxi). The drain had, in fact, to dispose of all surface water accumulating in the northern half of the palace, for, as will be described later, the gutter from the garden connected with it (p. 122).

The southern courtyard was closely similar in structure to the northern court, except that its colonnade flanked only the north and east sides. Excavation here has not been extensive, but sufficient was uncovered to show that the stylobate and gutter had been largely removed; only one stylobate block was found in position.

In both courtyards there had been so much destruction in the later Roman times that garden features of the earlier period seem to have been obliterated. Nevertheless it must be assumed that these courtyards, like the main central garden, were laid out with bushes and shrubs, and perhaps with climbing plants trained to grow up the blank walls. There is no evidence of a water-supply to suggest the presence of fountains, but a large semi-circular basin of Purbeck marble (Vol. II, fig. 21) was found in the robber trench for the south gutter in the northern courtyard, and another basin in the same stone, once supported on legs, was recovered together with other architectural fragments from the Third-Period well dug in the south-east corner of the southern courtyard (Vol. II, fig. 22, no. 4). Neither basin need necessarily have been used in the respective courts but the possibility remains that they were.

The verandas have suffered much from continued use, to such an extent that their original floors have been completely removed. On analogy with other parts of the building, however, they are likely to have been floored only with cream-coloured mortar.

THE RANGE OF ROOMS (fig. 34, p. 211)

Between the peristyles and the eastern limit of the building lay a range 27 ft. (8.2 m.) wide by 132 ft. (40.2 m.) long, containing eleven rooms. All that now survives are the flint footings of the walls and the clay and rubble make-up for the floors, with the exception of rooms E 10 and E 11 where the original pink mortar floors are still in an excellent state of preservation. The original nature of the other floors is completely unknown, but small fragments of a broken-up black and white mosaic in room E 6 may indicate that one, if not all of the rooms, was once mosaic-floored.

The positions of the doorways is similarly uncertain, but on the reconstruction (fig. 34) an attempt has been made to interpret the plan in terms of a functioning unit by suggesting likely door positions. The plan divides neatly into blocks, each consisting of one large and two small rooms which, it is suggested, were interconnected and served perhaps as individual suites. If so, there would be two suites belonging to the north courtyard and one to the south. This would leave unassigned room E 7 which might however have been considered as an integral part of the southern suite. Room E 8 is evidently a corridor joining the southern courtyard to the eastern corridor. Access at this point was needed, but it seems unnecessary to suppose that there were many doors opening eastwards. One would also have been required to provide a way through to the north courtyard, but this would have been sufficient. The intention of the architect who planned this area was clearly to provide private courtyards with rooms opening off; too many links with the service corridor would have ruined the effect.

Reconstruction of the superstructure

The nature of the superstructure is fairly easy to reconstruct on the basis of the known plan. The colonnades are of the same proportions as those found around the main garden, where it can be shown that the columns rise to a height of approximately 12 ft. (3.66 m.). Since the adjacent rooms would have required light, a height of about 20 ft. (6.1 m.) to the eaves would seem to be a reasonable estimate to allow room for a clear-story above the highest part of the adjacent veranda roof.

There would have been no problem in roofing the range with a simple continuous ridged roof, but slight difficulties occur at either end where the roof would have joined the Aisled Hall and the Entrance Hall. Had the ridge continued to butt up to these structures, part of the roof would have obscured the lunettes with which the buildings are thought to have been provided. The simplest solution is to assume that the main ridge terminated on gable ends based on the wall north of rooms E 1 and E 2, and the wall south of room E 9. Rooms E 10 and E 11 and the corridor on the north side of rooms E 1 and E 2 could then have been covered by a single pitched roof similar to the veranda roofs.

The corridor which runs along the east side of the range was probably roofed in a manner similar to the internal verandas, though it cannot be decided whether the roof was supported on a colonnade, a balustrade or simply a blank wall pierced by windows. Since no stylobate and no fragments of columns have been found, a blank wall seems to be the most likely explanation. Moreover a large quantity of plain wall plaster was found lying in the rubble on the external road; this too suggests a wall, for it is difficult to see how else it could have got there. A wall of this kind would also have had the advantage of giving a little more privacy to the neighbouring rooms.

Very little painted wall plaster survived except for a few fragments of green, red and yellow from room E 2, and large areas of plain red and white from the rubble lying on the adjacent road-surface which had fallen, presumably from the external face of the eastern wall (Vol. II, p. 78).

THE BATH SUITE AND ADJACENT AREAS

The least known part of the East Wing is the bath suite and its adjacent courtyard, which began life in the first period as part of the proto-palace and was incorporated, in a modified state, into the south end of the wing. For purposes of description, it is easier to consider the southernmost block of rooms first and then to return to the area between it and the Entrance Hall.

Some comments have already been offered concerning the state of the baths in the First Period (pp. 61 ff.); here it is necessary only to consider the nature of the Second-Period alterations. It will be seen from the plan (fig. 34) that the main rooms were contained within a square block measuring 58 ft. by 59 ft. (17.6 × 18 m.) externally. The three northern rooms, nos. 10–12, seem to have continued in use as hot rooms unchanged from their Period 1 state, unless their decoration (above, pp. 66 ff.) dated to the later period. The corridor (no. 13), and the cold room with its tiled floor (no. 14) again remained much as they had previously been. The main alteration came in the areas of the rooms 15 and 16, where the dividing wall was demolished and a new floor of pink mortar was laid on a foundation of pitched stone rubble. The effect was to create a large square room off which all the others opened.

To the north of the main block room 9 seems to have continued in use as a heated room, but what happened beyond is far from clear. It has been suggested above (p. 63) that a large plunge bath existed in Period 1 surrounded by a mortar-lined bench, but it must be admitted that even if this explanation is correct there is absolutely no proof of the date at which the bath was inserted — it could just as easily be of Period 2 date built in the shell of a Period 1 room. The problem cannot be resolved on the evidence available.

On the north side of the main road, however, the picture is a little clearer, for here two of the old veranda walls along the west side of the courtyard were demolished. The western wall must have been destroyed to give space for the construction of the new colonnade while the eastern wall was demolished to the new floor-level but was for the most part preserved below it. This left one of the old walls to serve as the limiting wall of the wing, and it was against this that the new west wall of the northern part of the wing abutted. At one point a large foundation pit had been dug up against the old wall and filled with a solid masonry footing composed of courses of greensand lumps set in a pink mortar. The lower courses of the demolished eastern wall were incorporated in it. The foundation has been traced so far as excavation was possible, but the proximity of the modern road has made further examination out of the question. In the main, the road and sidewalk are so low that the concrete foundation is likely to have been totally destroyed.

The eastern range of the Period 1 building is less well understood, but there seems to have been no major change when the Flavian palace was butted up to it, except that the floor-levels were all raised and at one point a new floor of pink mortar was laid. In the absence of further evidence we can only suppose that the range of rooms and its two flanking corridors

K

continued to be used much the same as before. The only major change was that the eastern-most corridor was possibly terminated halfway along its length on a new cross-wall, the southern part of the corridor apparently now being demolished. Functionally then, the northern part of the old proto-palace continued in use as a courtyard surrounded by colonnades, a range of rooms to the east and an eastern flanking corridor. In fact the arrange-ment was identical to that on the north side of the Entrance Hall, and we are forced to conclude that this part of the new palace was modelled on the old to give the wing a sem-blance of symmetry about the centre line.

Between the old palace and the Entrance Hall was a slightly wedge-shaped piece of land delineated on the west by a length of wall, continuous with the front wall of the Entrance Hall, which butted neatly against the old work to the south. Its eastern side was closed by a range of three rooms, reproducing in general form the arrangement on the north side of the Hall and linking with the rooms in the old proto-palace. If the ground plan looks a little awkward, the visual effect would have been a happy blend of new and old. Of the rooms themselves, there is little to be said. Excavation has been minimal but there appear to be three rooms, nos. E 12–14, of which the southernmost is presumably a linking corridor. The treatment of the open space to the west of the range is uncertain, largely because much of the contemporary surface has been destroyed by recent levelling, but the possibility remains that it was laid out as a narrow colonnaded courtyard with a colonnade along its southern and eastern sides similar to the courtyard on the north side of the Entrance Hall. Such a treatment would have retained the symmetry which was evidently so important to the planners, but proof will never be forthcoming.

It would be unwise to attempt a detailed reconstruction of the wing south of the Entrance Hall in view of what little is yet known of its plan. However, certain general points are clear. The courtyard and the adjacent range of rooms are likely to have been roofed in much the same way as the areas north of the Entrance Hall, and the easternmost veranda was probably identical in appearance to its continuation further north. Much less is known of the baths, to the south, but they were probably roofed with a combination of vaults and pitched roofs in much the same way as they would have been in the earlier period. The possibility that a new east-facing façade was added cannot be ruled out. Visually some form of balancing structure was needed to act as an equivalent to the imposing mass of the Aisled Hall.

THE FORMAL GARDEN

The wings of the palace, just described, enclosed an area of 258 ft. (78.4 m.) by 320 ft. (97.6 m.) which was laid out as a formal garden. The features incorporated into the design can be divided into: (a) the colonnades, (b) the floral arrangement and paths, (c) the water supply, and (d) the garden furniture.

THE COLONNADES   (figs. 35–38, p. 211, and pls. XXXII–XXXIV)

In general terms it can be said that the garden was totally enclosed by colonnaded verandas, on the west side the colonnade being based on the 5 ft.-high (1.52 m.) retaining wall which ran in front of the West Wing, while on the other three sides the columns were

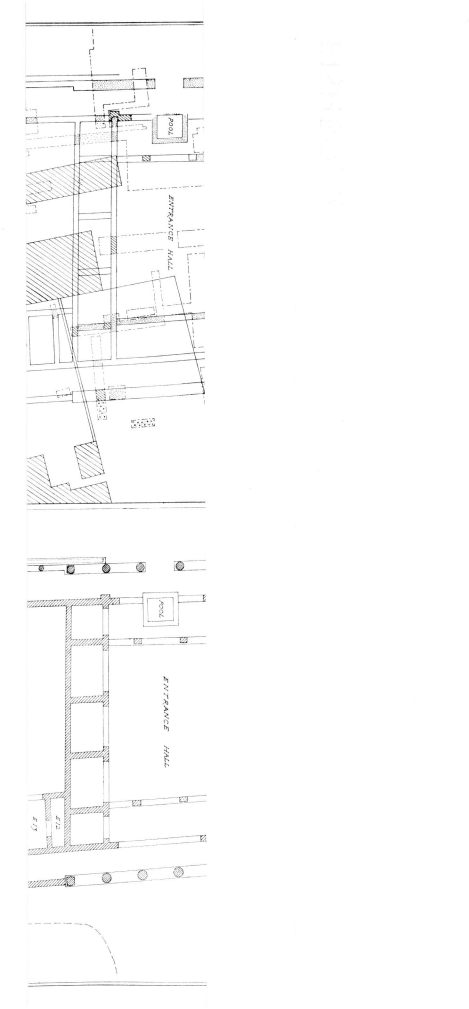

supported on a ground-level stylobate. The regularity of the arrangement was broken only in the centre of the East and West Wings, where larger columns and pedimented fronts focussed attention on the two principal points on the main axis. The top levels of the West Wing wall (pl. XXXIII) have been completely destroyed, but in all probability a stylobate of normal type capped the top of the revetting wall and served as a base for the columns. On the north, east and presumably south sides of the garden a rubble foundation marked the position of the ground-level stylobate which had been almost entirely removed late in the Roman period (pl. XXXIV). Along the north side the foundation consisted of a trench-built footing 2 ft. (o.6 m.) wide and 2 ft. 6 in. (o.76 m.) deep, constructed of greensand and chalk blocks; the eastern foundation was of flints set in a creamy-yellow mortar (pl. XXXIV). In the north-west corner the stylobate survived in position for a length of 45 ft. 6 in. (13.8 m.). It consisted of blocks of Bembridge limestone 15 in. (o.4 m.) thick and varying in their other dimensions, but always with their front faces aligned in a straight and regular line.

Of extreme importance was the fact that in this corner three column bases survived in position on the stylobate (pl. XXXII) providing the only certain evidence of column spacing from the entire excavation. Moreover, in the rubble lying around fragments of the caps were also recovered. From these remains it is possible to deduce that the columns were erected at 11 ft. 9 in. (3.6 m.) centres and that the normal height was approximately 12 ft. (3.96 m.). As shown above, these general proportions can be applied to the colonnades in other parts of the palace and fit comfortably with the dimensions dictated by the ground-plan. The fact that the West Wing veranda floor was some 5 ft. (1.5 m.) above the adjacent North Wing veranda created slight difficulty with the arrangements of the roof lines at this point. The problem was however overcome by making the westernmost column of the north colonnade of greater diameter than the others and therefore proportionally higher. This implies, as the illustration (fig. 35), demonstrates that the roof of the northern colonnade rose in two steps to meet the western columns, in this way providing sufficient head-room to allow a flight of steps between the two levels. It would have been necessary, at two points, to attach the architrave to the drum of a column, but this could easily have been accomplished by means of brackets and is by no means unusual in Roman architecture. It may be thought that the appearance of the junction would have been rather unsightly, but it should be remembered that the corner was partly masked by a water tank (p. 129) and by a tree (p. 127).

Although the excavation has been extensive no fragments of masonry entablature belonging to the colonnade have been recovered. Had one existed some fragments would surely have been found. In all probability therefore, it was of timber. So, too, would have been the structure upon which the tiled roof of the veranda was based. When it is remembered that the total length of the colonnade around the garden approximated to 1,200 ft. (366 m.) some idea is obtained of the vast quantities of timber and tiles which would have been required.

Apart from the gaps opposite the Entrance Hall and the Audience Chamber, the entire colonnade was originally fronted with a ground-level gutter of large stone blocks up to 5 ft. (1.5 m.) in length, hollowed out on their upper surfaces to form a continuous channel. The slope of the gutter was so arranged that the rain-water from the northern half of the courtyard gravitated to the north-east corner, where it was collected in a tile-built drain (pl. XXXIVa)

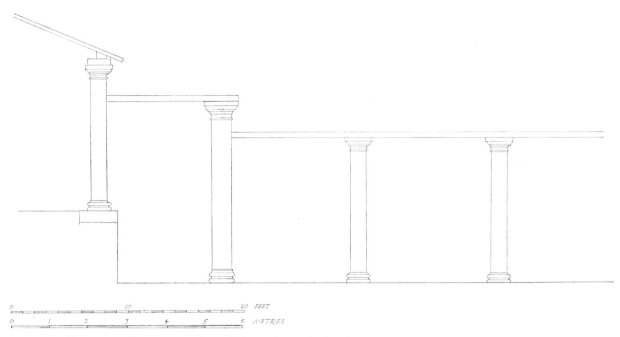

FIG. 35.   Reconstruction of the colonnade in the north-west corner of the garden

and led beneath the veranda floor into the open gutter in the northern courtyard of the East Wing, and from here it passed through a deeper tile-built drain below the rest of the wing, eventually emptying into the stream. The rain-water collected in the two courtyards in the North Wing as well as that from the southern courtyard of the East Wing also emptied into the garden gutter through small link drains beneath the veranda floors. Thus almost all the rain falling on the roofs of the north half of the palace would have drained through the single opening leading from the East Wing. The southern half of the garden and building would probably have been drained in a similar way, presumably with the water collecting in the south-east corner and passing from here, by means of a subterranean drain, to the sea.

For the efficient functioning of so delicate a system, it was necessary for the slope of the gutters and the capacity of the drains to be calculated with the utmost accuracy. Fortunately, sufficient survives to show that from the centre of the West Wing to the north-west corner of the garden there was a fall from 19.40 ft. (5.803 m.) to 18.63 ft. (5.505 m.), from here to the drain in the north-east corner the fall was 18.63 ft. (5.505 m.) to 16.84 ft. (4.902 m.), and from the centre of the East Wing to this point it was from 17.38 ft. (5.194 m.) to 16.83 ft. (4.902 m.). Clearly, then, the water would have flowed, but not too rapidly. The sub-floor drains are not well-preserved, but all seem to have been built in a similar fashion with roof tiles, flanges uppermost, used as a base, each overlapping the next so that the water would flow freely. The walls of the drains were built of coursed greensand blocks and courses of roof tiles set in clay (pl. XXXI). No trace of covering survived, but roof tiles or bricks would have been satisfactory. Capacities cannot be given with precision largely because the upper courses of the drains may well have been removed, but knowing the width of each and the maximum surviving height of their sides certain comparative figures can be offered. The drains from the North Wing courtyards and the southern East Wing court were only 60 sq. in. (0.42 sq. m.) in cross-section, presumably because the volume of water passing through them was relatively slight. That leading from the north-east corner of the garden was at least 150 sq. in. (1 sq. m.) reflecting the larger volume of water, whilst the final stretch of drain beneath the East Wing which had to take all the surface run-off was in the order of 240 sq. in. (1.5 sq. m.) across. Clearly, the engineers had considered the problem carefully.

The inner walls of the colonnades were originally plastered and painted, but with the exception of a quantity of painted plaster from the west end of the north colonnade little now survives. At the west end, however, the walls were painted with a white dado splashed with red and yellow. The top was marked by a wide band of deep red. The area above was also painted white but was divided into a series of rectangular panels by bands of red. Within each panel was set a simple diamond-shape delineated by bands of graded yellow or sometimes of pale green. The painting differs noticeably from the internal decor of the rooms in that it is predominantly light-toned, no doubt to reflect the light. The very simple and unobtrusive design was evidently chosen so as not to detract from the strong vertical emphasis of the columns, seen when the colonnade was viewed from the garden (Vol. II, pp. 72 ff.).

THE PATHS, BEDDING TRENCHES AND OTHER GARDEN FEATURES
(fig. 38, p. 211, and pls. XXXV–XL)

The entire area of the garden was an artificial platform created by removing the natural clay and gravel from the western part of the site and dumping it over the low-lying eastern part. The surface resulting from such an extensive levelling was therefore bare clay with patches of gravel in which practically nothing would have grown well. It seems that at this stage the plan of the arrangement to be taken by the hedges and shrubs was marked out by means of trenches, 9–12 in. (0.2–0.3 m.) wide and up to 2 ft. (0.6 m.) deep, which were then filled with the grey silty top-soil from a stockpile, created before the levelling began, mixed with crushed chalk in order to counteract the acidity of the local conditions. We must suppose that the shrubs were then planted while their bedding trenches could still be seen, and finally the areas to be turfed or planted were covered by a layer of soil 1 ft. (0.3 m.) thick, brought right up to the bushes and therefore sealing the bedding trenches.

It was because these elaborate preparations were made that so much of the garden plan survived and was recoverable by excavation. In practice, however, certain difficulties were encountered. In the first place, while the bedding trenches over the western part of the site were extremely well-preserved by virtue of the fact that they had been cut into clean clay and were buried below a build-up of rubble and plough-soil, those of the central and eastern areas were more difficult to trace, partly because medieval and recent ploughing had disturbed all but the bottom 6 in. (0.15 m.) or so of the slots and partly because, in the eastern area in particular, the trenches had been cut into redeposited clays and silts, closely similar to the natural soil with which they were filled. Nevertheless most of the original plan still survived and was recovered. In practice the technique of excavation was to remove mechanically the accumulation of plough-soil to 6 in. (0.15 m.) above the level of the garden and then to excavate to the surface of the Roman top-soil by hand. When the areas of soil had been cleaned and examined they were removed, leaving frequent temporary vertical sections and horizontal surfaces to be checked for discolorations or other disturbances caused by human or plant activity. In this way work proceeded until the underlying clay was reached, at which stage the plans of the bedding trenches became apparent. When these had been planned and photographed, the filling of each trench was carefully removed leaving longitudinal and cross sections for reference. Finally, all temporary sections were removed. Because of the unique character of the remains, certain precautions were taken. Instead of collecting samples and sending them to experts for analysis it was possible to persuade a soil scientist, Miss Rose Finey, and a botanist, Mr J. Greig, to excavate parts of the garden themselves and collect their own samples, thereby gaining a deeper knowledge of the environment. It was also decided to leave certain areas of the bedding trenches un-disturbed for future excavations.

The general plan of the garden can be seen clearly in fig. 38 and there is no need to give a general description, but certain points of detail need emphasis. The main feature of the arrangement was a 40-ft. (12.2-m.) wide central pathway running the full width of the garden from the Entrance Hall in the East Wing to the Audience Chamber in the West (pl. xxxv). The north façade, which has been completely excavated, incorporates an alternate arrangement of rectangular and semi-circular recesses delineated by two parallel bedding trenches, except for the first and last semi-circles which were outlined by only a single trench. Between adjacent recesses the façade had been widened to contain three bedding trenches. A careful examination of the area within each recess failed to trace any evidence of plant-roots, with the exception of the easternmost recess where two shallow bedding pits were recovered (pl. xxxvia), suggesting perhaps the presence of shrubs or small trees, a feature which was evidently not repeated elsewhere. Very little of the southern façade lay within the area available for excavation, most of it being beneath modern gardens, but sufficient of the eastern end of the façade was examined to show that it repeated almost exactly the plan of the northern side (pl. xxxviia). A limited trial excavation in the garden of no. 74 Fishbourne Road also encountered the north-west corner of the southern façade in its expected position. Such regularity has allowed the luxury of reconstructing on paper, albeit tentatively, the missing section.

In front of the West and North Wings ran a pathway 14 ft. (4.3 m.) wide, branching from the main path close to the Audience Chamber (pl. xxxix). It was enclosed by continuous bedding trenches, three rows on the west and north and two on the east and south On both sides of the western path the rows closest to the path were indented at regular intervals to create ornamental niches to enliven the view. The north path was treated in this way along its northern side, but the south boundary trenches were generally continuous and straight.

The problem of the plants which originally grew in the bedding trenches will be discussed later, but for the time being we may reasonably assume them to have been bushes of some kind, forming a hedge. The plan of the bedding trenches therefore implies paths lined with rows of bushes. How high the bushes grew or how they were trained, whether they were cut into animals or letters or quite plainly, remain a matter of uncertainty, but along the West Wing it was noticed that the bedding trench closest to the wall was deeper than the others and the outermost trench was the shallowest, a fact which may imply that the hedges increased in height the closer they were to the wall. This accords well with Pliny's description of his Tuscan garden,[1] in which he describes a boundary wall hidden by rows of bushes of increasing height. As if to emphasize the point, the external face of the West Wing wall at Fishbourne was plastered and painted with a dark-green background against which boldly-drawn foliage is shown, painted in varying shades of green. Clearly, the intention here was to camouflage the wall so that even if it was glimpsed behind the bushes it would not detract from the feeling of the garden.

The treatment of the eastern side of the garden differed slightly from the north and west. Against the gutter three rows of bedding trenches were laid out, but while the northern part of the façade was indented in a manner similar to that employed elsewhere, the southern length consisted simply of three parallel trenches (pl. XLa). A further difference was that the inner and middle trenches were filled not with the grey marled loam but with black occupation material. There are various possible explanations for this, the most likely being that the inner trenches were planted with shrubs which demanded a richer type of soil, such as roses. Another, less likely explanation, is that these trenches were dug out and refilled at a later date, but this seems to be an unnecessary complication. If a climbing plant, such as a rose, had in fact been grown here it would have provided a context for the post-holes which occur rather sporadically along the façade, for some type of timber structure might well have been provided to support them.

In front of the bedding trenches just described was a pathway 8 ft. (2.4 m.) wide, linking the east end of the north path with the central path, close to the Entrance Hall. Unlike the other paths, its garden (i.e. western) side was not delineated by bedding trenches of the normal kind. But careful excavation showed that the Roman top-soil started on a straight line and that parallel to its edge were several discontinuous bedding slots of V-shaped section, 5 in. (0.14 m.) wide and cut to a depth of 4–5 in. (c. 0.15 m.) into the underlying clay make-up. Evidently some type of shallow-rooted bedding plant had been grown here, but of what species we cannot now be certain.

The eastern front was enlivened by a further decorative element represented now by a row of holes, 18–24 in. (0.46–0.6 m.) in diameter, laid out on a straight line, 14 ft. (4.3 m.) from the edge of the path, each hole being 7 ft. (2.1 m.) from the next. The holes ran the full length of the eastern side (pl. XXXVIIb) and at the north-west corner the line turned at right-angles, running west for a distance of 40 ft. (12.2 m.) along the northern path. Two types of hole were represented: one, evidently a post-hole, was packed with greensand blocks around a void which would have once taken a post some 5 in. (0.15 m.) in diameter, the others were more irregular, 12 in. (0.3 m.) deep and filled with black soil, presumably to serve as bedding pits for trees or shrubs. The two types have been differentiated on the plan (fig. 38), where it will be seen that the bedding pits occurred alternately with the post-holes, but only along the southern half of the line, the break coming at a point corresponding exactly with the change in layout of the bedding trenches flanking the east side of the path. The explanation of these facts would seem to be that some form of rustic timber framework stood along the east side of the garden, punctuated towards the central path with trees arranged alternately with the posts. The arrangement is remarkably similar to one in Pliny's Tuscan

[1] Pliny, *Letters*, Book v, letter 6.

Garden, where he says there was a row of 'fruit trees alternating with posts, giving an impression of rural simplicity in surroundings of otherwise studied formality'.[1] It may be that slighter climbing plants grew around the more northern of the posts, but no trace of bedding trenches or pits survives with the exception of a continuous bedding trench 10 in. (0.25 m.) deep which lay in front of part of the northern row. The overall effect would have been to create a façade of foliage becoming denser, and perhaps higher, towards the central path, where it suddenly gave way to a clear view of the front of the Entrance Hall. This western façade would have been backed and emphasized by another, based on the bedding trenches against the east colonnade where, as we have seen above, there is some evidence to suggest that bushes gave way to climbing plants as the central path was approached. There can be little doubt therefore that the garden was carefully planned to emphasize and display the surrounding architecture and that the principal planned views were from the centre of the West Wing, looking east.

So far, only the northern half of the garden, where it has been possible to carry out excavation on a large scale, has been considered. The southern half is largely inaccessible, but from what little evidence is available it would seem that the arrangement of this area corresponded closely to the northern half. Trial trenches across the east side of the garden have discovered bedding trenches of the same type as those found to the north of the central path and there is good evidence to suggest that a continuous façade existed along the southern side of the central path, but further than this it is not possible to go. Trial trenches in the south-east corner of the garden, dug as close as possible to the modern main road, failed to trace features similar to those found on the north side of the garden; instead they brought to light a 10 ft. (3 m.) wide gravel path with a post-hole on either side. Unfortunately, it cannot yet be said to what date these features belong; the path was laid over a layer of turf and therefore might well be later than the original garden.

At the south-east corner of the central path, where the south bedding trenches end and the east trenches begin, several post-holes were found, evidently originally supporting some kind of rustic gate leading to the southern part of the garden. Each post was packed with a number of limestone blocks, almost all of which were derived from the Corinthian capitals described below (Vol. ii, pp. 11 ff.). Although it is impossible to say that the posts were definitely erected at the time when the main garden was laid out, rather than at a later date, the general plan makes it likely that they were part of the primary concept and thus date to the early Flavian period. That other fragments from the same capitals were found in bedding trenches in front of the North Wing adds support to the view.

At the west end of the central path, on the centre-line, immediately in front of the Audience Chamber, a masonry base, $4\frac{1}{2}$ ft. square (1.37 m.) was found. It was built of roof tiles and was infilled with boulders of stone and fragments of tile laid in yellow clay (fig. 36). The external face was rendered with pink mortar. At a later date an additional skin of roof tiles set in pink mortar was added externally, with a projection extending to the west. From its central position there can be little doubt that the base belongs to the initial plan of the garden and must have supported an ornamental feature of some kind, such as a basin or more likely a statue. No positive evidence of either survives.

[1] Pliny, *Letters*, Book v, letter 6.

In an equivalent position at the east end of the path a circular pit was found, measuring about 4 ft. (1.2 m.) in diameter and 3 ft. (1 m.) deep, and filled with a fine, slightly stony, soil. If the pit is contemporary with the construction of the garden, as its central position would suggest, it must have supported an upstanding feature of some kind — possibly a tree or shrub — to provide a focus for the view along the path from the west.

From the above description it will be seen that the garden was divided into two halves, each surrounded by paths and bedding trenches. The areas enclosed were large, but how they were laid out remains uncertain. It is known that they were originally covered with a layer of soil 12 in. (0.3 m.) or so thick, but in spite of extensive excavation no trace of large-scale planting was found; in fact only one bedding pit was discovered towards the western side of the north half. It measured 2½ ft. (0.76 m.) across by 2 ft. (0.6 m.) deep and was

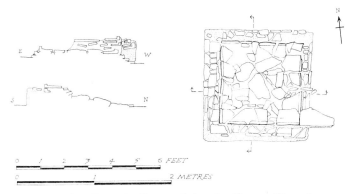

Fig. 36. Base in front of the Audience Chamber

filled with grey loam similar to the bedding trenches. That only one bedding pit should survive and be easily recognizable strongly suggests that no others ever existed. What manner of plant the bedding pit supported remains completely unknown, but some kind of solitary tree would seem to be most likely, matched perhaps by one similarly placed in the southern half of the garden. The surrounding areas could have been treated in one or two ways: either sown with grass or planted with shrubs to form a wilderness of the type shown on the wall painting in the famous Garden Room of Livia at the Prima Porta. On balance, the first possibility would appear to be more likely, partly because of the lack of bedding pits which the shrubs would surely have required, but mainly because a wilderness would have obscured the view of the east façade, over which so much trouble had been taken.

Another tree probably stood in the extreme north-west corner of the garden close to the water tank (p. 129) at the end of the row of bedding trenches fronting the West Wing. At this point, excavation disclosed a large pit, 5 ft. by 7 ft. (1.5 × 2.1 m.) dug to an irregular bottom at a depth of 4 ft. 6 in. (1.4 m.) below the contemporary surface. The bottom of the pit had been filled with a layer of builders' rubble, presumably to aid drainage, sealed by a 3-ft. (0.9-m.) thick layer of turf which merged with turf sealing the adjacent bedding trenches overlapping the foundation off-set of the tank. The bottom of the pit was broken by fissures and holes which could well have been formed by the penetration of roots, but in the soft wet clay they were distorted by pressure from the weight of soil above. It seems, therefore, that the pit was dug when the garden was laid out, probably to take a tree, the function of which would have been to mask the tank and the rather clumsy line of the veranda roof behind. A tree in this position, matched by the one in the south-west corner, would have given a pleasing emphasis to the limits of the West Wing when viewed from the Entrance Hall, and would thus have provided added visual significance to the central approach to the Audience Chamber.

Samples of soil collected from various parts of the garden were examined by Mr Grieg in the hope of finding Roman pollen from the flowers and shrubs preserved. As was expected, however, the relatively dry soil conditions were such that most of the pollen had been destroyed by aerobic bacteria, but Mr Grieg's report (Vol. II, pp. 372 ff.) lists a few species whose pollen was either produced in very large quantities or was resistant to decay. They include heather, hawkweed, and daisy. In fact only the weeds of cultivation survived, the pollen from the flowering plants having completely rotted. The reasons for this are discussed below (Vol. II, p. 375). To reconstruct the garden, therefore, we have to rely upon three classes of indirect evidence: a consideration of the Fishbourne soil, contemporary descriptions of Roman gardens and contemporary wall paintings.

It has already been stated that for the most part the bedding trenches at Fishbourne were filled with a loam which had been carefully marled to create slightly alkaline conditions, the implication surely being that they were prepared for a lime-loving plant. Moreover, the manner in which the trenches were laid out strongly suggests that we are dealing with a hedging shrub of some kind. Now Pliny, describing the gardens of his Laurentine and Tuscan villas, constantly refers to hedges of box used to border his pathways,[1] and since box would grow well in the alkaline conditions created at Fishbourne, we may tentatively suggest its use here. Box is known to have grown wild in Britain before the Conquest, and its occurrence on Roman sites is well attested. The rich occupation soil used to fill the trenches along the East Wing, together with the presence of posts, presumably for lattice work, suggest the growth here of a different type of plant, quite possibly a climbing rose. There can be no doubt, judging by the Elder Pliny's comments and by wall paintings from Herculaneum[2] and indeed from Fishbourne that roses were popular in sunlit positions such as this, but unfortunately no firm proof is forthcoming to show that roses were grown at Fishbourne. Uncertainty also attaches to the type of trees which were planted in a line across the eastern side of the garden, but again Pliny mentions the presence of fruit trees in a similar position in his Tuscan villa,[3] and certainly the posts with which they alternated at Fishbourne imply that the trees were trained — a treatment suitable for fruit trees. At any event we cannot doubt that in such a visually significant position the trees would presumably have been chosen largely for their flowering quality.

Of the other plants with which the garden would have been adorned, there is little to be said. It seems likely from the archaeological traces that bedding plants lined the western side of the east path, and it may be that flowering plants of some kind were used to infill the strips between the hedges. A wide choice would have been available to the gardeners but in the absence of any decisive evidence at Fishbourne further discussion would be groundless.

[1] Pliny, *Letters*, Book V, letter 6.
[2] Bajardi, *Le pitture antiche di Ercolano*, vol. 2, 131.
[3] Pliny, *Letters*, Book V, letter 6.

THE WATER SUPPLY   (figs. 37 and 38, pls. XXXVIII, XLI)

The garden in its heyday was supplied with piped water which would have served orna-mental basins and fountains set around the pathways. Some doubt still attaches to the source of the water, but in all probability it was drawn from the spring which lies to the north-east of the building, near the present pond. It would have been necessary to pump it to the top of a water-tower to provide a sufficient head to feed by gravity the collection tank sited in the north-west corner of the garden. How the water was conveyed between these two points is still partly uncertain. Over the initial stretch of low-lying land an aqueduct supported on piers would have been required leading to the centre of the North Wing, where the water was fed into a ground-level culvert. No evidence of the supposed aqueduct has been found but the culvert was traced as far as the north-west corner of the wing (fig. 37). It was built of a base of flanged roof tiles with the sides constructed of broken roof tiles set in yellow clay, with traces of pink mortar rendering still surviving (pl. XLIa). Much of the structure had been destroyed when the trench for the water main was dug in 1960, but substantial parts survived for study. The nature of the culvert along the west side of the wing is largely un-known because of later building activity and destruction, but a short length of masonry built of tiles set in pink mortar with a well-built eastern face survived, barely 1 ft. (0.3 m.) from, and parallel to, the end wall of the wing. The implication is that the culvert here incorporated the main structural wall as its eastern side. Before the south-west corner of the wing was reached, the system had changed to a 4-in. (0.1-m.) bore ceramic water-pipe bedded in clay which led across the corner of the West Wing, cutting somewhat roughly through the masonry, and then passed beneath the steps to the collection tank (pl. XLIc). The tank itself has now vanished, but its masonry substructure still survives, consisting of a wall 18 in. (0.46 m.) thick enclosing three sides of a square measuring 10 ft. (3 m.) across; the fourth side is the West Wing revetting wall against which the structure abuts. In so far as the building sequence is concerned, it is clear that the stylobate, gutters and colonnade were erected before the construction of the tank, for its walls would have once passed across the gutter blocks, presumably by means of a small arch, and butted against the first column of the north colonnade (pl. XXXVIIIb). But it is equally apparent that the tank was thought of as part of the initial layout of the palace, partly because the surface of the column against which the tank foundation impinged was only roughly finished, and partly because the turf of the Roman garden sealed the foundation offset of the wall. The nature of the tank itself cannot now be assessed; it may have been of masonry, but is more likely to have been of timber, lined perhaps, with lead. It would have served two functions, acting both as a distribution point for the water supplied to the various parts of the garden and as a settlement tank for sediment which might otherwise have clogged the buried mains.

Three water-pipes led from the tank (pl. XXXVIII), one passing along the north side of the north path and turning at the north-east corner to run along the east path, a second along the west side of the west path, and a third (the first part of which has not been fully traced) along the centre of the north and east paths, gradually converging on the eastern bedding trenches south of the central path. As originally laid, the main consisted of ceramic pipes 18 in. (0.46 m.) long, socketed together with the joints sealed by a fine white mortar. They were laid in shallow trenches cut into the natural clay, but along the eastern part of

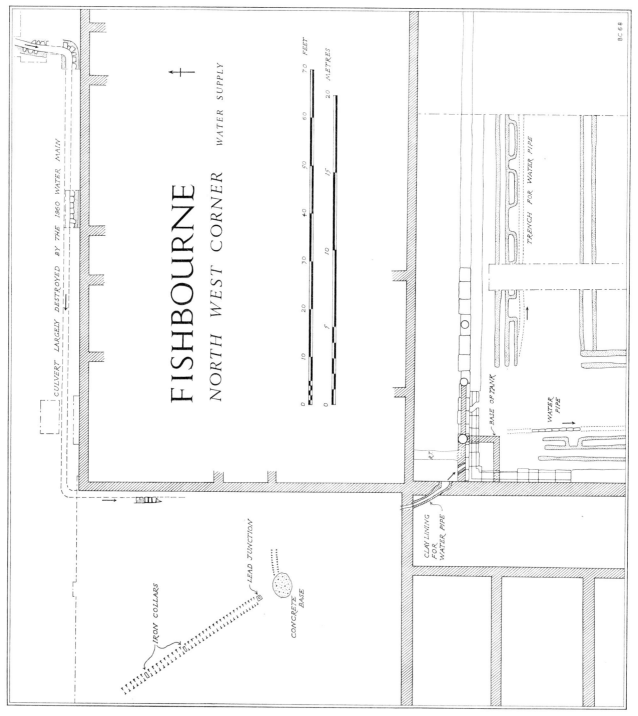

FISHBOURNE
NORTH WEST CORNER   WATER SUPPLY

FIG. 37

the site, when the natural was buried below layers of make-up, the pipes were packed around with clay to ensure that they remained water-tight.

The function of the system was to provide water under pressure for a series of basins or fountains which would have been placed against the inner hedgerows. No basins survive in position and since they would have required no foundation it is impossible to locate precisely their original positions. One possibility is that they were placed in the recesses in the hedges, but of this there is no proof. The reason why the basins were aligned against the inner hedgerow was to facilitate the removal of waste water, which must have drained into the open gutter in front of the colonnade. Most of the pipes belonging to the innermost mains serving the west, north and northern half of the east paths were removed in late Roman times, with the exception of short lengths in the north-east and north-west corners and isolated pipes elsewhere along the line. Even so, it is possible to show that the western main ran across the front of the Audience Chamber and therefore presumably served basins along the entire western front. Similarly, the northern main would have functioned along the entire north path and the northern half of the east side, but by the time the pipe reached the central path its pressure would have been spent. Therefore to provide water for the basins of the southern half of the east path, and probably for those on the south path as well, a separate main was constructed running, untapped from the tank, along the north and east paths to take up its position against the hedge south of the central path. From here on it would have provided water for the basins. That the pipe was, over most of its length, untapped is clearly demonstrated by a length of more than 100 ft. (30 m.) which still survives in position, embedded in the eastern path.

At the north-east corner both the inner and outer mains were joined to short lengths of pipe which led towards the stylobate gutter, the length from the inner main running beneath the line of the outer. The only reasonable explanation would seem to be that these off-shoots provided the means by which the northern part of the circuit could be drained if necessary. This would have been an advantage at times when the pipes needed to be cleaned out or when the fountains were turned off and drained.

In all, there would have been more than 1,500 ft. (460 m.) of ceramic water-pipes used in the garden. That is approximately 1,000 single pipes, each of which was carefully laid to the correct gradient. That such an enormous and costly piece of work was ever undertaken emphasizes the importance which must have been attached to the provision of fountains in the garden. The word 'fountains' has been used to imply a structure by which water was made to spurt into the air. At Fishbourne the fountains could never have been very elaborate, but the 4-in. (0.10-m.) bore pipe with a 4 ft. (1.2 m.) head of water behind it could have made a moderate show: if the outlet was narrow the water might have gushed 3 or 4 ft. (1–1.2 m.) into the air. It is unfortunate that nothing of the actual mechanism survives at Fishbourne, nor are we even able to say how many fountains were provided along each main. All that remains are fragments of four ornamental marble basins into which the fountains may once have played (Vol. II, pp. 37 ff.).

THE SOUTHERN GARDEN

Although the work carried out in the garden of no. 69 Fishbourne Road was sufficient to demonstrate the presence of a southern garden overlooked by the South Wing, it was not until April 1969 that the full extent of the terrace became apparent (fig. 39). It must, however, be stated at the outset that the examination of this area is far from complete. At the time of writing (May 1969) new discoveries are currently being made and while the general structure of the problem is now clear much detailed work remains to be done. For this reason it is proposed here merely to summarize the main features of the site and to leave detailed description and a consideration of the material for a separate volume, to be produced when the work has been completed.

Immediately south of the South Wing and bath suite an artificial terrace extended for a distance of 350 ft. (106 m.) to the sea. It had been created by dumping up to 5 ft. (1.5 m.) of silt, gravel and clay over the original First-Period surface and revetting it along the south side with timber piles, behind which were piled heaps of massive limestone and greensand blocks. The east and west limits of the terrace are currently being examined. A builders' trench, across the line of the supposed west side, has suggested the possibility of a veranda about 10 ft. (3 m.) wide, but the point cannot yet be checked. No excavation has so far been possible across the east side but the contours of the land hereabouts suggest the southward continuation of the easternmost wall of the palace together, perhaps, with its flanking road.

The surface of the terrace bears evidence of landscaping. Towards the centre lay a pond more than 30 ft. (9 m.) across, apparently fed by a copious spring hereabouts. A gully (once thought to be the edge of the terrace) led towards the pond from the north-east, where there may well have been another, somewhat larger, pool extending along the south side of the bath suite, where limited excavation produced evidence of extensive water-lain silts up to 4 ft. (1.2 m.) deep. At one point within this area a square base was found composed of flints set in cream-coloured mortar, which may possibly have taken a free-standing column or statue (fig. 27). Beyond the south-west corner of the central pond a 50 ft. (15 m.) length of ceramic water-pipe was traced running south towards the sea, serving either as a drain for the pool or a separate water supply for fountains. Other features, including minor gullies (? bedding trenches) and a gravel path, were also sectioned.

Finally, a trial trench dug in 1966 in the meadow south of the 'Woolpack' sectioned a well (fig. 51, section 2) which had been constructed in an approximately rectangular pit, 4 ft. 9 in. (1.45 m.) across, dug to a depth of 6 ft. (1.83 m.) below the contemporary surface. The framework consisted of squared re-used timbers, 3 ft. (0.9 m.) long, the ends of each pair overlapping the ends of the pair below. Only the two lowest frames, which were still below the water-table, survived, the upper members having rotted. The well was filled with a uniform grey stony silt containing occasional fragments of tile and pottery of little value for precise dating but of first-century character. That a well could be dug so close to the sea is an interesting comment on the force of the fresh-water springs hereabouts.

The timbers which framed the well were evidently re-used from another structure. Two are well-preserved: one has a tenon projecting from one end but its other end and the ends of the second timber were sawn square when the timbers were being prepared for re-use. In their original context the opposed sides of both were slotted to receive the ends of timbers

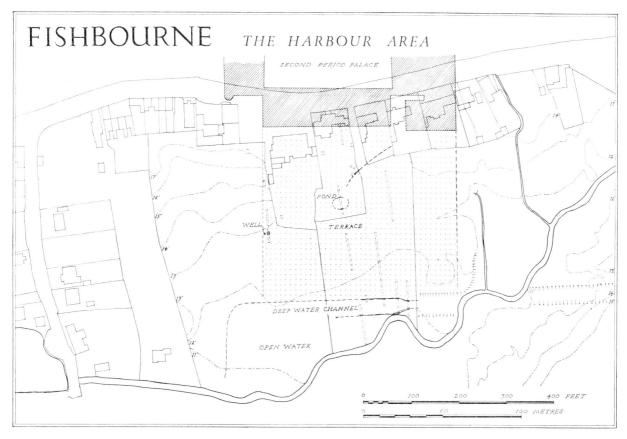

FISHBOURNE   THE HARBOUR AREA

FIG. 39.   Area of the First-Period harbour and the Second-Period
Southern Garden (interim plan)

set at right-angles. On one side the slots were cut with vertical edges, whilst on the other, one end was ramped down so that the tenon of the attached timber could be slid into position. The nature of the structure to which the timbers originally belonged is unknown.

Immediately to the south of the terrace a deep-water channel had been constructed by dredging away up to 2 ft. (0.6 m.) of the natural gravel in a strip 32 ft. (9.75 m.) wide, narrowing at the eastern end to 16 ft. (4.88 m.), thus creating, from the top of the terrace to the bottom of the channel, a vertical interval of 6–7 ft. (*c.* 2 m.). The stratigraphy shows clearly that the area south of the terrace, including the deep-water channel, had been flooded with sea water in the Roman period, which must have lapped close to the surface of the terrace. By what mechanism the water was retained in the basin remains to be examined. At the eastern end of the excavated section of the channel, at the point where it narrowed to 16 ft. (4.88 m.), the southern side as well as the north was revetted with timber and ballast, showing that the large expanse of water was here narrowed to a canalized stream. It is even possible that it was provided with a lock at this point, but extensive excavation will be required before the problem can be solved. The canal has been traced for a distance of at least 1,300 ft. (396 m.) further east. The silt layers in the old canal bed are particularly prolific of occupation material, including animal bones, quantities of pottery, leather and wooden objects. A full report on the material recovered so far must be reserved for the third volume.

From the above brief survey it will be immediately apparent that the South Wing was provided with its own private garden, exceeding in size the formal garden which lay to the north. The evidence so far available shows that it sloped down to a wharf to which boats of considerable size could have sailed. The garden itself seems to have been laid out in an informal way with pools, minor streams, and probably with clumps of trees and shrubs. It formed, in contrast to the northern garden, a completely 'natural' garden with a sea-scape beyond, of the type so popular in Italy at the time.

APPROACHES AND ENVIRONMENT

THE ROADWAY AND THE EASTERN FRONT   (fig. 34, p. 212, pl. XLII)

It has been suggested above that the Entrance Hall was sited so as to make use of the earlier road, which probably led from Chichester to the site. That the early road existed beneath and east of the Hall is proven, but its course beyond the present eastern limit of the site has not been traced. Nevertheless it is a reasonable assumption that it ran towards the east gate of Chichester. The remetalled version of the road broadened considerably when it reached the front of the Entrance Hall, at which point two side roads converged: one from the north, the other from the south, both running along the front of the palace immediately adjacent to its easternmost wall. The roads, some 16 ft. (4.9 m.) wide, were constructed of a clean rammed gravel up to 18 in. (0.46 m.) thick in the centre. For the most part two distinct layers of metalling were recognizable, but since there was no evidence of considerable wear on the lower surface, nor any silt between, no great time-lag could have existed between the deposition of the two layers.

The surface of the side road was slightly cambered in such a way that most of the surface water would have drained off to the east, where a spread of gravel, continuous with the road surface but only 4 in. (0.1 m.) thick, sloped gradually down to a drainage ditch running along its eastern side. At one point on the edge of the camber a soak-away pit, 4 ft. (1.2 m.) square and 3 ft. (0.9 m.) deep, was provided, filled with large blocks of loose rubble and linked, by a trench filled in a similar manner, to the ditch. In periods of exceptionally heavy rainfall the soak-away would have prevented volumes of surface water, flowing off the north road, from flooding the main road in front of the Entrance Hall. Some water would inevitably have drained towards the wall of the palace, and as rain-water from the roof gradually eroded a deeper channel along the base of the wall, the problem would have become worse. This was foreseen by the builders, who adopted the novel procedure of providing two arched openings (pl. XLII*b*) through the foundations of the wall (fig. 34) below ground-level, presumably to prevent pressure from ground-water building up, and on either side of the footing they built a shallow rumble drain filled with greensand blocks (pl. XLII*a*). This would have meant that water accumulating against the wall would have seeped down into the rubble below and that any excess would have drained through the arches into the rubble-packed trench immediately to the west, thus relieving pressure which might otherwise have affected the stability of the footings.

The north side-road has been examined over most of its length and traced to beyond the north-east corner of the building. Functionally it would have provided access from the main road to the Aisled Hall and also to the east–west service road, to which it led. There is no evidence that its line continued beyond this point. The road leading south has not been fully traced, but it has been examined at various points. At the extreme south-east corner of the building where excavation has been reasonably extensive, it could be shown that a layer of gravel metalling spread over the destroyed footings of the proto-palace walls. A little further to the south, the ground had been consolidated at this time with a mass of greensand rubble surfaced with a thin spread of gravel. The indications suggest that a hard standing, projecting out towards the sea, may have been constructed at this point, served by the southern road. Further excavation is required before the area can be fully understood. Trial excavation immediately south of the bath block showed no trace of metalling; indeed layers of silt were found which were clearly deposited under water. This raises the problem of how fuel was transported to the furnaces nearby, but it may be that the faggots were simply carried by hand from the service road along the south side of the building to the flues. There would have been no insuperable difficulties in such an arrangement. The space between the bath block and adjacent building, which had been metalled in the first period when the baths had served the proto-palace, was remetalled in the palace period after a layer of greensand rubble had been laid down to bring the level up to the new floor-level adopted elsewhere at this time. It was in this region that the flues were situated.

THE AREA NORTH OF THE NORTH WING (fig. 15, p. 212)

Trial trenches were dug out at intervals across the area to the north of the North Wing, but no large-scale excavations have been undertaken. The eastern part of the area, which was low-lying and liable to flood, was made up with tips of rubble and clay extending for a distance of some 80 ft. (24 m.) beyond the north wall of the palace. At a distance of 30 ft. (9 m.) lay the south edge of a gravelled road some 20 ft. (6 m.) wide, which runs in an east–west direction, presumably joining the main north–south service road. The east–west road has not been fully traced but it leads to an expanse of gravel metalling extending over the area immediately adjacent to the north-west corner of the wing, close to the ovens. To the north of the road, on the extreme edge of the marsh, another area of gravel and rubble metalling, 15 ft. (4.6 m.) wide, was seen in two of the trenches. Its extent has not been fully traced, but it aligns with the fence found further to the west (described below, p. 138) and indeed a post-hole was found in it. Both facts suggest that it functioned as a fenced boundary to the palace area.

THE NORTH-WEST CORNER OF THE SITE — THE KITCHEN GARDEN, THE OVENS AND THE BOUNDARY FENCE (fig. 40, p. 212, pl. XLIa)

In the angle between the North and West Wings is an open area covered with a 12 in. (0.3 m.) thick layer of black soil devoid of features. The layer had been created by the deposition of occupation refuse over a considerable period of time, but the mixed nature of the layer indicated continuous disturbance. One possibility is that the area functioned as a

L

kitchen garden. The palace must have possessed one and the present area would have been conveniently situated.

The area was served with water drawn from the main aqueduct supplying the garden. At one point a rough base of concrete about 4 ft. (1.2 m.) across was discovered. It was set in a pit cut into the natural clay and must once have supported a basin or tank of some kind. It was linked to the culvert by a pipe, presumably of socketed tiles, for which only the trench now remains. From the base another trench led towards an area of hard-packed greensand make-up, some 55 ft. (16.7 m.) away to the north-west. This pipe was of wood jointed by means of iron collars (Vol. II, p. 128). Two collars were found 10 ft. (3 m.) apart, the third is missing and in place of the fourth was a lead junction consisting of a plate of lead which had been nailed on to the end of the wooden pipe; in the centre was a hole around which had been soldered a vertical circular collar, which would originally have joined to a further length of lead pipe leading from the tank (Vol. II, p. 144). It is not exactly clear how the system functioned, but water was apparently led into an open tank placed on the concrete base, and from here a subsidiary pipe led perhaps to a second tank standing on the base of greensand blocks. If, as we have suggested, the area around functioned as a kitchen garden, the water supply from the first tank would have been very useful, particularly in the height of summer when this part of the site would have dried out rapidly. The function of the second tank is less certain, but it was sited conveniently close to the ovens and may perhaps have been used at some stage in the baking process.

The oven itself is now much mutilated, partly by an old farm ditch and partly by the 1960 water-main trench. The surviving fragments (pl. XLIb) comprise a single foundation built of greensand blocks with occasional tiles at the corners, packed in clay and measuring 17 ft. (5.2 m.) square. The foundation was divided into four by two channels which crossed a little off-centre, the east, west and north arms of the channels being 2 ft. 3 in. (0.69 m.) wide, the south being 4 ft. 6 in. (1.37 m.). The entire structure had been set into a shallow pit, 18 in. (0.46 m.) below the surrounding surface, and all around, particularly within the channels, was a mass of black charcoaly soil mixed with quantities of broken pottery of late first-century date. Since the foundation nowhere survives to a height greater than two courses, it is impossible to say accurately how the superstructure would have looked and functioned. One point, however, is significant: even though the channels were choked with burnt material, there was no sign of scorching on the walls or floors, and therefore the channels cannot have served as flues. One explanation is that they were ventilation channels running beneath the flues. Alternatively they may represent ash-pits for oven rakings. A close parallel to this type of arrangement occurs in the Pompeii bakery in Region I, insula iii, where the oven chamber itself is raised above an ash pit so as to be at a convenient working height (Mau, 1899, figs. 203 and 209). In size and in the provision of a nearby water supply the Fishbourne and Pompeii structures are also similar. In the absence of further evidence we may tentatively suggest that the Fishbourne structure also served as a bread-oven. It would have been large enough to produce loaves on the scale required by a palace of this size.

About 35 ft. (10.7 m.) to the south-west was another oven of simpler form consisting of an oval chamber and short flue constructed of hard-baked clay. It had been set into the clay make-up, but was otherwise undated. The adjacent area has not been extensively excavated and it may be that other ovens survive. The whole area between and around the ovens had

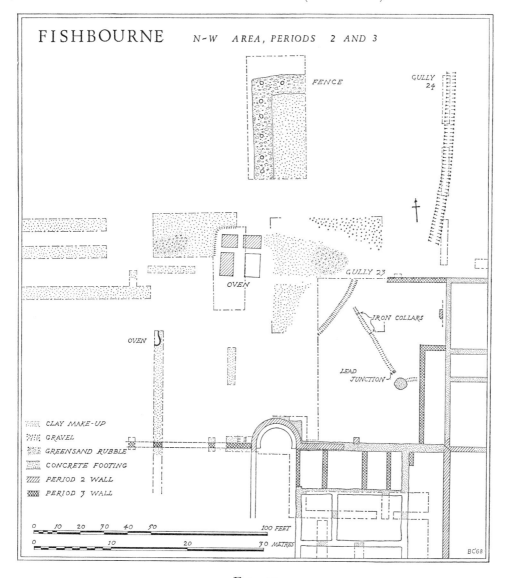

FIG. 40

been raised, in the period when the palace was built, by the deposition of an 18–24 in. (*c.* 0.5 m.) thick layer of clay make-up mixed with greensand blocks. In some areas the green-sand had been packed tightly into the top of the clay to give a hard metalled surface in areas where exceptional wear was expected. One such area seems to have been a path leading towards the large oven from the west. The extent of the make-up is shown on fig. 40. Along all sides it appears gradually to peter out, merging with the surrounding natural surface. No gullies are known to cross it, but a drainage gully which runs along the west side of the West Wing projects a little into the area and this may well be joined by a narrow gully (gully 23) about 15 in. (0.4 m.) wide which runs diagonally across the site, and effectively divides the supposed kitchen-garden area from the hard standing to the east of the oven. A further gully, gully 24, lay to the north. It was 2 ft. (0.6 m.) deep and filled with grey occupation soil containing Flavian pottery.

A problem is posed by the date of the wall which runs west from the apse at the north-west corner of the West Wing. The wall is built of greensand blocks laid in a shallow trench cut into the top of the Second-Period clay make-up and it runs across the drainage gully along the west side of the building. It is therefore structurally later than the initial phase of the Second-Period complex, but it need not be much later and could, in fact, be a southern boundary wall for the working area containing the ovens. It may be significant that its line corresponds approximately with the southern edge of the make-up. A more difficult question is raised by the wall of similar structure which once ran west from the north-west corner of the North Wing. It was represented only by a shallow robber trench which could be traced for about 20 ft. (6 m.) from the corner, beyond which it was totally destroyed by the 1960 water-main as the two converged. How far the wall once ran is unknown, but it may have butted up to the large oven. If contemporary with the palace, it would have formed the northern boundary to the supposed kitchen garden.

Immediately north of the large oven, beneath the site of the public lavatory built in 1969, a total excavation of the area revealed an L-shaped foundation of greensand rubble a foot thick (0.3 m.) tightly packed in a matrix of clay, continuous with a spread of clay make-up defined by the foundation. The foundation was pierced by seven post-holes, each apparently 12 in. (0.3 m.) in diameter and 12–18 in. (0.3–0.46 m.) deep. It would appear that the posts were set up first and the rubble spread and packed around them. The north–south line of six posts aligns with the westernmost wall of the palace, while the east–west line, represented by two posts, lines up exactly with a post set in a similar rubble footing sectioned some distance to the east (fig. 15).

It seems reasonable to suppose that the fence defines the boundary of the palace enclosure, 80 ft. (24.4 m.) north of the North Wing and parallel to it. It can be shown that the make-up spreading north from the wing consistently ended on this line while the gravel service road (fig. 15) lay exactly between the fence and the building. It is possible that the north–south arm of the fence returned south to the apse at the north-west corner of the West Wing, leaving the ovens outside the enclosure. Unfortunately the crucial area has been totally destroyed by a recent farm ditch.

WEST OF THE WEST WING

The area immediately to the west of the West Wing has been trial trenched and can be shown to be without make-up or features, with the exception of a U-shaped drainage gully 2 ft. (0.6 m.) wide and 1 ft. (0.3 m.) deep, which ran immediately outside the west wall of the wing, presumably to carry off rain-water from the roof and empty it into the sea. West of this, the area was open.

In January 1964[1] pieces of greensand were noticed on the spoil-heap of a soak-away which workmen were digging on a building-site, 120 yards west of the West Wing of the palace (fig. 41). An examination of the pit itself showed a thin layer of greensand fragments

[1] This description is contributed by Mr Richard Bradley, who undertook the work of excavation.

overlying the natural clay and part of a robbed wall, with flint and mortar footings. By this stage both houses on this site, now 104 A and B Fishbourne Road, had been built and so the extent of this wall, which ran on a north–south alignment, could not be determined.

It was, however, reported that another wall had been found in alterations to the garden of the adjoining house, 104 Fishbourne Road, and a small area was kindly made available

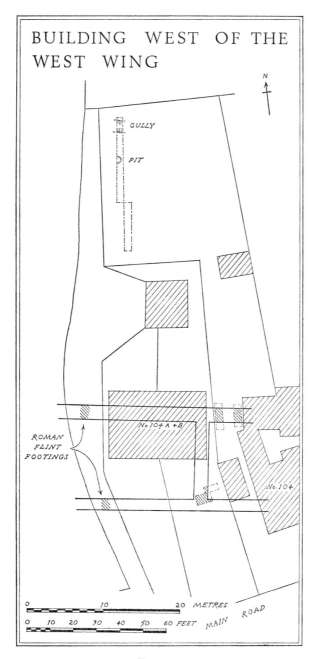

Fig. 41

for excavation.[1] It became clear that the wall in question was of a post-medieval date but overlay a second robber wall running east–west. A further section in the summer of 1964 confirmed the line of this wall and again demonstrated its relationship to a superficial spread of greensand fragments. Though no further excavation was possible at this time, the line of this second wall again appeared sectioned by a mains trench to the west of the new houses. A second wall was briefly observed at the same time running parallel to it, 45 ft. (13.7 m.) to the south, but no dating evidence was obtained.

Finally, in December 1968, it was possible to carry on excavations in the garden of 104 Fishbourne Road,[2] in an area 100 ft. (30 m.) to the north of the 1964 trenches. This work was intended to check the possibility that the three walls recorded might belong to a detached wing of the palace, running parallel to the excavated West Wing. In fact no trace of any major structure was found, though a further superficial spread of greensand fragments was recorded, this time in association with a shallow pit and an undated drainage gully.

Thus a structure can be defined, built in the same material and on the same alignment as the palace. Its northern limit has been roughly defined by the negative results of the 1968 excavation and a sharp fall in the ground below the more southerly east–west wall may give an indication of its overall extent, for though the mains trench could not be fully recorded before it was refilled it showed no obvious traces of terracing. Finally, it may be mentioned that both east–west robber trenches were almost 6 ft. (1.8 m.) in width and may be suggestive of the positions of major load-bearing walls. Unfortunately we do not have the width of the single north–south wall for comparison. Of the extent of the building to east and west we have no information save that it must be in excess of 70 ft. (21 m.).

The discovery raises a series of extremely interesting questions to which, without further evidence, there can be no firm answers. Nevertheless the style of building is so similar to that of the palace that the two may tentatively be assumed to be largely contemporary. It will be evident from the foregoing description of the palace that no traces of servants' quarters, storerooms or workshops have been found on the main site, and yet they must have existed to serve so vast a palace. They are unlikely to have been sited east of the building, for visual reasons, and excavation has shown that they did not lie to the north or south. Therefore the west side would have been the most likely site and it is thus quite possible that the foundations just described are part of such a service wing. Further than this it is not possible to go on the available evidence, but it is to be hoped that such a significant part of the site will one day be excavated on a much larger scale.

THE INTERIOR DECORATION OF THE PALACE

Although the original palace building suffered considerably, first from alterations, then from destruction and robbing and later from ploughing, a remarkable amount of detail of the interior decoration has survived. In the following sections the various types of decorative finishes are discussed. The main problem to be faced is one of dating. The building continued in use for 200 years, during which time many changes were made. In the case of the mosaic floors, the originals can easily be distinguished from those which came later, partly

---

[1] By kind permission of Mrs M. Grey.   [2] By kind permission of Mr R. Gribbon, who also gave valuable assistance in the excavation.

on stratigraphical grounds and partly on stylistic considerations, but the same is not true of the marble, stucco and wall painting, the remains of which were found in the destruction rubble filling the rooms and in the surrounding robber trenches. From contexts such as these they could, in theory, date to any period; indeed there is undisputed evidence that some of the rooms were later repainted. This makes the problems of assigning dates to the wall finishes very difficult. Nevertheless, the quality of the stucco and marble work is such that the only reasonable context for its introduction is in the adornment of the late first-century palace. The status of the building in the succeeding century does not seem to have been sufficiently high to have supported such exotic craftsmanship. The date of the wall painting poses more difficult questions, but these are best considered individually below.

WALL PAINTING   (Vol. ii, pp. 50–82, and figs. 27–35)

The surviving Flavian wall painting has been briefly mentioned in the descriptive sections dealing with each room above, and it is discussed and analysed in more detail in the second volume (pp. 50–82) where all periods of wall painting are considered. Here it is necessary simply to offer some general remarks about the style and quality of the Flavian work.

In general it may be said that the painting was of exceptionally high quality and offers much in common, particularly in the choice of colour, with the Neronian painting of the proto-palace. There are, however, a number of new features which do not appear at the early date. The painting may be divided into three broad styles:

Style 1 consists of walls painted to represent elaborate arrangements of inlaid marble. In all examples a dado is provided, composed either of a single 'marble', the individual 'sheets' being divided by simple vertical lines, or of a series of different, but tonally related, 'marbles' divided by simple 'mouldings'. Often at the base of the dado is a separate skirting. The top of the dado is always marked by a continuous horizontal moulding ranging from carefully-toned examples to simple stylizations.

The treatment of the upper part of the walls can be divided into two variants: (a) panels of plain colour ornamented with simple frame lines in the manner of the Neronian painting; (b) panels meant to represent elaborate marbles set within complex frames composed of fillets of marble. Sometimes these panels are relieved by adjacent panels of plain colour.

Variant (a) is best represented by the simple treatment of the Aisled Hall and the corridor around the western courtyard in the North Wing, while most of the other rooms in the North Wing were decorated as variant (b).

Style 2 is similar to style 1 but the painting is altogether simpler. The dados are usually continuous bands of splashed colour with no vertical divisions and no attempt at depicting mouldings, while the walls above are usually painted white but are divided simply into rectangular panels which might be further decorated with very stylized panels or frame lines. Good examples occur in the corridor flanking the west side of the West Wing and the veranda in front of the North Wing.

Style 3 is by far the most delicate and accomplished. The walls appear to have been painted in an overall plain yellow, upon which are shown small isolated panels, the commonest being of complex bright colours, usually framed within reds of different tones. Simply framed areas of flowers and foliage also occur, the flower painting being of extremely high quality. Occasionally small pictures are included, one of which is a scene showing a villa set against a seascape, brilliantly painted in brown, white and blue in a style identical to that of the famous harbour scene from Stabiae. Painting of this kind was found in the dump of builders' rubble west of the North Wing, but fragments have also been found in room N 5. It is by no means common and it may be that only one or two rooms were decorated in this style.

There can be little doubt that all the internal wall-surfaces and indeed most of the external faces were originally painted. The fragments that survive all belong to one of the above styles. The implication must be that an army of painters were brought to Fishbourne from the continent to carry out the work, and it is therefore hardly surprising that the quality of the Fishbourne work is equal to much of that from the metropolitan areas.

STUCCO WORK   (Vol. II, pp. 50–51, and fig. 26)

Altogether nine fragments of moulded stucco were found, in addition to a quantity of plain-ribbed stucco from the Audience Chamber in the West Wing. Eight of the pieces belong to one moulding, the ninth is of a different type. All were found in the robber trenches around rooms N 2 and N 7 in the North Wing.

The largest surviving pieces (Vol. II, fig. 26, and pl. XVIIa) belong to a moulding which would probably have been placed between the wall and ceiling. It depicts a simple, squared cornice, below which is a repetitive frieze, each element showing two birds holding long-stalked fruit in their beaks and facing a central vase which appears to contain fruit. Each panel is divided from the next by a vertical stalk which splits at its lower end into two branches, each terminating in an acorn. Below the frieze is a narrow continuous panel ornamented with a motif incorporating elongated beads divided by narrow reels.

The second type of stucco moulding is represented now only by a small fragment (Vol. II, fig. 26, no. 2). It had been set into an angle formed in the mortar of the wall and is presumably therefore not part of a more extensive moulding. It consists of a simple egg and dart motif impressed into a fine hard white mortar. A stamp comprising two or more eggs must have been used, because on the surviving fragment a vertical break is apparent along the right-hand dart, the panel to the right being impressed rather more deeply.

MARBLE MOULDINGS AND VENEER   (Vol. II, pp. 16–33, and figs. 8–16)

Marble was used in a variety of ways as internal decoration in the palace, but three basic types can be recognized: (a) mouldings of cornices and other frames, (b) panels with moulded borders and plain or inscribed surfaces, (c) geometric shapes in the form of sheets or strips of stone. The range of stone commonly employed was limited to blue Purbeck marble, a white Phrygian marble, a blue-veined marble, possibly of Italian origin, and a green-veined marble from the Pyrenees. A dull grey shale from the Weald occurred among the plain wall veneer and more rarely were found marbles from Laconia, Skyros, Seravezza and the Haute Garonne (Vol. II, pp. 16 ff.).

Mouldings. A complete list of mouldings from the palace is given below, where the individual pieces are illustrated (Vol. II, figs. 7–10). It will be seen that the mouldings can be divided into three categories based on the type of stone from which they were carved. The most common types are the rather heavy mouldings of Purbeck marble (Vol. II, fig. 9, nos. 15–18). The solidity of some of the pieces and the complete lack of cramp holes to attach them to the wall strongly suggests that the blocks were used vertically, presumably as frames for doors and windows, rather than horizontally as cornices.

The mouldings carved in the white crystalline marble are altogether finer and more precisely cut (Vol. II, fig. 8). At least two of the blocks bear evidence of cramp holes cut and bored to take iron cramps, $\frac{1}{4}$ in. (0.6 cm.) in diameter, and one block ends neatly in a stopped moulding. Here the implication is that the mouldings served as cornices, but whether above doors or windows is unknown.

The third type of stone used for mouldings is the grey-veined white crystalline marble. Only two blocks of this stone are known, both carved with the same carefully constructed cornice mould and both with cramp holes cut into their upper faces. One of the blocks represents the end member of a cornice with its moulding returning across the end, but there is no evidence of stopping. Like the blocks of plain white marble, these would seem to have been used as cornices.

In summary, therefore, it may be suggested that the finer imported marbles served as cornices while the rather duller and cheaper Purbeck marble may have been used only as the vertical members of framing mouldings.

Mouldings of Purbeck marble are more common in Britain than might at first appear. Close parallels to the Fishbourne examples are known from the sites of Silchester, Chichester, Chester, Verulamium, Lincoln, and Colchester, but the only villa so far to produce an example is Angmering.

Moulded panels. A number of fragments of marble panels have been recovered, of which most pieces belong to square or rectangular slabs carved along the outer edges of the exposed face with a simple framing mould. Examples occur in Purbeck marble, white crystalline marble and the green-veined Pyrenean marble. In no case does the centre of the slab survive but in all probability the enclosed area was plain, or like no. 38 was enlivened by concentric moulded bands. A second type of decorated panel was found, represented now by three fragments of Purbeck marble (nos. 27–9), on which the surface decoration consisted of incised V-sectioned lines arranged in a pattern which might originally have represented a square-within-square motif. Unfortunately insufficient survives to be sure. Presumably both types were used as wall inlay.

A rather different form of moulded marble sheet was represented by the two slabs of blue-veined marble re-used in the floor of the Third-Period cold bath in the East Wing. The slabs were carefully finished with their opposed edges moulded with simple beading (Vol. II, pl. VIa). How such a piece could have been arranged to show the two edges is very difficult to understand. It is more likely that one edge was cut first, found to be unsatisfactory, and the slab turned over and a new edge cut, so as not to waste valuable material. The explanation might seem over-elaborate, but it is supported by the fact that one of the edges is certainly of inferior workmanship and appears to be unfinished. The re-use of the slabs in a bath constructed in the early second century is a fair indication of their first-century date. How and where they were used in the original building, however, is not certain but the possibility exists that they may once have edged the pool in the western bay of the Entrance Hall.

A similarly moulded fragment of white crystalline marble was found in the North Wing (no. 36). One of its vertical edges had been chamfered off either to enable an adjacent slab to overlap it or, more likely, to fit a mitred corner. Its original use and position must remain unknown, but the piece could have formed a skirting either to a wall or a recessed panel. An even simpler piece with a domed edge was found nearby.

The only elaborately carved panel (Vol. II, fig. 23, no. 1) to be found came to light in a third-century rubbish deposit to the west of the North Wing. All that now survives of it is a small fragment some 5 in. (c. 0.15 m.) across and $3\frac{1}{2}$ in. (9.0 cm.) thick, carved on its upper surface with two somewhat stylized leaves in positive relief, both bearing a pattern of raised veins. The tip of a third leaf-shaped object survives, but unlike the others it was flat and undecorated, and may indeed not have been a leaf at all. Only one roughly flattened edge survived, the others all being broken. The straight edge was evidently not the side of the panel, which would have been more carefully finished or moulded; more likely it was simply the junction between two slabs implying that the original composition was quite large. The size of the leaves would support this view. Nothing more can be said of the original form or position of the monument of which the fragment once formed a part, but there can be very little doubt from the monumental size and quality of the piece that the structure was of some considerable significance and would have occupied a position of importance within the palace.

Marble inlay. Fragments of marble wall inlay were found scattered over various parts of the site, but two concentrations appeared; one on the floor of room N 10 and in the adjacent robber trenches, the other in front of the west façade of the Entrance Hall. Although the latter group could have been merely a dump of material collected from another part of the site, it is quite clear that the heap of marble fragments in room N 10 lay exactly as they had fallen when the building was burnt down in the late third century, some pieces actually retaining the positions, relative to others, that they had occupied when in position on the wall.

Numerical analysis of the marble from the room is included below (Vol. II, pp. 26–30) and the matter need not be considered in detail here. Suffice it to say that four basic marbles were presented: Purbeck marble and a grey Wealden shale were used mainly as side strips, the Purbeck also acting as area infills, a white crystalline marble was used as narrow edging strips, and green-veined Pyrenean marble appeared in slabs cut to different shapes, principally triangles of various kinds and diamonds as well as long strips. Sufficient survives to enable something to be said of the general pattern which the various elements comprised. It seems that the inlay was generally set flat into the wall surface in a single plane, but some of the white edging strips had a domed upper edge which would have protruded slightly, thus catching the light and giving the appearance of a slight change in relief. However, a few fragments survived of a white marble strip some 3 cm. wide and 1 cm. thick, with a single domed edge. These pieces would evidently have been used only to edge a recessed panel. That they were few in number would suggest that changes in relief rarely occurred; indeed it might be that the entire marble panel was recessed slightly into the wall-surface, the strips being used only as an outer frame. The way in which some of the fragments were lying when found shows that the basic arrangement, in one part at least, consisted of a shape of Pyrenean marble framed by thin edging strips of white marble, the edges of which had been cut diagonally to give a neatly mitred join. Outside the edging strip was a wide strip of grey shale. The effect of such a juxtaposition would have been to emphasize the quality and colour of the central shape by surrounding it with sharply contrasting materials. In broad terms this would seem to have been the general style behind the rest of the design.

The exact form of the original pattern cannot be accurately reconstructed from the surviving pieces, but certain of the motifs of which it was comprised can be isolated. The occurrence of diamond shapes and triangles strongly suggests that one recurrent theme was the diamond set in a square or rectangular framework, thus creating triangular shapes in the corners which would be infilled with a contrasting stone. The same basic theme was emphasized by the long strips of Pyrenean marble cut at such an angle across the end that placed together they, too, would delimit a diamond shape. One of the diamond-shaped elements (Vol. II, fig. 13) also shows that the sharp apices, which would have touched the ends of the enclosing rectangle, were sometimes removed and replaced by inset semi-circles of a different stone. Another pattern, the hexagon with a circle set inside it, was evidently incorporated somewhere in the design, as is shown by the elements of Purbeck marble which would have filled the space between the two shapes. The tangential segments of circles might also have been part of this particular motif.

Many of the individual patterns, which must somehow have been combined to form the total composition, can be paralleled on continental walls and floors.

How widespread marble inlay was in the Flavian palace cannot now be gauged, but the general scatter of fragments over most of the main area of the North Wing suggests that many of the rooms were ornamented with inset panels. The only one which seems to have survived to the late third century, however, was the panel from room N 10 discussed above. The others had presumably been allowed to fall into disrepair or had been deliberately removed and replaced with painted plaster, either because fashions had changed or, more likely, because further supplies of marble for patching were no longer available in the later period. Outside the area of the North Wing, marble inlay was seldom found, with the exception of the small group of pieces, mainly slabs of Purbeck marble, found amid the rubble lying in front of the west façade of the Entrance Hall. It is difficult to see how marble would have been used hereabouts. Conceivably it might have been inset in the pedimented front of the Hall, but the small elements would have been out of place so high up. More likely the pieces were collected from some other position and dumped or dropped here at a later date.

THE MOSAIC FLOORS   (pls. LXXIV–LXXXII)

In the description given above of the component parts of the building, the individual mosaic pavements have been described. Here it is intended to discuss the general style, dating and significance of the floors as a group. Substantial remains of fifteen floors belonging to the Flavian period now survive, but smaller fragments, sometimes only borders, of many others occur, showing that originally most of the rooms would have been mosaic-floored. Stratigraphical and structural considerations leave no doubt that the earliest group of floors were laid in the same period as the erection of the palace and were thus primary. An interesting constructional detail which all have is the single row of large brick tesserae around the outer edge of the floor up against the walls. It is a feature common only to the primary floors and implies that the floors were laid before the walls were plastered, the plaster hiding the edging row.

The materials of which the floors were constructed were limited largely to a hard white chalk and a dark grey stone derived probably from the Weald. Colours were only rarely used: blue was usually of Purbeck marble although the mosaic in room N 20 also incorporated a greyer blue, possibly made of lias limestone; red was usually cut from the silt-stone said to be of Mediterranean origin but brick was used as well; the same silt-stone also provided different tones of yellow and purple, which were only occasionally used. The tesserae were consistently 0.8–1.0 cm. square, with the exception of those used in the Audience Chamber which were between 0.5–0.8 cm. across.

Stylistically the floors form a remarkably homogeneous group quite consistent with the Flavian date proposed for them, but for the purpose of discussion it is better to consider them as two groups: the plain black and white floors and the coloured floors. The black and white floors are typical of those found in Italy and parts of Europe in the first century, both in their general absence of colour and in their choice of motifs. Similarly the overall repetitive patterns shown almost invariably by the Fishbourne floors is a characteristic which became common in the latter part of the first century A.D. in the metropolitan area.[1]

The Black and White Mosaics:

A. Patterns

The general patterns can be divided into five groups:

(a) *squares set in a framework of diagonal lines forming diamond-shapes.* To this group belong the mosaics in rooms ? N 1 (pl. LXXIX), N 3 (pl. LXXVIIa), N 12 (pl LXXVIII) and W 8 (pl. LXXVI), the simplest of these being the one in room N 3 (pl. LXXVIIa) in which the squares are regularly spaced within a simple linear framework. Room W 8 creates a more elaborate appearance by setting one group of squares diagonally to the others and by doubling the width and complexity of the framing pattern, but it still adheres to the same general principle. The mosaic in room N 12, on the other hand, is altogether more elaborate with cross-shaped motifs between the squares and with the framing pattern so arranged as to give the impression of boxes in perspective. The very fragmentary floor in room N 1 does not certainly belong to this group but in general style it is not too out of place here. The limited use of colour (red and blue) as an infilling for squares serves to distinguish it from the other floors in this category. It would be tedious and unnecessary to quote detailed parallels for these floors. The style recurs so frequently among the mosaics of Pompeii that it was evidently the general rule rather than the exception in the late first century. Its popularity continued into the second century: several of the mosaics from Hadrian's villa at Tivoli

---

[1] For extensive surveys of contemporary Italian mosaics see Blake, 1930 and 1936. Because these excellent corpora offer a wide selection of close parallels to the Fishbourne floors, references can be cut to a minimum.

are based on the same general arrangement, and two in particular (Blake, 1936, pl. II, nos. 1 and 2) are close to the Fishbourne floors, nos. N 12 and N 3. Examples are also known north of the Alps, e.g. in the Procurator's Palace in Trier (Parlasca, 1959, Taf. 16.3) and in Gaul, particularly at Nizy-le-Comte (Stern, 1957, no. 49 A, pl. XVII) and Reims (Stern, 1957, no. 37, pl. XV). A close parallel to the room W 8 floor occurs at Besançon (Stern, 1960, no. 297 A).

(b) *squares set alternately within meander patterns*. To this group belong the floors in rooms W 3 (pl. LXXV) and N 13 (pl. LXXXa). Both appear to be simply constructed with squares, some containing a variety of geometric motifs placed diagonally, others a fine meander pattern, set alternately against a background of linking meander designs. The arrangement is common enough, occurring at Trieste, Rome, and Ostia early in the second century, while meanders in different arrangements are well represented at Pompeii. In Gaul, all-over meander pavements of the first and second centuries occur sporadically, e.g. at Bavay (Stern, 1957, no. 121, pl. XLI) and Bous (Stern, 1960, no. 175 B, pl. XV).

(c) *simple repetitive pattern of overlapping rectangles*. The design is easier to illustrate than to describe, but simply stated it is comprised of four overlapping rectangles around a square, all set within a larger square. The arrangement, repeated many times, constitutes the entire floor in room N 19 (pl. LXXXd) and the fragment in room N 22 (pl. LXXXa) may well be of the same type. As might be expected, such a simple arrangement occurred frequently in the Roman world. First-century examples are found at Ostia and Pompeii, it continues in use throughout the second century at Hadrian's villa at Tivoli, and at Ostia, and is found even later at Nyon. The same pattern was used again at Fishbourne in the borders of the floor in room N 12 (pl. LXXVIII).

(d) *chequer-board composed of solid squares of two different sizes*. This type of arrangement survives only in room N 4 (pl. LXXVIIb). Although it is basically very simple, close parallels are not frequent in the rest of the Roman world. To some extent, however, it is similar in feeling, if not in detail, to the coloured floor in floor N 21.

(e) *separate mats depicting chequer-boards alternately black on white and white on black*. This pattern occurs most clearly in room W 6 (pl. LXXIVc) where the 'mat' can be seen in relation to the main decorated panel, most of which has been destroyed. A similar arrangement probably existed in room N 9 (pl. XXIIIa) but only the corner now survives. The pattern is of some particular interest because of its apparent late appearance in Italy. The floors of the so-called Bridge of Caligula, on the Palatine, dated to the Domitianic period, are among the earliest examples known but by the early second century it had become more widespread, occurring in such well-dated contexts as the Markets of Trajan. It would seem, therefore, on present evidence, that the examples at Fishbourne must be regarded as lying towards the beginning of the sequence.

B. *Motifs*

If the overall patterns of the black and white floors at Fishbourne are relatively limited, the individual motifs which they incorporate are various. It is convenient here to discuss them in list form:

(a) *the running scroll.* A running scroll of simple vine leaves occurs twice at Fishbourne, in rooms W 5 (pl. LXXIV*b*) and W 8 (pl. LXXVI), in both cases serving as separate limiting panels outside the main patterned area. The tendrils are simple but the nodes from which they sprout are infilled alternately with red and yellow, enlivening an otherwise dull arrangement. Vine scrolls such as this occur frequently in the Pompeian houses, principally as thresholds, continuing in use in the later period at such sites as Este and Trieste.

(b) *Compass-designed rosettes.* The only floor on which this motif occurs is the mosaic in room N 12 (pl. LXXVIII). The type recurs so frequently from the first century onwards that general comparisons are pointless, but for an extremely close parallel see Pompeii, VII, iv, 31.

(c) *Rosettes of leaves and scrolls.* Two identical examples, found in room N 12 (pl. LXXVIII), come close to being arabesques which were to become so popular in the early second century, particularly among the floors in Hadrian's villa. The extreme corner of the panel surviving in the Audience Chamber may once have contained a rosette of this kind, but too little survives to be sure.

(d) *Triangles placed base to apex.* These occur as the infillings of the cross motifs in room N 12 (pl. LXXVIII) and around the edge of the decorated panel in room W 6 (pl. LXXIV*c*). The arrangement was of widespread popularity from the first to the fourth century.

(e) *Squares diagonally within squares.* This arrangement was used consistently in room W 8 (pl. LXXVI), room N 1 (pl. LXXIX) and recurred several times in room N 12 (pl. LXXVIII). It was extremely popular from the first century onwards.

(f) *Squares arranged concentrically.* These occurred in slightly different forms in rooms N 12 (pl. LXXVIII), N 1 (pl. LXXIX), N 3 (pl. LXXVII*a*) and W 8 (pl. LXXVI). The motif is exceptionally common.

(g) *Four squares overlapping a central square.* This pattern was found only on the mosaic in room N 3 (pl. LXXVII*a*). It cannot be easily paralleled, but it is too simple to be of any dating or stylistic value.

(h) *Crosses infilled in various ways.* These occur only in room N 12 (pl. LXXVIII). The arrangement is by no means common, but on mosaics from Ancona and Rimini guilloche-filled crosses dominate the designs. Both floors are thought to be of second-century date on stylistic grounds. The infilling at Fishbourne is either of solid black bands against white or of triangles arranged base to apex.

(i) *Triangle upside-down within a triangle.* The motif occurs frequently in room W 8 (pl. LXXVI). It has no particular dating significance, being found throughout the Roman period.

The above list includes the major form of decorative motifs found on the black and white floors at Fishbourne. Other motifs were used as infill in the squares between the meanders in rooms W 3 (pl. LXXV) and N 13 (pl. LXXX*c*) but these are either too incomplete or too generalized to be defined.

The Polychrome Mosaics

Although limited colour was used in the predominantly black and white floors in rooms N 1 (pl. LXXIX), W 5 (pl. LXXIVb) and W 8 (pl. LXXVI), only three mosaics can be described as truly polychrome: the geometric mosaic in room N 21 (pl. LXXXII) and the more elaborate floors in the Audience Chamber, room W 14 (pl. XIX) and in room N 20 (pl. LXXXI). All were different in style. Strictly speaking, the small floor in room N 21 (pl. LXXXII) was more akin to the geometric floors elsewhere in the palace and should perhaps be classed in the same category as the floor in room N 1 in which large slabs of red and blue were used against a black and white background. The only difference between the two is that in room N 20 the design was in reverse, i.e. white on black and the structure was simpler. There are no close parallels to this floor.

The mosaic in room N 20 (pls. LXXXI, XXVI, XXVII, XCI) is by far the most interesting in the building, not only because of its colour but also because of its highly advanced design. Basically the arrangement is simple, a circular panel contained within a square with motifs incorporating tendrils filling the corners. Such patterns, while by no means common, are known in Italy in the first century at Cividale, Pompeii and Brescello and in second-century contexts at Hadrian's villa, Ostia, Rome and Bologna.[1] It is the subtle use of colours and the elaborate motifs which serve to distinguish the Fishbourne floor. The spandrel motifs, consisting of fish and dolphins on either side of vases with vine tendrils beneath, are impossible to parallel. The vase and vines recur frequently enough (cf. the Alexandrian mosaic) and the *cantharus* from which vines sprout is found on several thresholds in the Pompeian houses, but the use of fish as well is exceptionally rare. The two-ply guilloche which encloses the circular panel is also an unusual feature, for although the motif was in the repertoire of the late first-century mosaicist, its execution, particularly in graded colour, seems generally to have been avoided — presumably because of the technical difficulties inherent in laying a guilloche attractively and accurately in a circular band (but see Cividale). The Fishbourne floor is one of the few known where the technique was practised. Inside the guilloche came a band of rosettes alternating with vine leaves; parallels are again impossible to find, emphasizing once more the unique quality of the Fishbourne mosaic. It is sad that the entire centre panel had been destroyed in the late Roman period. One wonders what motif the designer would have dared to display against so rich a border. It would need to have been exciting to avoid anti-climax.

If a relatively unimportant room in the North Wing could have had so fine a mosaic, the floor in the Audience Chamber must have been magnificent, but apart from a length of two-ply guilloche and the corner of a panel containing a rosette it has been completely destroyed. The minute tesserae and the skill and care with which they were laid surpasses the technical quality of all the other floors of the building. We must suppose that the artistic quality of the design was also of this high standard.

Sufficient will have been said to show that the Fishbourne mosaics compare in design and quality with the late first-century mosaics of Italy. In no way do they lag behind the metropolitan development and indeed in some respects they incorporate motifs which were just

[1] See Blake, 1930, pls. 38, 39, 41, and Blake, 1936, pls. 13, 14, 18.

becoming fashionable in Rome itself. We must therefore conclude that the floors were laid by immigrant craftsmen thoroughly conversant with the most up-to-date developments at home, and of sufficient skill to construct floors indistinguishable from Italian examples.

SUMMARY AND DISCUSSION

The description of the Second-Period remains, given above, is sufficient to show that from about A.D. 75 until about A.D. 100 a palace existed at Fishbourne, covering an area of about 10 acres (at least 16 acres if it is correct to assume that the remains found to the west are the servants' quarters of the palace). It was constructed in the form of a hollow square with four ranges of rooms enclosing a large central garden. The detailed arrangements of the plan leave little doubt that the architect thought of the building in terms of its function, distinguishing carefully between the official and semi-public areas and the private ranges where perhaps visitors and the owner may have lived. In the East Wing the public regions were the Entrance Hall and possibly the Aisled Hall, together with the linking corridor which fronted the street. Once through the Entrance Hall the visitor would have seen in front of him the garden with the West Wing spread out on its higher terrace behind. Both elements were clearly part of the public areas, and both were laid out visually and functionally in one, linking with the Entrance Hall. The central pathway from the Hall to the Audience Chamber would have been the communicating axis of the plan but there was nothing to prevent the visitor from wandering at will in the garden or strolling in its enclosing colonnades. The West Wing was similarly at his disposal and having once climbed the steps in front of the Audience Chamber he would have been able to enter any of the adjacent rooms which opened on to the flanking colonnade.

The North Wing, on the other hand, was planned with a view to creating a series of private environments based on small colonnaded courtyards, cut off from the main building except for small communicating doors. Visually the wing hid behind the colonnade which fronted its southern side, and to a visitor in the garden all that could be seen were the clear-stories and gables of the building beyond. The same thinking was evidently behind the planning of the rooms in the East Wing, lying between the two public halls, and possibly also that part between the Entrance Hall and the baths to the south. But instead of large suites of rooms with their own courtyards, such as occur in the North Wing, the rooms of the East Wing were divided into smaller suites which would have shared larger communal courtyards.

Although very little is known of the South Wing, it is possible to show that it, too, was cut off from the main building and evidently faced south across its own private terrace to the sea beyond. The bath suite lay conveniently close at hand. Without a doubt, from a residential point of view, the wing would have been the most attractive in the whole palace and for this reason it is not impossible that it was occupied by the owner of the building as his private accommodation.

It would seem, therefore, that the palace divided naturally into three parts: the official public part, residential units perhaps for visitors, and a private range for the owner. To this we must add a kitchen and servants' range, lying somewhere to the west out of sight, presumably with separate access along the north side of the palace from the western service road.

If the emphasis of the residential quarters was on quiet inturned luxury based on the inward-looking peristyle of traditional Roman building, the character of the public areas was of monumentality and contrived vistas, clearly designed in the newest Hellenistic style to impress. The parallels are not with the domestic architecture of Pompeii or the Gaulish towns such as Vaison (Sautel, 1954), nor with the larger countryside villas of Gaul like Chiragan (Grenier, 1934, 832–7) or Le Jardin de Grassi (Benoit, 1947 and Rolland, 1958), even though, with their large garden peristyles, they are close in size to Fishbourne. The real similarities lie with the palaces of the Emperors in Rome, and particularly with Domitian's palace (MacDonald, 1965). The three basic architectural elements, the Audience Chamber, the Entrance Hall and the Aisled Hall, were all planned in what would have been considered to be a racy modern style, even in Rome itself. The Entrance Hall, for example, was huge and no one entering it for the first time could have failed to be overawed by its sheer volume or excited by the prospects glimpsed through its arcades.[1] In some ways it even resembled the Octagon Room in Nero's Domus Aurea (Boëthius, 1960) with its cunning suggestion of unexplored spaces opening off all around. But the eye was forced to the central axis, first by a wide central arch and then by a pool immediately beyond — a homely touch reminiscent of the *impluvium* in the Roman house of the old style — for the visitor was meant to look across the hedge-lined path through the centre of the garden to the façade of the Audience Chamber beyond, a towering structure so arranged that it would always be seen outlined against the sky. The approaches were brilliantly planned, whether consciously or subconsciously, to have a most forceful psychological effect on a visitor walking towards the Audience Chamber. As he stepped out from the Entrance Hall the first overwhelming impression would have been of space and loneliness, for suddenly he would be in a vast garden, the building having receded almost out of his span of vision — except for the centre of the West Wing. The low hedges would only have increased the feeling of space. And then would have come the long walk across the garden closed in on both sides by hedges, each recess seeming from a distance to provide a turning off, only to prove to be a blind end when one came level with it. Gradually the front of the Audience Chamber would have come closer, appearing as a dark opening behind a colonnade. Then the steps would have to be mounted and finally the visitor would have to enter the Hall itself. It may be that the psychological implications of the plan have been over-emphasized, but it is extremely difficult to believe that the architect was not trying to impress and disarm the visitor by creating strong visual contrasts and a sense of loneliness which in some could have caused near-panic.

The Audience Chamber itself was a masterpiece of design with a high vaulted roof painted in bright blues and purples, and an apsidal recess covered by a semi-dome in the far wall. MacDonald has described in vivid terms how a similar hall in the palace of Domitian was designed to show the Emperor sitting in state in the recess, covered by a soaring vault like a god with only the heavens above (MacDonald, 1965, 56–63). Some such feeling must have been in the mind of the Fishbourne architect. The implication of the room will be returned to below.

---

[1] Structurally it is similar in many respects to the Entrance Hall belonging to the First Period of the Roman baths at Bath (Cunliffe, 1969).

M

The Aisled Hall is quite a different problem, tucked away as it is in the north-east corner of the site. But in spite of its somewhat out of the way position the massive nature of its architecture implies a hall of some significance, and we can only suppose that it once served as an assembly room, or perhaps even a shrine. Again, there is a close parallel for the provision of such a room in the Palace of Domitian.

Finally some mention must be made of the wide corridor to the west of the West Wing which terminates in apsidal recesses. Its function is obscure but it is remarkably like the so-called *hippodromos* attached to the south-east side of Domitian's palace, wherein one might have expected exercise to be taken. The provision of such a structure at Fishbourne serves to emphasize its close relationship with contemporary Italian styles.

The brilliance of the architecture was matched by the elegant simplicity of the garden with its wide paths served by fountains, and its screens of trees and climbing plants providing quiet shady walks. Similar features, if on a smaller scale, would have been provided in the other courtyards within the North and East Wings and presumably also on the terrace south of the South Wing. Apart from the sheer bulk of soil shifted, which would have been costly enough, the provision of carefully prepared bedding trenches for the plants and of an extensive system of water-pipes to serve the fountains would have required specialists who, in all probability, had to be called in from abroad. Within the rooms, the quality of the craftsmanship was high. Between 60 and 70 mosaic pavements were laid, all in a style comparable to good, above-average, work in Italy. Some of the rooms were decorated with inlaid marble wall panels, others had stucco moulding and most were provided with marble framing for doors and windows. Everywhere, inside and out, painted walls abounded, all of good quality. One fragment even seems to be by the same hand that painted the famous harbour scene at Stabiae. Evidently no expense was spared and scores of craftsmen were brought in from far afield to adorn the building in the most up-to-date styles used in Italy itself. The cost must have been enormous. An architect giving an estimate today for the site-work and construction of the basic superstructure, using normal modern materials, suggested that the palace would cost about one million pounds to build. Add to this the expense of all the interior decoration and cost of laying out the gardens, together with any sea-scaping which may have been done, and the actual figure would be in the order of two million pounds. The estimate, however approximate, gives some idea of the order of magnitude of the building.

Seen in a local Romano-British context the palace was of staggering size. The average masonry farm-building, such as Lockleys or Welwyn would have fitted neatly into one of the smaller courtyards, and even the more elaborate houses, such as Angmering or the Fishbourne proto-palace, were dwarfed by comparison. Admittedly, by the fourth century some Romano-British villas began to approach the size of Fishbourne, but never do they seem to have adopted the grand architectural principles seen here; at best they were buildings in the local vernacular. The palace, then, is at present unique in Britain, but sufficient will have been said to show that it corresponded in size, concept and decoration to the large villas and palaces on the Italian mainland, and in particular there are several close similarities between Fishbourne and the almost contemporary palace of Domitian in Rome. There can be no doubt that Fishbourne was palatial architecture in the most up-to-date Roman manner.

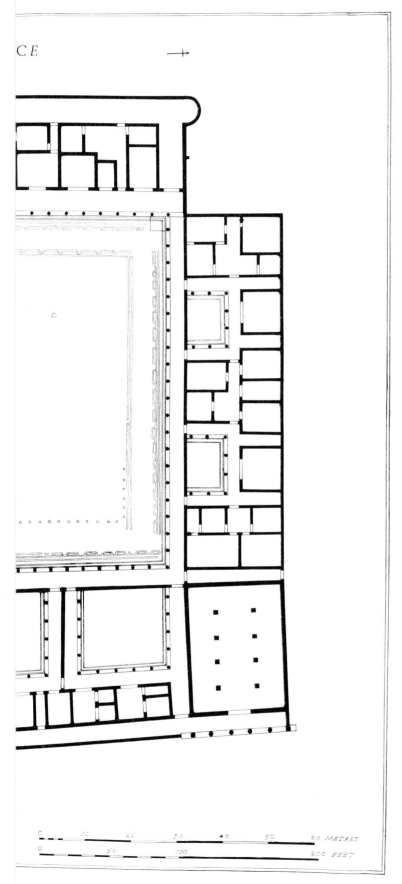

It remains to consider the problems of ownership and function. Two points seem to be of considerable importance, first that the palace grew out of an earlier 'proto-palace' which in turn replaced a moderately comfortable timber house, and second that it was centred upon an Audience Chamber comparable to those in the imperial palaces. The implications, then, are of a continuity of function and perhaps ownership, and of use by a high-ranking official thoroughly conversant with Roman taste, whose illusions of grandeur were acceptable to the central government. The imperial governor is one possibility, but at this time it would have been Frontinus or Agricola, whose pre-occupation with the west and north would surely have prevented the leisurely use of a southern residence. Moreover, for an official residence to be placed in the territory of Cogidubnus, on the very door-step of his town, would have been an enormous insult to a king whose loyalty was so prized. It is indeed far more reasonable to suggest that the palace was owned by Cogidubnus himself. Its growth from a modest late-Claudian timber house may well have echoed the fortunes of the king, on whom territories and honours were forced by Rome. Moreover, the Audience Chamber would have been quite in keeping for a local king who was also a Roman senator (*legatus Augusti*). If this attribution is correct, it is interesting to speculate why, early in the reign of Vespasian, the small proto-palace should have been so enormously enlarged. It may, however, be that under Vespasian the king received his senatorship, perhaps as a reward for support in A.D. 69 when Vespasian was struggling for power. It was not unlike Vespasian to react in this way to his supporters, and a sudden rise in status would neatly explain the change from the proto-palace, suitable for a king, to a palace more fitting for a king and senator. The matter will always remain in the realms of speculation, but the explanation has the virtue of being internally consistent.

Functionally, the layout of the palace is easy to explain. Part of it was administrative, with the West Wing forming the official block where the owner could sit in audience and where guests could be entertained in the adjacent rooms. A palace of this kind would also have needed guest-rooms, several suites of which were provided in the North and East Wings, cut off from the public areas. We may also assume that the owner lived in the building, presumably in the south range with its own private terrace leading down to the sea and with the baths close at hand. Thus the building, as we at present know it, could have served all the functions which might be expected of a palace.

It will be shown below that by the beginning of the second century a series of far-ranging changes had been initiated, implying a drastic change of function and presumably ownership. The occasion could reasonably have been the death of Cogidubnus, for when the old client king died his territory would have been incorporated into the province and the need for a local palace would thus have been removed.[1] The building certainly continued in use, but such were the changes that the architectural magnificence and the functional arrangement of the unified palace were destroyed. Whether the family of Cogidubnus continued to live here or whether the building was sold to one or more different owners must remain unknown.

---

[1] Dr Wilson, following Prof. E. Birley, suggests that the two experienced *legati juridici*, C. Salvius Liberalis and L. Javolenus Priscus, were in Britain between 78 and 86 to incorporate the kingdom of Cogidubnus into the province following his death (Wilson, 1956, 100 ff.). While it remains a possibility that this was true of Priscus, here between 84–6, had Liberalis been involved (78–81) it would hardly have given time for the palace to be completed before the king died.

PART IV

The Third Period *c.* A.D. 100–280

THE NATURE OF THE THIRD PERIOD ALTERATIONS

THE alterations to which the original palace was subjected are here referred to simply as the Third Period, but the term tends to belie the complexity of the later structural development of the site. In summary, it may be said that from about A.D. 100 until the time of the final destruction in the late third century, the palace, and particularly the North Wing, was altered many times. On some occasions the changes were drastic in that parts of the old structure were demolished, but generally the alterations were relatively insubstantial, the shell of the old building remaining largely intact while new floors were laid or partition walls erected to divide up large rooms.

While it is evident that these alterations succeed the palace in its original form, it is not always possible to arrive at the sequence in which they were made. It is even more difficult to assign accurate dates to the individual changes. Nevertheless, in broad terms, four phases can be recognized in the North Wing: the first modifications, at the beginning of the second century; more drastic changes about the middle of the century; further minor alterations early in the third century, and a final phase of building work beginning in the late third century, but left unfinished because of the fire which destroyed the building. These phases are summarized in fig. 45.

The alterations in the East Wing, though simpler, can also be related to the main sequence, but discussion of the complex evidence involved is best left to the detailed description below. The changes in the West Wing were very slight and cannot be closely dated.

In the following pages the structural sequence of the individual wings is given separately, the changes being described as far as possible in chronological order.

THE NORTH WING
(Figs. 43–5)

The four phases into which the alterations in the North Wing can be divided must not be thought of as discrete, for in all probability the changes were continuous, but such subtleties are not discoverable by archaeological means. For the sake of convenience this Third Period has been divided into four phases, but it should be remembered that while the sequence is *generally* correct, the rigidity of classification is imposed by the observer.

PERIOD 3A: EARLY SECOND CENTURY

THE NORTH WING BATHS   (fig. 43, p. 212, and pl. XLV)

In the first phase the structure of the old palace seems to have undergone very little change, except at the east end where a new bath suite was inserted into the corridor or alley which originally divided the North Wing proper from the Aisled Hall. The structural alterations were not very considerable, but the corridor was divided into three elongated rooms by means of two east–west dividing walls. The northern wall was built of greensand blocks, while the southern wall was apparently based on a foundation of large relaid stylobate blocks, two of which still survive in position: the wall itself has since disappeared.

Caldarium (pl. XLVa). The northern room, which served as the *caldarium*, was floored with a thin layer of pink mortar laid directly above a compact layer of greensand chippings of the Second Period. The floor served as the basement for a hypocaust, represented now by a few *pilae* tiles still in position. Hot air was supplied by means of a flue outside the east wall, built of broken roof tiles, with elongated cheek walls large enough to support a hot-water boiler above.

Tepidarium. Insufficient of the southern wall of the *caldarium* survives to show whether it was perforated by vents to allow the hot air to pass into the middle room, but some such arrangement would have been likely. If so, the middle room would have been the *tepidarium*. Unfortunately its floor has been entirely destroyed and no trace of the original arrangement survives. Opening out of the west side of the room, however, is a small bath, 5 ft. (1.5 m.) square, which probably functioned as a warm bath attached to the *tepidarium*. It was built of re-used material, including a stylobate block in its south-west corner and several roof tiles used as semi-bonding courses between the ashlar masonry. The floor was of 8-in. (20-cm.) square *pilae* tiles set in pink mortar and the walls were internally rendered with pink mortar, there being an angular 'quarter-round' moulding at the junction of the wall and floor.

Frigidarium. To the south of the *tepidarium* lay another room, the floor of which has been totally destroyed. In all probability it served as a *frigidarium*. Water was supplied from the east by means of a wooden water-pipe (see below) and the room was provided with a drain composed of two re-used gutter blocks running through the southern boundary wall of the North Wing, leading into the gutter surrounding the garden. The re-use of large gutter blocks would seem to be rather unnecessary when a simple ceramic drain could easily have been provided, but one possible explanation for this is that the southern part of the room functioned as a latrine, the seats of which could conveniently have been built of timber above the gutter.

Immediately to the east of the *tepidarium* was a small room built in the north-west corner of the reduced Aisled Hall. Since it is more likely to belong to the Hall rather than the baths, it will be described later (p. 158).

The building materials of which the bath suite was constructed were largely re-used from the original building, but the *pilae* tiles and box-tiles (Vol. II, p. 45 ff.) must have been imported specifically for the job. The secondary use of stylobate and gutter blocks in the new walls and drains of the bath suite implies that somewhere in the old palace a colonnade was being demolished, but it is impossible to say which it was. It is unlikely that as early as this the east courtyard of the North Wing was being pulled down; a more reasonable possibility is that the blocks come from one of the colonnades around the garden.

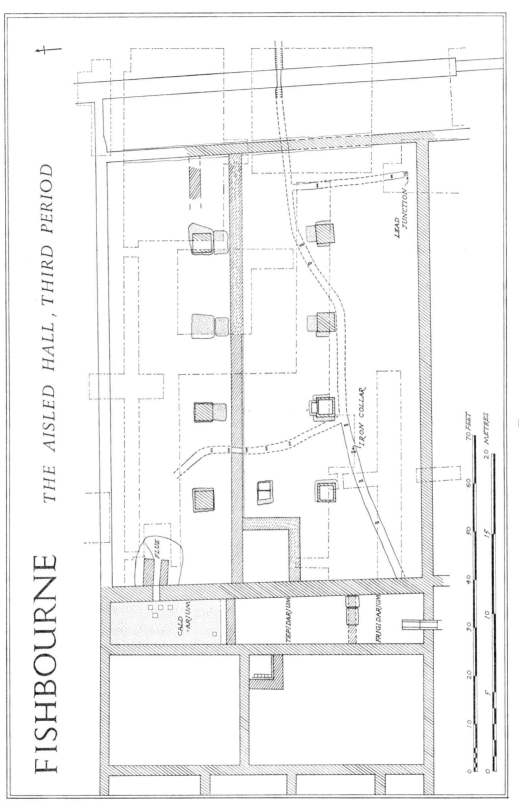

FISHBOURNE   THE AISLED HALL, THIRD PERIOD

FIG. 43

Painted Plaster.   The plaster recovered from the vicinity of the small plunge bath shows that its chamber was decorated with a deep red dado or skirting with a white wall above. The wall was divided into panels by vertical bands of deep red, each panel being outlined with a thin orange-red frame line. A 'moulding' painted in graded reds probably belonged to the cornice surmounting the panels. A few fragments of window or door embrasures were also recovered (Vol. II, p. 69).

The *tepidarium* itself was decorated in basically the same style as its adjacent bath with the additional use of black and yellow areas, and white splashed with large spots of red and yellow, presumably giving some relief from the somewhat austere red and white decor (Vol. II, p. 78).

Water Supply (fig. 43).   Water was supplied to the baths from the east by means of a wooden water-pipe which was laid in a ragged trench cut through the eastern wall of the Aisled Hall. Once within the Hall the pipe divided into three branches, the main one to the *frigidarium*, one to the hot water boiler constructed over the flue, and the third to the south-east corner of the Hall. The main branch, to the *frigidarium*, was traced over most of its length and could be seen to swerve so as to negotiate one of the pier bases. In the last 36 ft. (11 m.) six iron collars, 6 in. (*c.* 15 cm.) in diameter, were found, representing the joints between one wooden section and the next; the spacing clearly implies that the individual sections were of varying lengths. The pipe to the hot water boiler branched from the main pipe, but the junction between the two could not be traced. Five of its collars, 3¾ in. (9.5 cm.) in diameter, were discovered *in situ*. The pipe had been laid through the newly-constructed north wall of the Hall in a neatly-built slot overlaid by ashlar masonry in such a way as to strongly suggest the broad contemporaneity of both wall and pipe. It appears then to have skirted the stoking area of the flue, approaching the north cheek wall of the boiler support from the north. The third pipe lay in the south-east corner of the Hall where two iron collars, 4⅜ in. (11.0 cm.) in diameter, survived in position. Close to the southern collar was a lead junction unit, consisting of a perforated lead sheet provided with a vertical lead attachment, through which the water would have emptied. It may well be that this third supply belonged to a slightly later period, during which the East Wing baths were functioning. If so, it could have provided a flow of fresh water in the latrine which is thought to have been constructed immediately to the south (p. 172). For details and illustrations of the iron and lead fittings see Vol. II, pp. 126–8 and 144.

THE AISLED HALL   (fig. 43, p. 212)

The Aisled Hall, like the rest of the palace, was subjected to a series of alterations during the Third Period, but insufficient evidence survives to provide any close indication of the date of the individual changes within the bracket A.D. 100–280. In general terms, however, the sequence and the broad date range are clear.

The only major alteration was the reduction in width of the Hall from 66 ft. (20.1 m.) to 38 ft. (11.6 m.) by the construction of a new north wall across the building south of the northern row of piers, which would by now have been removed. The new wall so changed the proportions of the building that the old southern row of piers now became the central roof supports. Clearly the entire roof line and superstructure must have been remodelled at this time. The new north wall, which had to take the thrust of the roof, was substantially built of ashlar masonry on a deep footing of pitched greensand placed dry in a wide foundation trench. Its western length survived to a height of several courses above the foundation offset, but the eastern part was deeply robbed. In the north-west corner a small room, 10 ft. by 11 ft. (3.0 × 3.35 m.), had been built at the same time as the new north wall. Although it had been entirely robbed to its shallow footings, sufficient of the north wall survived to show that the two had once been bonded together. The function of the room is unknown, but it could perhaps have been an *apodyterium* for the baths. Indeed, it may even be that the reduced Hall now served as an exercise hall for the newly-constructed bath suite. The idea is not unreasonable, but it is totally beyond proof.

The original eastern end of the Hall underwent considerable modification during the Third Period. At an early stage, possibly contemporary with the reduction in width just described, the eastern colonnade was removed and a compacted gravel was spread over the foundations up to the line of the inner corridor wall, in effect widening the road at this point and implying that the original façade had been completely demolished. That the metalling was laid at all is an indication that traffic continued up to the Hall at this time.

No attempt was made to refloor the Hall in the Third Period. The water pipes were set in trenches cut through the accumulated builders' rubble and more rubble was spread discontinuously to fill up hollows and create a roughly level surface. Dating depends on the fact that the water pipe serving the boiler, which belongs to the early second-century layout of the baths, was laid neatly through the new north wall in such a way as to show that the wall either post-dated the water pipe or was broadly contemporary with it. It is more reasonable to suppose that the reproportioned Hall is contemporary with the construction of the bath suite. Both were major building projects and both seem to have been planned in relation to each other. Moreover, as suggested above, they may have functioned as a single unit.

The area to the north of the new north wall of the Hall remained, at this time, open and must have served partly as a stoking yard for the furnace at its west end. At the east end a short length of wall was found, built on a shallow footing cut into the Second Period make-up. Its date is unknown but it could possibly have been a late Second Period addition removed during the Third Period alterations.

THE ROOMS OF THE NORTH WING   (figs. 44 and 45, p. 212, and pls. XLIII, XLIV, LXXXIV)

Room N 13.   Room N 13, which in its original state contained a black and white geometric mosaic, was in this period refloored with a completely new floor of a most unusual type, but before the mosaic was laid large areas of the original floor were destroyed — presumably to provide tesserae for the new work. The new floor (pls. XLIII, LXXXIV) consisted of a decorated panel, measuring 13 ft. square (3.96 m.) set within a red tessellated surround. In the centre roundel was a Medusa head contained within a braided guilloche enclosed in a square frame, the spandrels being filled with complex pelta motifs. This centre square was set within a larger square, the two being joined at their corners by chequer-board patterns between which, on each side, are pairs of octagonal panels each containing a stylized leaf, a flower or a Solomon's knot. The whole square was framed by bands of repetitive motifs including segmented circles, triangles arranged base-to-apex, stylized tendrils, squares divided diagonally into two differently coloured halves and semi-circles touching each other tangentially. These bands were arranged along the four sides of the floor so as to emphasize the direction from which it was intended to be viewed.

The quality of the craftsmanship is, to say the least, crude. The colours of the tesserae are ill-matched and in some places pieces of flint have been used. Elsewhere mistakes have been made in the layout. The north-east chequer-board, for example, was made too large, causing the framework of the adjacent octagonal panel to be squeezed up and one line of its border had actually to be omitted so that the design would fit. Other minor mistakes abound. But in spite of all this the design and style are exceptionally lively, giving the floor an intensely vigorous and pleasing appearance.

Dating depends entirely upon the fact that tesserae made of samian pottery were included in the design. These were examined individually by Mr B. R. Hartley, who was of the opinion that no vessel dating to after the period A.D. 90–100 was used. This in itself merely provides a *terminus post quem*, but taken in conjunction with dating evidence of a similar nature for the later floors, discussed below (p. 164), it suggests that the mosaic might reasonably be dated to the beginning of the second century. Stylistic arguments cannot be used for close dating, but it is clear that the piece is of local workmanship, and is far less assured in style and quality than the Dolphin and Shell mosaics, which must post-date the middle of the second century. It is therefore best to see it as the first faltering steps in mosaic art in Britain, closely influenced by the earlier mosaics still surviving elsewhere in the building but laid at a time before assurance and tradition had created a local skilled school. On these grounds some support is provided for the early second-century date proposed above.

The West Corridor. Early in the Third-Period development of the North Wing a corridor was built along part of the west side of the North Wing to link the North Wing to the West. It was 9½ ft. (2.9 m.) wide and was floored throughout with a red tessellated pavement decorated with a chequer-board pattern picked out with greensand tesserae (pl. LXXXVII), very similar in design to that found on the Flavian mosaic in room W 6. The Third-Period walls on the north and west were only slightly built in a shallow foundation trench cut into the Second-Period ground-surface. They had been entirely robbed and no indication of superstructure survived. It is, however, most unlikely that the wall stood in masonry to full height, and indeed it may only have been a footing for a veranda.

Exact dating is not possible. The veranda walls were cut into rubbish deposits of the late first century, but since the floor was not lifted no datable material could be recovered from below it. Nor can the style of the design be used for close dating. Chequer-board patterns of this form are known during the reign of Domitian and become relatively common in the metropolitan area early in the second century, but the pattern continues in use for a considerable period and is known in fourth-century contexts. The Fishbourne floor could therefore belong anywhere within the Third Period: it is, however, thought to be early on the grounds that a corridor here would be necessary to by-pass the north-west corner of the garden, which was turned into a rubbish dump early in the second century (see Vol. II, p. 161). Moreover, its design closely follows that of the Second-Period floor, which implies (though by no means proves) that it was laid before a local school with a more up-to-date pattern book arose.

PERIOD 3 B: MID-SECOND CENTURY
(Figs. 44 and 45)

Period 3 B was a time of maximum alteration to the structure and decoration of the old palace. Two major pieces of work were undertaken at this time: the demolition of the eastern part of the North Wing and the complete refitting of the western part.

THE EASTERN END OF THE NORTH WING   (figs. 44 and 45, p. 212)

Sometime in the second century the eastern courtyard was obliterated, the colonnade being dismantled and the stylobate and gutter blocks removed for use elsewhere. A new wall was then built from the south-west corner of room N 15, south to the southern limit of the wing. This new wall now marked the eastern limit of the wing, everything to the east of it being demolished to ground-level. Normally over the demolished area at least two, and sometimes three or more, courses of ashlar masonry remained above the level of the flint footings and since the area was soon to become covered in rubbish, the surviving masonry disappeared from view and was thus protected from later robbing.

The dating of the demolition depends on several factors. In the first place a reasonable period of time must have elapsed to allow for the construction and use of the bath suite before it was demolished. The ash layer which had eventually been allowed to clog the flue produced a moderately worn coin of Hadrian (Vol. II, p. 97) which is unlikely to have been dropped much before the middle of the second century. Secondly, the area of the demolished rooms was soon covered with a layer of occupation rubbish containing pottery of mid-second century date and later, and finally some time must be allowed for the Flavian mosaic in room N 20 to wear out in the centre and be patched with fragments of tiles and a layer of clay. On all these counts demolition can most reasonably be dated to about the middle of the second century.

THE WESTERN END OF THE NORTH WING   (fig. 44, p. 212)

It is probable that in this period the major structural alterations were made: these are most conveniently described in terms of the individual rooms beginning at the west end.

Room N 1 seems to have remained unchanged at this period, unless the thin layer of discontinuous white mortar, evident in patches beneath the later hypocaust, dates from this time.

Slabs of painted plaster remained *in situ* on both the east and west sides of the room, kept in position by the fallen rubble even after the walls had been robbed from behind (pl. XLVIa). The nature of the base of the plaster shows that it belongs to the period of the mortar floor, thus post-dating the early use of the building but pre-dating the latest alterations. At this stage the base of the wall was painted with a skirting of deep purple-red, followed by a pink strip over-painted with purple flowers, and a dark green strip, both dividing the skirting from the main wall colour of pale green. This background was overpainted with simplified flowers in pink and white, and composite bands of deep red sandwiched between pink or bright blue between red. Brown and blue were also used for freehand painting. Other unrelated colour combinations included yellow splashed with red-brown (Vol. II, p. 58).

The overall effect is far less assured than that achieved by the Flavian painters and both the plaster backing and painting appear to be of inferior quality, although they have suffered much from fire.

Room N 2 (pls. LVIa, LXXXVIa) was at some stage refloored with a new mosaic after the original Second-Period floor had been removed. Only two small fragments of the later floor survive. One piece in the south-east corner of the room shows a white background with random stars of black tesserae, the other fragment in the northern half of the room depicts a chequer pattern of alternating squares of black and white. The rest of the design is totally beyond recovery.

Room N 3 was largely untouched except that the original doorway in the south end of the east wall was blocked up and a new doorway was cut in the centre of the north wall. All that now remains is the sill composed of the original ashlar masonry covered with pink mortar. It may be to this period that the quarter-round moulding of pink mortar was provided to seal the junction of the wall and the floor.

Room N 4 was at this time extended in size by the demolition of its original north wall and the construction of a new north wall in line with the north wall of room N 3. The original Second-Period black and white mosaic was retained, but subsequently had to be patched on two separate occasions with fillings of pink mortar. At some stage, possibly from Period 3 B onwards, the newly-proportioned room was turned into a workshop. In the south-east corner a large oven was constructed (pl. LXa) against a square masonry infilling. The flue, paved with tiles, still survives together with 1-ft. (0.3-m.) wide cheek walls of tile and limestone blocks. The oven, however, is destroyed and nothing remains to indicate its original superstructure or function. It is rather too massively built to be a bread-oven and may therefore be connected with whatever industrial processes were undertaken in the room.

In the northern part of the room was a hearth, built of tiles and mortar. Like the oven, it cannot be precisely dated within the third period. Fragments of wall plaster roughly finished and painted in a pale green probably belong to this period.

Room N 5 (pl. XLVb). The old Second-Period room ceased to exist in the Third Period, at which time it was divided into four parts, three constituting rooms whilst the fourth, the strip referred to above, was added to room N 4. The dividing walls were built of greensand blocks, presumably derived from the demolished east end, laid on a rubble footing which had been rammed into shallow foundation trenches cut into the Second-Period floor make-up.

Of the three new rooms thus created, room N 5a was the most elaborately fitted. It was floored with a new mosaic pavement (pls. XLVIb, LXXXb, LXXXIXb) generally rectangular in shape but with its short sides convex, set within a red tessellated surround. The floor is of a somewhat unusual design, consisting of two large scallop shells, in white, yellow and red, on either side of a central panel which appears to contain ill-drawn fish flanked by a border of lozenges. The workmanship and design are not particularly good but the floor can at least claim originality. The use of large scallop shells as major decorative elements can best be paralleled in this country by the second-century mosaic at Verulamium (Wheeler and Wheeler, 1936, pl. XXXIX). Another interpretation of the design is that the 'fish tails' are in fact the feet of a knobbly-kneed peacock whose tail is spread out to form the side 'scallops'. The idea is perhaps a little more attractive, but the problem is unlikely ever to be solved. Dating must rest entirely on the sherds of samian pottery broken up for use as tesserae, which Mr B. Hartley dates to about the middle of the second century. Like similar pieces used in the Dolphin mosaic (see below, p. 164) they include no late Antonine or Trajanic or earlier pieces, a fact which strongly suggests that the mosaicists were working towards the middle of the century and were using broadly contemporary sherds. The marked contrast with the date of the samian tesserae used in the Medusa mosaic is an added indication of the validity of this method of dating, at least at Fishbourne.

Stratigraphically the shell mosaic was laid after the dividing walls were inserted into room N 5, and since no traces survive of earlier floors or occupation levels contemporary with the wall it may safely be assumed that the walls and mosaic are of the same date.

Rooms N 5b and c do not appear to have been specially floored, but discontinuous patches of mortar in N 5c suggest local patching of the Second-Period floor matrix which here served as a floor.

Since the room was remodelled during the Third Period, it is probable that most of the painted wall plaster belongs to the time of the second-century alterations. Although a large quantity survives, the pieces are very small, the largest being little more than $2\frac{1}{2}$ in. (4 cm.) across, making reconstruction impossible. Even so, it is possible to see that bright streaky blue was fairly common, occasionally with over-painted white lines. Blue is shown adjacent to areas of purple carefully painted with closely-spaced leaves in bold brush strokes of whitish-green and green. Areas of plain green are also shown next to red, painted over with floral designs in green, yellow and white. Other main variants are described below. Stylistically, the decor is totally dissimilar to the painting of the Flavian palace, but it corresponds closely in colour range and style to the paintings in rooms N 1 and N 7, which on other grounds are thought to be of a similar mid second-century date (Vol. II, p. 59).

Room N 6.   In the Second Period, room N 6 served as a corridor, but by the time of Period 3 B it seems that a layer of occupation soil had had time to accumulate here before two cross-walls were inserted to divide the old corridor into two rooms of approximately equal size. In the northern room a new layer of floor make-up, consisting of pitched greensand blocks, was laid together with the foundations of the cross-wall, and both were cemented together with the same hard pink mortar. Some of the greensand blocks used in the wall footing were actually broken fragments of gutter blocks, perhaps from the eastern courtyard in the North Wing which was being demolished at this time. On the pink mortar floor a group of regularly-placed hypocaust *pilae* were based to serve as the support for a suspended floor, since destroyed. The source of heat for the room would have been provided by a fire in the southern room, connected by means of a flue to the hypocaust. The flue itself was destroyed in the early third century, but soot and charcoal together with lenses of burnt clay were found sealed beneath the tessellated floor with which the room was later floored.

The superstructure of the two dividing walls had been largely removed, but a doorway survived in the southern wall; the northern wall would have been pierced only by the flue.

No positive trace of a door leading into the hypocaust chamber survives, but the arrangement of the patterned border to the mosaic in room N 7, to be described below, indicates the presence of a doorway in the east wall of the hypocaust chamber towards its northern end.

Thus, a small heated room was created in the north end of the corridor, its flue being sited immediately to the south. This suggests that the smoke and fumes were allowed to escape into the veranda surrounding the old western courtyard, both from this flue and the flue, which will be described later, which heated a similar hypocaust on the other side of room N 7. The implication must be that at this time the courtyard was of no great amenity value. Furthermore the fact that the flues were not sited outside the building to the north might suggest that the reconstituted North Wing faced north and that it was necessary to keep this northern area clear of unsightly clutter.

There is no direct dating evidence for the construction of the hypocaust system, but it follows a period during which dirt was allowed to accumulate in the Period 2 corridor and if the door in the east wall was inserted at the time of construction, the fact that the border of the mid second-century Dolphin mosaic was designed to create a 'mat' in front of the door implies that the hypocaust dates to the middle of the century or slightly earlier. The evidence, such as it is, may be tenuous but it is internally consistent.

Room N 7 (pls. XLVII-LIII, LXXXIII, LXXXVIII). At this stage the south wall of room N 7 was rebuilt to form a wide entrance, on either side of which the wall was expanded so as to create the appearance of flanking pilasters. The masonry had been largely destroyed by later robbing, but sufficient survived to give the broad outline of the plan at this point. This fact, together with the inaccessibility of the lower levels of the wall due to the presence of well-preserved mosaic and tessellated pavements immediately adjacent to it, made it impossible to say for certain that the entrance belonged to the Third Period rather than the Second. But since the Second-Period footing for the south wall of room N 16 shows no such embellishments, and both rooms were presumably of equivalent status and position in the Second Period, it is safer to assume that the surviving south entrance to room N 7 was a Third-Period remodelling. Between the flanking piers a flight of three steps would originally have risen from the level of the veranda to that of the mosaic with which the room was floored. The steps would have been of timber; all that now survives is the mortar seating for them and a few patches of charred timber belonging to the uppermost step.

The room was floored with a mosaic pavement, 13 ft. square (3.96 m.) set within a simple grey and white chequer-board composed of small tesserae of the same size as those in the main design. The central element of the floor is a circular panel enclosed in a braided guilloche, depicting a cupid holding a trident and sitting astride a dolphin (pl. L). The panel is set within a large square delineated by a twisted guilloche and between it and the panel are four semi-circular panels and four quadrants, each enclosed by a simple twisted guilloche. The semi-circular panels contain fabulous sea beasts: two have sea-horses drawn in black and white with red mouths (pl. XLVIII), while the other two depict multi-coloured sea-panthers (pl. XLIX). One animal of each pair is larger and more boldly drawn, the reason being that the mosaicists were apparently attempting to distinguish between males and females. The point is clearly made with the sea-panthers: the male has fangs and claws while the female is altogether more docile in appearance. The quadrants, placed in the corners of the squares, are filled with simple scallops of red, yellow and black outlined in white (pl. LIII*a*).

The concave-sided squares formed between these panels were filled with black and white vases drawn against a white background (pl. LI). The vases, though generally similar, all differ in detail from each other. They share in common rather emaciated tendrils growing from the bases, and handles confused with similar tendrils, giving the vases a somewhat organic appearance.

The main square enclosed by the twisted guilloche is bounded by a frame of concave-sided triangles arranged base-to-apex, outside which is a border of tendrils. Each sprig of tendrils starts near simple vases placed in the centres of each of the four sides (pl. LII). They differ considerably in detail but the general arrangement, not always adhered to, is for a simple black leaf to alternate with a coloured flower. At one point in the north border a small black bird is shown (pl. LIII*b*), standing on one of the leaves.

The space between the tendril border and the walls of the room is filled with a black and white chequer pattern of squares about 1 ft. (0.3 m.) across, but in front of the south side of the floor, and between it and the side entrance, the chequer is replaced by a pattern of squares set diagonally within larger squares, forming a 'mat' in front of the entrance. Another variation of the simple chequer pattern occurred in the north-west corner, at the point where a small side-door would probably have led into room N 6 (pl. LXXXIII).

The general arrangement of the mosaic is known in first-century A.D. Mediterranean contexts and becomes common in the second century in various parts of the Empire. By the middle of the second century there seems to have been schools of mosaicists working regularly in Britain, particularly at Verulamium, where several mosaics of this kind are known. The Dolphin mosaic may well have been laid by a similar school of craftsmen perhaps working locally. Internal dating evidence depends entirely upon the fragment of samian ware used occasionally as tesserae. These have been examined by Mr B. Hartley, who reports that the majority of them are assignable to the middle of the second century. No late Antonine sherds were incorporated and only a few fragments were Trajanic; thus the strong indication is that this floor, like the shell mosaic, dates to the middle of the second century.

It is difficult to be sure how much of the surviving painted wall plaster belongs to the Flavian period and how much is of second-century date, but since there is good reason to suppose that the south wall was remodelled during the Third Period it may well be that the room was totally redecorated at this time. Moreover it is abundantly clear from the position of the room and the quality of its reflooring that it became the principal chamber in the reconstituted building — such a room would surely have been repainted.

The basic design consists of areas of painted 'inlaid marble' set within borders of other colours. The 'marbles' vary: they include deep purple with a coarse blue graining, pale purple with grey, red and blue textures and dark red over-painted with curvilinear graining in green and blue. The framing bands also show considerable variety but are usually composite and frequently include black, white and bright blue. Evidently the main design was not dissimilar in concept to the Flavian painting but in technique, particularly the brush work, and in choice of colour it is much closer to the second-century work in rooms N 1 and N 5. A second style of painting was also recognizable from the fragments recovered from within the room. It consisted of plain bright red painted with stylized floral designs in white and green. Some of the pieces definitely curve in two directions, implying that they belong to the internal rendering of an apsidal recess of relatively small proportions. These pieces are decorated with a continuous row of scored pendant semi-circles dividing the deep red from a whitish-grey; the junction is enlivened with pale green designs which have suffered considerably from weathering. While it remains a distinct possibility that some of the painting of this second type belongs to the ceiling rather than wall, the curved pieces would be more appropriate to a wall-niche (Vol. II, pp. 61–2).

Room N 8 (pl. LIV*a*).   The original Second-Period corridor on the east side of room N 7 was, in the Third Period, treated in exactly the same way as the comparable corridor on the west side, that is it was divided into two rectangular rooms by the insertion of two cross-walls, the northern room being provided with a hypocaust while the southern room housed the necessary flue. Both cross-walls were built in shallow foundation trenches cut into the earlier floor make-up but both have since been completely robbed, the southern robber trench being overlaid at a later date by a tessellated floor. In the southern part of the hypocaust chamber the *pilae* were regularly spaced in five rows at an equal distance apart, but in the northern part the spacing and orientation were haphazard. The explanation is not altogether clear, but one possibility is that part of the floor collapsed into the hypocaust and was replaced from above, the restricted space available determining the placing of the rebuilt *pilae*.

No trace of the flue was visible in the southern room except for charcoal and burnt clay which could be seen in the sides of the robber trenches beneath the later tessellated floor, but since the floor was not lifted, a detailed examination of the Period 3 B layers beneath it could not be made nor could any direct dating evidence be obtained. The stratigraphical sequence, however, shows that the hypocaust and its flue post-dated the Second-Period arrangement yet went out of use when a new tessellated floor was laid in (it will be argued below) the early third century. On this evidence alone the changes are assigned to Period 3 B.

Both divisions of the room seem to have been replastered during the Third Period, presumably consequent upon the insertion of the heating system. The style of painting here closely resembles that of the East Wing baths put up towards the middle of the second century. The room was provided with a dado of pink splashed with red and divided from the upper part of the wall by a wide deep red band. Above this the wall was painted white, divided into panels by red bands, the panels being individually framed with inner thin black lines concentric with the red border. (Vol. II, p. 62).

Rooms N 9, 10 and 11 (pls. LIV*b*, LV, LVI*c*). It is difficult to date the changes which took place in rooms N 9–11 within the Third Period. It may be that the rooms were refloored in Phase 3 B, but no dating evidence of any kind survives and the possibility exists that the floors were later. However, in view of the fact that the major alterations elsewhere were undertaken in Period 3 B, it remains a strong possibility that the refitting took place at this time.

The original Second-Period mosaic in room N 9 had almost entirely worn out or had been destroyed by the time that the new floor of pink mortar was laid (pl. LV*a*). There was a little preparation for it: a layer of rubble was put down and on it a 3-in. (7.5-cm.) thick layer of pink mortar was spread. A separate quarter-round moulding of the same pink mortar was then laid to seal the junctions of the wall and floor. At some later stage after the floor in the south-east corner of the room had worn through it was patched with fragments of tile (pl. xxiiia).

Room N 10 was at this stage divided into two unequal halves by a timber partition about 11 in. (0.28 m.) wide, based presumably on a horizontal sill beam laid on the matrix of the Second-Period floor after the original mosaic had been removed (pl. lvb). Against the beam, on both sides, a spread of rubble had been laid, upon which was based a red tessellated floor set in a thin layer of pink mortar. All trace of the beam had gone but its position was clearly marked by the floor and its make-up ending against it with straight faces.

Room N 11 was divided in a similar way with a beam 10–11 in. (0.25–0.28 m.) wide. The northern room thus created was floored with red tesserae set in pink mortar laid on a rubble foundation, beneath which was a 1½–2-in. (4–5-cm.) thick layer of dirty soil, possibly representing an occupation accumulation. The southern room was similarly floored with tesserae but towards the centre was a simple mosaic panel 6 ft. 9 in. (2.06 m.) square (pls. lvic, lxxxvb, xca). Although the pattern has suffered considerably from later ploughing, sufficient remains to show that the design included a central rosette enclosed by an irregular meander pattern which was in turn surrounded by a border incorporating ill-drawn sub-geometric designs difficult to describe. The floor was rather inexpertly designed and the style, such as it is, cannot be closely dated. Nor is there any other form of dating evidence available for it. A few scraps of samian were used as tesserae, but none can be precisely dated and all that can be said is that it dates to after the beginning of the second century.

The floors of both halves of room N 11 have subsided drastically into the filling of a First-Period gully beneath. To this fact alone can be assigned the relatively good preservation of the floors, which would otherwise have been ploughed away in the post-Roman period.

It seems unlikely on the available evidence that the rooms were elaborately repainted during the Third Period. The painting from rooms N 9 and N 11 is characteristically Flavian while that from room N 10 is largely plain white and deep red — suitable contrast for the areas of marble wall inlay with which the room was adorned — and could be of any period. How the division of rooms N 10 and N 11 affected the decor cannot now be assessed (Vol. ii, p. 66).

Room N 14 (pls. lvib, lviib, lxxxvic). Very little is known of the original floor of room N 14, except that it was covered with a black and white mosaic and that some of the white tesserae in the western part of the room were arranged diagonally to the walls (pl. lvib). During the Third Period an interesting change took place: the room was divided by a timber beam into a continuous corridor and an elongated chamber, the latter being floored with a black and white mosaic (pl. lviib) closely similar to the Second-Period floor in room N 12. Indeed, it is so similar that originally it was thought to be of Second-Period date, but a close examination of its southern edge showed two rows of white tesserae of the original floor in position below the later floor. The quality of the craftsmanship is, in fact, inferior to the larger mosaic in room N 12, particularly in the neatness of the infillings of the white diamonds. The motifs in the later floor are much more varied, and patterns based on circles were evidently now more popular. A further point of difference is that the row of red tesserae which invariably bordered the Second-Period mosaics was not repeated here.

The implications of the floor are interesting. It was either a relaid version of the floor which first occupied the room or it was a deliberate attempt to copy the Second-Period mosaic in room N 12, using materials robbed from elsewhere. In either case it suggests, as indeed does the late survival of the room N 12 floor, that this particular type of design was still acceptable in the second century.

The northern part of room N 14 served as a corridor. At some stage in the Third Period it was floored with red tesserae (pl. LVI*b*), but no date can be assigned to the reflooring nor can it be proved to be of the same period as the relaying of the black and white mosaic just discussed. In fact the entire series of changes in room N 14 are without dating evidence.

The original Second-Period doorways must have provided access to and from the east and west ends of the room. A door was also provided through the centre of the partition wall between the two parts of the original room. No trace of the sill survives, but the edge of the black and white mosaic became worn against the point where the door sill is thought to have been, and had to be patched with red tesserae. Another door was provided immediately to the south between rooms N 14 and N 13, again in the centre of the wall. It is represented now by a sill of ashlar masonry surviving to a height of 3 in. (7.6 cm.) above the floor-level, between deep robber trenches on either side.

Room N 12. The Second-Period mosaic floor of room N 12 was kept intact throughout the Third Period except for a few careful, though sometimes not altogether accurate, patches of the original design. At some stage, however, the room was divided into two by a partition wall of timber (pl. XXIV*a*), the surface of which had been plastered and painted. The northern room was provided with a quarter-round moulding between the base of the wall and floor, but less trouble seems to have been taken with the southern room. Two doorways were provided, one in the centre of the original north wall and one through the eastern end of the partition wall. Of the northern door the charred timber sill still survives in position, together with a rough tessellated patch of mosaic floor immediately adjacent to it. The other door is shown only by the tessellated patches on either side of the position which its sill once occupied.

The western courtyard and its verandas. For reasons which will become apparent later it is thought that the alterations which the veranda underwent in the Third Period are best assigned to Phase 3 C. It may well be that its original Second-Period form persisted until this time.

The east end of the reconstituted wing (fig. 44, p. 212)

Immediately east of rooms N 11, 13 and 14 two new rooms were created by inserting two walls, one running from the south-west corner of room N 16 to join with the south wall of the wing, the other continuing the line of the partition wall which divided room N 14 to join the new north-south wall. The walls were built in standard Third-Period style, of greensand masonry based upon a shallow footing of rammed greensand blocks. Stratigraphically the walls succeeded the demolition and removal of the masonry of the original courtyard. In plan the additions merely tidied up the east end of the wing, which would otherwise have been ragged after the destruction of the east end of the old building. Probably the walls were built soon after the demolition and are thus best dated to the middle of the second century. Some support for this is provided by the occupation layer, containing late second- to early third-century pottery, which overlapped the outside of the footing of the north–south wall and was continuous with the rubbish deposited over the destroyed east end.

The additional walls created two rooms. The southern room was rectangular with an earth and rubble floor, while the northern room was in fact an L-shaped corridor flanking room N 11 and providing access from the central corridor to the north side of the building. It was floored with a 3-in. (7.6-cm.) thick layer of yellow mortar, surviving now only in the south-east angle.

The lead-angled tank (pl. LVIIa).   Eight feet (2.4 m.) to the east of the new east limit o the wing the remains of a wooden tank were discovered, set into the contemporary ground-surface to a depth of 6 in. (15.2 cm.). It measured $17\frac{1}{2}$ in. by 15 in., by about 15 in. in height (45 × 38 × 38 cm.). The internal angles of the tank were strengthened by angled strips of lead nailed with iron tacks to the wood. The tacks seem to have been specially made for the job, with short shanks and large flat heads which could not be pulled through the lead sheeting (Vol. II, p. 144).

The tank must belong to the Third Period on stratigraphical grounds, but no precise date can be given, nor can its function be discovered.

FEATURES TO THE NORTH OF THE NORTH WING   (figs. 15 and 44)

Immediately north of the building, adjacent to the north wall of room N 9, was a rectangular room built of greensand masonry set in a shallow foundation trench 3 in. (7.6 cm). deep cut into the top of occupation layers of the Second Period. Traces of pink mortar survived between some of the stones. Immediately to the east a 6–8-in. (15–20-cm.) thick spread of consolidated gravel lay up to the wall, again sealing occupation material of Second-Period date. These additions must belong to some time during the Third Period but the exact date and function are uncertain.

Further east four other walls, three north–south and one east–west, all post-dating the deposition of the Period 2 make-up, have been sectioned in trial trenches and contractors' excavations. They were all built of greensand ashlar laid in pink mortar set on a footing of pitched greensand blocks. Between and around them was a layer of compacted gravel 6–8 in. (15–20 cm.) thick, laid after the wall had been constructed, sealing the clay make-up of Period 2.

Without extensive excavation it will be difficult to say more of the plan or function of these walls. They belong to the Period 3 alterations, and the pink mortar suggests that they may have been deliberately water-proofed, but further than this it is not possible to go.

PERIOD 3 C: EARLY THIRD CENTURY
(Figs. 44 and 45, pp. 212–13)

It may be said that in Period 3 B the North Wing acquired the form which it was to retain throughout the rest of the period of occupation. The subsequent alterations were of a minor character. Only those rooms and corridors which were altered are mentioned here; the rest of the building continued in use unchanged.

Room N 6. The Period 3 B hypocaust in room N 6 ceased to function in Period 3 C, when its flue was demolished and a new floor of red tesserae laid above the demolition and occupation rubbish which had been allowed to accumulate here. Since no new flue was provided, the hypocaust room could no longer be heated but there is no evidence to suggest that the floor was destroyed or that the room was in any way changed. The dating of these alterations depends upon the discovery of a very slightly-worn *denarius* of the eastern coinage of Septimius Severus, issued in A.D. 196–7, which had been dropped immediately before the mortar matrix for the tessellated floor was laid. The coin therefore provides a *terminus post quem* of about A.D. 200. Since the tessellated floor had had time to wear before the final destruction of the building about 280, it is reasonable to suggest a date early in the third century for the alterations. This is the only direct evidence for the dating of Period 3 C.

Room N 8 (pls. LVIII*b*, LXXXV*a*, LXXXIX*a*). The two divisions of room N 8 were treated in exactly the same way as were those of room N 6. The flue was abandoned and the southern room was floored with a small rectangular mosaic bordered by a red tessellated surround. Here again there is no indication that the hypocaust chamber was in any way altered during this period, except that it was no longer heated. The southern wall of the southern room was demolished, its footings were removed and the mortar matrix upon which the mosaic was to be set was laid across the filling of the robber trench. A careful examination of the point where the matrix joined that beneath the tessellated floor of the veranda showed that while some faulting had occurred over the loose filling of the 'robber', giving the appearance of a vertical junction in some places, the mortar in both areas had in fact been laid at the same time, showing beyond doubt that the tessellation of the veranda was contemporary with the Period 3 C reflooring of the southern room.

The mosaic panel measured 7 ft. 4 in. by 5 ft. 6 in. (2.22 × 1.68 m.). Its centre motif consisted of a Solomon's knot enclosed within a circular braided guilloche, the roundel being set against a plain white background on which are shown four pairs of dolphins, each pair facing a central vase. Enclosing this is a simple black frame with scallop shell motifs in the corners. On two sides are further panels containing diamond-within-rectangle motifs. The craftsmanship is somewhat irregular and the composition is dull and lifeless.

Since the mosaic floor was well-preserved, it was not lifted and therefore no dating evidence could be recovered from beneath it. However, it post-dated Period 3 B and showed signs of use before the late third-century destruction. It is thus likely to belong to the same phase as the early third-century alterations to room N 6 described above. Some support is provided for this dating by the fact that no tesserae made from samian sherds were incorporated in it. In isolation this means nothing, but taken in conjunction with the evidence for use of samian in mosaics elsewhere in the building it could add strength to the view that the floor dated to the third century, after samian ware had gone out of common use.

One further detail requires comment. The removal of the southern wall of the room gives the superficial appearance of the room being now one with the corridor; however, a strip of pink mortar had been left between them, suggesting that the two may have been divided by a timber partition based on a sill beam. Alternatively, the sill may have been no more than a threshold.

N*

The Western Courtyard and its Verandas (fig. 44, pl. LVIIIa).   During Phase C of the Third Period the Second-Period colonnade was removed, its place being taken by a wall of ashlar masonry. How high the wall originally stood cannot now be demonstrated, but it seems reasonable to suppose that it served only as a dwarf wall to support vertical timbers which in turn would have taken the inward-sloping veranda roof. A wall standing to full height would have been unnecessary and moreover would have cut out too much light. The new wall was built on the original stylobate but apart from the west side, where the stylobate and part of the wall survive intact, both have since been largely removed, leaving only a ragged robber trench. Nevertheless the existence of a north and east wall are demanded by the height of the adjacent tessellated floor, which would have oversailed the stylobate and must therefore have been retained by a wall standing on it. At what stage the Second-Period gutter blocks in front of the stylobate were removed is uncertain, but it was evidently before the final destruction, for the northern part of the trench of the western side was packed with clay and the northern robber trench contained a 5–8-in. (12–20-cm.) thick silting of black soil with chips of tile and greensand which had accumulated before the destruction. It is thus far more reasonable to suppose that the gutter was dismantled at about the same time as the colonnade was pulled down.

The old western veranda was at this stage divided from the north and east verandas by a wall continuous with the wall which replaced the northern colonnade. Another wall was built parallel to it, 8 ft. (2.4 m.) to the south, thus dividing the corridor into two unequal parts. Both were built of re-used greensand blocks laid on a pitched footing. The southern wall incorporated a fragment of a broken column drum, derived presumably from the demolished colonnade. The northern room functioned as a small kitchen at this stage, with an oven built of baked clay set in a hollow in the south-east corner of the room (pl. LVIIIa). Since the oven had been largely destroyed in the final phase, no trace of its super-structure survived. The southern room bears no evidence of its function at this time, nor does it seem to have been floored apart from the original mortar floor of the Second Period.

The north and east arms of the old veranda retained their original function, but were floored with red tesserae set in a pink mortar. It has been shown above (p. 169) that this matrix was laid at the same time as the seating for the mosaic in room N 8 and therefore must belong to Period 3 C, which on other evidence is assigned to the early part of the third century. No other dating evidence of any kind survives for the changes to the courtyard and its surrounding verandas.

It is probably to this period that the square masonry foundation in the courtyard belongs. It is about 6 ft. (1.8 m.) square and is composed of a foundation of alternate layers of greensand rubble and pink mortar laid in a foundation pit cut to a depth of 1 ft. 10 in. (0.55 m.) in the clay make-up of the courtyard. The surface of the foundation has been brought to a level with fragments of tile set in pink mortar. It shows some signs of wear, but no other indication of function survives. One possibility is that it served as a base for a wine-press, but this is speculation.

PERIOD 3 D: LATER THIRD CENTURY
(Figs. 44 and 45, p. 213)

The final series of alterations took place either together at one time or individually at several different phases throughout the third quarter of the third century.

The West Veranda. The old west veranda, which in the Period 3 C had been divided into two separate rooms, was further modified by the demolition of the dividing wall and the destruction of the oven in what was originally the northern room. A new floor level of cream mortar up to 2 in. (5 cm.) thick was laid, covering the destroyed oven and wall footing and extending discontinuously to the south. Into this floor an oval pit was cut which served for a short period to contain a fire. It cannot correctly be described as an oven, because it was not especially lined with clay or any other material nor is there any evidence of a superstructure. All that remains is a pit, the sides and bottom of which have been burnt.

Room N 5. It was late in the Third Period that the western wall, which had earlier been inserted to divide up room N 5, was demolished and a discontinuous occupation spread was allowed to accumulate. It may be that the demolition was in some way connected with the alterations in room N 1.

Room N 1 (pl. LIX). The last change to be made in the North Wing was the building of a hypocaust in room N 1. Until this time the room seems to have been neglected and a layer of occupation rubbish allowed to accumulate, although at one stage a mortar lens represented a previous attempt at partial re-flooring.

The new hypocaust basement floor, of upturned roof tiles, was laid on the existing floor-surface. It measured 8 ft. (2.4 m.) square and from its corners diagonal channels, similarly floored, were constructed leading to the corners of the room, there presumably to join with chimneys let into the masonry. The walls have been robbed and no trace of vertical chimneys survive, but their existence is demanded by the arrangements of the vents. The hot air was intended to be introduced by a separate channel leading through the north wall and into the north side of the chamber. It, too, was floored with roof tiles, reverse side up. The walls of the basement and channels were built of two faces of greensand blocks set in clay and bonded with two courses of roof tiles. The walls stood to a maximum height of 1 ft. 5 in. (0.43 m.). The roof of the inlet vent survives tolerably intact, showing that it had originally been covered with a corbelling of roof tiles. The external spaces between the walls of the vents were filled with soil and rubble up to the level of the tops of the channel walls. During excavation the south and east infillings were removed to expose the early floor beneath, but apart from a few sherds of nondescript second-century coarse ware no dating evidence was obtained. The *pilae* upon which the floor of the hypocaust was to be based were constructed of broken fragments of roof tile roughly squared. Apparently no standard 8-in. (20-cm.) square *pilae* were available.

Excavation immediately to the north of the room, at the point where the flue should have been, showed that although the ground had been levelled, the stokery and flue had never been constructed. Moreover the north end of the inlet channel showed no traces of having been subjected to heat: the clay in which the tiles had been set remained a yellow colour, and ash and charcoal were completely lacking. The implication must be that the hypocaust was never fired. A further relevant point emerged when the hypocaust chamber itself was excavated — no fragments of the broken-up suspended floor were found. This strongly suggests, but does not prove, that the room was never floored. In fact the entire project was, for some reason, left unfinished.

The excavation of room N 3 showed that two large heaps of yellow gritty mortar had been mixed ready for use, and one of them even showed the impression of a plank which had been set up to prevent the mortar from spilling too far over the floor. In all probability this was the mortar which was to be used to form the new floor of the hypocaust room. The reason for the job being left unfinished was evidently that the entire North Wing was burnt to the ground. The dating of the alteration depends entirely upon the acceptance of this fact. Admittedly it might be argued that the work had been abandoned for some time before the fire, but this is unlikely in the face of the evidence discussed below which suggests that the building was in use up to the moment of destruction. Since it will be shown that the latest pottery in use at the time of the fire must be dated to the period A.D. 260–80, the same date-bracket can be assigned to the construction of the hypocaust.

THE EAST WING IN THE THIRD PERIOD

The northern part of the East Wing from the Entrance Hall to the Aisled Hall shows clear evidence of continued use throughout the Third Period. What happened to the south of the Entrance Hall is, however, far less certain. Excavation in this area has necessarily been very restricted and no trace of Third-Period alterations or occupation has been discovered. Indeed in the present state of knowledge it would seem that the southern part of the wing was abandoned at an early date, but in the absence of positive evidence it would be as well to be cautious.

THE BATH SUITE   (figs. 46–7, p. 213, and pls. LXb–LXV)

During the Third Period the north courtyard and its verandas were completely remodelled to form a suite of heated baths. The structural implications in terms of the old Second-Period superstructure are that, while the old walls were left standing and utilized in the new arrangement, the colonnade and the veranda roof which it supported were removed, leaving the stylobate in position. The area to be occupied by the new baths was defined by Second-Period walls on the east, west and south, and by a new Third-Period wall built on a wide rubble footing, which completed the square on the north side. Within the area thus enclosed the new suite was built. The basic arrangement was achieved simply by building walls of ashlar masonry, 1½ ft. (0.46 m.) thick, on the south and east stylobates, and by dividing the space between these walls and the old Second-Period walls by a series of cross-walls, creating two ranges each of four rectangular rooms. Additional rooms were built out into the courtyard in the north-east corner of the enclosure. The stokeries and boilers were all hidden within the old rooms of the east range.

The South Range (pls. LXb, LXI, LXIIa)

The south range of four rooms, inserted into the Second-Period veranda, were each defined by well preserved walls built of greensand blocks set in a cream-coloured mortar. The masonry was particularly well laid, great care having been taken to make the individual courses level. This is well demonstrated by the piece of wall on the north side of room C, built on the stylobate which had already subsided some 4 in. (10 cm.) into the soft filling of the First-Period stream below. The lower course of masonry was so arranged that it exactly compensated for the subsidence, leaving its upper surface dead level. Continued subsidence throughout the Third Period has since thrown the level out of true again. Where the walls were not based on the stylobate, footings of rammed greensand blocks set in mortar were provided.

Room A. There is little to be said of room A except that its walls have been largely destroyed by later robbing.

Room B. Room B has been entirely excavated (pl. LXI). Its three Third Period walls are preserved to a maximum height of three courses above the foundation offset. In the eastern wall there was originally a doorway, 4 ft. 8 in. (1.42 m.) wide, which had later been blocked with less regular greensand masonry (pl. LXIb). The room contained three features: the bottom part of an amphora partly buried in the floor and two tile cists (pl. LXb) built against the south and east walls. The latter were constructed of roof tiles set a few inches into the floor but with no form of binding or packing evident. No new floor had been provided with the alterations, the floor-level consisting at this time simply of mortary rubble trampled into the underlying clay make-up.

Rooms C and D. At the beginning of the Third Period, rooms C and D seem to have been a single rectangular room, but sometime during the Third Period it was divided into two units by means of a timber partition, the western room being floored with a 3 in. (7.6 cm.) layer of pink mortar. All that now survives of the partition is a projection from the north wall of the room built of tile and greensand fragments set in mortar, which probably once supported a timber vertical from which a door might have swung. The mortar floor of room C was kept clean, but rubbish was allowed to accumulate on the floor of room D.

The East Range (pls. LXII–LXV)

The four rooms inserted into the eastern veranda of the old building were built in much the same way as the rooms of the southern range. There was, however, one difference, for whereas the stylobate originally served as the base for much of the western wall of the range, sufficient of the masonry survived at the north end to show that for a distance of at least 3 ft. (0.9 m.) the stylobate was missing and the wall was built directly on the footing beneath the stylobate blocks. Although it may be that much of the stylobate along this side had been removed before the bath suite was built, it is possible that only one or two blocks were taken away so as to build the main east–west wall across the courtyard and veranda, the rest of the stylobate being left in position. In support of this it may be said that the short length of north–south wall ends abruptly in such a way as to suggest that it was merely infilling for a missing block, the southerly continuation of the wall being built on the stylobate, which has since been robbed out.

Room E. Room E, at the south end of the east range, was completely featureless. Since it is unlikely to have opened out of the *caldarium* to the north, it is best thought of as functionally part of the southern range.

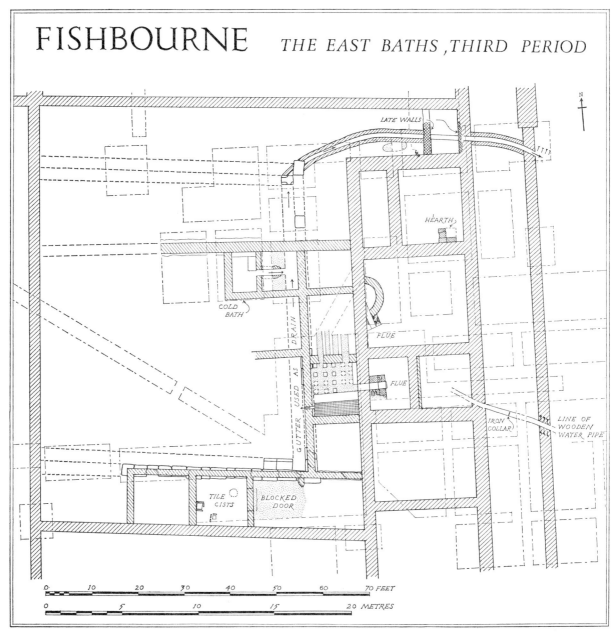

FISHBOURNE THE EAST BATHS, THIRD PERIOD

FIG. 46

Room F. Immediately north of room E was a small *caldarium* divided into two separate parts by a sleeper wall. The southern part served as a hot plunge bath. It measured 9 ft. by 3 ft. (2.7 × 0.9 m.) and was floored with a red tessellated pavement which sloped to the west side towards a drain formed by a single ceramic water-pipe laid across the stylobate footings. The seating for a second pipe survived immediately next to it, showing that the waste water was emptied into the old Second-Period gutter. The two pipes were laid at an angle to each other so as to form a U-bend in order to prevent draughts from entering the room (pl. LXIIb).

The northern part of the room was provided with a suspended floor supported on regularly spaced *pilae* built on a basement floor of hard pink mortar (pl. LXIII). The upper floor nowhere survives in position, but from the rubble filling the room was recovered a large quantity of broken pink mortar, presumably belonging to the floor which had been deliberately broken up when the building was abandoned (see p. 189).

The *caldarium* was heated through the east wall from a separate stoking chamber built into room E 4 of the old east range. The original Second-Period walls would have been still standing at this time, but for some reason the eastern wall of the room was widened by an additional facing of ashlar which survived the later robbing. Why such a widening was necessary is by no means clear, unless it was to provide a support for a water-tank. The point will be further discussed below (p. 177). The flue was well preserved (pl. LXIIIb). It was built entirely of roof tiles set in clay. From its length and massiveness it was clearly intended to support a water boiler, which would have supplied the hot water for use in the small bath, as well as heating the air circulating beneath the hypocaust floor.

Room G. Room G, opening directly from the north side of the *caldarium*, served as the *tepidarium*. The two rooms were divided by a wall of ashlar masonry rendered with pink mortar, through which basement ducts had been provided to allow the hot air from the *caldarium* to pass into the space beneath the floor of the *tepidarium* (fig. 47). The floor of the *tepidarium* was supported on longitudinal blocks of masonry composed of tiles set in pink mortar, leaving channels for the hot air to flow between. At regular intervals the masonry supports were perforated by through-ducts, created simply by setting a hollow box-tile through the width of the support, so that the hot air in the main channels, joined to the vents leading from the *caldarium*, could pass into the two subsidiary channels beneath the centre of the floor. The masonry support flanking the eastern wall of the room was also provided with through-ducts of box-tiles placed side by side to allow the hot air to be fed into the jacketing of vertical wall flues with which the room would originally have been provided (pl. LXIIIa). In this case the box-tiles were not mortared to the basement floor as were those used elsewhere in the room, but were raised up some 3 in. (7.6 cm.) on a plinth of roof tiles, the reason being to draw off more easily the air which would rise to the ceiling of the channels. The arrangement was thus both simple and effective.

The tiles used to fit out the suite were imported specifically for the job, apart from the roof tiles which could well be re-used material. Several basic types of box-tile were used but all were decorated with roller-stamped designs differing completely from tiles used in the First-Period baths to the south or the early second-century baths at the end of the North Wing. The building material will be discussed in more detail below (Vol. II, pp. 43 ff.).

The *tepidarium* was painted in a similar style to the plunge bath (p. 177) with a deep red dado surmounted by a predominantly white wall divided into panels by red bands and thin black frame lines. There are also fragments of yellow painting, but how these fitted with the general design is uncertain (Vol. II, p. 78).

Room H. Room H, immediately to the north of the *tepidarium*, was floored with a rough white mortar and rubble floor showing no trace of internal features. Projecting beyond the east wall of rooms G and H into the Second-Period room E 3 was a shallow apse built in Third-Period style of re-used greensand blocks and floored with broken tiles set in pink mortar. A subsidiary source of heat was provided by means of a tile-built flue inserted into its south side. As the plan will show, the presence of the apse poses certain structural problems, for it straddles both rooms G and H, and if the wall between them stood to its full height it is difficult to see how the apse functioned. If, however, the dividing wall was merely a sleeper wall which did not project above floor-level, the apse could have held a semi-circular tepid bath opening out of the centre of the east wall of a long *tepidarium*. Another implication of this would be that the *tepidarium* was a unit of carefully-graded heat, the southern part of the room closest to the *caldarium* being the warmest while the north end ('room H') possessed no under-floor heating at all.

The 'sleeper wall' is known only from its 20-in. (0.5-m.) wide robber trench, no part of the actual structure remaining in position, nor are there any pitched footings similar to those which elsewhere underlie Third-Period walls. The implication must be that no superstructure was supported on it. Furthermore a sleeper wall in this position could have served the dual function of terminating the north side of the hypocaust basement, as suggested above, and at the same time containing a culvert to allow waste water from the tepid bath in the apse to drain away into the gutter. A drain in this direction would have been essential since no other possibility for draining the apsidal bath is known. An explanation in these terms would explain all the observed features and would be in keeping with the general subtlety of the architectural design.

Rooms I and J. Rooms I and J are strictly both part of the *frigidarium* built along the north boundary wall of the bath suite, adjacent to the north end of the *tepidarium*. Room I, which served as an ante-room, would originally have been floored at a height of about 15 in. (0.38 m.) above its surviving floor in order to hide the drains beneath. Since no trace of this floor now survives, nor is there any evidence of rubble packing around the drains to support a floor of tiles of mortar, it may be that timber planks were used, laid on joists set into flanking north and south walls. Beneath this floor was a well-built masonry drain leading from the cold plunge bath and emptying into the old Second-Period gutter (pls. LXIV*b*, LXV*b*). It was constructed of a base of roof tiles, side-walls of ashlar masonry and a capping of corbelled roof tiles. The inner faces of the masonry were rendered with pink mortar and a quarter-round moulding of similar mortar was provided to seal the angles between the walls and floor. Although the old open gutter in front of the Second-Period stylobate was later removed (pl. LXV*b*), it is evident that during the Third Period it was both present and functioning, for it is most unlikely that such a well-built drain would have emptied into an unlined robber trench. It was, in fact, correctly graded to suit the level of the gutter.

The small quantity of painted wall plaster recovered from the room show that it was fairly elaborately painted with areas of grey marbling splashed red, black and yellow, and red marbling splashed black, both probably serving as a dado. Above were bands of composite colours including blue, black and white, but little survives from the upper part of the walls (Vol. II, p. 75).

The west end of the *frigidarium* (room J) was occupied by a cold plunge bath measuring 7 ft. 3 in. by 5 ft. 3 in. (2.21 × 1.60 m.), from which the drain led (pl. LXIV*a*). The bath was floored, somewhat irregularly, with re-used tiles of various kinds, mostly *pilae* tiles, together with three slabs of marble. Of these one was a square slab of a coarse white crystalline stone, while the other two were of a much finer blue-veined marble with beaded edges — evidently re-used from the old palace (p. 111, and Vol. II, p. 24). The bath was provided with a bench along the north end, built of re-used semi-circular tiles set in pink mortar, and a rectangular seat projecting into the north-east corner. It, too, was built of re-used tiles.

The walls were rendered with a red mortar which in places survived to a height of 12 in. (0.3 m.) above the floor, even though the walls themselves had been robbed to their footings. From the robber trenches and from the filling of the bath itself were recovered large quantities of pink wall plaster which once covered the upper parts of the walls. A quantitative analysis suggests that the lower $3\frac{1}{2}$–4 ft. (1.07–1.22 m.) was painted deep red, while above this the walls were painted plain white with simple panelling picked out in a thin black line (Vol. II, p. 76).

Room K. Room K, of unknown extent, was built in the angle between the *frigidarium* and the *tepidarium*. It appears to have had no special internal features and was floored with a mortary rubble from which the surface has since been worn. It is, however, reasonably certain from its position that the room was a general concourse serving as an *apodyterium* and Entrance Hall. A visitor to the baths would have undressed here before passing through a door into the eastern part of the *frigidarium* from which point he could have chosen whether to begin his bathing with a swim in the cold bath or whether to start with the heat treatment.

The water supply (fig. 47)

The water supply to the baths was brought in from the east through a wooden water-pipe, jointed with circular iron collars, laid in a trench cut through the floor make-up and footings of the easternmost corridor belonging to the old palace. The ultimate source, which must be somewhere to the east, is unknown. The pipe has been traced into room E 5, but from here its course could not be followed. It is, however, certain that both of the flues, one serving the *caldarium* and the other heating the apsidal bath of the *tepidarium*, were provided with boilers supported over their cheek-walls. It is not unreasonable, therefore, to suppose that the pipe emptied into a communal tank from which the two boilers could be filled. No trace of the tank survives, but a possible site for it is on the wall between rooms E 4 and E 5, which had been specially strengthened with an added thickness of masonry in the Third Period. The strengthening masonry is difficult to explain structurally unless it was to support a tank, but positive evidence will never be forthcoming.

The drainage system and latrines (figs. 46–7)

The drainage system of the baths was based entirely upon the open gutter of the Second-Period courtyard and the culvert, which in the original palace period allowed the rainwater to drain away beneath the floors of the wing into the ditch. Only three of the original gutter blocks have survived the post-Third Period robbing, one in the north-east corner of the courtyard and two close to the south-east corner, both of which had had their inner flanges removed, suggesting that they might have been relaid here at some time, possibly the beginning of the Third Period. Nevertheless, the arrangement of the drains leaves no doubt that the gutter remained functional throughout the Third Period.

As we have seen, the three rooms of differing heats were each provided with a bath requiring drainage. The bath in the *caldarium* emptied its waste through a ceramic pipe, but the plunge bath of the *frigidarium* was larger and was accordingly provided with a more substantial drain. How the apsidal bath in the *tepidarium* was emptied is less certain, unless its drain ran beneath the floor of the *tepidarium* in the manner discussed above.

It remains a possibility that the baths were provided with latrines, but it must be admitted that no certain trace of any survives except for the amphora, set into the floor of room B, which could have been used as a urinal. Since the general flow of the waste water was towards the north-east corner, it is most unlikely that the rooms of the south range served as latrines, for this would have meant the sewage passing beneath the floors of the bath suite, an arrangement which could hardly have been acceptable. Indeed, the only reasonable site for latrines would have been along the culvert to the north of the baths.

In the old corridor, immediately north of rooms E 1 and E 2, through which the culvert passed a cross-wall had been constructed during the Third Period (pl. LXV*a*). The wall poses certain interesting problems, for it was built across the main culvert to serve as a revetment after the culvert walls and the adjacent clay and rubble make-up had been completely removed down to the level of the tiles of the culvert floor, which were left in position. The footings of the Second-Period wall on the east side of this excavation had been strengthened at this time, but the drain was allowed to pass through unhindered. Superficially it would appear as though these alterations destroyed the functioning of the culvert and thus marked the end of the useful life of the baths but there is a strong possibility that the alterations were connected with the construction of a latrine. The siting, at the end of a corridor 'down-stream' from the baths, is ideal but the fact that the wall was built across the drain raises problems. One factor, which might have required such a construction, should not be overlooked: that is that the base of the drain had subsided in places to such an extent that the sewage might have flowed back towards the baths. Plate LXV*a* shows clearly that the base of the culvert passing through the east wall was in fact higher than it was further to the west. However, the construction of the cross-wall would have prevented a flow-back and if a vent was built through it about 12 in. (0.3 m.) above the base it would have caused a head of waste water from the baths to build up behind it, the overflowing of which would have acted as an excellent sluicing for the latrine. Thus the apparent incongruities of the surviving features can be explained in terms of an efficiently functioning latrine. Such a structure would have required seats and an upper flooring of timber, but subsequent destruction has removed any trace which might have survived.

It should also be noted that a fresh water supply was provided by means of a water pipe leading to the south-east corner of the Aisled Hall (p. 157). It may well be that the pipe was in some way connected to the latrine for reasons of hygiene.

Superstructure

There is little to be said in detail of the superstructure of the baths, but a few general points can be made. The basic idea of the plan seems to have been to enclose the baths within four

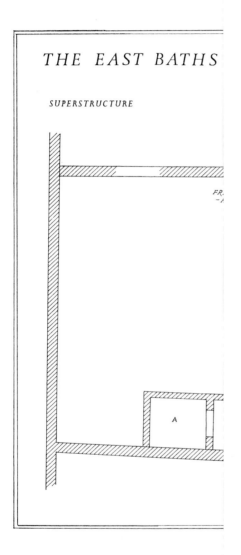

THE EAST BATHS

SUPERSTRUCTURE

F.R.

A

boundary walls, constructing the main rooms along two sides of the enclosure, leaving the rest free to serve perhaps as an exercise courtyard. The roofing of the south range could have been accomplished quite simply with a pent-house roof sloping down from the south wall, turning at the corner to cover room E. The *frigidarium* and Entrance Hall were probably covered by a single gabled roof. This leaves the problem of how the heated rooms were roofed. Traditionally one might have expected them to be covered with a single barrel-vault of masonry, and indeed quantities of plaster and voussoir blocks of tufa tend to support this view, but of the detailed structural arrangement we are ignorant.

Dating and significance

The evidence for the initial dating of the baths depends upon two sources: pottery and the patterned flue tiles. Fortunately, in room D a thin occupation layer containing pottery had been allowed to accumulate before the wall was built. Pottery was not common, but sufficient was recovered to show that it was predominantly Hadrianic in date. Since the layer appears to be an occupation accumulation rather than a deliberate deposit, which might contain a quantity of earlier material, it is fair to assume that the bath building was in existence soon after the beginning of the Antonine period at the latest. The patterned flue tiles tend to support this dating. Although their occurrence cannot be dated as precisely as pottery, it is generally accepted that roller-stamped tiles were manufactured in the first half of the second century. The construction of the bath building may therefore be tentatively dated to within the range *c.* A.D. 130–60.

The erection of what must be described as an elaborate and well-planned bath suite at Fishbourne at this time requires comment for, as we have seen, another range of baths had been inserted into the east end of the North Wing during this same broad period. Two possible explanations present themselves: either both were in use at the same time or one set replaced the other. If they are contemporary the implication must be that in the early second century the old palace was divided up into at least two flats, both provided with their own baths. Furthermore, if the original Period 1 and 2 baths were still functioning as well, it might be supposed that three separate flats had been carved out of the original building. The theory is attractive, but on balance the facts are against it. In the first place there is no evidence at all for the continued use of the palace baths into the second century, and secondly the North Wing bath was completely demolished by about the middle of the second century. It is therefore more in keeping with the available evidence to suggest that the north baths were built to replace the original south baths about A.D. 100 and were in turn rendered obsolete by the construction of the east baths, on a grander scale, sometime towards the middle of the century. This proposed sequence of rapid replacement requires some explanation. It is difficult to see why the First- and Second-Period baths were abandoned (if indeed they were), but they were built very close to the water-table near the edge of the inlet. They must always have been damp and any minor increase in the height of the water-table or an exceptionally high tide could easily have caused flooding, added to which they were sited inconveniently far from the centre of occupation. A combination of factors such as these would have argued against their survival for long. The reason why the baths at the east end of the North Wing were demolished is more readily apparent. The east end of the North Wing had been built over the remains of a substantial timber building and its surrounding drainage ditches belonging to the First Period. It was not long before subsidence occurred which, by the middle of the second century, had become so serious that it is difficult to see how some of the shallow-based Third-Period walls could have remained standing. The decision to demolish the contorted east end would therefore have been forced on the occupiers, but would have left them without a bath suite. It is to this context that the construction of the East Wing baths probably belongs. The quality and scale of the new work would be in keeping with the changes which were being undertaken at this time in the refitted part of the North Wing and must indicate a period of relative wealth and prosperity.

THE AISLED HALL

It was suggested above (pp. 157 ff.) that the reconstructed Hall might have been used for purposes of exercise connected with the North Wing bath suite constructed at the beginning of the second century. Since the Hall appears to have remained standing after these baths were demolished, it is a distinct possibility that it continued to function as a room for recreation and exercise throughout the life of the East Wing baths. It was conveniently connected to them by means of corridors, and such a facility would not have been out of place in a suite as elaborate as this.

THE REST OF THE EAST WING DURING THE THIRD PERIOD (figs. 46 and 48, p. 213)

Apart from the construction of the baths, there were no other major alterations made to the structure of the East Wing during the remainder of its life. Nevertheless, evidence for demolitions and minor readjustments exists which is best considered in terms of the individual parts of the old palace.

The east range of rooms north of the Entrance Hall.   The easternmost wall of the wing, bordering the street, still survives to street-level in fine ashlar masonry, whereas elsewhere in the wing building-stone of this quality had all been removed by stone robbers after the abandonment of the building. Although proof is lacking, the most reasonable explanation for this is that the wall was demolished during the Third Period and its lower courses, which remained in position, were covered by the general rubble and gravel which accumulated over the area soon afterwards. The explanation carries with it the further implication that the main structure of the east range was standing at the time of abandonment.

Only two features of Third-Period date are known within the range, with the exception of the flues and apse of the baths. In room E 2 a hearth of tiles was built against the south wall and in the corridor to the north another hearth of oval shape was created.

None of the rooms in the East Wing was refloored during the Third Period and indeed in practically every case the old floors had been allowed to wear out or were deliberately removed before the final abandonment. Evidently the wing was not used for habitation, though it could still have served as storage space. A close examination of the rubble sealing the building showed that very few fragments of roof tile and no rafter nails were to be found, implying that the roof had been removed before the building was abandoned. There is no indication as to when the demolition occurred, but the strong possibility remains that the wing was roofless throughout much of the Third Period and only the partly dismantled shell of the old building survived to the final destruction.

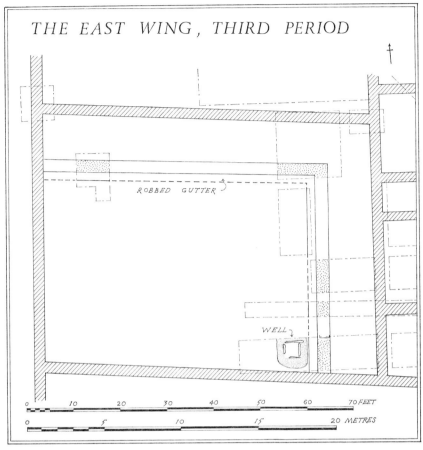

THE EAST WING, THIRD PERIOD

ROBBED GUTTER

WELL

0   10   20   30   40   50   60   70 FEET

0   5   10   15   20 METRES

Fig. 48

The courtyard south of the bath suite (fig. 48, p. 213). Towards the beginning of the Third Period a well was constructed in the south-east corner of the courtyard, close to the southern wall and the gutter. The well-pit, measuring some 6½ ft. (1.99 m.) across, was dug to a depth of 7 ft. (2.13 m.) below the contemporary surface down into the water-bearing gravel, cutting partly into the filling of the old First-Period stream (pl. LXVI). Within the pit the well itself was built with a series of rough oak timbers, each pair placed at right-angles to the pair beneath, the shoulder-jointed ends of one pair projecting beyond the sides of the timbers upon which they rested. In this way a loose framework was built up to the surface. All that survived in position were the partly-rotted timbers of the two lower frames, but the shaft itself, some 3 ft. (0.9 m.) across, could easily be traced by virtue of its different filling. Between the timber framework and the well-pit a filling of gravel and rubble, includ-ing tiles and mortar from a destroyed arch, had been tightly packed, serving perhaps to filter the surface water percolating into the well.

The well went out of use during the second century or early third century and was filled with rubbish and debris containing coarse ware datable to the early third century, part of a column base showing evidence of patching (Vol. ii, p. 5) and a fragment belonging to a Purbeck marble basin (Vol. ii, p. 40). The pottery does not occur in sufficiently large quantities to give a close date for the abandonment of the well: the sherds could easily have been dropped into the water whilst the well was still in use.

The area around the well was used as a rubbish tip from the late second to the late third century, giving rise to a layer of debris up to 12 in. (0.3 m.) thick, which was spread particularly densely over the floor of the veranda, but thinned out across the courtyard. Quantities of building material and iron slag were mixed up with the occupation layer, showing that some demolition as well as iron smelting was going on at the time, but the exact locations of these activities have not been traced.

The pottery recovered from the layer is predominantly late Antonine in character but fragments of Rhenish, Nene Valley and New Forest beakers show that rubbish continued to be deposited well into the third century. After this a turf-line, some 4–6 in. (10–15 cm.) thick, accumulated over the entire area before the adjacent superstructure collapsed or was abandoned, giving rise to a sealing layer of mortary rubble.

The Entrance Hall (fig. 34, p. 213).   The continued existence of the Hall in the centre of the East Wing as a major thoroughfare throughout the Third Period cannot be doubted, but the exact nature of its superstructure in this period is a matter of uncertainty. One fact, however, is clear: the story is one of gradual decline and collapse rather than of major modification. This is not to say that no structural repairs of the original building were undertaken. It may be that from time to time the roofs were patched or the walls rendered, but no evidence of such work could be expected to survive — everything points to a long period of gradual decay.

Along with much of the easternmost wall of the wing it would appear that the colonnade in front of the Hall was demolished to ground-level and gradually gravel and rubble washing off the road sealed the footings and spread into the veranda. Everywhere, where the floor of the Hall was examined, the original Second-Period surfacing had been removed down to the underlying clay make-up. Discontinuous patches of mortar, representing attempts at reflooring, occurred in the north-eastern part of the Hall, but elsewhere the traffic had worn deeply into the clay. By some undefined stage in the Third Period its volume seems to have decreased sufficiently to allow a layer of silty soil, possibly a turf-line, to accumulate over the northern half of the Hall while the southern half was kept clear by pedestrians or carts hugging the south wall. This was followed by the collapse of the main roof (or its deliberate demolition) which resulted in the deposition of a mass of roof tiles and some building rubble over the entire floor. The rubble lay where it had fallen and the traffic continued across it, wearing the tile and stones smooth and grinding the fallen mortar into powder (pl. lxvii). At this stage the walls were still standing, and moreover the wear of the tiles lying on the east side of the western bay of the Hall shows that the piers still formed obstacles which caused visitors to funnel between them. It was some time after this that the superstructure of the walls was destroyed, creating a layer of mortary rubble which sealed everything.

The sequence in the Third Period is therefore clear enough: a period of considerable wear followed by a lessening of traffic, allowing grass to grow, then the collapse of the old roof with the traffic continuing over the rubble, and finally (probably early in the fourth century) the demolition of the superstructure. Little dating evidence survives to define the sequence, except a few sherds of third-century coarse ware and two coins of the same date from the turf-line before the roof fell in. In general terms, then, a broad correlation with the mid to late third-century turf-line in the courtyard to the north is suggested.

The East Wing south of the Entrance Hall. So little has been seen of the southern part of the East Wing, and the area has been subjected to so much levelling and disturbance in post-Roman times that it is impossible to trace its development during the Third Period. All that can be said is that there is no evidence of post-Flavian alterations. Furthermore, of the few fragments of pottery recovered from destruction levels, all were of generalized second-century types. This need, of course, prove nothing but with the absence of later Roman material, even from the disturbed upper levels, it may tentatively be suggested that the area was abandoned and perhaps gutted at the beginning of the Third Period.

THE WEST WING IN THE THIRD PERIOD
(Fig. 49, p. 213)

That the West Wing continued in use into the Third Period is evident from the alterations made to its fabric and from the fact that a new corridor was built at the west end of the North Wing to join it, in a rather more convenient fashion, to the rooms in the West Wing. The alterations were, however, of a very minor character.

In the range of rooms proper the awkwardly-shaped room W 3 was divided by a partition wall built of re-used masonry (pl. XIIIa), which cut off its southern recess. The partition had been built directly on the mosaic floor with no foundations and when, after abandonment, it had been largely removed, sufficient of its basal mortar survived in position to demonstrate its former presence. The rectangular room created by the division continued to be entered through an original door in the south-west corner. At some stage, part of the mosaic floor close to the door sill was carefully and neatly patched with red tesserae. To the south, in room W 6, a small buttress of tiles and mortar had been built out from the west wall of the room. Its function must remain unknown but it may have served as a support for a vertical timber, connected perhaps with fitted furniture (pl. XVIb).

The only other alterations to the known part of the range are connected with the wide corridor which ran along the north side of the wing, joining the east corridor to the west. During the Third Period it was divided by four cross-walls of rough ashlar masonry into four separate compartments of varying size. Although in most cases only the footings survive, the remains show evidence of centrally-placed doorways. Two additional blocks of masonry should be assigned to this period: one was built into the south-east corner of the western-most room, the other was constructed in the north-west angle of the eastern corridor. The former was of tiles set in pink mortar, the latter of greensand masonry rendered externally with pink mortar. Their functions remain unknown. No precise dating evidence survives for these alterations but between the walls, and contemporary with their use, were occupation layers containing pottery of second- and early third-century date.

One further point should be mentioned here. From the west side of the apse a wall has been traced for a distance of 25 ft. (7.62 m.) continuing the line of the northernmost wall of the West Wing. It was built of greensand blocks set in a shallow foundation trench cut into the top of the Second-Period clay make-up, but is otherwise undated. While it could be of Second-Period date, built to define the southern limit of the supposed kitchen garden, the possibility remains that it belongs to the Third-Period alterations. The matter is considered above (p. 138).

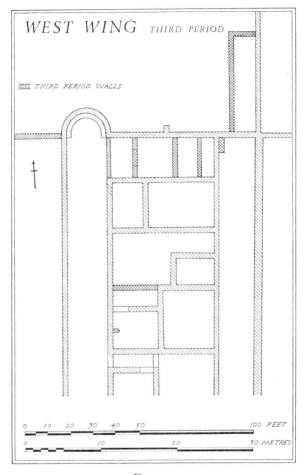

Fig. 49

THE GARDEN
(Fig. 35)

It is most unlikely that the huge formal garden could have been kept up during the Third Period (see Vol. II, p. 161). The expense would have been enormous and the scale quite out of proportion with the Third Period standard of living evident elsewhere on the site. Traces of an overgrown garden are not easily discoverable by archaeological methods, but two pieces of evidence, the dumping of rubbish in the north-west angle of the garden and the construction of a boundary-fence along the north side of the central path, suggest a radical change in the character of the garden area. The extreme north-west angle of the garden was covered to a depth of up to 2 ft. (0.6 m.) with a mass of occupation rubbish which had been carried out of the building and dumped on to the path, gradually spilling over the bedding trenches on either side, eventually clogging up the gutter and burying the enclosed area of the garden to a depth of 6–9 in. (15–22 cm.). The date of the deposit ranges from the Hadrianic period well into the third century, and must represent the household refuse cleared out of the North Wing during the Third Period. The whole length of the west path was also used as a tip, but for much smaller quantities of rubbish. At one point an irregular pit, 6 ft. (1.83 m.) in diameter and 5 ft. 3 in. (1.6 m.) deep, had been dug, cutting through and destroying the inner row of bedding trenches. Into it, rubbish containing third-century pottery and part of a column had been thrown (pl. LXXI*c*).

The north side of the central path still functioned as a boundary in the Third Period. It was delineated by a row of irregularly-spaced posts, of which the holes for seven survive, cut to a depth of between 3 and 8 in. (8–20 cm.) below the surviving surface. The central part of the garden had, however, been lowered some inches by medieval and recent plough-ing, perhaps completely destroying some of the intermediate post-holes. Strictly all that can be said of dating is that three of the posts stratigraphically post-date the construction of the bedding trenches, and since they are evidently in no way concerned with the garden arrange-ments they must belong to a period after the garden had ceased to exist. But the fact that the alignment itself so closely follows the north side of the path indicates that the construction of the fence is unlikely to have taken place long after the garden went out of use. On this evidence alone a Third-Period date is suggested.

SUMMARY OF THE THIRD-PERIOD OCCUPATION

The Third Period at Fishbourne — a period lasting some 180 years — saw a number of changes. At the beginning was the huge Flavian palace, by the end it had been converted into a comfortable stylish villa impressive enough by contemporary standards but small compared with its former state.

At the beginning of the second century the changes began with the construction of a suite of baths in the corridor between the North Wing and the Aisled Hall suggesting, perhaps, that the old bath suite was abandoned. The Aisled Hall was reduced in size but modifica-tions made to the structure of the North Wing at this time were insignificant. Major changes occurred towards the middle of the century, by which time the subsidence had so weakened the east end of the North Wing that it had to be demolished, together with the baths built only fifty years or so before. To compensate, a new and more elaborate bath building was constructed in the old northern courtyard of the East Wing. The style of the baths shows that the standard of living remained distinctly higher at Fishbourne than elsewhere in the con-temporary countryside, where bath suites are practically unknown. The living accommoda-tion was also modified and refitted at this period, some of the rooms being refloored with mosaics of good quality. By the late second century it could be said that the building at Fishbourne was still one of the foremost country houses in Britain — it had developed its own individual style, owing relatively little to the palace out of which it had grown.

Minor improvements to the North Wing continued to be made in the early part of the third century, and by the third quarter of the century modifications were still being carried out. It seems that a new programme of widespread rebuilding was initiated at this time, including the construction of a new hypocaust in the North Wing, a reglazing of many of the rooms and possibly the systematic demolition of the West Wing. It was at this stage that the fire struck — putting an end to everything.

The history of the Third Period has necessarily been based on the results derived from the excavation of the northern half of the old palace, but from the little that is known of the rest it is fair to assume that the nucleus of the late development lay in the north. Indeed, it is highly probable that the southern regions were abandoned or destroyed at an early stage.

PART V

The Destruction of the Building and the Subsequent History of the Site

DESTRUCTION AND DEMOLITION

THE END OF THE NORTH WING (fig. 43, p. 213)

BY the third quarter of the third century the occupied part of the North Wing had reached its final form. Habitation was now restricted to the western two-thirds of the old building and nearly two centuries of use and alterations had completely reproportioned the structure, giving rise to a compact entity probably facing north with its working rooms and kitchens on the south side. Alterations were still being undertaken when the building was burnt down.

The evidence for the fire is dramatic and conclusive. The whole of the occupied area was blanketed by a layer of charred roof timbers, rafter nails and discoloured fragments of roof tiles (pl. LXXIa) representing the debris of the collapsed roof. The sequence of destruction seems to be that the roof caught fire and as it burnt lead fittings melted and dripped in large puddles to the floors (pl. LXIX). The burning timbers then gave way and fell in, under the weight of the tiles, and continued to burn, discolouring large patches of the mosaics and tessellated floors. A careful excavation of the collapsed roof showed that none of the individual burnt rafters could be traced, with the exception of short lengths, 12–18 in. (0.3–0.46 m.) long. The explanation became apparent when the fallen tiles were considered, for no complete tiles at all were found and the fragments had obviously been disturbed after the burning so that highly oxidized tiles were immediately adjacent to pieces which had been re-fired under reducing conditions. This could not have happened to a fallen roof which had continued to burn *in situ* on the floor, for a short period, and had then been left undisturbed. The answer must be that the occupants returned after the fire and raked through the ashes, removing any articles of value. Complete roof tiles might have been carried off at this stage, or at some later period.

A fire of this intensity must have caused widespread damage to other parts of the structure beside the roof. The doors, for example, would have caught fire. In front of room N 7, masses of charcoal and several iron hinges (Vol. II, fig. 5) represent the remnants of the large doors that would have given access to the corridor on the south, and in rooms N 10 and N 11 quantities of double-ended iron studs of different sizes, used to decorate woodwork, may have come either from doorways opening through the timber partitions or from the partitions themselves (Vol. II, fig. 55). Elsewhere, e.g. the door at the west end of corridor N 14, both doors in room N 12 and the door leading into room N 6, remains of the charred timber sills survived in position (pl. LXVIIIb).

o

The fire must have caused considerable damage to the upstanding walls, but since the walls have been robbed there is little that can be said on the matter. The surviving wall plaster, however, shows that not all the walls were severely scorched; some certainly were but others had managed to escape the flames, depending presumably upon how the roof fell and the direction of the wind.

Although it is clear that the ruins were picked over soon after the fire, a number of objects were recovered during excavation which give an interesting indication of the last activities in the building before destruction. The heaps of mortar in room N 3, which were probably mixed ready for use in room N 1, have already been mentioned (p. 172). Other signs of building activity were found in room N 9 where large quantities of glass window-panes had been stacked up, presumably for use somewhere within the building. The fire had severely cracked some of them while others, closer to the flames, had been contorted and partially melted by the intensity of the heat. Most of the objects were, however, recovered from rooms N 12, N 3 and N 4, which at this stage during the life of the building served as the work-shops or store-rooms. Against the southern wall of room N 12 a group of pots lay scattered (pl. LXX) but so arranged as to suggest that they had either fallen from a shelf or had been smashed in position by falling debris. Closely associated with the pots were angle-brackets of iron of a type which would have been used as strengtheners for a wooden box or tray (Vol. II, fig. 62). The implication is that the pots may have been standing on a tray or in a box when the building collapsed. A few feet away a dish lay on the floor close to a buckled iron collar from a water-pipe. The pots all show clear evidence of having been subjected to considerable heat after they had been smashed, causing joining pieces to be re-fired to different colours. One of the large jars contained lentils which survived in a much-charred condition (Vol. II, p. 376). The dating significance of the pottery will be considered below (p. 220).

In the northern half of room N 12 a group of iron objects had been left lying on the floor, including three hippo-sandals and a length of chain attached to a padlock (Vol. II, fig. 64). Room N 3 also produced a group of iron objects, mainly brackets and large nails, but from the northern part of the room came two iron axle-caps with slots for the linchpins (Vol. II, fig. 61). They were found 5 ft. 6 in. (1.68 m.) apart and were orientated in such a way as to suggest that the entire wooden axle lay on the floor when the fire began. A number of other iron objects were found beneath the destruction-level, but these are discussed in detail below (Vol. II, p. 134).

Room N 4 served more as a workshop than as a store-room. Its oven and hearth have already been mentioned, but at the time of destruction it also contained two large limestone blocks (pl. LXVIIIa) which had simply been placed on the floor. Both showed clear signs of their upper surfaces having been considerably worn, suggesting that they may have been used as benches or anvils connected with whatever constructional functions were carried out in the room.

Surprisingly little decorative or architectural material was found in the rubble, apart from quantities of painted wall plaster. On the floor of room N 10 an area of marble wall inlay had peeled off the wall just before the roof fell in, and lay buried beneath the collapsed tiles on the tessellated floor, and several marble mouldings were found in rooms N 10 and 11, mixed up with the rubble. Some pieces of fluted marble inlay were also recovered from the rubble over the ovens in the western corridor of the old courtyard, but the general impression is that a lot of detailing of this kind, surviving from the old Second-Period decor, must have been salvaged after the fire. How many larger architectural features were still in use by the end of the Third Period cannot be ascertained; one column base was found on the floor of room N 3 and another lay amid the rubble in the north-west corner of the gutter robber trench, but they were not part of the collapsed superstructure since both could be shown to have been in position before the fire. It is unlikely that features of this kind survived in their original positions after the mid second-century alterations.

The date of the fire in the North Wing depends upon the assessment of the group of pottery found on the floor of room N 12 beneath the destruction debris. Since there can be no doubt that the vessels were all currently in use when the building was burnt down, they can be used as a reliable indication of the final date of occupation. The significance of the individual types is considered in some detail below and need not be repeated here. Suffice it to say that the group as a whole can be dated to the period A.D. 270–90 (see p. 220).

THE DESTRUCTION OF THE EAST WING BATH SUITE (p. 213)

The fire in the North Wing did not spread to the east bath suite, presumably because by this time the two buildings were completely detached. Nevertheless it would appear that the destruction of the North Wing in the late third century led to the immediate abandonment of the bath suite and to its systematic demolition. The suspended floors were broken up and the debris lay scattered about and tipped in heaps in the room containing the *caldarium* flue and the room immediately to the east of it, so that usable tiles from the hypocaust and the wall flues of the heated rooms could be salvaged. The other parts of the building were not ransacked in this way and there is positive evidence that no large-scale attempt was made to remove the stone blocks of the walls themselves, the robbers being content at this stage to remove only tiles. Altogether, 43 coins have been recovered from demolition layers, all of which apart from early strays date to the period from 268 to 296. The conclusion is clear enough; as soon as the North Wing had been destroyed by fire the bath suite became useless and could be dismantled. The dating evidence for the two events is completely consistent with the view that one event was consequent upon the other (pp. 220–1).

THE LATE OCCUPATION IN THE EAST WING (fig. 46, p. 213)

Unlike the North Wing, where the late third-century fire marks the end of occupation, the contemporary demolition of the East Wing bath suite was followed by a period of occupation confined, apparently, to rooms E 1–3. It may be that the two hearths, in room E 2 and the corridor to the north of it, belong to this phase, but it is impossible to be sure. The most notable feature of the late habitation is a 6–9-in. (15–23-cm.) thick layer of occupation debris which had been allowed to accumulate in room E 3, sealing the destroyed remnants of the Third-Period *tepidarium* apse. The occupation, therefore, stratigraphically post-dates the end of the Third Period, a fact which is confirmed by the pottery from the layer which belongs to the late third–early fourth century (Vol. II, pp. 165 ff.) and includes several diagnostic New Forest types absent elsewhere on the site (p. 221).

O*

The nature of this late occupation is limited in extent and appears to be of no considerable duration. It is best explained as a temporary and rather squalid use of the shell of the old building after the site had become largely derelict, perhaps by the gang of labourers responsible for the systematic demolition of the superstructure following the fire. The work of demolition was considerable and would have been spread over months, if not years. It is not unreasonable to suppose that the men concerned used part of the old building as a shelter for eating and sleeping until the job was complete.

THE END OF THE AISLED HALL   (fig. 43, p. 214)

The demolition of the east end of the North Wing in the middle of the second century left the Hall, in its reduced and re-roofed state, isolated from the inhabited area of the building. It was probably for this reason that the fire did not spread, that is always supposing that the Hall was still standing at the time. Unfortunately there is no close dating evidence for the last stages in the life of the Hall. A few scraps of generalized third-century coarse ware were found on its floors, but the area had been kept very clean and it would be unwise to argue closely with so little evidence to go on. There is, however, one point which might be marginally relevant. A heap of white tesserae had been piled up in the north-east corner of the building before the destruction. As we will see (below, p. 191), white tesserae were being uprooted from one of the rooms in the West Wing at the time of the fire. It therefore remains a possibility that as part of the phase of rebuilding which was under way at the time of the fire tesserae were being removed from the West Wing and temporarily stored in the Hall before being carted off. If so, the demolition of the Hall and the fire both came after this event. The link is tenuous and accordingly weak, but it is consistent with the known facts.

The physical evidence for the destruction of the Hall consists of a layer of roof tiles and mortary rubble lying to a maximum depth of 15 in. (0.38 m.) above the Hall floor. The almost complete absence of greensand building blocks strongly suggests that the walls were still standing at this stage. There is no certain way of saying whether the roof collapsed accidentally or whether the debris layer is the result of a deliberate act of demolition. The relative lack of rafter nails points to careful demolition in which useful timber and tiles were removed while rotten timbers and broken tiles were discarded on the spot. In all probability this followed the fire and was contemporary with the pulling down of the east bath suite.

THE END OF THE WEST WING   (fig. 49, p. 214)

The nature of the end of the West Wing poses a number of problems, largely because the whole area has suffered considerably from post-Roman ploughing. With very few exceptions, agricultural activities have removed all trace of destruction levels and in many areas even the floors and their underlying make-up have been ploughed away. The only evidence upon which to assess the final phase is therefore restricted to those areas where, for varying reasons, destruction levels survive. Even so, the evidence is inconclusive.

In the apse of the Audience Chamber and in rooms W 11 and W 12 deposits of rubble survive which show no trace whatsoever of burning, but in both cases the rubble is atypical. In the apse only 2–3 in. (5–7.6 cm.) of rubble survives above the floor and this is confined to fallen stucco from the ceiling, whereas rooms W 11 and 12 are filled with rubble from the collapsed hypocaust and superstructure which evidently accumulated at some stage before the roof fell in. Where traces of collapsed roof occur, in rooms W 3 and W 6, no burnt rafters or rafter nails were found. On the other hand, there are some traces of burning. In the corridor behind the Audience Chamber fragments of painted plaster were recovered which had evidently fallen from a badly scorched wall, the mosaic in room W 8 showed areas of burning, and traces of a charred door sill survived between rooms W 7 and W 9. Admittedly these features can all be explained away in one way or another, but taken in conjunction they are suggestive of destruction by fire, presumably the North Wing fire, which could easily have spread to the adjacent building. But even if destruction by fire is accepted and it is assumed that ploughing has been responsible for removing most of the traces, certain problems remain. There is clear evidence, for example, that loose tesserae were being stockpiled in room W 6. Moreover, the total absence of rafter nails from the region of rooms W 3 and W 6, where some rubble does survive, is surprising because unlike large tiles which can be dragged off by extra-deep ploughing, or charcoal which might be dispersed and broken down by a combination of roots, worms and ploughing, rafter nails would tend to survive if they had once blanketed the floors of the West Wing in the same quantities as they did the North Wing.

One possible explanation presents itself, that the West Wing was actively undergoing demolition when the fire struck. The heaps of tesserae show that the floors were being removed at this time and it could well be that parts of the roof had already been taken down as well. The explanation attractively supports the facts and may well approach the truth, but it must remain unproven.

THE ROBBING OF THE MASONRY (p. 214)

The late third-century destruction was followed at once by the removal of tiles from the ruins and by the partial demolition of the unburnt structures again to recover tile fittings of various kinds. This much is clear from the stratigraphy above the latest floors which shows the rubbish of the collapsed or demolished roofs lying in the different rooms retained by the walls, which were still at this time standing. Then followed a period of apparent abandonment, during which mortar peeled off the walls in small pieces, presumably under the influence of natural weathering, and fell into the rooms together with soil which had begun to accumulate. This phase is not always apparent, but in several parts of the North Wing, where a sufficient profile had escaped the later ploughing, it was well-marked. How long a period it represents is uncertain but since no well-defined turf-line had formed, it may not be more than a few years — it could be as little as a few months.

The rubble filling the rooms to a depth of 2–2½ ft. (0.6–0.76 m.) tended to protect the painted plaster of the wall-faces. This was particularly clear along the west wall of room N 12 and around the cold plunge of the east bath suite, where the lower 2 ft. (0.6 m.) of the plaster facing was well preserved.

The phase of apparent neglect was followed by a period of active stone robbing, during which time all the upstanding walls were removed down to their flint rubble footings. The robbing was so thorough and methodical that where the ashlar masonry had not been removed there is usually some good explanation. In the case of the east end of the North

Wing, the reason for the survival of the lowest courses was that the walls had been demolished to ground-level in an earlier period and the stumps of the walls could no longer be seen. In the west end of the North Wing the short lengths of foundation courses, which survive between deep robber trenches, represent the positions of doors: to a stone robber working from above it would have been a waste of effort to remove all the debris clogging a door simply to get at the few dozen ashlar blocks below its sill. Even so, in some cases this was done and all trace of the doorways consequently obliterated. The section of wall between rooms N 3 and N 4, which still survives to a height of several courses, had escaped robbing because at the time of the fire its upper part had collapsed into room N 4 only to be overlaid by the mortar peeling off the adjacent walls. By the time the stone robbers arrived there was no trace of it to be seen.

The care with which the walls were robbed is shown by the robber trench along the west side of room N 12, which had followed the wall with such precision that the plaster rendering, supported by the rubble accumulation in the rooms, remained standing to a height of 2 ft. (0.6 m.). Only after the wall had been removed did the plaster fall away and collapse into the bottom of the robber trench (pl. LXXIb). In the case of the plaster facing on the west wall of room N 1, the robber trench had been filled back before the plaster could collapse and consequently it was preserved exactly in its original position, even though the wall behind it had been removed (pl. XLVIa).

At what date the robbing took place is uncertain, but it could not have been long after the fire. In all probability it was contemporary with the late third- to early fourth-century occupation found in room E 3 of the East Wing which, it is argued above, might have been the result of temporary habitation by the stone robbers. It might be added that of the very small number of fourth-century coins recovered from the site all except one belong to the first quarter of the century (Vol. II, p. 98). The implication is that after c. 310–20 all activity had ceased.

SUMMARY OF THE DESTRUCTION

The end of Roman Fishbourne is clear. In about A.D. 280–90 the North Wing was gripped in a disastrous fire which destroyed the entire upper part of the building, leaving only the walls standing. It seems that the fire spread to the West Wing, where there is some evidence that partial demolition was going on. Both the Aisled Hall and the East Wing bath suite were sufficiently detached to prevent the fire in the North Wing from spreading. Immediately following the disaster, people returned to the ruins to remove useful tiles and any other valuable fittings which had survived, but no attempt was made to rebuild. Indeed, the baths and very probably the Hall were gutted at this time and left abandoned. Then followed a period of systematic stone robbing resulting in the total dismantling of all the standing superstructure. It appears that the work-gang involved camped in the shell of the East Wing until their activities were completed. By the 320s the site was finally abandoned.

Two questions need some consideration: what caused the fire and why was the building not re-inhabited? The fire could, of course, have been the result of an accident — a careless builder perhaps — but it remains a possibility that it might have been started by raiders. Fishbourne is very close to the sea and, judging by the number of coin hoards of the period deposited along the south coast, threat of pirate attack was in the air. It is possible that the destruction of the villa at Preston was a direct result of these troubled times. Events became so serious by the mid-280s that Carausius was appointed for the task of 'ridding the shores of Belgica and Armorica of pirates' — a briefing which clearly implies that the pirates had broken through the Straits of Dover and were raiding the southern shores. A context therefore exists for the destruction of Fishbourne, but proof will remain lacking.

We are unlikely ever to know why the building was not re-occupied. Several factors would have had a bearing on the decision: the extent of the destruction may have made rebuilding impracticable, it may have been thought unsafe to live so close to an undefended shore and, of even more significance, it seems that a rise in sea-level was causing flooding, both of the southern part of the site and of the area to the north of the building. All told, Fishbourne was no longer considered to be a suitable place for occupation.

FISHBOURNE FROM THE FIFTH CENTURY

HUMAN BURIALS   (fig. 50)

The early fourth-century demolition left the site of the old palace as heaps of weed-grown rubble and for some time it must have remained thus, weathering and plant action gradually smoothing out the contours. While the ponding up of spring water to the north turned a large expanse of land into a bog, the encroachment of the sea on the south side led eventually to the formation of an extensive salt marsh separating the site from the open navigable creek.

At some later date at least four bodies were buried haphazardly in the rubble, the archaeological details of which may be summarized as follows:

Grave 1.   An extended inhumation lying supine, with the hands folded across the pelvis. The body was orientated north–south with the head at the north, facing east. No grave goods were found, nor were there any traces of a coffin. The grave had been cut into the filling of a robber trench for the east wall of room N 11 and was sealed by ploughsoil.

Grave 2 (pl. LXXIIa).   An extended inhumation lying supine, with the hands folded across the pelvis. The body was orientated north–south with the head at the north, facing east. No grave goods were found, nor were there any traces of a coffin. The grave had been cut through the rubble which had accumulated on the floor of room N 9, to a depth of 10 in. (25 cm.) below the surface of the pink mortar floor. It was sealed by the ploughsoil.

Grave 3 (pl. LXXIIb).   An extended inhumation lying supine, with the hands folded across the pelvis. The body was orientated east–west with the head at the west, facing south. No grave goods were found, nor were there any traces of a coffin. The grave had been cut into the rubble which had accumulated against the north wall of the veranda fronting the North Wing immediately east of room N 4, but not deep enough to penetrate the floor. It was sealed by the ploughsoil. A number of disarticulated fragments of human bones were found close by.

Grave 4 (pl. LXXIIc). An inhumation with knees flexed, lying supine with the hands folded across the pelvis. The body was orientated north–south with the head to the north facing east. No grave goods were found, nor were there any traces of a coffin; indeed the layout of the burial would preclude one. The grave had been cut through the rubble which had accumulated in the north-west corner of the garden and was sealed by the ploughsoil.

The general characteristics of the burials are therefore inhumation, an essentially non-east–west orientation, no grave goods and probably no coffins. As to their date all that can be said is that they post-date the early fourth century and are earlier than the ploughsoil, which began to accumulate at least as early as the eleventh century. This is not much to go on, but their orientation suggests that they are likely to be non-Christian, which together with the fact that they are inhumed points more to a late or sub-Roman date than to the Saxon period. Further than this it is not possible to go.

MEDIEVAL AGRICULTURE AND STONE ROBBING   (fig. 50)

The entire site was covered with a layer of finely broken rubble mixed with a large amount of soil, which had evidently been created by ploughing activities over a long period. This ploughsoil varied in thickness according to the topography of the Roman levels beneath. Thus over the high West Wing it was a mere 2–3 in. (5–7.6 cm.) thick, whilst immediately to the east of the West Wing revetting wall it occurred to a depth of some 3 ft. (1 m.), gradually thinning out again across the garden, but thickening as the East Wing approached until it reached an average thickness of 18 in. (0.5 m.).

Mixed up with the ploughsoil was a quantity of small abraded sherds of medieval and later pottery presumably derived from the manuring of the fields with household debris. The pottery ranged in date from the eleventh to the sixteenth century, nondescript green-glazed sherds of the thirteenth and fourteenth centuries predominating. Medieval and later coins, including a short cross penny of Henry II or III, a groat of Henry VI, and a half groat of Henry VII or VIII, were found together with a number of Nuremburg tokens of the sixteenth century.

Medieval agricultural features impinged upon the Roman structure in several places. The west end of a strip field (field 2) some 68 ft. (20.74 m.) wide, was clearly to be seen over the West Wing, where ploughing had gouged deeply into the Roman floors completely destroying them and leaving well-defined edges with the non-ploughed areas. Immediately to the south lay the edge of another field (field 3) 15 ft. (4.57 m.) away from the first. It, too, ended more or less on a line with the west end of field 2. Its width could not be measured at this end, where a modern garden wall prevented further excavation, but a length of a shallow gully was traced over the East Wing of the Roman building aligned with the field and possibly representing its south side. If so, this field would be almost exactly the same width, 68 ft. (20.74 m.), as field 2. The south side of another field (field 1) could also be traced cutting into the floors of the Roman West Wing, some 16 ft. (4.88 m.) north of the north side of field 2. Its northern boundary was clearly marked by a shallow gully, containing sherds of thirteenth–fourteenth-century pottery, which had been gouged through the floors of the North Wing. The gully was short but its line was continued by a series of ragged pits, possibly resulting from tree-root penetration. The width of field 1 was identical to that of the other two fields. Plough-ruts scoring through the Roman surfaces appeared in small areas in fields 1 and 3.

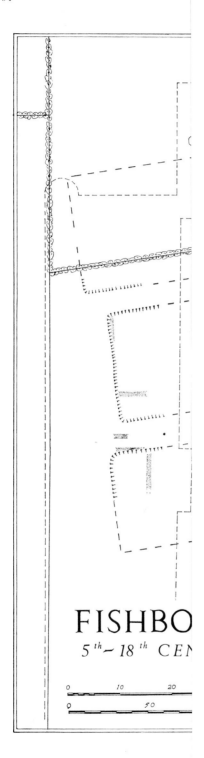

FISHBO

5 *th* ~ 18 *th* CEN

0   *10*   20

0   *50*

There is, therefore, clear evidence of three separate medieval fields, each about 68 ft. (20.74 m.) wide, separated from each other by unploughed baulks, 15–16 ft. (c. 4.7 m.) wide. Fig. 50 shows that their alignment was closely followed by the present-day boundaries, which were probably set out when the area was enclosed in the eighteenth century. The easternmost hedge must mark the approximate end of the strip fields, since it follows the line of the stream which would have been in existence since Roman times. The maximum length of the strips is therefore 450 ft. (137 m.), but the actual length is likely to be less to allow a headland for the plough to turn. If the present (i.e. enclosure date) western boundary followed the medieval boundary, as would appear probable, the headland at the east end would have been between 30 and 40 ft. (9–12 m.), the same as it is at the west end.

During the ploughing across the West Wing, the medieval inhabitants would have encountered the Roman flint footings which stood here to a few inches above the level of the Roman floors. Considerable stone robbing activities followed, resulting in the almost total removal of certain lengths of the footings. The robbing is dated by several sherds of thirteenth–fourteenth-century pots from the bottom of the robber trenches. The other wings were largely untouched at this time because the flint cobble footings, which had escaped late Roman robbing, were up to 2 ft. (0.6 m.) below floor level and were therefore unlikely to be found during normal agricultural activity. Only one wall in the East Wing, on the south side of room E 9, suffered from deep medieval robbing.

RECENT TIMES

At the time of the Enclosures, the new fields were delineated by deep V-shaped ditches, which served to drain the area, flanked by thorn hedges. These features survived largely intact until excavation began in 1961. The relative lack of seventeenth–nineteenth-century pottery, together with the formation of a 9–12-in. (0.2–0.3-m.) thick stone-free topsoil, suggests that ploughing ceased and the area reverted to pasture. The construction of a stable as part of the outbuildings of the eighteenth-century farmhouse built in the south-east corner of the site may be an added indication of the predominantly pastoral activities. It was in the early nineteenth century that a system of land-drains was cut through the ill-drained area over the old Roman garden. The stratigraphy shows that they were dug at a time long after ploughing had ceased.

Apart from ribbon development along the main road, the site changed little in the nineteenth and early twentieth centuries, until, in 1960, the trench for the water-main sliced through the Roman building.

CONSERVATION AND PRESERVATION

In 1963, a large part of the site of the palace was bought by Mr I. D. Margary and donated to the Sussex Archaeological Trust. Two years later work began on the construction of a series of modern buildings designed to display the Roman remains, and on 31 May 1968 the site was opened to the public. The presentation and consolidation of the structures posed problems for which, frequently, no precedents existed, but with the aid of a number of professional consultants the difficulties were gradually overcome. In the following pages a general outline of the work will be given, which will serve to summarize the state of the site when archaeological work was concluded in April 1969.

THE MODERN BUILDING

Since most of the well-preserved floors lay in the North Wing of the Roman palace, it was decided to concentrate the work of preservation upon that area by enclosing it entirely within a modern protective cover-building in which the physical atmosphere could, to some extent, be regulated. The work of designing the cover, and all the other buildings which were later to be erected, was placed in the hands of the Trust's architects, Carden, Godfrey and Macfadyen Ltd.

It was felt that the cover-building should be based as exactly as possible on the Roman foundations to give an idea of the mass of the Roman wing, while in no way attempting to reproduce it architecturally. It was further agreed that there should be no internal supports. In consequence, it was necessary to span a width of 70 ft. (21.3 m.), the entire building being 270 ft. (82.3 m.) long. The resulting structure incorporated a scissor-strutted Blandform beam roof of laminated timber, supported on a framework of vertical timbers based on concrete footings which, except at the east end, followed exactly the footings for the outer walls of the Roman wing. The roof was sheathed in aluminium and boarded internally while the south and east walls were predominantly of glass. Originally it was intended that the north wall should be similarly built, but the presence of a high-power, 18 in. (0.46 m.) water-main immediately outside required the wall to be more substantially constructed of brick-faced concrete. The happy combination of materials and design have created a building admirably suited to its function: it is light and airy, the faceting of the roof gives a feeling of life and space where a simple ceiling would have been dull and claustrophobic, and the simplicity of the work, while pleasing in its own right, in no way detracts from the Roman features which it is designed to protect.

It was realized that construction work on this scale raised the possibilities of damage to the Roman work, but these were considerably lessened by leaving a soil-cover of between 18 in. and 3 ft. (0.46–0.6 m.) over the entire site while work was in progress. The two east–west foundation trenches were then dug precisely along the lines of the Roman robber trenches, down to the level of the flint cobble footings. In most cases the robber trenches had already been excavated archaeologically, but where the original filling still remained it was removed under archaeological supervision. The sides of the trenches were then shuttered and the modern reinforced concrete foundation was created with special strengthening at the points where the load-bearing vertical timbers were to stand. Generally the process worked efficiently and safely, with the exception of one occurrence when an unexpected rise in the water-table caused the shuttering on the east side of room N 3 to collapse, with the result that the sides of the trench fell in, destroying the edge of the mosaic. Fortunately, only the plain white border was involved and the fragments were rescued and re-set later. Once the footing had set the superstructure was erected, great care being taken to ensure that the soil within the building was in no way penetrated or subjected to extreme weight. Only after the structure was completed was the soil within removed and the Roman features re-exposed.

One of the most serious difficulties to be encountered was the high water-table in the area. The site lies astride one of the many streams which drain the South Downs, and at times of heavy rainfall the water-table rises rapidly to within a foot of the undisturbed soil-level. Since it was essential that the North Wing building should be well-drained, two lateral drains were dug, clear of the building, on the north and south sides to collect the water and empty it into the stream, the bed of which had to be lowered to accommodate to the required level. The drains were carefully sited to be clear of Roman structures and their sections were recorded.

The position of the site in relation to the present-day lines of communication determined that public access could be provided only from the west. This in turn led to the decision to site the concourse, museum and Custodian's house in the angle between the North and West Wings, where they would be unobtrusive when viewed from within the Roman garden but would still serve as a reception area between the entrance and the Roman North Wing. An added advantage of the position was that no Roman structure was known to occupy the area. Even so, before the buildings were erected the site was archaeologically excavated almost in its entirety.

THE PRESERVATION OF THE UNCOVERED AREAS

The East and West Wings were re-covered with soil after excavation. As a temporary measure they have been re-sown with grass-seed in the expectation that eventually the Trust may one day wish either to cover all or part of the wings with a new building or to lay out the position of the walls on the surface with some suitable markers.

The garden. Apart from a relatively small strip of soil along the east side of the garden, south of the central pathway, the whole of that part of the garden which belongs to the Trust has been levelled to the Roman ground-surface, and laid out as it is thought to have been in the Roman period. In practice this means that the northern half of the actual garden was thus treated. The Roman paths were gravelled and the lines of most of the bedding trenches were marked with bushes of box which, we are assured, will eventually grow into continuous hedges. The single bedding pit now supports a cypress tree, while the line of post-holes and bedding pits across the east side of the garden is represented by flowering cherry trees growing against a timber frame. The shallow bedding slots found lining the west side of the east path have been marked by a bed of acanthus but the whole of the central area, which produced no evidence of its original layout, has been turfed. The intention behind this work has been simply to lay out the plan of the garden as it was discovered by excavation, using the types of plants which the Romans commonly employed for this purpose in their contemporary gardens.

The colonnades surrounding the garden were variously treated. The revetting wall in front of the West Wing, still surviving to a height of 3 ft. 6 in. (1.07 m.), was consolidated by a team of masons working under the direction of a skilled craftsman provided by the Ministry of Public Building and Works.[1] In places the wall had suffered badly from robbing and weathering, causing it to slip forwards into the robber trench left after the gutter in front of it had been removed. At points such as this, concrete underpinning was required. The upstanding parts of the wall were treated differently according to the state of the masonry.

---

[1] The work was directly supervised by Mr R. Sanders under the general guidance of Mr W. Taylor, the area superintendent.

Where the facing survived in position, repointing and the resetting of the top course of blocks was all that was necessary, but where only core-work survived the outer skin had to be removed and reset completely, keeping as close to the original appearance as possible. At the north end of the wall the masonry was in such a weak state that even the facing-stones had to be removed and completely reset. Everywhere a lime mortar was used which dried to a light-grey colour. It can be readily distinguished from the Roman mortar, which is more yellow in appearance and contains a more pebbly aggregate.

The west end of the north colonnade posed different problems. The stylobate and gutter were in a sufficient state of preservation to leave untreated, but the walls and column bases on them were very badly shattered and weathered and had to be removed for consolidation. Of the three column bases the first and second from the west were treated by the Ministry of Public Building and Works masons, who cleaned the stonework thoroughly and joined the broken fragments with Akemi and dowels of delta metal, making good the deeper voids with stone dust and white cement, but leaving the missing areas unmade up. The third base was made up completely and is now incorporated in the reconstructed column on show in the museum, together with one of the original capitals found close to it in the rubble. The lengths of ashlar masonry between the columns and the walls forming the base of the water-tank were dismantled, the stonework thoroughly dried and impregnated with Moviol,[1] and the features rebuilt exactly as they once were.

With the exception of a single gutter block in position in front of the Entrance Hall and the concrete footing of the stylobate close by, which has been consolidated and exposed, the rest of the northern and eastern stylobate and gutter had been completely destroyed in the Roman period. The position of the stylobate is to be marked out with modern paving slabs, while the missing gutter is delineated by concrete edging strips retaining loose gravel.

The treatment and consolidation of the walls and floors of the North Wing

The construction of the cover-building and of the two external drains provided some control of the atmosphere within the North Wing, but even so the exceptionally high water-table tended to create a high humidity which could only be reduced by an extensive system of air-blowers and ventilation louvres. The problems of frost fracturing which would arise under these conditions at sub-zero temperatures were overcome by the addition of air-heaters designed to cut in when the internal temperature reached 55°F.

The treatment of the floors and walls was conditioned by a number of considerations. First, as much of the original structure that was sound should be left untouched; second, features that were weak or likely to decay should be given the minimum of consolidation treatment sufficient to preserve them; third, that restoration should be carried out only where it was necessary to preserve ancient features or make the remains more intelligible; and fourth, that non-floored areas should be treated so as to prevent the creation of dust and to control the problems of rising damp.

The mosaic floors (pl. LXXIIIb). The mosaic floors were found to be in various states of stability. In some cases the adhesion between the tesserae and the underlying matrix was good, whilst in others the tesserae had become detached from their bedding. Clearly, there-

---

[1] The masonry was treated by Mrs M. Rule under whose supervision the wall was rebuilt.

fore, different degrees of treatment were required. In the case of the well-preserved floors, such as those in rooms N 1, N 2, N 3, N 4, N 5, N 7 and N 8, all that was required was for the interstices to be raked clean and regrouted with a slurry of cement to give the individual tesserae good lateral adhesion and to prevent the downward penetration of water when the floors were being cleaned. The general policy adopted towards repair was that where individual or small groups of tesserae were missing or loose they were replaced with Roman tesserae collected during excavation; larger holes 5 in. (12.5 cm.) or more across, were simply infilled with a cement, but where large areas of the original matrix survived intact bearing the impressions of the tesserae, as in rooms N 1, N 3 and N 4, the edge of the mosaic was retained by a fillet of cement and the whole of the missing area left in the state in which it was found. The Dolphin floor required special treatment. In some parts of it, where subsidence had created deep vertical cracks and faults through the floor, cement had to be pumped into the voids beneath while the tesserae along the edges of the cracks, where the mortar was weak, had to be lifted and reset. A strip of about 2 ft. (0.6 m.) wide along the north side of the room, which had subsided, was lifted in sections, using a fine scrim stuck to the surface, and relaid on a new bedding.

The mosaics in room N 13 presented a special problem, for here two floors remained, one superimposed on the other, the upper floor being in a very weak state. All that could be done was a regrouting of both surfaces and a strengthening of the exposed edges of the upper floor. Such a treatment retains the exact quality of the original but is not, of necessity, as strong as if the technique adopted elsewhere had been employed.

The seven remaining floors, nos. N 11, N 12, N 14, N 19, N 20, N 21 and N 22, were all in a very friable state largely because of their nearness to the modern surface, but partly because some of them had subsided violently into earlier features beneath. Numbers N 11, N 12 and N 14 were all lifted in sections, on average 2 ft. (0.6 m.) square, using a technique of gluing a fine scrim on to the surface, undercutting the section and sliding it on to a sheet of hardboard. The sections were then reversed and cleaned and finally reset in their original positions in a slurry of cement laid on a new bedding of concrete. The technique of lifting only small sections without rolling them has the great advantage that the pieces can be lifted and turned easily by one man. They are also far more manageable when they are relaid; indeed this is the only convenient method for replacing a mosaic in its original position — a team of two experienced workers could re-lay an area of 10 sq. ft. in a day. Needless to say, success depends upon rigorous recording. The method employed here was to attach battens around the walls, marking them with a series of grid numbers with which the lifted sections could be numbered. The scrim was sufficiently transparent for the design of each piece to be seen, thus greatly facilitating the re-laying. One possible disadvantage of lifting floors in small sections is that the cuts are many, but if the breaks are made along the lines of the design rather than arbitrarily, and the re-laying is sufficiently careful, no joints need be obvious.

The mosaic in room N 19 had suffered considerably from recent agriculture and from the water-main trench which had been gouged through it. In this case, it was decided to repair the smaller holes as extensively as possible and regrout the whole floor, infilling the missing areas with cement. Wherever possible the lines of the black design were made good to emphasize the pattern.

The mosaic in room N 20 was found to be in an even more ruined condition: not only had its corner been removed by the water-main, and large parts of the centre worn away, but there had also been considerable subsidence into voids beneath, giving rise to contortion and stretching of the floor. It was clear when the floor was first uncovered in 1961 that it would have to be lifted, partly because of its condition and partly because there was at that time a possibility that the site would be developed as a housing estate. The work was carried out by sticking unbleached calico to the surface with PVA[1] and then undercutting the floor, rolling it back across a wooden drum on to a sheet of hardboard. Four separate sections were subsequently lifted in this way, the largest measuring 10 ft. (3 m.) by 4 ft. (1.2 m.). Two of the sections were backed with a 2 in. (5 cm.) thick slab composed of an aluminium silicate cement poured on to the under-surface of the tesserae and reinforced with a $1\frac{1}{2}$ in. (4 cm.) mesh grid of welded stainless steel rods. The other two sections were left unbacked. In 1968 the entire floor was reassembled in its original position, but whereas the unbacked sections were easily relaid directly on to a cement slurry, the large cement-backed slabs were more difficult to place because of their weight, which prevented easy manoeuvrability. Even though great care was taken to remove stresses by laying them on a bed of sand, the backing cracked in several places. Nevertheless, with careful, limited repair, and the replacement of small areas of missing tesserae, the result is satisfactory. The difficulties encountered in re-laying the large cement-backed slabs in room N 20 contrast with the ease with which the floor in room N 12 was able to be replaced in small sections directly on to a cement bed.

The mosaic in room N 21 posed a different series of problems. It was tolerably well-preserved but had subsided in two places into the voids left by rotting post-stumps of the First Period beneath. The subsidence, while considerably weakening the floor, was an essential part of the history of the site and therefore had to be preserved. Thus before the floor was lifted a contour-plan was made of it in relation to datum battens fixed in position beyond the edges of the room. The floor was then lifted in small sections in the manner described above. Next the old matrix was removed and was replaced by a seating of concrete following the exact contours of the original matrix. Finally sections of the mosaic floor were relaid in a slurry of cement on the new concrete base. The small fragments of mosaic in room N 22 were treated in a similar manner.

The tessellated floors and corridors were generally well preserved, but most of the edges had suffered to a greater or lesser extent from the later stone robbing, which had tended to allow the unsupported edges of the floors to collapse into the trenches. It was decided therefore to make good the missing areas, using Roman tesserae collected from the excavations so far as possible. When these ran out new tesserae were chipped from Roman tiles, using a mosaicist's hammer. The first results were rather too fresh in appearance, but this was overcome by tumbling them together in a concrete mixer for a short period. To make sure the difference between the old and the new work will always be apparent, the relaid tesserae were set on a base of waterproof cement which insures that they remain dry while the original tesserae, laid in their bedding of porous mortar, take on a brighter appearance because of the rising damp.

The work of lifting the mosaic in room N 20 was undertaken as part of the archaeological excavation in 1961, the sections being subsequently cleaned and reset by Mrs M. R. Rule.

[1] Plastic 6/530, ex R. A. Brand and Co.

The rest of the mosaic consolidation, which took place in 1966–8, was carried out by Art Pavements Ltd, under the personal direction of the managing director, Mr W. Novis.[1] The nature and extent of the treatment of each individual floor was arrived at by site discussion, but the actual processes involved and the high quality of the finished floors resulted entirely from the thorough and loving care which Mr Novis and his team of craftsmen lavished on them.

Mortar floors.   Wherever mortar floors or patches of mortar matrix survived, as in rooms N 1, N 3, N 4, N 6, N 8 and N 9, they were carefully cleaned and left untreated. At the junctions between the walls and floors, where the floor had usually broken away as the result of robbing, the gap was made good with a modern mortar of the appropriate colour, but always sufficiently different from the Roman work for the distinction to show.

Other floors.   The remaining floors were variously treated. The exposed clay and rubble make-up in room N 5, the western courtyard and the southern part of corridor N 29 was simply covered with a loose gravel, but the south part of room N 6 which had originally contained a tessellated floor, removed during excavation, was refloored with a red mortar finish. The floors and courtyards at the east end of the wing had, with certain exceptions, been largely destroyed in antiquity and, since important features of the First Period lay beneath them, the areas had been extensively excavated to the natural ground surface, leaving only the walls of the Second Period still surviving. It was therefore decided to seal the entire area with concrete surfaced with fine cement toppings which differed in colour and texture from room to room. The verandas and corridors were treated with a uniform topping to emphasize their similarity of function and the courtyard was surfaced with an exposed aggregate concrete, the aggregate being the same brown gravel as that used to cover the western courtyard. The position of the stylobate was marked with paving slabs and the line of the gutter in front of it was delineated with toppings of different colours.

Walls.   The walls of the North Wing that were still standing were repointed where necessary and their top courses were reset, using a grey gritty lime mortar to contrast with the yellowish-cream Roman mortar. The walls of the hypocaust in room N 1 were similarly treated. Elsewhere, where the walls had been robbed, it was necessary to adopt an entirely different treatment. Since the ashlar masonry removed by the stone robbers invariably went down well below the floor-levels, robbing had left the edges of the floors vulnerable. It would therefore have been unwise to have attempted to expose the tops of the footings, since this would have meant leaving the floors as raised islands surrounded by robber trenches. Instead, the technique adopted was to fill the robber trenches with rubble to the level of the floors and to create the appearance of a wall in an exposed aggregate concrete strip the width of a wall, made by pouring concrete between two edging strips of the same material. To make the distinction between walls of the Second and Third Periods, a different coloured matrix was used, care being taken to butt or bond the concrete 'walls' in the same way as their Roman predecessors. The result of such a treatment was to protect the floors and give the feeling of walls dividing them, while in no way attempting to copy the ashlar of a true Roman wall.

---

[1] The Fishbourne Management Committee wish to record their grateful thanks to Mr Novis for his considerable personal help and interest.

The stylobate and gutter of the western courtyard

The western courtyard had suffered considerably from robbing but the entire western stylobate remained in position and sufficient fragments of gutter blocks were found to show that the stylobate had once been fronted with a continuous ground-level gutter. To create the appearance of the courtyard in its original state, and to protect the exposed edges of the tessellated veranda floor, the north and east sides of the stylobate were rebuilt in modern concrete blocks carefully toned and textured so as not to clash with the genuine blocks. In front of the stylobate a gutter of pre-cast blocks, similarly coloured and textured, was laid in the old robber trench.

Painted wall plaster (pl. LXXIIIa)

Although most of the walls of the palace had once been plastered and painted, the fire and the consequent robbing had caused almost all of the plaster to flake off. In only one place, in the south-west corner of room N 14, did plaster still survive *in situ* on a wall, but it had been so affected by the fire that it was in a very crumbly state when found. The painted face was therefore removed by sticking fine scrim to the surface with animal glue[1] and cutting away the mortar behind. After the weak backing mortar had been removed, the plaster was impregnated with Vinamul 9910[2] and the sheets reset in their original positions using a lime mortar slurry backed on to a thick lime mortar.

A strip of painted plaster at the base of the east wall of room N 1 still survived in a vertical position even after the wall to which it had been attached was removed by stone robbers. During conservation the painted face was exposed, before the filling of the robber trench was removed, and protected with scrim stuck on with Vinamul, and attached to supporting battens behind. Once stable, the filling was removed and the back face of the plaster cleaned. Next it was backed with lime mortar, then the robber trench was filled with a weak concrete, to which the plaster face was firmly attached, allowing the supporting scrim to be removed. Finally the face of the paint was cleaned and treated with soluble nylon.

Different problems were presented by the west wall of room N 12, where the plaster facing on both sides of the wall had collapsed into the robber trench. It was decided to leave a length as it had fallen after first lifting it and inserting a damp-course, and to reconstruct an adjacent length in a vertical position on a rebuilt wall-core. The techniques and materials used do not differ from those employed in treating the other areas of plaster, described above.

Biological and chemical problems

To begin with, large numbers of seeds present in the soil germinated and grew to luxurious proportions under the greenhouse conditions provided by the cover-building. Weeding at regular intervals throughout the first year soon reduced the problem to negligible proportions. More serious problems were posed by the growth of algae and fungi on the walls and floors, but these were eventually controlled with chemical sprays.[3] Worm activity tended to be

[1] This proved generally unsatisfactory.
[2] Ex Vinyl Products.

[3] A 1% solution of sodium pentachlorphenate (ex John Line) was found to be effective in destroying the algae growth.

considerable when the floors were freshly exposed. In room N 12, for example, there were on average eight worm-holes per square foot, but the worms rapidly vacated the North Wing, persuaded no doubt by the chemical sprays and the regrouting of the mosaics.

The high water-table and the dry atmosphere within the building tend to encourage the efflorescence of mineral salts on the surfaces of the porous floors and walls. At present no damage seems to be occasioned and all that can be done is the constant brushing of the surfaces affected.

CONCLUSIONS

It has been thought advisable to offer above a broad outline of the problems posed by the consolidation and presentation of a monument to the public. We have been concerned here only with matters directly related to the archaeological remains, not with the wider problems of design and communication. Some effort has been made to summarize the post-excavation treatment to which the ancient features have been subjected, partly because such information is essential so that future generations of archaeologists will understand how the excavated remains were transmuted to their present state, and partly because our experience may be of some use to those facing similar problems in the future — if only to serve as a warning of the complexities involved.

APPENDICES

APPENDIX 1: COMMENTARY ON THE SECTIONS

INTRODUCTION

During the excavations about half a mile of archaeological sections were drawn: those published here as figs. 51–59 are merely a representative selection, chosen to demonstrate significant relationships and structures. They have been arranged as far as possible to follow the chronological development of the site, but clearly a single section often reflects many or most of the periods represented. Originally it was intended to insert references to the relevant parts of the sections in the descriptive text but, when this was begun in practice it soon became clear that such a system was too cumbersome. In some cases it would have meant inserting three or four lines of references at frequent intervals into an already overloaded text. It was finally decided to adopt the method presented in the following pages, namely to provide a separate commentary on the sections arranged in an order which can easily be cross-referenced to the main text. Although the commentary does not make particularly inspiring reading it does provide a useful visual cross-check with the plans and verbal description. Fig. 60 offers a key-plan showing the position of all of the published sections, in relation to each other and the outline of the Flavian building.

Individual trenches are nowhere numbered except on the sections, since the trench is merely an observer-imposed structure of no direct relevance to the ancient features, nor does it form a useful basis for description. Nevertheless for ease of reference in the commentary the trench and layer numbers are quoted. A full set of correlation tables are available with the excavation archive in the site museum. To have published them here would have been enormously expensive and quite unjustifiable.

GENERAL ENVIRONMENT

(a) A SUMMARY SECTION ACROSS THE FISHBOURNE VALLEY (p. 6):

Section 1 is a general composite section.

(b) THE SILTING OF THE HARBOUR BEFORE THE ROMAN OCCUPATION (p. 6):

Section 2 (Tr. F 3) layers 8, 9, 13; layer 8 is a beach-line, probably of Iron Age date.

Section 3 (Tr. 281) shows silty soil of the valley floor, layer 15, at the beginning of the Roman period.

Section 4 (Tr. H 11) cuts through the shingle of the shore-line, layer 8, into silts below, layer 9.

(c) FLOODING LATE IN THE ROMAN PERIOD (p. 8):

Section 2—(Tr. F 3) layers 9 and 13 are pre-Roman silting. Layer 8 is a beach-line, probably of Iron Age or very early Roman date. Above this comes the make-up for the southern garden of the Palace, layer 7.

Section 3—(Tr. 281) layer 3 is a grey-brown silt overlapping the gravel road of the second period, layer 5, and sealing a lens of building debris, layer 4.

Section 4—(Tr. H 11) layer 3 is a silt overlapping the edge of the Period 2 make-up, layer 6.

PERIOD 1 A

(*a*) THE STREAM   (pp. 38 ff.):

The stream was sectioned at several points along its length; a selection of sections are shown here, sections 5–9.

Section 5—(Tr. 44) the shallow stream bed became filled with an inch or two of a gravelly silt, layer 15, but generally it was kept free of silt by the flow of the water. Later, gully 4 was cut into it, layers 11 and 9.

Section 6—(Tr. 215) the stream here contains a thin layer of silt, layer 19, followed by deliberate filling, layers 15–18.

Section 7 (Tr. 272) shows position of bridge (see below, p. 46). The original stream flooded to give rise to silt, layer 12. The stream in the later period, after the bridge was constructed, deposited layer 16.

Section 8 (Trs. 81 and 77) sections stream where it may have been artificially deepened. In the bottom is a thick black organic silt, layer 11 (for content see Vol. II, p. 377), then follows a deliberate infilling.

Section 9—(Tr. 260) an irregular stream bed, thought to have been re-cut after the Period 1 A road went out of use. The stream certainly flowed across the truncated ends of the early road, layer 27. Silts formed within its course, layers 44 and 47. Later the road was relaid, layer 24, across the silted-up stream.

(*b*) THE ROADS AND PATHS — PERIOD 1 A   (pp. 38 ff.):

The south road appears in:

Section 9 (Tr. 260) layers 27 and 35 cut by the opened-up stream and the later gully 10.

Section 13—the metalling, lying on the natural soil, is represented by Tr. 258 layer 30 and Tr. 259 layer 26.

Section 14 (Tr. 292) shows the road further west. Its original Period 1 A metalling is layer 5, contemporary with its side ditch, gully 16.

Section 17—(Tr. 177) the early road metalling is layer 27.

The north road appears in:

Section 16—(Tr. 80) the Period 1 A metalling is layer 13. The side ditches, gullies 7 and 9, have been recut.

Section 39 Tr. 345 layer 16 and Tr. 343 layer 16.

The path north of Building 2:

Section 25—(Tr. 172) layer 11 represents the natural surface with roof-tile fragments trampled into it.

Section 24—(Tr. 171) layer 17 is the same as above.

Section 23—(Tr. 224) further towards the stream the path was metalled with gravel, layer 18.

The north-south road along the eastern edge of the site:

Section 11 (Tr. 283) layers 21 and possibly 12.

Section 12 (Tr. 71) layer 9.

(c) TIMBER BUILDING 1 (p. 39):

The long parallel foundation trenches in which the vertical timbers were placed are shown in *Sections 10* and *11*, cut into the natural and filled with redeposited natural gravelly clay. In one case (Tr. 294) one of the timbers was sectioned. The foundation trenches and voids are sealed by Period 1 B floors, e.g. *Section 11* (Tr. 294) layers 22 and 23.

(d) TIMBER BUILDING 2 (p. 41)

The post pits of Timber Building 2 are shown in *Sections 23* and *26*.

Section 23 shows two of the post pits, in the centre of which are voids for the timbers, layers 15 and 17, into which the superimposed occupation layers, layer 13, and Second-Period make-up, layer 11, have subsided.

Section 26, however, sections post pits which have had the posts dug out and have been filled with occupation debris of Period 1 B, layers 17, 20, and 22. The compaction of the debris has allowed the Period 2 make-up layers to slump down.

(e) GULLIES 2 AND 3 (p. 43):

These flank the path north of Timber Building 2. They are shown in *Sections 23, 24* and *25*.

Section 23 (Tr. 224) gully 3 lies below Second Period wall, only partly seen.

Section 24 (Tr. 171) shows gully 2 filled with silty occupation material, layer 16, which merges with the occupation layer 7 over the path.

Section 25 (Tr. 172) demonstrates more clearly the silting; it shows a clean grey silt in the bottom, layer 15, with occupation material of Period 1 B above, layer 12.

(f) GULLY 8 AND 8a (p. 43):

Not shown on the sections.

(g) GULLY 12 (p. 43):

Section 22—(Tr. 167) layer 16 is the clean primary silt of the gully. It is sealed by a thin occupation spread of Period 1 B date, layer 13.

(h) GULLY 13 (p. 45):

Not shown on section.

(i) GULLY 14 (p. 45):

The section — *Section 39* layer 17 — shows the gully atypically. Here it appears to have been deliberately emptied of its filling at the time of the Second-Period building, and filled with flints, clay and gravel to consolidate the ground immediately in front of the colonnade.

(j) GULLY 15 (p. 45):

The bottom of the original gully appears in *Section 31* layer 13. Its upper levels have been cut away by the late widening, layers 11, 12, etc. The same features are shown more clearly by *Section 41*, where layer 13 represents the bottom filling of the original gully.

(k)   GULLY 16   (p. 45):

Section 14—(Tr. 292) layers 17 and 18 represent the lower filling of the original gully. The angle of rest in the silting is marked by layer 15, a thin turf accumulation.

(l)   OTHER FEATURES — THE ?FOUNDATION TRENCH   (p. 45):

Section 29 (Tr. 311) layer 25.

PERIOD 1 B

(a)   THE ROADS, THE BRIDGE AND THE STREAM   (pp. 46 ff.)

The south road:

Section 9 (Tr. 260) shows that the road, layer 27, went out of use and the ford was cleared away to improve the flow of the stream. Gully 10 was also cut through the original metalling. Although to the west of the stream the centre part of the road was clear of soil and rubbish, soil began to accumulate over the edges, e.g. *Section 17* (Tr. 177) layer 26 and *Section 13* (Tr. 258) layer 26 and (Tr. 259) layer 28.

The north road and bridge:

Section 16—(Tr. 80) layer 10 represents a remetalling of the original road, probably broadly contemporary with the recutting of the side ditches, gullies 7 and 9.
The timbers of the bridge appear in *Section 7* (Tr. 272) together with the revetment of greensand blocks immediately behind. Up to this revetment was laid a gravel causeway, layers 9 and 10.

(b)   TIMBER BUILDING 4   (p. 47):

Section 12—the floors of the building appear as Tr. 70 layer 19a and Tr. 69 layer 23, together with their adjacent sill beam slots. The destruction of the building is represented by Tr. 70 layers 15 and 17 and Tr. 69 layers 22 and 14.

(c)   TIMBER BUILDING 5   (p. 48):

Section 10 (Tr. 257) shows beam slot and adjacent clay floor; Tr. 256 shows floor surface sealing Period 1 A timber building. The dry-stone footing to the east of the building appears in Trs. 278 and 257.

Section 11—(Tr. 287) layer 14 is filling of the beam slot filled with clay from the demolished superstructure continuous with Tr. 294 layer 21 which slumps into the eastern beam slot. Below are the floor levels, Tr. 294 layers 22 and 23. The dry-stone footing is shown in Tr. 283.

(d)   TIMBER BUILDING 6   (p. 49):

Does not appear on published sections.

(e)   TIMBER BUILDING 7 IN AREA 1   (p. 51):

For general stratigraphy in the area see *Section 32* (Tr. 351). The building does not appear but the contemporary First-Period levels are layers 38 and below.

(f)   THE SITE OF THE TIMBER BUILDING 2   (p. 51):

The building is demolished and occupation layers accumulate, *Section 23* (Tr. 225) layer 13 and (Tr. 224) layer 12; *Section 26* (Tr. 189) layer 12.

P

(*g*) GULLY 6 (p. 51):

Section 32 (Tr. 351) layer 42, grey silty occupation material. The gully here is very shallow.

(*h*) GULLIES 7 AND 9 (p. 51):

It is difficult to be sure whether these gullies, as found, are recut versions of earlier ones. The general stratigraphy would suggest this.

Section 16—(Tr. 98) layer 17 is clean silt in the bottom of gully 9 and (Tr. 93) shows silting in bottom of gully 7.

(*i*) GULLY 10 (p. 52):

Sectioned many times, usually filled with occupation rubbish.

Section 8 (Tr. 75) layer 9; *Section 9* (Tr. 260) layers 36 and 39 — this section shows gully cutting through the early road; *Section 10* (Tr. 256) layer 30; *Section 12* (Tr. 68) layer 13.

(*j*) THE DITCHED ENCLOSURE (p. 52):

Section 27 (Tr. 121) shows profile of ditch with thin lens of occupation material in the bottom, layer 26. Above are layers of deliberate filling, e.g. layers 24, 23, 21, 20, dating to the Second Period.

Section 29 (Tr. 311) has a similar profile but wider, with occupation material, layer 22, in the bottom. The natural silting of the sides accounts for layers 19, 20 and 21, but above this the filling is deliberate, consisting of tips of clay, gravel and soil sealed by a single layer of clay, layer 17. The bank of gravel is layer 23 with a turf facing, layer 24.

Section 28 (Tr. 113) shows the truncated ditch (gully 18) which is probably the north–south continuation of ditch 21. The lower silt is layer 16, above which is a grey gravelly filling, layer 15. The upper levels were sheared off during the Second-Period levelling.

(*k*) DITCH 22 (p. 53):

Section 30—(Tr. 279) the ditch, cut into the natural silty clay, almost vertically-sided. In the bottom was a layer of silt, layer 12, above which came a filling of clay, layers 5, 11, with lenses of chalk, layer 10.

(*l*) AREA SOUTH OF MODERN MAIN ROAD (p. 53):

Section 4 (Tr. H 5) shows the silty topsoil, layer 6, of this area.

(*m*) AREA NORTH OF THE MAIN SITE (p. 54):

The details are not published on sections.

PERIOD 1 C

(*a*) THE ROADS AND THE STREAM (p. 55):

The stream was at this time filled; see *Section 8* (Tr. 77) layers 9 and 10, *Section 6* (Tr. 215) layers 15–18. A new diversion ditch was dug, *Section 15* (Tr. 267) layer 13.

The southern road was relaid over the stream, *Section 9* (Tr. 260) layer 24, and east of the stream it was remetalled, *Section 14* (Tr. 292) layer 4.

(*b*) AREAS 1 AND 4 (p. 56):

Gully 4 appears most clearly on *Section 6* (Tr. 214), where it can be seen to be clearly later than the filling of the stream. It was deliberately filled with clay and gravel in Period 2, layers 21 and 22. No silt in the bottom suggests that it was either newly dug or had just been cleared out. It also can be seen in *Section 5* (Tr. 44), where it had been cut into the old stream bed, which itself had not been filled in at this point. Some silt had formed, layer 11, and occupation rubbish had been tipped in, layer 9.

Gully 1 is shown in *Section 24* (Tr. 194). The lower silt, layer 16, is sealed by miscellaneous rubble and gravel thrown in in Period 2, layers 15 and 12.

The levelling and gravelling east of gully 4 is shown in *Section 32* (Tr. 351) layer 40.

(*c*) AREAS 2 AND 5 (p. 57):

The fence posts do not appear on the published sections.

Gully 15, re-excavated and possibly turned into a pond, is shown on *Section 31* (Tr. 308) layers 10, 11 and 12, and *Section 41* (Tr. 357) layers 10, 11, 12 and 14. Apart from lenses of occupation the filling was of silts and silty clays.

(*d*) THE BUILDERS' WORKING YARD (p. 58):

The debris from the stone-sawing appears in *Section 12* (Tr. 69) layer 13 and (Tr. 68) layer 9. Greensand chippings occur extensively on the roads and paths: *Section 13* (Tr. 258) layer 23, (Tr. 259) layer 25; *Section 17* (Tr. 177) layer 42; *Section 12* (Tr. 71) layer 7, (Tr. 70) layer 8; *Section 11* (Tr. 283) layer 11.

(*e*) THE FIRST MASONRY BUILDING: AREA 3 (pp. 61 ff.):

The structural details of the first masonry building appear on *Sections 17–21*.

Upstanding walls: *Section 21* (Tr. 199) with building spread, layer 19, and occupation layers next to the wall, layer 16; *Section 19* (Tr. D 2) shows the wall of the buttress. Elsewhere in *Section 19* the footings of dry-stone work belonging to the bath building walls can be seen.

Building spreads of mortar: *Section 17* (Tr. 177) layer 31, belonging to a wall robbed before the deposition of the Period 2 make-up; *Section 18* (Tr. 176) layer 34; *Section 19* (Tr. D 2) layer 5; *Section 20* (Tr. 400) layer 16 — here rubble and mortar; *Section 21* (Tr. 199) layer 19.

Floor make-up within bath rooms: shows particularly well in *Section 19* (Tr. D 1) layers 3 and 4, (Tr. D 9) layers 3, 4 and 8, (Tr. D 13) layers 10 and 11, (Tr. D 30) layer 7.

Make-up in ? stoking area north of the baths: *Section 19* (Tr. D 2) layer 4.

Make-up within verandas of peristyle: *Section 18* (Tr. 176) layers 4 and 7; *Section 17* (Tr. 177) layer 61.

Make-up in courtyard: *Section 18* (Tr. 176) layer 33, but in the southern part of the courtyard there is no make-up, only an occupation accumulation; *Section 21* (Tr. 199) layer 16.

Soil accumulation to the north of the building: *Section 17* (Tr. 177) layer 26, continues to form but close to the building a thin trample of clay and gravel occurs, layer 44, over the earlier turf-line, layer 36; *Section 20* (Tr. 400) layer 15.

(*f*) THE SECOND MASONRY BUILDING (p. 69):

Wall footings: *Section 37* (Tr. 347) marked as flint footings; *Section 34* (Tr. 265) shown beneath later floor make-up.

The contemporary make-up layers are shown in *Section 34* (Tr. 265), (Tr. 264) layer 6.
The slot: *Section 34* (Tr. 264) layer 12.
The gully 19 is shown on *Section 35* (Tr. 126) layer 21.

PERIOD 2

(*a*) PREPARATION OF THE SITE AND THE BUILDING SEQUENCES (p. 78):

Many of the sections show evidence of layers of make-up deposited as a preparation for the Second-Period building. In relation to the proto-palace in *Section 17* (Tr. 177) layers 5, 10, 13, 31, 33, 43, 57, 58, 63, etc., all seal the earlier building levels, some slumping into the trench left after one of the First-Period walls had been removed. The same section shows the flint footings for the Second-Period palace dug whilst the make-up was being deposited. In *Section 21*, (Tr. 199) layer 21, which includes a column shaft, was laid down between two standing Period 1 walls whilst on either side the ground-level was raised with (Tr. 199) layers 10 and 15 and (Tr. 205) layers 6, 12, 18, 25, 28, 31 and 32. *Section 20* shows the relationship between the walls of the two different periods; the Period 1 C wall relates to the original ground-surface while the Period 2 wall was not erected until after the occupation layer 14 had been deposited. Then the level was made up with tips of rubble, layers 3, 5, 6, 11, 12, and 13.
The terracing of the garden wall into the slope of the land appears in *Sections 33* and *34*.

(*b*) BUILDING MATERIALS AND TECHNIQUES (p. 80):

Walls: Second-Period walls with flint cobble footings and ashlar masonry appear in several sections, e.g. *Section 22*, particularly Trs. 171, 172 and 173, and *Section 24* (Tr. 194), in the eastern half of the North Wing where early demolition had prevented the robbing of the ashlar. Also well preserved were the main east wall of the building, *Section 12* (Tr. 70) and *Section 32* (Tr. 351) and the Entrance Hall, e.g. *Section 13*, where the sequence of make-up in relation to construction is particularly well shown — the footings are taken down to the natural through the lower make-up levels.
Sometimes the ashlar was not exactly aligned with the footings below, e.g. *Section 9* (Tr. 260) and *Section 24* (Tr. 194).
Stylobates were on shallow foundations: *Section 8* (Tr. 81); *Section 42* (Tr. 326); *Section 40* (Tr. 346); *Section 39* (Tr. 343).
The revetting wall in front of the West Wing appears in *Sections 33, 36, 37* and *38*.
Floor make-up for the North Wing mosaics: *Section 22* (Tr. 168) layer 8, (Tr. 169) layers 5 and 9, (Tr. 171) layers 5 and 10, (Tr. 172) layer 4, (Tr. 173) layer 6, (Tr. 174) layer 7.
Courtyard make-up of clay, etc.: *Section 26* (Tr. 197) layers 9 and 11, (Tr. 189) layers 4, 9 and 10.
The above details are a selection only of those shown.

(*c*) THE WEST WING (pp. 83 ff.):

Details summarized on *Sections 33–7*, e.g. *Section 33*, floor make-up of greensand rubble topped with mortar (Tr. 127) layers 13, 14, 6 and 7, with a thin matrix of pink mortar (Tr. 127) layers 12 and 5, in which the tesserae were set. Similarly *Section 34* (Trs. 265 and 266) shows a matrix of pink mortar over rubble and mortar make-up relating to the wall of the Audience Chamber apse. The verandas on the east and west sides were floored with clay and gravel, probably originally with a surfacing of mortar: *Section 33* (Tr. 127 E) layers 3 and 6; *Section 34* (Tr. 264) layer 5; *Section 35* (Tr. 126) layers 14 and 18 and *Section 36* (Tr. 352) layers 3a and 3b.

(*d*) THE NORTH WING   (pp. 93 ff.):

Details are summarized on *Sections 23–6* and *42–5*.
Make-up layers: *Section 22* (Trs. 167 and 168) layers 8, 9 and 10, (Tr. 169) layers 5, 9, 11 and 15, (Tr. 170) layers 5, 8, 9, and 14, (Tr. 171) layers 5, 8, 10 and 11, (Tr. 172) layers 4 and 7, (Tr. 173) layers 6 and 9, (Tr. 174) layers 7 and 9; *Section 23* (Tr. 225) layers 11 and 13, (Tr. 224) layers 10, 11, 12, 13, and 14; *Section 24* (Tr. 200) layers 4, 5, 7, 10, 11 and 12, (Tr. 194) layers 7, 9 and 14, (Tr. 171) layers 5, 6 and 8; *Section 25* (Tr. 172) layers 5 and 14; *Section 26* (Tr. 197) layers 9 and 11, (Tr. 189) layers 4, 9, 10 and 16; *Section 42* (Tr. 326) layers 7 and 8; *Section 44* (Tr. 107) layer 8, (Tr. 111) layers 15 and 16; *Section 45* (Tr. 110) layer 11.
Original mosaics are shown set in their pink mortar matrix in *Section 22* (Trs. 173 and 174).

(*e*) THE SOUTH WING   (pp. 103 ff.):

The robber trench for the stylobate and gutter on the south side appears in *Section 4* (Tr. H 6) layer 2.
Make-up layers for the terrace are shown in *Section 4* (Tr. H 6) layers 3, 4 and 5, (Tr. H 5) layers 3a, 4 and ?5 and (Tr. H 11) layer 6.

(*f*) THE EAST WING   (pp. 105 ff.):

Aisled Hall (p. 106): make-up layers shown in *Section 6* (Tr. 214) layers 7, 8, 13, 21 and 22, (Tr. 215) layers 8 and 11, (Tr. 216) layers 12 and 13; *Section 5* (Tr. 44) layers 3, 4, 5, 7 and 8; *Section 32* (Tr. 351) layers 5, 6, 10, 33 and 39.

Entrance Hall (p. 110): make-up layers shown in *Section 13* (Tr. 258) layers 6, 7, 14, 16, 17, 18, 19 and 20, (Tr. 259) layers 15, 21, 22, 27, 9, 10, 19 and 20; *Section 17* (Tr. 177) layers 21, 25 and 40. The pool in the Hall is in *Section 17* (Tr. 177), foundations of greensand are layer 23, the side walls layer 41. Layers of make-up are also sectioned in *Section 10* (Tr. 256) and *Section 11* (Tr. 294).

Peristyles (p. 116): southern courtyard north of Entrance Hall: stylobate and gutter robber appear in *Section 8* (Tr. 81).

Range of rooms (p. 117): make-up layers shown in *Section 12* (Tr. 70) layer 12, (Tr. 69) layers 5, 8, 9, 10 and 11, (Tr. 68) layers 4 and 8. *Section 8* shows two of the original pink mortar floors, layer 3.

Bath suite (p. 119): the ? stoking area remetalled, *Section 19* (Tr. D 2) layers 2 and 3. Wall in Tr. D 30 demolished and new layers of make-up deposited, (Tr. D 29) layer 8 and (Tr. D 30) layers 4 and 5.

(*g*) THE GARDEN   (pp. 120 ff.):

Colonnades (p. 120): see West Wing revetting wall (above) and *Section 39* (Tr. 343) stylobate, and *Section 40* (Tr. 346) stylobate.

Bedding trenches and topsoil (p. 123): *Section 38* (Tr. 320) layers 8, 9, 12, 16, 17 and 18; *Section 39* (Tr. 345) layers 4, 5 and 15, (Tr. 343) layers 7, 8 and 9; *Section 40* (Tr. 346) layers 7, 9, 15 and 17; *Section 41* (Tr. 357) layer 5; *Section 18* (Tr. 176) layers 19, 20 and 21.

Water supply (p. 129): water pipes, *Section 38* (Tr. 320); *Section 39* (Tr. 345) layer 8 and *Section 40* (Tr. 346).

(h) APPROACHES AND ENVIRONMENT   (pp. 134 ff.):

Road along east side (p. 134): *Section 10* (Tr. 278) layer 3 and (Tr. 257) layer 4 and make-up beneath; *Section 11* (Tr. 283) layer 7 and (Tr. 287) layer 4 and make-up beneath; *Section 12* (Tr. 68) layers 4 and 5 and (Tr. 69) layers 6 and 7 and make-up beneath; *Section 32* (Tr. 351) gravel in east end of trench.

North-west corner of site (p. 135): general make-up layers appear on *Section 27* (Tr. 121) layers 9, 19, 20, 21 and 23.

West of the West Wing (p. 138): gully shown on *Section 34* (Tr. 280) layer 8.

South of the South Wing (p. 132): see South Wing, above p. 103.

North of the North Wing (p. 135): *Section 3* (Tr. 281) shows road, layer 5, together with make-up layers 6, 16, 18, 19 and 20.

PERIOD 3

(a) NORTH WING — PERIOD 3 A   (pp. 154 ff.):

The floor of the *caldarium*: *Section 22* (Tr. 175) layer 6 with later collapsed tiles and rubble over it, layers 4 and 5. The cheek of the flue is shown to the east of the wall in (Tr. 175).

(b) AISLED HALL   (p. 157):

Robber trench for one of the inserted walls of Third-Period date appears on *Section 6* (Tr. 214) layer 20.

(c) THE ROOMS OF THE NORTH WING IN PERIOD 3A   (p. 158):

No Period 3 A alterations shown on illustrated sections.

(d) THE EAST END OF THE NORTH WING IN PERIOD 3 B   (p. 160):

Section 22 (Trs. 171–5) shows the survival of ashlar masonry up to floor-level, in contrast with other parts of the North Wing where the ashlar was removed by stone robbers.

(e) THE WEST END OF THE NORTH WING IN PERIOD 3 B   (p. 160):

Details are summarized in *Sections 44* and *45*. New dividing walls, now marked by robber trenches, were inserted, *Section 44*. In the north room a new pink mortar floor was laid, upon which the *pilae* were set. To the south, the original Period 2 matrix, layer 15, served as a floor over which occupation material accumulated, layer 10.

Section 45 shows one cross wall of large stone blocks set in pink mortar continuous with the floor to the north, while to the south the robber trench of the other cross wall survives. Between are complex layers of ash, occupation material, etc., layers 7, 8, 9, and 10. Towards the top a coin of Severus was found.

(f) THE EAST END OF THE RECONSTITUTED WING   (p. 167):

Shallow footings of the new wall are shown in *Section 26* (Tr. 197) sitting immediately on layer 9.

(g) ROOMS OF NORTH WING IN PERIOD 3 C   (pp. 168 ff.):

Section 44 (Tr. 111) shows new floor of red tesserae, layer 4, set in pink mortar and sealing the Period 3 B occupation levels as well as the robber trench for the south wall. The matrix is continuous with that of the veranda.

Section 45 shows a similar red tessellated floor in a pink mortar matrix, layer 4, sealing the earlier layers. It respects the robber trench, showing that the wall was still standing. To the south is the new tessellated floor, on a pink mortar matrix, belonging to the veranda.

(h) THE WESTERN COURTYARD AND ITS VERANDAS (p. 170):

The reflooring of the verandas has just been mentioned. The new tessellation also shows in *Section 42* (Tr. 326), in the extreme eastern end. The height of this veranda floor implies that it once abutted a wall built on the second period stylobate.

Section 43 (Tr. 336) shows how the robber trench for the stylobate gutter was here filled with clay and rubble, layer 11, while on the stylobate itself was built a wall, now represented by the basal mortar, layer 12, and the robber trench, layer 9. Immediately to the west of the robber are a series of occupation layers and floors relating to the two ovens.

The greensand and pink mortar foundation shown on *Section 42* may be of this date.

(i) PERIOD 3 D ALTERATIONS (p. 171):

In the west veranda, *Section 43* (Tr. 336), occupation layers, layer 15, and floors, layer 18, can be seen sealing the early oven.

(j) THE EAST WING BATH SUITE (p. 172):

Not shown on the published sections, but the Second-Period drain which still functioned appears on *Section 16* (Tr. 93), layer 6.

(k) THE COURTYARDS SOUTH OF THE BATH SUITE (p. 181):

Section 8—(Tr. 77) a well was dug through all the Second-Period layers. It was sealed by a later occupation layer, layer 3a.

(l) THE ENTRANCE HALL (p. 182):

Mortar refloorings appear on *Section 9* (Tr. 260) layers 9 and 11. The turf accumulation is shown on *Section 9* (Tr. 260) layer 8 and *Section 13* (Tr. 259) layers 8 and 16. The collapsed roof worn by traffic is best shown on *Section 13* (Tr. 258) layer 10.

(m) THE WEST WING IN THE THIRD PERIOD (p. 183):

Section 29 (Tr. 311) shows a wall of greensand blocks laid on the Second-Period make-up, layer 17. It may be of Third-Period date.

DESTRUCTION AND LATER

(a) NORTH WING (pp. 187 ff.):

Destruction layers appear on *Section 23* (Tr. 225) layer 3, (Tr. 224) layers 4 and 9; *Section 25* (Tr. 172) layer 3; *Section 42* (Tr. 326) layers 3 and 4; *Section 43* (Tr. 336) layer 3; *Section 44* (Tr. 111) layer 4 and layer sealing the hypocaust basement in Tr. 107; *Section 45* (Tr. 110) layer above the tessellated floor.

(b) EAST WING BATH SUITE (p. 189):

Destruction layers do not appear on published sections, but for the late occupation see *Section 16* (Tr. 98) layer 3, (Tr. 80) layer 4, (Tr. 93) layer 5.

(c) THE END OF THE AISLED HALL (p. 190):
The collapsed roof is shown in *Section 6* (Trs. 214–16) layer 5.

(d) THE END OF THE WEST WING (p. 190):
Little destruction rubble has escaped ploughing, but see *Section 33* (Tr. 127) layer 3 and *Section 34* (Tr. 266) layers 4, 17 and 7 and (Tr. 280) layer 2.
Rubble tipped in front of the revetting wall: *Section 33* (Tr. 127 E) layers 8 and 10; *Section 38* (Tr. 320) layer 14.

(e) ROBBING (p. 191):
Robber trenches are shown on many of the sections. They are not specifically listed here as they are easily recognizable.

SECTION 22 (TRENCHES 167-175)

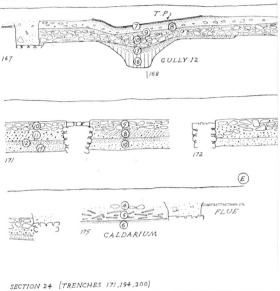

SECTION 27 (TRENCH 121)

SECTION 29 (TRENCH 311)

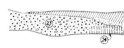

SECTION 24 (TRENCHES 171,194,200)

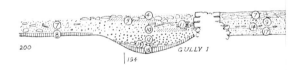

SECTION 31 (TRENCH 308)

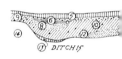

SECTION 26 (TRENCHES 197,189)

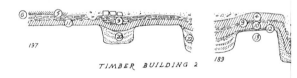

	STONE BLOCKS		CLAY
	MORTAR		SILT OR TU
	BUILDING DEBRIS		GRAVEL

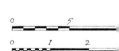

F

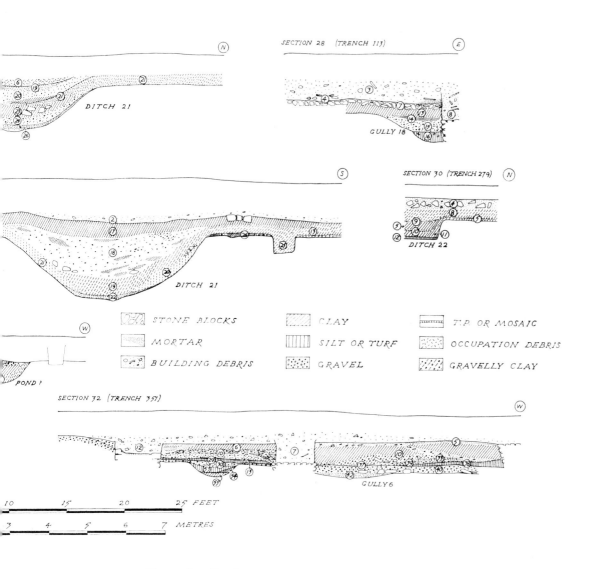

SECTION 28 (TRENCH 113)

DITCH 21

GULLY 18

SECTION 30 (TRENCH 279)

DITCH 21

DITCH 22

STONE BLOCKS   CLAY   TIP OR MOSAIC

MORTAR   SILT OR TURF   OCCUPATION DEBRIS

BUILDING DEBRIS   GRAVEL   GRAVELLY CLAY

POND ?

SECTION 32 (TRENCH 357)

GULLY 6

10   15   20   25 FEET

3   4   5   6   7 METRES

Fig. 56.   Sections 27–32

APPENDIX 2

DETAILS OF THE POST-PITS OF TIMBER BUILDING 2
(pp. 41–2, fig. 9)

The numbers given refer to fig. 9, from which the diameters of the pits can readily be measured.

ROW A

A 1   17 in. (0.43 m.) deep — post dug out and pit filled with clay and occupation material (*Section 26*).

A 2   2 ft. 3 in. (0.69 m.) deep—post dug out and pit filled with occupation material (*Section 26*).

A 3   2 ft. 6 in. (0.76 m.) deep—post dug out and pit filled with occupation material (*Section 26*).

A 4   2 ft. 6 in. (0.76 m.) deep — post dug out and pit filled with occupation material.

A 5–7   Not excavated.

A 8   Corner only sectioned: the post had been dug out.

A 9   Edge only sectioned: post dug out and pit filled with occupation rubbish.

A 10–11   Not excavated.

A 12   Corner only sectioned: post dug out and pit filled with occupation rubbish.

A 13   The edge only seen in section.

ROW B

B 1   Post clearly defined, *c.* 2 ft. (0.6 m.) deep. Packing of post-pit of redeposited clay and gravel.

B 2   Packing of redeposited clay. The edge of the post, of undefined depth, just showed in the section.

B 3   Packing of redeposited clay unexcavated. The post-hole was clearly defined to a depth of 2 ft. 3 in. (0.69 m.). Both post and pit had been partly cut into by a later pit of Period 1 B date containing mortar and clay, possibly from a destruction level (pl. 11*a*).

B 4   Post had been dug out, leaving a pit 2 ft. 9 in. (0.84 m.) deep filled with clay and occupation rubbish, but the position of the bottom of the post was just visible for 6 in.

B 5   Post had been dug out, leaving a pit 2 ft. (0.6 m.) deep filled largely with redeposited natural clay.

B 6   Not excavated to level of post-pit.

B 7   Post had been dug out and the pit, 2 ft. 6 in. (0.76 m.) deep, had been filled with clay and occupation material.

B 8   Not excavated.

B 9   Post and foundation pit clearly defined (pl. 1*b*): the post was 2 ft. (0.6 m.) deep. The packing of the pit was of redeposited natural gravel.

B 10–11   Not excavated.

B 12   Post position was clearly visible surrounded by a packing of redeposited natural gravel. The depth of the pit was 2 ft. (0.6 m.) (*Section 23*).

B 13   Position of the post could be traced in plan against the foundation pit packing of redeposited gravel. The feature was not excavated to the bottom.

ROW C

C 1   Post-pit dug to a depth of 2 ft. 3 in. (0.69 m.) and packed back with clay around the post.

C 2   Post has been dug out to a depth of 2 ft. 6 in. (0.76 m.) and the pit filled with tips of occupation rubbish and clay.

C 3   Post position could be traced. The pit, dug to a depth of 2 ft. 3 in. (0.69 m.), was packed back with redeposited natural clay.

C 4   Post has been dug out to a depth of 3 ft. 3 in. (1 m.) and the pit filled with tips of occupation rubbish interleaved with clay.

C 5   Post has been dug out to a depth of 2 ft. (0.6 m.) and the pit filled with occupation rubbish sealing a thick lens of clay.

C 6   The edge only seen but the post appears to have been dug out.

C 7–9   Not excavated.

C 10   Top of post-pit was traced but not excavated.

C 11   Post-pit, filled with redeposited natural gravel, excavated to its bottom, 18 in. (0.46 m.) down. No trace of the post seen.

C 12   Post clearly visible in the pit, 2 ft. (0.6 m.) deep, packed with redeposited natural gravel (*Section 23*).

C 13   Post clearly visible in the pit, 2 ft. (0.6 m.) deep, packed with redeposited natural gravel.

ROW D

D 1   Post position visible in pit packed with redeposited natural clay. Depth not ascertained.

D 2   Post position visible in large pit dug to a depth of 2 ft. 3 in. (0.69 m.) and packed back with redeposited clay.

D 3   The post had been dug out and the pit filled with occupation material and clay, but the impression made by the bottom of the post could be traced as a rectangular indentation in the bottom of the pit at a depth of 1 ft. 6 in. (0.46 m.).

D 4   The post had been dug out and the pit filled with clay and occupation material. The depth of the pit exceeded 2 ft. 6 in. (0.76 m.).

D 5   The post had been dug out and the pit filled with clay and occupation material. Depth 2 ft. 3 in. (0.69 m.).

D 6   Only the edge sectioned, but the post appears to have been dug out.

D 7–10   Not excavated.

D 11–12   Post-pits traced, filled with redeposited natural gravel, but no trace of the posts could be seen in the upper foot (0.3 m.) of the filling. Excavation below this was not attempted.

D 13   Post not traced because of overburden of masonry.

ROW E

E 1   Post position visible in pit packed with redeposited clay. Not fully excavated.

E 2   Not excavated.

E 3   Post position visible in pit packed with redeposited clay. Bottom at 2 ft. 3 in. (0.69 m.).

E 4	Post void visible in pit packed with clay. The bottom of the pit is below 1 ft. 9 in. (0.53 m.).
E 5	Post dug out and pit filled with layers of occupation debris and tips of clay to a depth of 2 ft. 6 in. (0.76 m.).
E 6	Edge of pit only sectioned. The post has apparently been dug out.
E 7–11	Not excavated.
E 12–13	Surface of post pits were traced but not fully excavated. They were filled with redeposited natural gravel.

ROW F

F 1–2	Not excavated.
F 3	Post position visible in pit packed with redeposited clay. The pit had been dug to a depth of 2 ft. 3 in. (0.69 m.).
F 4–13	Not excavated.

SOUTHERN ROW

Four posts out of alignment with those of the main building were found along the southern side Each post was placed in a rectangular post-pit dug to a depth of about 2 ft. 9 in. (0.84 m.) below the contemporary surface. Three of the post positions were traced. The posts had been packed around with redeposited natural gravel and clay. The fourth post was not traced in the packing of its pit, largely because of local disturbances by later features.

ISOLATED POSTS

Two isolated posts were found:

(a) Between B 3–4 and C 3–4. Small post in post-pit 18 in. (0.46 m.) deep, packed with clay.

(b) Between D 4–5 and E 4–5. Small ? post dug out and its pit filled with tips of occupation rubbish and clay. Depth exceeds 2 ft. (0.6 m.).

APPENDIX 3
SUMMARY OF THE DATING EVIDENCE

PERIOD 1 A.   *c.* A.D. 43–5

Very few tightly stratified deposits of this date occur. A selection of the coarse ware is shown in Vol. II, fig. 73; to this should be added the decorated Arretine sherd (Vol. II, fig. 121, no. 1) and the three decorated form 29s (Vol. II, fig. 126, nos. 1–3) which belong to the period A.D. 40–55.

An early initial occupation date of A.D. 43–5 is preferred on the grounds that (a) the two first timber buildings are of military type (pp. 39 ff.), (b) a few military fittings have been recovered (Vol. II, fig. 43, nos. 75–84), (c) the high proportion of copies of Claudian coins, 4 : 1, is closer to military sites, e.g. Cirencester, than to civil sites, e.g. Verulamium or Canterbury (Vol. II, p. 97), and (d) a high percentage of the earliest Terra Sigillata is of 'Arretine' type suggesting a very early date (Vol. II, pp. 260–4). While, therefore, it is impossible to argue from the material in which year occupation began, a strong case can be made out for a military origin, which implies settlement in the invasion year. The general dating of the pottery in no way conflicts with this.

PERIOD 1 B.   *c.* A.D. 45–65/70 and 1 C, *c.* A.D. 65/70–5

Period 1 B covers a considerable period of time and has accordingly produced masses of material from the rubbish tipped close to the occupied area. The coarse ware pottery from Periods 1 B–C is illustrated in full (Vol. II, figs. 83–104, and pp. 175–216). But while the coarse ware supports the dating it does not determine it. Over much of the site no stratigraphical distinction can be made between Periods 1 B and C. Therefore the coin list (Vol. II, p. 96) reflects the duration of both periods with its 32 coins of Claudius and earlier, seven of Nero and six of Vespasian, none of which was minted after 72–3.

Gully 10, which was filled with rubbish in Period 1 B and sealed with masons' working debris of Period 1 C, provides the only dating evidence for the beginning of Period 1 C. Of the 12 coins recovered, two are pre-Claudian, 7 + ? 2 are Claudian and only one is Neronian. Clearly Period 1 C cannot have begun before Neronian coins were in circulation but the Period 1 C building existed for a time before massive rebuilding began in *c.* 75. A date of *c.* 65–70 for the beginning of 1 C is therefore consistent with all the evidence. Two datable sherds of decorated samian (Vol. II, figs. 126–7, nos. 4 and 7) from the gully are Claudian, the rest of the samian and coarse ware is generally Claudian to Neronian.

The other gullies cannot be closely tied down. Gully 2 contains a Claudian coin. Gully 3 has produced one illegible coin of Vespasian and decorated samian dating to 50–65 (Vol. II, fig. 127, no. 13). Gully 4 contained one coin of Nero. Gully 9 contained a decorated samian vessel dating 55–75 (Vol. II, fig. 127, no. 10). The occupation levels sealing the destroyed Timber Building 2 produced a coin of Vespasian. Ditch 21 contained a sherd of decorated samian dating 50–65 (Vol. II, fig. 127, no. 15). From the general occupation layers were recovered a quantity of coarse ware (Vol. II, figs. 83–104, types 1–198), decorated samian (Vol. II, figs. 126–8, nos. 4–21) and stamped samian noted in the section on samian stamps (Vol. II, pp. 299 ff.). The pottery evenly spans the period 43–75: its upper limit is considered below.

PERIOD 2 CONSTRUCTION.   A.D. 75–80

The construction of the palace sealed the First Period levels mentioned above and contained within the make-up levels occupation material derived from the period of construction as well as redeposited material from earlier levels. Altogether, from within and below the primary make-up levels, 86 coins have been recovered of which the latest are of Vespasian's fourth consulship in A.D. 73. The absence of any later issues from among the 12 Vespasianic coins tends to suggest that building had begun soon after 73 (Vol. II, p. 98). The latest work to be carried out, the laying of the garden turf and the metalling of the road, produced four coins, one of Nero, one of Vespasian and two of Domitian. Since it could be argued that the garden topsoil was not a closed deposition and metalling could have been patched at any time, too much weight should not be placed on this group, but they do suggest that general site work, as opposed to construction, was still being carried out in the early 80s. Thus, on the coin evidence, the major building activity fits within the bracket 75–80.

The samian evidence is in complete agreement, though the date bracket is necessarily wider. Of the relevant decorated sherds (Vol. II, figs. 128–9, nos. 22–46), the latest vessels mostly lie within the range A.D. 70–85, the most distinctive group being comparable to vessels in the Pompeii hoard sealed in the eruption of Vesuvius in A.D. 79. The stamped samian, though less well dated, is consistent with the date of the decorated wares, but three stamps, nos. 56 B, 84 A and 96 A, are not yet known to occur before about 75 and are common only in the Flavian period. If this dating proves to be correct the Fishbourne building is more likely to have begun nearer 80 than 75.

PERIOD 2 OCCUPATION.   c. A.D. 80–100

The first occupation of the palace was unfortunately neat and hygienic, the rubbish being removed from the vicinity of the building and tipped beyond the limits of the present excavation. This is reflected by the dearth of Flavian coins after c. 74 (only seven from the entire site) and the general lack of distinctive Flavian coarse ware types. Of the decorated samian, however, about half is generally dated to the late first century. Presumably fine tableware of this kind remained in use unbroken for some time after manufacture, until the early second century when rubbish began to encroach on the palace.

PERIOD 3 A–D.   c. A.D. 100–280/290

The relative dating evidence for the North Wing during the Third Period has been summarized in the descriptive text above (pp. 154–172). Here it is necessary to give only the evidence by which the sequence is calibrated.

Period 3 A is not closely datable but the mosaic pavement in room N 13, which stylistically is of this period, incorporates tesserae of samian ware dated by Mr B. R. Hartley to A.D. 90–100. A date early in the second century is indicated, particularly when mosaic styles and the internal development sequence of the building are taken into consideration.

It is probably at this time that the rubbish began to accumulate in the north-west corner of the garden. The coarse wares, key group 3 (Vol. II, fig. 74), show a predominance of early second-century types, while of the distinctive decorated samian (Vol. II, figs. 131–5, nos. 56, 60, 67, 74, 76, 84, 85, 87, 89) only two sherds out of the nine date to after 140.

The impression given by the coarse ware, that rubbish tipping ceased at the beginning of Period 3 C towards the end of the second century, is borne out by the samian. The coins are all first century: one each of Claudius, Vespasian and Nerva.

Period 3 B marks the major reorganization of the North Wing. Floors are relaid, including the dolphin mosaic in room N 7 and the shell mosaic in room N 5, both with tesserae of largely Hadrianic samian ware. The east end of the North Wing was demolished and occupation layers accumulated containing pottery of mid-late second-century date (key group 4, Vol. ii, fig. 75, and decorated samian, Vol. ii, figs. 133–5, nos. 73, 78, 80, 94). The tip seems to have been in use for only a short time since distinctive third-century coarse ware types are rare. The two coins, one Republican and one of Vespasian, are unhelpful.

The bath building at the east end of the North Wing, which had been constructed in Period 3 A, was also demolished and sealed by occupation rubbish. The last layer of ash in its flue contained a coin of Hadrian, now much corroded. It is suggested that the bath suite in the north part of the East Wing was built at this time (*c.* 150) on the grounds that it incorporated roller-stamped flue tiles usually thought to be of Antonine date elsewhere (Vol. ii, p. 49), and the occupation layer through which one of the footings cut contained sherds of Hadrianic samian.

Period 3 C was marked by certain minor alterations. A new floor laid in room N 6 sealed a slightly worn coin of Severus minted in 196–7, suggesting a date early in the third century for the floor. The absence of samian tesserae in the contemporary mosaic in room N 8 might be thought to support a date in the third rather than second century, but the point cannot be conclusive (p. 169).

Period 3 D alterations are assigned together in this period only by virtue of the fact that the work appears to have been halted by the fire (pp. 171–2).

DESTRUCTION.   *c.* A.D. 280/290

The fire which destroyed the North Wing is dated by a group of coarse ware vessels sealed beneath the collapsed roofs of the North Wing (p. 188 and key group 6, Vol. ii, fig. 77). The pots cannot be closely dated but should best be placed in the bracket 270–90 on the grounds that while New Forest colour-coated wares occur there is nothing distinctive of the early fourth century. In general support of a *c.* 280 date, a late (pre-destruction) occupation layer in the Entrance Hall contained two coins, one of Claudius II (268–70) the other of Tetricus I (270–3). Similarly the occupation layer in East Wing courtyard 2 which formed in the third century contained several late third-century coarse ware types (key group 5, Vol. ii, fig. 76) together with three coins: a barbarous radiate, one of Tetricus II (271–3) and one of Claudius II (268–70). Both layers were deposited before the demolition of the superstructure, which is thought to have followed close upon the fire.

ROBBING

The robbing of the East Wing bath suite (p. 189) is archaeologically well defined. Altogether 43 coins were recovered, ending with a single coin of Allectus which suggests an end date in the late 290s for this phase of the robbing (Vol. ii, p. 98) before the common issues of the early fourth century had come into circulation. The general robbing of the walls yielded 23 coins, ending with a follis of Maximian I (Vol. II, p. 98). While, therefore, on coin evidence, the two acts of demolition were largely contemporary, being confined to the decade or two immediately following the fire, the stratigraphy shows that the bath suite was gutted first before the walls were pulled down. Key group 7 (Vol. II, fig. 78), deposited during the robbing, contains generalized late third-century types normally in use at the end of the century and even later.

FOURTH CENTURY AND LATER

The fourth century was for Fishbourne a time of abandonment. This much is shown, not only by the total absence of occupation or building layers post-dating the late third-century robbing, but also by the lack of fourth-century coins, normally so prolific. Altogether only six have been found from the entire site and must represent casual losses. The density is about the same as that of the thirteenth- and sixteenth-century coins and jettons, 11 of which were recovered from the ploughsoil (Vol. II, p. 97).

PLATE I

a. General view of Timber Building 1; looking north (p. 39)

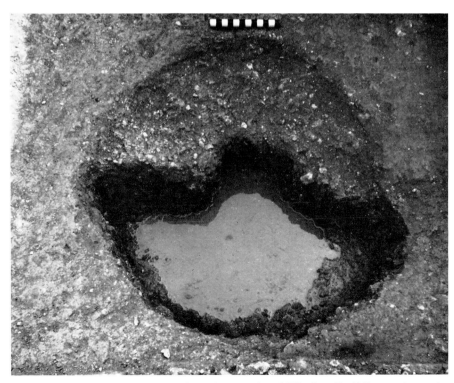

b. Half-sectioned post void and post pit of Timber Building 2 (p. 41)

PLATE II

b. Gully 15 looking west (p. 45)

a. Timber Building 2, post rows A and B looking west (p. 41)

PLATE III

a. The northern road east of the stream: the Period 1 B metalling (p. 46)

b. Post voids for the west revetment of the Period 1 B bridge. The remaining unexcavated part of the causeway can be seen in the foreground and in the section behind the rod (p. 46)

PLATE IV

b. Period 1 A gully 12, partly sectioned, and the subsidence of the later floors into its soft filling; looking south (p. 43)

a. Period 1 C gully 11 and 1 B drystone footing behind the second period wall; looking east. The two large post holes on the right-hand side belong to the Period 1 C fence (pp. 57–8)

PLATE V

b. Slots for the sill beams of the south end of Timber Building 4. The row of post holes in front of the rod belong to Timber Building 1; looking east (p. 47)

a. The drystone footing fronting Timber Building 5. The large post holes on the left-hand side belong to the Period 1 C fence; looking north (p. 57)

PLATE VI

b. The metalling of the Period I C south road where it crosses the filled-in stream; looking west (p. 55)

a. Rotted sill beams for north wall of Timber Building 4; vertical view (p. 47)

PLATE VII

a. The debris layer belonging to the Period 1 C builders' working yard; looking north-east (p. 58)

b. Pink mortar floor and wall rendering of room 8 in the proto-palace. The left half of the picture shows the robber trench for the wall; looking west (p. 63)

PLATE VIII

a. Buttress on the north wall of room 11 in the proto-palace; looking east (p. 61)

b. Footings for the Period 1 C wall between rooms 10 and 11 in the proto-palace; looking east (p. 61)

PLATE IX

b. Period 1 C culvert beneath the Audience Chamber in the West Wing; looking west (p. 71)

a. Collapsed roof lying to the north-west of the proto-palace; looking west

PLATE X

b. Period 1 C wall footings beneath W 14. Ditch 22 can be seen sectioned behind the rod; looking east (p. 69)

a. Period 1 C wall footing beneath make-up of room W 8; looking south (p. 69)

PLATE XI

Period 1 C wall footings in relation to the walls and floors of the West Wing of the Flavian Palace:

(a) in front of W 8 and W 13
looking north

(b) beneath W 14 looking east

(c) in front of and beneath W 7
looking west

PLATE XII

a. North wall of room E 9 showing ashlar masonry partly off
the line of the flint footings; looking north (p. 82)

b. North wall of room N 11 showing fragments of column bases
re-used; looking south (p. 82)

c. East wall of East Wing opposite rooms E 9 and 11;
looking west (p. 82)

PLATE XIII

b. Second-Period mosaic in room W 5 (p. 84)

a. Second-Period mosaic in room W 3 with part of a third period wall built on it, preserving a strip of tesserae from subsequent destruction; looking east (p. 84)

Plate XIV

a. Detail of south-west corner of the Second-Period mosaic in room W 8

b. General view of room W 8 showing the Second-Period mosaic and
subsequent destruction; looking east (p. 85)

PLATE XV

b. The West Wing looking north from the Audience Chamber (pp. 86–8)

a. The West Wing looking south from room W10 towards the Audience Chamber

PLATE XVI

a. Room W 12 showing stoke hole (right) and burnt door sill (left);
looking west (p. 86)

b. Second-Period mosaic in room W 6; looking west (p. 85)

PLATE XVII

b. The north-west corner of the garden showing junction of North Wing veranda with West Wing revetting wall; looking north (p. 89)

a. Second-Period corridor, W 13, showing subsequent mortar patching; looking west (p. 86)

PLATE XVIII

b. The junction of the two types of walling revetting the east front of the West Wing; looking east (p. 89)

a. Apsidal recess at the north end of the West Wing corridor. The bench lining the recess can be clearly seen; looking south (p. 89)

PLATE XIX

The apse of the Audience Chamber looking west, showing the position of the flanking bench within the apse and the corner of the mosaic still in position (p. 87)

PLATE XX

a.　Second-Period mosaic in room N 1; looking east (p. 93)

b.　Second-Period mosaic in room N 3; looking south (p. 93)

PLATE XXI

a. Rooms N 3 and 4; looking west (pp. 93–4)

b. Rooms N 3 and 4; looking south-east (pp. 93–4)

PLATE XXII

a. The western courtyard in the North Wing, looking south-west. The robber trench for the gutter can be clearly seen; the west stylobate is in position but on the north and east sides it has been robbed; the veranda floor is tessellated (p. 101)

b. Masonry projection north of room N 11; looking south (p. 102)

PLATE XXIII

a. South-east corner of the Second-Period mosaic in room N 9 (p. 95)

b. Second-Period mosaic in room N 13 beneath the Third-Period
Medusa floor; looking west (p. 97)

c. Second-Period mosaic in the north-west corner of room N 22 (p. 100)

PLATE XXIV

a. Second-Period mosaic in room N 12, looking east. The room was divided
in the Third Period by a timber partition (p. 96)

b. and *c.* Details of motifs: the left-hand side of *c* shows evidence of later
inaccurate patching

PLATE XXV

b. Second-Period polychrome mosaic in room N 21, looking west, showing subsidences caused by earlier post holes below, and the tile levelling for a door sill in the foreground (p. 100)

a. Second-Period mosaic in room N 19; looking north (p. 99)

PLATE XXVI

Second-Period polychrome mosaic in the room N 20; looking south (p. 99)

PLATE XXVII

Details of the Second-Period mosaic in room N 20 (p. 99 and pl. XCI)

Plate XXVIII

b. The Aisled Hall showing the structure of the original pier bases with their later additions; looking west (p. 106)

a. The front garden of no. 69 Fishbourne Road, showing the footing of one of the walls of the South Wing; looking east (p. 103)

PLATE XXIX

(c) the southern pier of the western
front (pp. 111–13)

(a) the inner sleeper wall of the western bay with a pier base in position

(b) the foundation for the pool

The Entrance Hall of the Palace

PLATE XXX

a. The north courtyard in the East Wing showing the original Second-Period stylobate in position with the robber trench for the gutter in front; looking south-west (p. 117)

b. The north courtyard in the East Wing showing the partially robbed gutter on the north side; looking north-east (p. 117)

PLATE XXXI

(c) the drain passing from the courtyard beneath one of the stylobate blocks still in position; looking east (p. 117)

(a) the structure of the drain, looking south;

(b) the drain passing through the east wall of the building; looking west

Drain leading from the north-east corner of the north courtyard in the East Wing

Plate XXXII

The north-west corner of the formal garden, looking west along the stylobate of the North Wing veranda to the revetting wall in front of the West Wing. Fragments of shattered columns lie in the foreground (p. 121)

PLATE XXXIII

a. The revetting wall in front of the West Wing where it turns into the garden to form the podium facing the Audience Chamber; looking west

b. The same feature looking south across the podium (p. 122)

PLATE XXXIV

b. The stylobate footing on the east side of the garden where it widens to take the monumental front of the Entrance Hall; one gutter block, the bedding trenches and a water pipe can be seen beyond; looking west (p. 125)

a. The north-east corner of the formal garden looking south along the flint-cobble footing for the stylobate. From the corner a tile-built drain leads the surface water away from the garden (p. 123)

Plate XXXV

General view across the centre of the formal garden towards the Audience Chamber, showing the bedding trenches for the hedges lining the north side of the central path (p. 124). The diagonal stone-filled trenches are nineteenth-century field drains (p. 195)

PLATE XXXVI

a. North façade of the central path; the easternmost recess with a bedding pit in the centre; looking north (p. 124)

b. North façade of the central path; one of the rectangular recesses; looking south (p. 124)

PLATE XXXVII

b. Stone-packed post holes and bedding pits flanking the east side of the formal garden; looking south (p. 125)

a. The south series of bedding trenches lining the central path; looking west (p. 124)

PLATE XXXVIII

a. The north-east corner of the garden showing the junction of the north and east paths and lengths of water pipe in position; looking south (p. 129)

b. The north-west corner of the garden showing the junction of the west and north paths with a length of water pipe in position along the west side of the west path; looking north (p. 129)

PLATE XXXIX

a. The west path looking north with the West Wing revetting wall
on the left

b. The junction of the central path and the west path seen from the West
Wing close to the Audience Chamber; looking north-east

PLATE XL

a. Bedding trenches, post holes and water pipe in front of the east stylobate footing; looking north

b. General view across the garden from the West Wing looking east. The modern North Wing cover-building is in the top left corner. In the centre foreground is a late Roman pit

PLATE XLI

b. The base of the oven west of the North Wing; looking east (p. 136)

c. The revetting wall of the West Wing showing the point where the clay-packed ceramic water pipe passed through it to the water tank. The pipe was subsequently removed; looking west (p. 129)

a. The culvert north of room N 8; looking east (p. 129)

PLATE XLII

a. The east wall of the East Wing with the rubble filled sub-floor drain alongside, looking east (p. 134)

b. Tile and greensand arch through the east wall of the East Wing; looking west (p. 134)

PLATE XLIII

Early second-century mosaic in room N 13; looking south (p. 158)

PLATE XLIV

Details of the early second-century mosaic in room N 13. (*a*) the central Medusa head with part of the Second-Period floor beneath; (*b*) and (*c*) flanking motifs. Because of an error in design (*c*) has had to be squashed up and part of its border omitted (p. 158)

PLATE XLV

a. Part of the *caldarium* and its flue, inserted into the east end of the North Wing in the early third century; looking north (p. 155)

b. General view of the west end of the North Wing in its final stage; looking north-west

PLATE XLVI

a. Painted wall plaster *in situ* on the west wall of room N 1 (p. 160)

b. Mid second-century mosaic in room N 5. West is at the top (p. 161)

Plate XLVII

Mid second-century mosaic in room N 7. North is at the top (pp. 163–5)

Plate XLVIII

a

b　　　　　　*a, b*.　Details of mosaic in room N 7

PLATE XLIX

a

b   *a, b.* Details of mosaic in room N 7

PLATE L

Central panel of mosaic in room N 7

PLATE LI

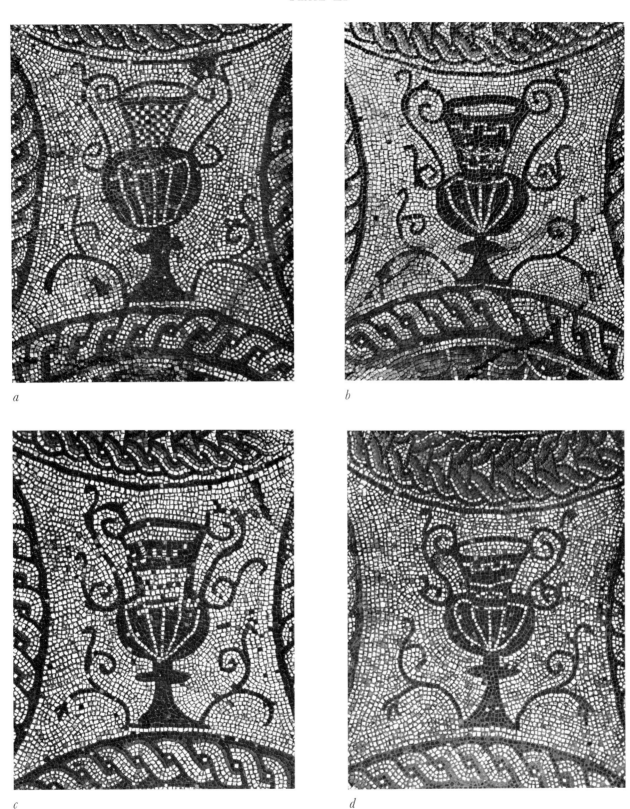

a–d. Details of mosaic in room N 7

PLATE LII

a–c. Details of the border and corners of the mosaic in room N 7

Plate LIII

a. Corner detail of mosaic in room N 7

b. Detail of north border of mosaic in room N 7 showing a solitary bird
standing on a broken tendril

PLATE LIV

a. Mid second-century hypocaust in room N 8; looking west (p. 165)

b. General view of rooms N 9–11; looking east (p. 165). The medieval ditch can be seen running diagonally across all three rooms (p. 194)

PLATE LV

a. The mortar floor of room N 9, on the north side of the room, cut away to expose the remains of the Second-Period mosaic beneath; looking south (p. 165)

b. Room N 10; looking south (p. 166)

PLATE LVI

a. Second-century mosaic in room N 2, south-east corner (p. 161)

b. North wall of room N 12 (below scale) showing tessellated floor of N 14 cut away to expose part of the Second-Period mosaic beneath; looking west (p. 166)

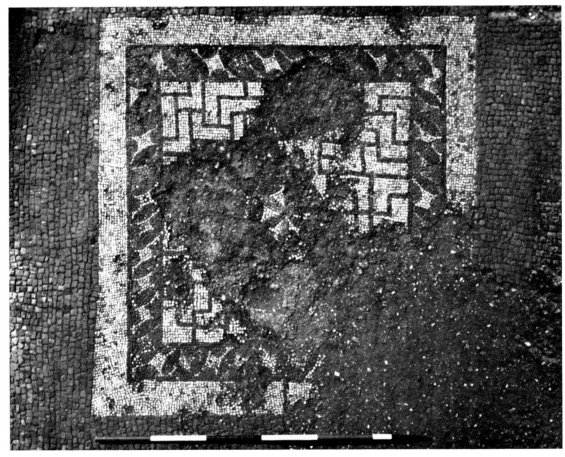

c. Mid second-century mosaic in room N 11. North is at the top (p. 166)

PLATE LVII

a. Lead angled tank east of reconstituted North Wing;
looking north (p. 165)

b. Second-century mosaic in room N 14; looking south (p. 166)

PLATE LVIII

a. Ovens inserted into the western veranda of the west courtyard in the North Wing;
looking east (p. 170)

b. Early third-century mosaic in room N 8; looking west (p. 169)

PLATE LIX

a. Flue of hypocaust in room N 1; looking north

b. General view of hypocaust in room N 1; looking south (p. 171)

PLATE LX

a. Oven in the south-east corner of room N 4; looking east (p. 161)

b. Tile cist in room B of the East Wing baths; looking west (p. 173)

PLATE LXI

a. Room B of the East Wing baths showing the north wall, the lowest course of which has been shaped to compensate for the subsidence of the stylobate into the soft filling of the earlier stream below; looking north (p. 173)

b. Room B of the East Wing baths showing the blocked door in the east wall; looking east (p. 173)

PLATE LXII

b. The *caldarium* of the East Wing baths (room F) showing the drain leading out of the plunge bath; looking east (pp. 174–5)

a. South range of East Wing baths built in the south veranda of the Second-Period courtyard; looking west (pp. 172 ff.)

PLATE LXIII

a. The wall between the *caldarium* and *tepidarium* in the East Wing bath suite; looking east (p. 175)

b. The flue serving the *caldarium* in the East Wing bath suite; looking west (p. 175)

PLATE LXIV

b. The drain leading from the cold plunge bath of the East Wing bath suite; looking west (p. 178)

a. The cold plunge bath of the East Wing bath suite; looking north (pp. 176–7)

PLATE LXV

a. The *caldarium* drain at the point where it once joined the open stylobate gutter, since removed and now represented by the robber trench in which the rod stands; looking north-west (p. 178)

b. The Second-Period culvert passing through the East Wing, seen here at the point where its sides have been removed and cross walls inserted to form a sump for a latrine; looking north (p. 178)

PLATE LXVI

a. The well in the southern courtyard of the East Wing, shown after the filling had been removed; looking north (p. 181)

b. The same well excavated to below the water table, showing the lowest timber frame still preserved in position (p. 181)

PLATE LXVII

General view of the west end of the Entrance Hall, looking south across the mass of collapsed roof tiles and rubble showing the wear caused by the constant passage of traffic in the third century (p. 182)

PLATE LXVIII

a. The north-west corner of room N 4 showing the two stone anvils still in position; looking south-west (p. 188)

b. Burnt door sill leading into room N 6; looking north (p. 187)

PLATE LXIX

a. Lead puddle formed by the dripping of molten lead on to the already worn tessellated corridor floor in front of room N 7; looking east (p. 187)

b. Lead puddle and collapsed iron work on the floor of room N 12; looking east (p. 188)

PLATE LXX

a. Group of smashed pots on the floor of room N 12; looking
south-west (p. 188)

b. Single smashed pot on the floor of room N 12; looking south (p. 188)

PLATE LXXI

a.   Mass of collapsed tile superstructure in the western courtyard
of the North Wing in front of room N 7; looking south (p. 187)

b.   Fallen wall plaster in the robber trench for the west wall of
room N 12; looking west (p. 192)

c.   Column fragment in the third-century pit cut through the
west path of the garden; looking south (p. 185)

PLATE LXXII

c. Skeleton 4; looking west (p. 193)

b. Skeleton 3; looking west (p. 193)

a. Skeleton 2; looking north (p. 193)

PLATE LXXIII

a. Reconstructing the plaster on the west wall of room N 12 (p. 202)

b. Mosaicists consolidating the mosaic floor of room N 12 (p. 198)

PLATE LXXIV

b. Second-Period mosaic in room W 5

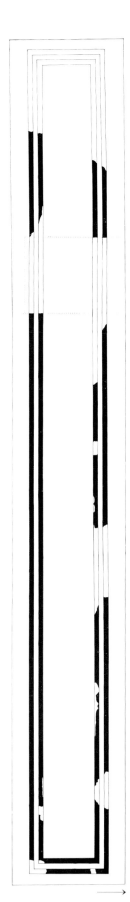

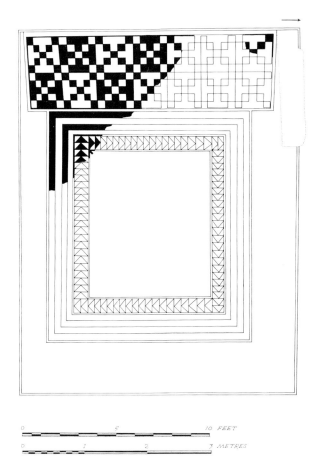

c. Second-Period mosaic in room W 6

a. Second-Period mosaic in room W 13

PLATE LXXV

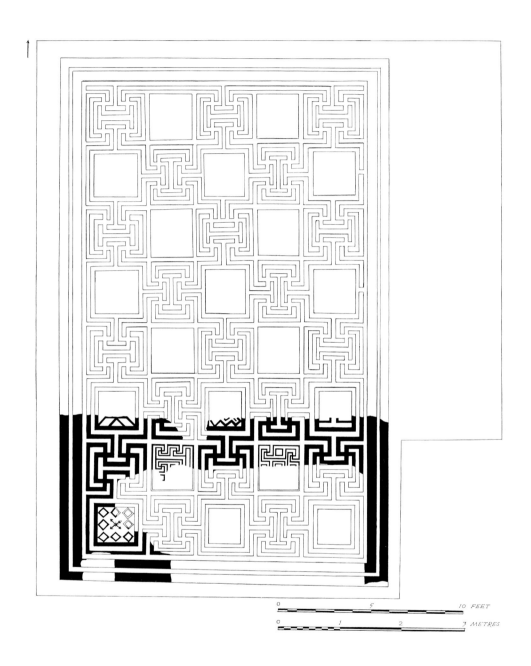

0   5   10 FEET

0   1   2   3 METRES

Second-Period mosaic in room W 3

PLATE LXXVI

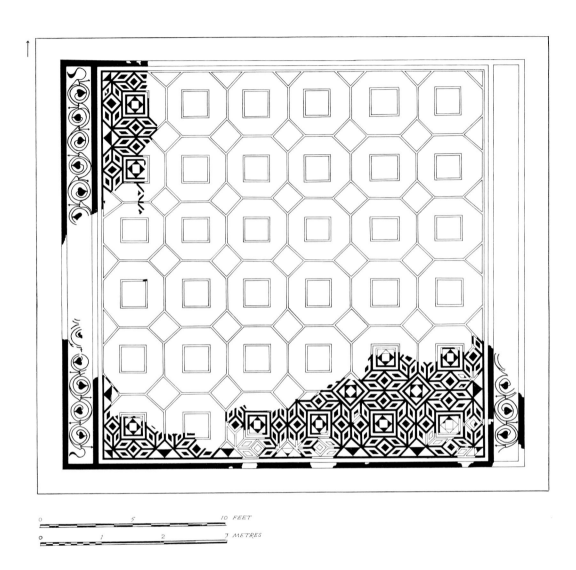

0   5   10 FEET

0   1   2   3 METRES

Second-Period mosaic in room W 8

PLATE LXXVII

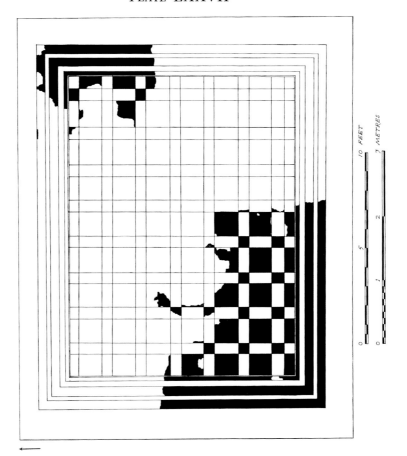

b. Second-Period mosaic in room N 4

a. Second-Period mosaic in room N 3

PLATE LXXVIII

Second-Period mosaic in room N 12, showing the
patches in the southern border

Plate LXXIX

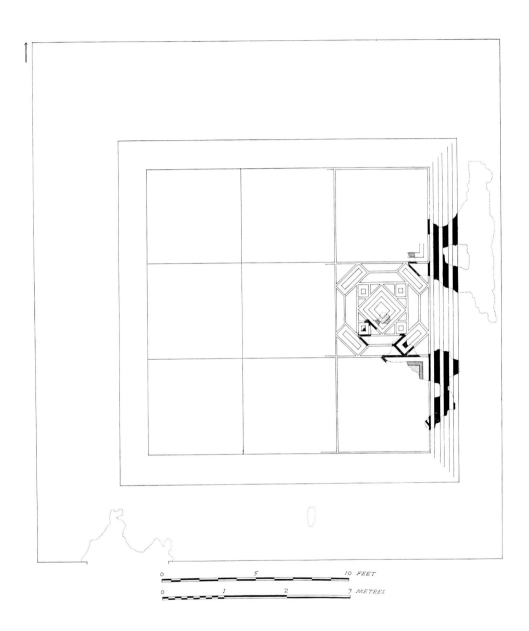

Second-Period mosaic in room N 1

PLATE LXXX

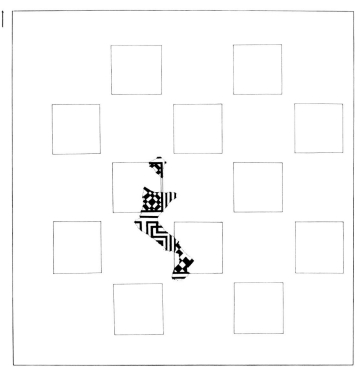

c. Second-Period mosaic in room N 13

a. Second-Period mosaic in
room N 22

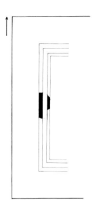

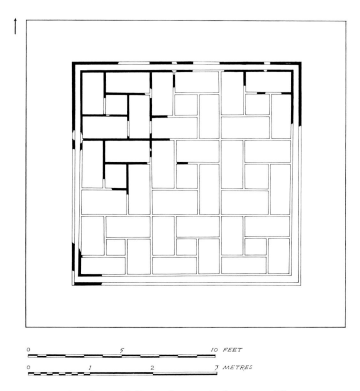

b. Second-Period mosaic in
room N 5

0   5   10 FEET

0   1   2   3 METRES

d. Second-Period mosaic in room N 19

PLATE LXXXI

Second-Period mosaic in room N 20

(N.B. This reconstruction drawing reflects the distortions suffered by the floor as
a result of severe subsidence during use)

PLATE LXXXII

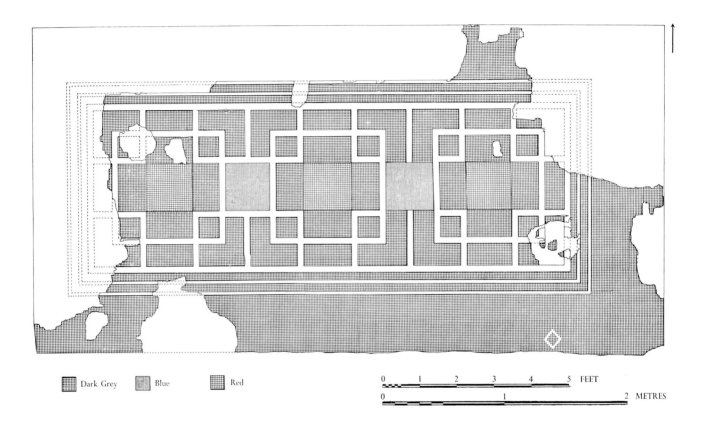

Dark Grey   Blue   Red

0   1   2   3   4   5   FEET

0   1   2   METRES

Second-Period mosaic in room N 21

PLATE LXXXIII

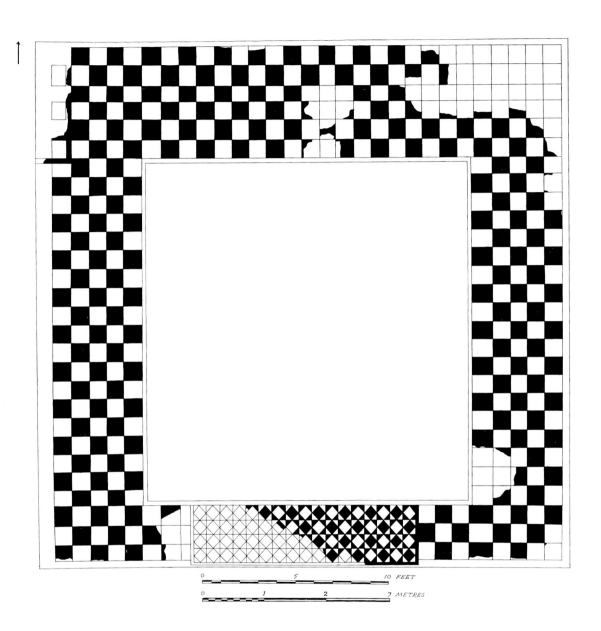

Third-Period mosaic in room N 7. The surround only is shown here; for the patterned centre see pl. XLVII

PLATE LXXXIV

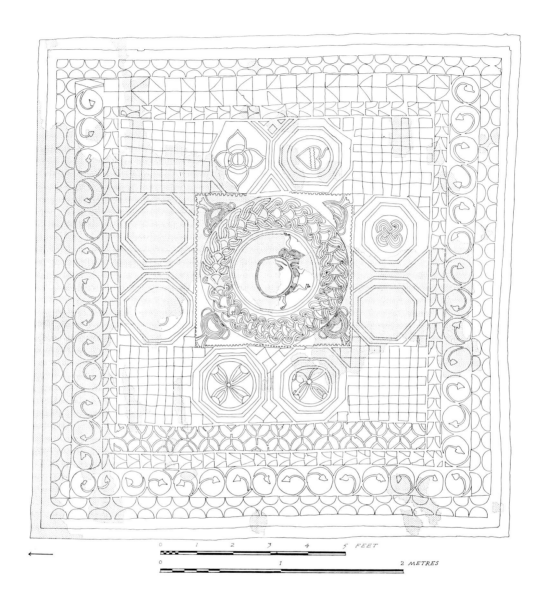

Third-Period mosaic in room N 13

PLATE LXXXV

a. Third-Period mosaic in room N 8: for diagram see pl. LXXXIX*a*

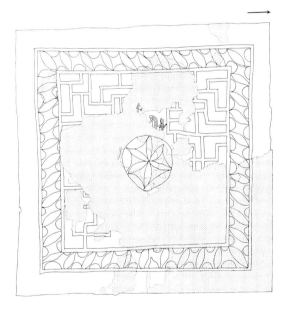

b. Third-Period mosaic in room N 11

Plate LXXXVI

a. Third-Period mosaic
in room N 2

b. Third-Period mosaic
in room N 5

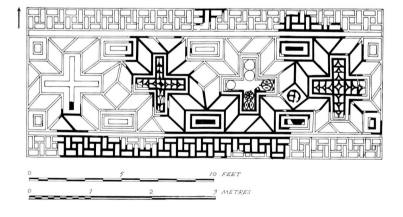

c. Third-Period mosaic in room N 14

PLATE LXXXVII

Red

Grey/
Brown

0   5   10 FEET

0   1   2   3 METRES

Third-Period tessellated floor in the corridor along
the west side of the North Wing

PLATE LXXXVIII

Third-Period mosaic in room N 7; for scale see pl. XLVII

Plate LXXXIX

a

b

a. Third-Period mosaic in room N 8; for scale and orientation see pl. LXXXV*a*

b. Third-Period mosaic in room N 5; for scale and orientation see pl. LXXXVI*b*

PLATE XC

a. Third-Period mosaic in room N 11

b. Third-Period mosaic in room N 13; general view looking north

c. Detail of Third-Period mosaic in room N 13, looking east at the central Medusa head. See pl. LXXXIV

PLATE XCI

b

d

c

a

a–d. General view and details of the Second-Period mosaic in room N 20; see pl. LXXXI